THIRD EDITION

INTRODUCTORY READINGS
FOR
COGNITIVE
PSYCHOLOGY

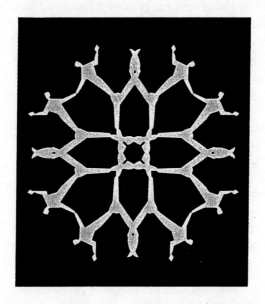

Edited, Selected, and with Introductions by
Richard P. Honeck
University of Cincinnati

Dushkin/McGraw-Hill

A Division of The McGraw-Hill Companies

For Joan

Third Edition

10 9 8 7 6 5 4 3 2

Library of Congress Cataloging-in-Publication Data

Main entry under title:
    Introductory readings for cognitive psychology/edited, selected, and with introductions by Richard P. Honeck.—3rd ed.
        Includes bibliographical references and index.
        1. Cognition. 2. Cognition and culture. 3. Psychology. I. Honeck, Richard P., *comp.*

153.4

97-075228

0-697-38642-2

 Printed on Recycled Paper

Preface

Introductory Readings for Cognitive Psychology, 3rd edition, is specifically designed for the student who is taking a first course in cognitive psychology. It can be used in conjunction with a textbook or on its own. Students in more advanced courses in cognitive psychology and related disciplines may also find this collection useful.

My major motivation for developing this anthology is to provide students with the opportunity to explore firsthand the scholarship that informs the field and the textbooks that describe it. Textbooks necessarily omit extended discussions of the background, methodology, and theorizing that appear in original pieces. Moreover, the excitement and the style of these pieces get filtered out in most texts. The readings in this volume capture this excitement, and it is my view that students will benefit from being directly exposed to the pursuits and passions of cognitive psychologists, the questions they grapple with, and the inner workings of their research.

This volume is composed of 32 short, accessible readings—mostly journal articles but also articles from edited volumes and excerpts from books. Twenty-one of the articles are new, while 11 popular articles from the previous edition were retained. All of the journal articles and edited chapters have been reprinted in their entirety. In selecting articles for this volume I have attempted to keep students' and instructors' concerns uppermost in my mind. One precondition for an article's inclusion was that it had to be written by an expert in a clear, explanatory way. Once this was established, I then used the following questions to guide my selections:

- Can the article be understood by students taking a first course in cognitive psychology?
- Is it well written, interesting, short, and not a rehash of material inevitably convered in textbooks?
- Is it informative about methodological problems?

Wide coverage of topics was another goal, as was the inclusion of articles that attempted to relate their content to real-world applications. In addition, new sections on perception and neurocognition and on the emotional mind have been added to this third edition. The former is in deference to the increasing rapproachement between cognitive psychology and neuropsychology. The section on emotion was included because of its interest and because cognitivists have been doing more and more work on the topic. Of necessity, some topics were left out. Generally, I did some gazing into the crystal ball of cognitive psychology's future in the twenty-first century, and many articles were selected accordingly.

The arrangement of the selections in *Introductory Readings for Cognitive Psychology,* 3rd edition, follows a sequence that is typical of textbooks in cognitive psychology—background, perception and neurocognition, memory, thought, emotion, and applications. Each section opens with an introduction that frames the selections and summarizes them as well. The student is invited to read these sections, or parts thereof, before and after reading a particular selection. There is also an introduction to the volume that addresses the question, What is cognitive psychology?

A word to the instructor   An *Instructor's Manual With Test Questions* is available through the publisher. It contains a synopsis of each selection, suggestions for generating in-class discussions of the selections, and multiple-choice and essay questions.

Acknowledgements   For the first edition, several people helped put this collection together. Michael J. Firment and Tammy J. S. Case helped in the editing. Dan Berch, William Dember, and Joel Warm at the University of Cincinnati made interesting and useful suggestions. Virginia Diehl of Western Illinois University and David E. Irwin of Michigan State University were generous with their advice. Mimi Egan, then program manager for the Dushkin Publishing Group, was, from beginning to end, efficient and encouraging in her handling of the project. And Shirley Doxsey typed a reference section for one of the articles. To all of these people, a hearty thanks.

For the second edition, the friendly and efficient assistance of Mimi Egan and David Dean is acknowledged, as well as that of David Brackley, then copy editor. Thanks are also owed students and instructors who commented on the first edition.

For the third edition, my thanks go to David Dean for his quick and cordial handling of all of the administrative details. I am also indebted to the following instructors, who provided some feedback on the second edition and made suggestions for the third:

Jo-Ellen Ashbury
Bethany College

Leanne Olson
Wisconsin Lutheran College

Jerwen Jou
University of Texas–Pan American

Derek Price
Wheaton College

Lisa M. Maxfield
California State University–Long Beach

Finally, it is my fondest hope that *Introductory Readings for Cognitive Psychology,* 3rd edition, will stimulate students, help them to see the relevance of the study of cognition to our everyday lives, and encourage them to explore further the general area of cognitive psychology.

R. P. H.

Contents

Part ❖ One
BACKGROUND

Part ❖ Two
PERCEPTION AND
NEUROCOGNITION

Part ❖ Three
MEMORY: REAL, FALSE, AND BROKEN

Part ❖ Four
VARIETIES OF THOUGHT

Kunst-Wilson and Zajonc, using empirical research in the area of unconscious detection, demonstrate that subjects can develop strong preferences for stimuli that have become familiar through repeated exposures and, further, that preferences can occur without conscious indentification of the stimuli. While the problem of nonreplicability is a disadvantage, the study provides a new interpretation of the term *affective.*

Part ❖ Six
APPLICATIONS

About the Editor

RICHARD P. HONECK is a professor of psychology in and serves on the graduate faculty of the Department of Psychology at the University of Cincinnati in Cincinnati, Ohio, where he has taught courses in cognitive psychology, psycholinguistics, the history of psychology, and statistics. He is a member of the Psychonomic Society, the Southern Society for Philosophy and Psychology, and Sigma Xi, and he also serves on the editorial board of *Metaphor and Symbol*. His research interests focus on cognition and psycholinguistics, and he has published numerous articles in these areas. His most recent contribution in this general area is *A Proverb in Mind: The Cognitive Science of Proverbial Wit and Wisdom* (Lawrence Erlbaum, 1997). He received a B.S. in psychology from the University of Wisconsin–Milwaukee in 1962 and an M.S. and a Ph.D. from the University of Wisconsin–Madison in 1966 and 1969, respectively.

AUTHORS

JOANNE ALEXANDER was a professor at the University of Michigan in Ann Arbor, Michigan.

MARK H. ASHCRAFT is a professor in the department of psychology at Cleveland State University. He is the author of numerous books and articles, including *Human Memory and Cognition,* 2d ed. (HarperCollins, 1994). He received his Ph.D. from the University of Kansas in 1975.

C. ASKEW is a professor at the University of Manchester.

JEAN BÉDARD is a professor at Leval University in Quebec, Canada. He received his Ph.D. in business administration from the University of Southern California.

STEPHEN J. CECI is a professor of human development and family studies at Cornell University. He is the author of *On Intelligence: A Bio-ecological Treatise on Intellectual Development* (Harvard University Press, 1996). In 1978 he received his Ph.D. from the University of Exeter in England.

CRAIG J. CHAMBERLIN is dean of the Department of Kinesiology and Physical Education at the University College of the Fraser Valley, Abbotsford, British Columbia, Canada. He has also taught in the School of Kinesiology and Physical Education at the University of Northern Colorado.

The late **WILLIAM G. CHASE** was a professor in the Department of Psychology at Carnegie-Mellon University in Pittsburgh, Pennsylvania.

MICHELENE T. H. CHI is a professor of psychology at the University of Pittsburgh and a senior scientist at the university's Learning Research and Development Center. Her research focuses on learning and conceptual change in science domains.

FERGUS I. M. CRAIK is a professor of psychology at the University of Toronto.

DEAN DELIS is a staff psychologist at the San Diego Veterans Administration Medical Center and an associate professor of psychiatry in the School of Medicine at the University of California, San Diego. He is coauthor, with Cassandra Phillips, of *The Passion Paradox: Patterns of Love and Power in Intimate Relationships* (Bantam Books, 1990).

JUDY S. DeLOACHE is a professor of psychology at the University of Illinois at Urbana–Champaign.

GEORG DEUTSCH is an associate professor of research in neurology and director of the Cerebral Blood Flow Laboratory at the University of Alabama in Birmingham. His main research interests concern brain/behavior relationships as studied by functional neuroimaging in normal subjects during different cognitive tasks and mental states. He is on the scientific advisory board for Stroke Groups of Texas, and he is a member of the Veterans Administration's Merit Review Board for Neurobiology.

K. ANDERS ERICSSON is an associate professor of psychology at the University of Colorado. The research reported in the *Science* paper that appears in this volume was completed when he worked as a research associate at Carnegie-Mellon University. He is coauthor, with Herbert A. Simon, of *Protocol Analysis: Verbal Reports as Data* (MIT Press, 1984).

The late **STEVE FALOON** was a professor in the Department of Psychology at Carnegie-Mellon University in Pittsburgh, Pennsylvania.

RONALD P. FISHER is a professor of psychology at Florida International University at Miami and a consulting editor for *Memory and Cognition* magazine. His research interests include applying theories of cognition to eyewitness testimony and investigative interviewing, and he has conducted training workshops in improved interviewing techniques to enhance eyewitness recollection in police departments in the United States and Israel.

JOHN FLEER is a partner and a civil trial attorney in the law firm of Bjork, Fleer, Lawrence, and Harris located in Oakland, California. He received his Ph.D. in clinical psychology from the University of Wyoming in 1977 and his J.D. from the University of California, Berkeley, in 1981. His research interests lie in the field of mental health and the law.

ELAINE FUNNELL is a professor whose research interests include the cognitive neuropsychology of language.

R. EDWARD GEISELMAN is a professor in the Department of Psychology at the University of California, Los Angeles.

ARTHUR C. GRAESSER is a professor in the Department of Psychology and an adjunct professor in the Department of Mathematical Sciences at the University of Memphis. His research interests concern cognitive science and discourse processing. He received his Ph.D. in psychology from the University of California, San Diego.

MARY HEGARTY is an associate professor of psychology at the University of California, Santa Barbara. Her research interests include spatial cognition, comprehension, reasoning, and individual differences. She received her Ph.D. at Carnegie-Mellon University.

EARL HUNT is a professor of psychology and an adjunct professor of computer science at the University of Washington in Seattle, Washington. His research interests include human cognition, mathematical modeling, and the application of technology and psychology in science instruction. He is the author of *Will We Be Smart Enough? A Cognitive Analysis of the Coming Workforce* (Russell Sage Foundation, 1995).

JOHN JONIDES is a professor of psychology and associate dean for research in the College of Literature, Science, and the Arts at the University of Michigan at Ann Arbor. His research interests are reasoning, memory, and perception. He received his Ph.D. in psychology from the University of Pennsylvania in 1975.

MARY KISTER KAISER is principal scientist of the Rotorcraft Human Factors Research Branch at NASA Ames Research Center in Mountain View, California. She received her Ph.D. in psychology from the University of Virginia, and she was a postdoctoral research scholar at the University of Michigan.

HOWARD H. KENDLER was a project director at the Office of Naval Research, a consultant to the U.S. Department of Defense, and a consultant to *Encyclopedia Brittanica* prior to becoming a professor of psychology at the University of California, Santa Barbara. His publications include *Psychology: A Science in Conflict* (Oxford University Press, 1981) and *Historical Foundations of Modern Psychology* (Dorsey Press, 1986).

NANCY H. KERR is a professor of psychology at Oglethorpe University in Atlanta, Georgia. She is a member of the American Psychological Society, the Psychonomic Society, and the European Sleep Research Society.

WILLIAM RAFT KUNST-WILSON taught at the University of Michigan, the University of Texas, and Rice University before becoming the executive vice president for Vyvx, Inc., a holding company for communications and telecommunications businesses. He is coeditor, with Robert Peterson and Wayne Hoyer, of *The Role of Affect in Consumer Behavior: Emerging Theories and Applications* (Lexington Books, 1985).

JUDITH H. LANGLOIS is a professor of psychology at the University of Texas at Austin. Her major research focuses on developmental psychology.

KENNETH R. LAUGHERY is the Herbert S. Autrey Professor of Psychology at Rice University.

ALAN M. LESLIE is a professor of psychology at Rutgers University. His research interests include the nature of cognitive architecture in early development, object cognition in infancy, and the cognitive neuropsychology of "theory of mind" concepts.

ANNE BOVENMYER LEWIS was an associate at the University of Colorado in Boulder, Colorado.

ROBERT S. LOCKHART is a professor at the University of Toronto in Toronto, Canada. His research interests include memory theory.

ELIZABETH F. LOFTUS is a professor in the Department of Psychology at the University of Washington in Seattle, Washington. She is coauthor, with Geoffrey R. Loftus, of *Human Memory: The*

Processing of Information (Lawrence Erlbaum, 1976) and the author of *Witness for the Defense* (St. Martin's Press, 1991).

RICHARD E. MAYER is a professor of psychology at the University of California, Santa Barbara. His research interests include mathematical and scientific thinking, learning from text and pictures, and learning computer programming languages. Among the books he has authored or edited are *Teaching and Learning Computer Programming*, *Educational Psychology: A Cognitive Approach* (Little, Brown, 1987) and *Thinking, Problem Solving, Cognition* (W. H. Freeman, 1983). He has served as editor of the *Educational Psychologist* and coeditor of *Instructional Science*.

RICHARD J. McNALLY is a professor of psychology in the Department of Psychology at Harvard University in Cambridge, Massachusetts. He has also taught at the University of Health Sciences/Chicago Medical School, where he established a research and treatment clinic for anxiety disorders.

JEFFERY SCOTT MIO is a professor at California State Polytechnic University.

KATHERINE NELSON is the editor of *Narratives from the Crib* (Harvard University Press, 1989) and *Event Knowledge: Structure and Function in Development* (Lawrence Erlbaum, 1986).

T. J. PERFECT has been published in the *Journal of Social Psychology* and *Applied Cognitive Psychology*.

DES POWER has contributed to numerous publications, including *Vox*.

KEITH RAYNER is Distinguished University Professor of Psychology at the University of Massachusetts.

LORI A. ROGGMAN, a developmental psychologist, is an assistant professor at Utah State University in Logan, Utah. She received her Ph.D. from the University of Texas at Austin.

DAVID J. SCHNEIDER is a professor in and chair of the Department of Psychology at Rice University in Houston, Texas. He has also taught at Amherst College, Brandeis University, Stanford University, Indiana University, and the University of Texas at San Antonio. He received his Ph.D. from Stanford University, and he is coauthor, with Albert H. Hastorf and Pheobe C. Ellsworth, of *Person Perception* (Addison-Wesley, 1979).

WALTER SCHNEIDER is a professor in the Department of Psychology at the University of Pittsburgh in Pittsburgh, Pennysylvania. His research interests include behavioral and brain imaging studies. He has contributed articles to such journals as the *International Journal of Imaging Science and Technology*.

MATTHEW D. SMITH is an associate of the Human Performance Studies program in the College of Education at the University of Alabama in Tuscaloosa, Alabama. His research interests focus on physical education teaching effectiveness and physical education teacher education.

SALLY P. SPRINGER is executive assistant to the chancellor at the University of California, Davis. She received her B.S. from Brooklyn College and her Ph.D. in psychology from Stanford University.

CHRISTINE M. TEMPLE is affiliated with the Developmental Neuropsychology Unit at the University of Essex in Wivenhoe Park, Colchester, England.

ENDEL TULVING, formerly a professor at the University of Toronto, is well known for his experimental and theoretical contributions to the study of human memory. He received his B.A. from the University of Toronto in 1953 and his Ph.D. from Harvard University in 1957. He briefly taught at Yale University during his tenure at the University of Toronto.

DANIEL M. WEGNER is a professor of psychology at the University of Virginia. He is the author of *White Bears and Other Unwanted Thoughts* (Viking/Penguin, 1989) and coeditor, with James W. Pennebaker, of *Handbook of Mental Control* (Prentice Hall, 1993).

MICHAEL S. WOGALTER is an associate professor of psychology at North Carolina State University.

DANIEL B. WRIGHT is a professor at the University of Bristol in the United Kingdom. He is the author of *Understanding Statistics: An Introduction for the Social Sciences* (Sage Publications, 1996).

R. B. ZAJONC is a professor of psychology in the Department of Psychology at the University of Michigan in Ann Arbor, Michigan, and director of the university's Institute for Social Research.

What Is Cognitive Psychology?

Cognitive psychology is generally acknowledged to be a part of cognitive science, which is an interdisciplinary approach to the mind. Cognitive science includes some aspects of computer science, philosophy, linguistics, anthropology, neurophysiology, and, of course, psychology.

But what *is* cognitive psychology? A simple answer is that it is the study of perception, learning, memory, reasoning, problem solving, deciding, and the like. This definition is serviceable enough. However, it does gloss over questions about whether or not a particular set of assumptions, methods, and theories—a paradigm—characterizes the field. Arguably, at this point in time, no such paradigm exists. Cognitive psychology is more like an undulating mass than a fixed target. Nevertheless, cognitive psychologists typically ask certain kinds of questions, such as the following:

- Does knowledge affect perception of a stimulus?
- What is memory? Are there different memory systems?
- What form does knowledge take?
- What facilitates or hinders remembering?
- How is language understood?
- How do people reason?
- How do people recognize patterns and categorize things?
- What factors influence problem solving?
- Are cognition and emotion separable systems?
- How do children learn word meanings?
- What happens when people read?
- Are people aware of what their minds do?

Although there are no overarching theories, such as a theory that could address all the above questions, there are smaller theories that apply to restricted domains, such as short-term memory, categorization, and reasoning. There are also "mini-theories" about particular phenomena, such as to explain why recall is generally different than recognition, how people discover analogies between things, why people tend to overlook misspellings of the word *the*, why pictures tend to be remembered better than words, how mental images are constructed, how tip-of-the-tongue phenomena can be explained, what makes for an expert in physics, and what young infants tend to notice. If anything, this set of mini-theories, the phenomena they address, the methods used to study the phenomena, and the assumptions brought to bear define the field.

THE LACK OF A FULL-BLOWN PARADIGM IS SOMEWHAT UNSETTLING. ONE WOULD hope for a more coherent, organized picture of the field. To some extent this organization is provided by the *information-processing view*. This is the predominant view among cognitive psychologists and the one most represented in *Introductory Readings for Cognitive Psychology*. The central assumption of this view is that inputs undergo a series of recodings. That is, mentally processing inputs involves changing them in various ways. For example, the letter *A* is processed not simply as a mark on a page but as having a certain sound associated with it, as the first letter of the alphabet, as the kind of grade someone might want to receive on a test, or as a best friend's middle initial. In this example, a stimulus has been imbued with different kinds of symbolic significance. However, the information "in" the stimulus is simply an initiating event; it is not "in" the recoded mental forms.

In this sense, the information-processing view forces the conclusion that the mind is different from the environment, shaped and constrained by it, but not a pale reflection of it. In order to account for the noncorrespondence between initiating inputs and eventual behavioral outputs, cognitive psychologists have invented elaborate mental structures and processes, including concepts such as long-term memory, working memory, automatic processing, pattern recognition, and serial processing. The metaphor that has most often been used to organize the information flow into and through the mind has been the computer metaphor. Thus, the information-processing view not only comports with but it has been aided and abetted by the computer revolution. Just as is the case with computers, humans are seen as systematically taking in, operating on, and outputting information by means of complex structures and processes. Ultimately, adoption of the computer metaphor makes the mind a computer, that is, a symbol-manipulating device, but a highly complex one. The strong form of this argument is that there is nothing special about the human mind—if its activity can be made explicit, then this activity can be simulated in a nonhuman machine.

ALTHOUGH THE INFORMATION-PROCESSING VIEW PREvails in cognitive psychology, it is not the only view. At least two minority positions can be discerned. The first and fast-growing alternative is *connectionism*, sometimes called *parallel distributed processing*. Connectionism is quite complicated, and here I will provide only a brief overview.

Connectionism is essentially a modern, mathematically sophisticated form of associationism. The basic assumption of connectionism is that behavior is a product of the strength of connections between input and output elements. The guiding metaphor is that the mind is the brain. In turn, the brain is viewed as a huge connection device in which billions of neurons trade electrochemical messages. These connections constitute the knowledge that an individual has. An input activates some subset of the elements, and the pattern and strength of this activation reflects "knowledge" about the input. A key premise is that activation is a matter of simultaneous (parallel) processing in a number of elements. From a neurophysiological perspective, such massive parallel processing is a virtual certainty. Thousands or millions of neurons may be responsible for even a seemingly simple act.

Like the information-processing view, connectionism allows for recoding of the stimulus, but unlike this view, connectionism is less likely to describe ouputs as being due to a series of information-processing stages in which formal rules are applied to inputs. Connectionists see behavior as exhibiting regularities, but these are explained in terms of the correlations between huge numbers of neuron-like elements. Behavior therefore becomes a probabilistic function of inputs that have been transformed by "hidden units," whose outputs are combined to yield a final output. Much, if not all, of this activity is seen as occurring outside the awareness of the person.

Thus, connectionism is similar to the information-processing view in that it assumes that inputs are successively recoded, but it is unlike the information-processing view in that it attempts to specify the (presumably) more continuous, correlational nature of the relationship between inputs and their recoded forms. In this respect, connectionists seem to pay more respect to the environment. Still, it must be noted that connectionism, like the information-processing view, is a mechanistic, largely computer-implemented approach to cognition. That is, connectionists attempt to model cognition by means of computer accessories. It is just that the "architecture" of the computer is different in a connectionistic system than it is in a conventional digital computer.

Connectionists are doing some exciting work in practically every area of cognitive psychology, some of it controversial. The major questions seem to be what phenomena connectionism can validly be applied to, whether or not it constitutes an unconstrained form of theorizing, and whether or not it actually mimics what real brains do. Nevertheless, it is clear that connectionism is a strong second force in cognitive psychology.

THE SECOND ALTERNATIVE TO THE INFORMATION-PROcessing view (and in sharp contrast to it) is the *ecological view*. The ecological view, built on the work of psychologist James J. Gibson, holds that much of perception, and therefore much of cognition, occurs in a direct way. That is, perception is caused by information in the stimulus, with special importance attached to movement information. Of course, perceptual systems have been "tuned" by millions of years of evolution to pick up certain information in the stimulus. The important implication is that perception is not due to mental factors—expectations, schemas, motives, mind sets, and the like. To use current jargon, there are no "top-down" components to perception. An organism's knowledge does not somehow meet the stimulus halfway and jointly produce a perception. The stimulus dictates the perception. Thus, perception is "bottom-up." The bottom-up axiom obviously contradicts the recoding axiom of the information-processing view. For the ecological psychologist, the environment is mirrored in the mind. Indeed, the mind is simply part of the environment. Some who take this view even maintain that memory is "in the stimulus." Organisms learn, but learning is generally seen as an "education of attention," such that successively finer discriminations of stimulus features are made.

The ecological view is a radical view, one that most cognitivists either reject or feel uncomfortable with. Nevertheless, research within this framework has generated a host of findings about perception and about some aspects of traditional cognition, and its advocates are a viable and vocal part of the community of cognitive psychologists.

THE FACE OF COGNITIVE PSYCHOLOGY IS CHANGING, AND not simply because of the impact of connectionism. The boundaries of cognitive psychology within cognitive science have been blurred. Several developments have brought this about. First, there is computer modeling. Since as far back as 1960, the mainstay of cognitive psychology has been laboratory experimentation. Although this is still the case, there is an increasing emphasis on computer mod-

eling of cognitive functions. Such modeling forces the theorist to be more precise about theoretical concepts and their relationships. Moreover, the pure complexity of cognition requires some way other than a verbal form of organizing the information contained in theories. Of course, modern computers have enormously increased in capacity, power, and scope, and so the marriage of cognitive theory and the computer is apt and was probably inevitable.

A second development is that the discipline of neuropsychology has been extended to include cognitive psychology, forming the new field of cognitive neuropsychology. This field looks at cognition largely by examining the effects of brain damage. However, because the effects of brain damage can only be observed once they occur, the methodology of cognitive neuropsychology involves single cases or small groups. The development of neuroimaging techniques has also played an important role in blending cognitive psychology and neuropsychology. These techniques allow the investigator to see where changes have occurred in the structure or function of the brain and to link these changes with cognitive activities. These changes have been linked to particular regions of the brain so often that cognitive neuropsychology has fostered an emphasis on "modularity," the idea that there are brain modules that are dedicated to carrying out particular cognitive functions.

A third development that has blurred cognitive psychology's borders is real-world application. The call for "relevance" that blossomed in the 1980s has become even stronger. Like cognitive neuropsychology, this development has produced its own set of issues, methods, and theories. For example, a great deal of research on autobiographical memory has been undertaken, which necessarily involves detailed studies of individuals' memories of their lives. This research has spawned new conceptions of the changes in memory that occur over a lifetime. There is also more interest in using cognitive psychology to help people solve complex everyday problems and to improve the general quality of life. Of course, for some time the area of human factors psychology has addressed issues concerning efficient human performance in practical situations. These efforts continue, with an emphasis on perceptual and attentional aspects of real-world tasks. However, the need to deal with more complicated everyday tasks, such as making medical diagnoses, and to automate some aspects of these tasks has forged a connection between cognitive psychology and computerization. The new area of "cognitive engineering" has partly emerged out of these concerns.

IT IS SAFE TO SAY THAT THE COGNITIVE SCIENCE IN COGnitive psychology has expanded and that, as a result, cognitive psychology will continue to change as we move into the twenty-first century. *Introductory Readings for Cognitive Psychology* reflects this scenario. The articles in this volume are divided into six sections: background; perception and neurocognition; memory: real, false, and broken; varieties of thought; the emotional mind; and applications.

The background section provides a sense of how cognitive psychology came about and where it might be headed. The recent history of the area is described as is the impact of connectionism. There is also some speculation about the future of cognitive psychology as a distinct discipline, an important question inasmuch as important developments are taking place in academic areas outside of psychology and in the larger society as well.

The section on perception and neurocognition bears witness to the merging of cognitive psychology and neuropsychology and to the development of new measurement techniques. The section begins with a description of classic work on so-called split-brain patients and what it has taught us about the left and right brain. Also included are case studies of a woman who has had a lifelong inability to recognize faces and of a cognitive psychologist who suffered a temporary inability to name some common items, owing to mild brain damage. A final article takes up the results of the newer methodologies to study eye movement that, in this case, have been used to examine reading.

The section on memory provides a wide-ranging set of articles on our mental lifeblood—our memory system. This section builds from a basic question about whether or not there are different kinds of memory systems. The first article asks, for example, is there a separate *episodic* memory system that is devoted to our personal, time-dated experiences? Other articles describe changes in this presumed system from childhood on. The current controversy surrounding the accuracy and permanence of memories is also taken up in articles that

document both the fragility of some memories and the endurance of others. A classic study demonstrates how short-term memory span can be "stretched" by various strategies.

The theme of the section on thought is that thought occurs in a variety of forms that undergo development from the simple to the complex. The first article traces young children's growing appreciation of the way in which one object comes to stand for something else. Succeeding articles explore the question of whether or not autistic individuals understand the concept of other people's minds and how metaphor can be used to convey humor. Other articles in this section examine complex problem solving in the realm of intuitive physics, mathematics, and expertise in general. Since, ideally, the acquisition of knowledge should be extendable beyond its original circumstances, the final article addresses the transfer of thinking skills from one domain to another.

Until recently, cognitive psychologists have largely ignored emotion. This has changed rather dramatically, as nearly every aspect of emotion has come under the cognitive microscope. The section on the emotional mind samples some of the efforts in this emerging area. Included is the issue of whether or not people can be emotionally affected by stimuli without necessarily recognizing them. Anxiety, a basic human condition, is also addressed, as are the theoretical status of emotionally based memories and the effects of mentally suppressing unwanted thoughts.

The final section, which is on practical applications, reflects the recent emphasis on this topic. Psychologists have "taken to the streets" for several reasons—everyday behavior and thought is a rich source of hypotheses; it is a testing ground for more laboratory-based ideas; it is interesting and deserving of study in its own right; and it satisfies a demand for relevance that comes from many segments of society, including cognitive scientists themselves. Theoretically, no aspect of our lives goes untouched by cognition, whether it is beauty, advertising, false memories, listening to music, eyewitness reports, and responding to warnings, all topics that are discussed in this section. The reader will find that many of the articles throughout this volume show a nice balance and interaction between practical interest and theoretical relevance.

On the Internet...

PsycINFO

PsycINFO is a department of the American Psychological Association (APA) dedicated to making it easier for researchers to locate psychological literature that is relevant to their research topics.
http://www.apa.org/psycinfo/

Resources for Psychology and Cognitive Sciences on the Internet

This large collection of psychology and cognitive science sites is maintained by the faculty staff of the Department of Kansei Engineering at Shinshu University in Nagano, Japan.
http://sasuke.shinshu-u.ac.jp/psych/

Part◆1

Background

Howard H. Kendler

◆

Walter Schneider

◆

Earl Hunt

Background

During much of the first half of the twentieth century, the predominant force in academic psychology was *behaviorism*. The favored topic during this era (the so-called great white rat era) was learning, and various theories of learning were fashioned. Most of these theories made the assumption that learning is a simple matter of strengthening stimulus-response (S-R) bonds. Depending upon the theory, bonds could be strengthened by repetition of the stimulus-response connection or by reinforcement of the response in the presence of the stimulus. Learning was thereby reduced to either Pavlovian or to operant conditioning, both of which incorporate repetition and reinforcement principles. Even though the theories differed somewhat on the principle emphasized, all behaviorists agreed on the following basic assumptions: naturally occurring phenomena operate according to mechanistic laws; behavior is a natural phenomenon and so it must operate by such laws as well; mental phenomena, if they exist, are subject to the same laws, but since these phenomena cannot be directly observed and seem to be unreliable and evanescent in any case, they cannot be the primary subject matter of psychology. The dominant belief came to be that psychology must deal only with publicly observable and therefore measurable pieces of behavior. In effect, behaviorism was an attempt to bring into psychology the attitudes and assumptions that seemed to have worked so well in other sciences, especially physiology and physics. Behaviorism was a kind of physics applied to people's movements. Indeed, it was John B. Watson, the founder of behaviorism, who described behavior as "bodies in motion." For the most part, such a view precluded the study of imagery, attention, reasoning, feelings, and anything else associated with cognition.

WORLD WAR II CHANGED ALL THAT, AND THE ROOTS OF COGNITIVE PSYCHOLOGY can be traced in part to the wartime experiences of psychologists. Academic psychologists, like other able-bodied men, were drafted during World War II, and many found themselves working to solve military problems. Needless to say, these were very practical problems, involving such questions as how to improve marksmanship, how to fly airplanes without crashing them, how to improve men's performance in battle conditions, how to keep morale up, and so on. Answering these questions often required psychologists to look more deeply into perceptual processes, decision making, problem solving, and the delicate interface between people and machines. For example, it became clear that perceptual-motor performance was greatly affected by visual and kinesthetic feedback, rather than reinforcement. This finding hastened the assimilation of *cybernetic theory* into psychology, since cybernetics is fundamentally concerned with the regulation of systems through feedback.

At the same time as these more practical psychological research projects were going on, a large group was gathered in England to work on the *Ultra Project*. The goal of this project was to break the intelligence codes being used by the Axis powers (Germany, Italy, and Japan). Mathematicians, logicians, engineers, and others set about working on Enigma, the typewriter-like machine that the Germans used to encrypt messages. As part of this effort, the first modern working computer, Colossus, was developed in order to do calculations that were too tedious to be done by hand. The Ultra Project was a success and played a major role in ending the war.

After the war, when many psychologists came back to practice their trade, they were changed people, with new sets of ideas, new questions, and, perhaps most important, a new perspective on humanity. This perspective emphasized the complexity of human behavior, with the corollary that mind would have to be studied in earnest in order to gain a complete picture of behavior. People were no longer viewed as mere bundles of stimulus-response associations; rather, they were seen as processors of information. The mind was seen as a huge transforming device that takes in information from the environment and radically changes it before outputting it in some behavioral form. And since information was involved, it would have to be described in some way. This issue was addressed by Claude Shannon and Warren Weaver, two electrical engineers, in their *mathematical theory of communication*, which was published in 1949. In this theory, communication was viewed as a process by which information is first encoded, transmitted over some channel, and finally decoded by a receiver (e.g., a radio or a human being). Information itself was defined as a reduction in uncertainty and was measured in terms of binary digits, or bits (a bit being anything that reduces uncertainty by one-half).

In conclusion, in the aftermath of World War II, cybernetics, information theory, and computers were conceptual forces to be reckoned with in psychology. Together, their impact resulted in a new, information-processing framework, which would eventually come to predominate in psychology. In the late 1950s, the linguist Noam Chomsky published *Syntactic Structures*, and that work, along with several papers by psychologist George A. Miller, challenged and undermined the behavioristic approach to language. Chomsky and Miller argued that language is rule-governed and that it is not an elongated chain of stimulus-response connections between words. For many psychologists, the work of Chomsky and Miller symbolized the eclipse of behaviorism. At the same time, however, some behaviorists were beginning to admit subjective or mediating variables into their theories. Indeed, some neobehaviorists, such as Clark L. Hull and Edward C. Tolman, had already done so before the war.

IT IS AGAINST THIS BACKGROUND OF WAR-RELATED DEVELopments, most of them originating outside of academic psychology, that Howard H. Kendler's selection from *Historical Foundations of Modern Psychology* can be appreciated. Kendler fills out the historical background just provided. He traces cognitive psychology back to Wilhelm Wundt in the latter part of the nineteenth century and to several major theorists in the middle part of the twentieth century, including George Miller and Jerome Bruner. He then describes the impact of human engineering (cybernetics, signal detection theory, man-machine systems), communications engineering (including information theory), Chomsky (his emphasis on biology, rules, the creativeness and the hierarchical nature of language), and computer science.

Kendler closes with the thesis that stimulus-response psychology was expanding to include cognition, that writers such as Robert S. Woodworth had, in fact, included the organism in the stimulus-response equation. Nevertheless, Kendler goes on, S-R psychology did not yield a full-fledged cognitive psychology. A revolution had to occur, and he traces that revolution to the failure of Hull's theory, to the desire for a less animal-oriented psychology, to the growing belief that mind cannot be ignored, and to the impact of the science historian Thomas Kuhn's views. Kuhn proposed that sciences advance through stages, including one in which the prevailing paradigm is overthrown due to factual anomalies in the paradigm. In psychology, the paradigm that was being overthrown was behaviorism.

COMPUTERS, OR RATHER THE ANALOGIES AND METAPHORS they have suggested to scientists, have played a major role in shaping modern cognitive psychology. Cognitive scientists have borrowed a number of computer-related concepts—input, sensory register, database, program, hardware, etc.—and have applied them to human cognition. Even more important, many psychologists have adopted the belief that at a formal/mathematical/logical level, there is no difference between computers and humans. Thus, computers should be capable of thinking just as a human does. But how does one arrive at this conclusion?

The conventional answer to this question was provided in a 1950 paper by Alan Turing entitled "Computing Machinery and Intelligence." Turing, a mathematician, was a leader in the Ultra Project, and he played a leading role in the development of Colossus. Although Turing's paper did not have a direct impact on cognitive psychology, it did indirectly influence it because a generation of mathematicians, philosophers, and computer scientists passed on its meaning to the new cognitive scientists. Turing couched his answer to the question of whether or not computers can think in terms of an imitation game, now called the *Turing Test*, in which an interrogator is called upon to guess, based on typewritten replies only, which of two people is a man and which is a woman. If a computer were substituted for the man or woman, could the interrogator tell the difference? In general, would the interrogator's task be made easier? Turing reasoned that if the output of the computer could not be distinguished from that of a human being, then the computer could be considered to be thoughtful. Thus, the computer could be credited with having simulated a human mind or at least some aspect of it. Turing stated that in 50 years (2000 A.D.) computers could play the imitation game well enough that the interrogator would not be able to distinguish between computer and human better than 70 percent of the time. Of course, the view that people's minds are "just" machines can be anathema for a number of reasons, which Turing considered in his paper.

THE COMPUTER THAT TURING HELPED FASHION IS THE digital computer, the kind that most of us are familiar with. Since its invention in the mid-1940s, the digital computer has moved far beyond its original conception as a fast mathematical calculator to a sophisticated, general-purpose manipulator of abstract symbols. This newer conception has required the development of a complex "architecture" for the computer, in which information (on-off electromagnetic pulses) is moved among various components, including a memory, a central processing unit

(CPU), and input-output devices. The proper movement of information requires instructions in the form of programs that tell the central processing unit what to do and when to do it. Active information is put into a register in the CPU. This describes the bare-bones operation of a digital computer. The process can get much more complex, with programs that translate other programs and various sorts of memory structures. The important point is that a digital computer has a highly complex, differentiated system—an architecture—for operating on discrete pieces of information. While computers are doing increasingly well at various expert tasks—diagnosing disease, finding oil, etc.—they do much less well at tasks that humans find easy or consider commonsensical, including talking, recognizing patterns in the environment, and getting around in the world. Every attempt to mimic human functioning with the digital computer seems to run up against the same sorts of problems, including the need for vast amounts of semantic information to be programmed in and recognition of the importance of cultural knowledge, context, and inference.

These sorts of problems and limitations, the arduousness of programming, and questions about the validity of the digital computer metaphor for mind have led some cognitive scientists to look for other models. Of course, cognitive science and cognitive psychology have always had their detractors. Those who take an ecological (Gibsonian) view, for example, are unhappy with the cognitivist's penchant for inventing mental processes and mental structures as explanatory mechanisms. Some are unhappy with the computer metaphor because in their view humans have special qualities that are not found in nonbiological mechanisms. Others are simply unhappy with the tendency toward reductionism—the notion that the mind can be reduced to a set of primitive elements and their relationships. Still others have criticized cognitive science on the grounds that it fixates on the mind at the expense of the environment, it ignores practical problems, and it has failed to produce general theories.

The strongest challenge to mainstream information-processing psychology (and the most recent) comes from *connectionism*, also known as *parallel distributed processing* and *neural network* views. For some psychologists, this challenge may well be a paradigm shift in the Kuhnian sense. This possibility is explored in Walter Schneider's paper "Connectionism: Is It a Paradigm Shift for Psychology?" After first describing some of the characteristics of a paradigm shift—for example, the rules for doing normal research are relaxed—Schneider lays out the nature of connectionistic models. Specifically, he pinpoints four key features of these models: processing occurs in certain elements, knowledge is a matter of the weights that govern the relationship among the elements, the units in the neural network combine their inputs according to mathematical rules, and learning occurs via rules that change the connections between elements. Schneider describes various examples of connectionistic learning, including the now-classic demonstration of "reading" by NET-TALK, a system that learned to associate English text with appropriate English phonology (speech sounds).

Schneider considers some new issues that are aroused by connectionism, including the question of how knowledge is stored (mental representation), the role of hidden units in transforming inputs into outputs, the optimal way to promote learning, and exactly how teaching should be done (e.g., supervised versus unsupervised learning). He also details the early pessimistic views about connectionism; the impact that connectionism is having on psychology in terms of conferences, journals, papers, etc.; and the theoretical machinery that it is yielding. The problems with connectionism are not overlooked by Schneider—the predictions it yields are often redundant; the models it contains in its architecture are unwieldy; and it has difficulty dealing with more complex, higher-order thinking skills. Schneider believes that connectionism is good for the field of cognitive psychology but, in his words, "It may be another field." He concludes that connectionism does represent a paradigm shift in psychology—one that is fraught with dangers as well as benefits.

THE FINAL SELECTION IN PART 1 LOOKS EVEN FURTHER into the crystal ball. In "Pulls and Pushes on Cognitive Psychology: The View Toward 2001," Earl Hunt focuses on "developments outside psychology that influence our opportunities." He claims that the "pushes" on cognitive psychology's opportunities come from biology and the physical sciences. For example, technological advancements have produced new means of inspecting the structure and function of the brain. Furthermore, progress in molecular genetics may allow further precision about the basis of thought. Hunt states that, in general, we can expect a decline in behavioral information-processing research and an upsurge in attempts to link biology and information processing.

Hunt sees the "pulls" on cognitive psychology as coming from mathematics and computer science. Regarding new computer developments, Hunt points to connectionism as a way of linking brain and mind. But this eventuality will require mathematical sophistication, as will neuroscientific advances. Unfortunately, this necessary proficiency in higher mathematics may put cognitive psychology out of reach for many students. Changes in government funding that impact negatively on information-processing psychology may also occur, although the need to understand more complex, real-world problem solving may salvage psychology in these areas. Finally, Hunt red-flags the computerization of work and the aging of the workforce. Computerization, he suggests, would raise questions about human-computer compatibility, and an aging population will have numerous ramifications both within and without psychology. Hunt concludes that "pure information-processing models, for the sake of building models, are probably on the way out," but he also feels that cognitive psychologists can still help provide some of the intellectual tools that society needs, if only they will take up the challenge.

1

Howard H. Kendler

Cognitive Psychology

Cognitive psychology was never born; it gradually coalesced. A variety of orientations, within and outside of psychology, merged to produce a new force in the 1950s that achieved a clear identity in 1966 with the publication of Ulric Neisser's *Cognitive Psychology.*

Today cognitive psychology, which seeks to understand how the mind works, represents the most popular orientation in psychology, receiving a level of support among a broad range of psychologists unmatched in its history. Because cognitive psychology represents a mingling of many different ideas, it fails to have the unity of systematic positions that have been dominated by a single spokesman (e.g., Titchenerian structuralism) or by a closely knit group (e.g., Gestalt psychology). Thus, cognitive psychologists do not speak with one voice; although they share a common orientation, they frequently disagree about important methodological and theoretical issues.

HISTORICAL ROOTS

The numerous historical roots of cognitive psychology can be divided into two main classes; those that emerged within psychology and those that originated in other disciplines.

Influences Within the History of Psychology

Several streams of psychological thought contributed to the development of this movement. These contributions include experimental methods for investigating the mind, theoretical interpretations of the mind, and a new field of psychology that became known as *human engineering.*

Experimental Analysis of the Mind.

Although Wundt denied that thinking could be introspectively observed he nevertheless assumed that mental activity could be inferred from both experimental and historical evidence. His complication experiment and the application of mental chronometry to the analysis of reaction time illustrated the logic of inferring mental activity from empirical evidence. Wundt's efforts anticipated the strategy that was to be followed by most contemporary cognitive psychologists.

General Theoretical Notions.

While conceptualizing the mind as a general system, psychologists differed about how it is organized and functions. Wundt and Titchener distinguished between different kinds of mental content (e.g., sensations, feelings). Functionalists, who were concerned with both mental activity and adjustment, stressed the importance of mental operations. Angell (1904) expressed this interest by suggesting that the major task of the functionalist is to discover "the typical *operations* of consciousness under actual life *conditions.*" Embedded in Angell's statement is a central concern of modern cognitive psychology—how the mind operates on information in order to solve a problem, whether it be simply the recall of a person's name or the proof of a complex mathematical principle.

In contrast to the functionalists' emphasis on mental acts and their adaptive significance, structural features of the mind were stressed by both Gestalt psychology and Tolman's cognitive behaviorism. The *psychological environment* of Gestalt psychology and Tolman's *cognitive map* were mental constructions designed to represent an organism's environment.

Mental structures and cognitive processes.

Psychologists who anticipated cognitive psychology all seemed to be proposing hypotheses about the workings of the mind. As a result, the distinction between mental structures and mental processes gradually became apparent although it is often subtle and sometimes even confusing. The distinction is analogous to the difference between anatomy and physiology. For example, anatomy describes the structure of the stomach while physiology describes the processes with which that organ digests food. Sir Frederic Bartlett (1886–1969), an English psychologist, introduced this distinction when investigating memory. He rejected the conception of remembering as a reproductive process

in which information is passively duplicated in memory. Bartlett (1932) proposed that memory is a reconstructivist process; when hearing a story a person transforms, or more technically, *encodes* the incoming information into a mental structure, a *schema,* that represents the interpretation of the story in line with the listener's preconceptions and attitudes. When recalling the story, the schema is *decoded,* transferred back into the remembered version. In this example the mental structure is the schema and the cognitive processes are encoding and decoding.

Jean Piaget (1896–1980), who was trained as a biologist, became interested in epistemological issues. Instead of treating epistemology as a speculative armchair discipline, Piaget decided to study it scientifically by empirically investigating the development of thought, or what he called *conceptual operations* from infancy through adolescence. In general, Piaget concluded that the growth of intelligence is not a continuous affair in which intellectual functioning gradually improves, but instead occurs in an invariant order of successive stages, each laying the foundation for the next.

Piaget hypothesizes that the structure of the mind undergoes qualitative changes just as a human embryo does during the period of gestation. The human embryo does not simply get larger; its structure changes dramatically. So do schemas, mental representations of objects, and their relations. Piaget's theory, like that of Freud's, was rich in ideas but vague in conception. His impact on modern cognitive psychology was twofold. His formulation stimulated interest in cognitive processes and thereby encouraged research and theorizing in the field of thought and intelligence. At the same time, Piaget's theory, based initially on naturalistic observations, appeared too ambiguous and therefore challenged cognitively oriented psychologists to formulate more precise theories of cognition.

George Miller (born 1920) published an influential paper entitled, *"The magical number seven, plus or minus two: Some limits on our capacity for processing information,"* in 1956. This paper sought to interpret the psychological phenomenon known as the *memory span,* the number of items an individual can recall after just one presentation. By analyzing a variety of findings, Miller concluded the magical number—seven plus or minus two—represented the storage capacity of short-term memory, a finding that was reported in 1871, but subsequently forgotten (Blumenthal, 1977). In other words, Miller suggested that the mind contains a mental structure analogous to a file with several slots with the exact number, depending on the individual, varying from five to nine.

In addition to postulating a memory structure, Miller proposed a process called *chunking,* which refers to the reorganization (encoding) of information to increase the number of items that can be packed into a single slot. For example, the task of remembering the phone number, 961-2834, can be made easier by chunking the number into five slots of information instead of seven; for example, 9-6-1-28-34 instead of 9-6-1-2-8-3-4.

Along with two collaborators, Eugene Galanter and Karl Pribram, Miller published *Plans and the Structure of Behavior* in 1960, which proposed that the *plan* should be substituted for the *stimulus-response (S-R) association* as the basic unit of behavior. A plan, in contrast to an S-R association, is a self-regulating system that uses available information to guide subsequent behavior. A thermostat is an example of a self-regulating system in which a target temperature (70°F) is maintained by the thermostat shutting down the furnace when that temperature is attained and starting the furnace when the temperature falls below that level. In an analogous manner, Miller, Galanter, and Pribram (1960) suggest that information feedback is basic to the execution of a plan. A plan has two functions: to compare the present situation with the desired goal and to activate routines of behavior that reduce the difference between the current situation and the goal state. A simple plan is illustrated in the task of hammering a nail into wood. The goal state is to have the head of the nail flush with the wood. The discrepancy between the goal state and the initial state when the point of the nail is resting against the wood is successively reduced by hammering the nail into the wood until the goal is achieved.

Another important book that encouraged the development of cognitive psychology was *A Study of Thinking* (1956) by Jerome Bruner (born 1915) and two collaborators, Jacqueline Goodnow and George Austin. They offered a mentalistic interpretation of concept learning that stressed a subject's strategy in marked opposition to the passive associationism that Hull had proposed in his interpretation of concept learning in 1920, and which had, from that time, tended to dominate this research area. Jerome Bruner felt that "the banning of 'mental' concepts from psychology was a fake seeking after the gods of the nineteenth-century physical sciences" (Bruner, 1980). Bruner and Miller helped found *The Center for Cognitive Studies* at Harvard in 1962. Establishing a physical presence as well as an active research program contributed to the launching of cognitive psychology.

Human Engineering.

A new branch of psychology, human engineering, developed in response to the needs of the military during and after World War II. The dominant attitude that prevailed at the beginning of the war was that the design of weapon systems, such as airplanes, submarines, radar, and the like, was a purely physical problem. This view proved to be naive. For example, one war plane that seemed to be perfectly engineered suffered a high rate of landing accidents. The reason was discovered to be due to the close proximity between two levers the pilot had to use for braking and retracting the landing gear. Instead of braking after landing the plane, the pilot, who had to keep his eyes on the runway, sometimes accidentally pulled the lever for retracting the landing gear and landed the plane on its belly. Such accidents could have been avoided had the reactions of the pilot been considered. The controls should have been designed, as psychologists would be quick to point out (Chapanis, Garner, & Morgan, 1949), so as to require entirely different arm movements for braking and retracting the landing gear. When the controls were redesigned accordingly, the source of the dangerous confusion was eliminated, and so were the accidents.

A core concept in human engineering is the *man-machine system* which stresses the principle that humans and machines operate as a single system. Thus, both psychological and engineering knowledge is essential for the effective design of machines. In addition, information processing, the flow of information through a man-machine system, was recognized as a basic variable in human engineering. If the necessary information does not reach the human, as was the case for the pilot who could not distinguish clearly between braking and retracting the landing gear, the man-machine system breaks down.

The radar operated advance warning system in Alaska is another example of a man-machine system. The radar operator's job is to detect any flying object traveling toward the United States. On his radar screen, which is similar to a TV screen, flying objects are seen as *blips,* points of light against a background of less intense light. In reacting to his scope, the radar operator must decide whether the activity observed indicates that a missile or plane is approaching. The task confronting the radar operator was conventionally conceptualized as purely a sensory problem. Did the operator see a blip or not? The analysis of this problem by signal detection theory (Green & Swets, 1966) suggested that nonsensory, as well as sensory processes are involved. When the blip is very faint, the operator is not sure he senses anything. A decision must be made to report or not to report a blip. One factor that will influence the decision is the relative cost of making one of the two mistakes: either not detecting a flying object (a miss) or reporting a blip when one is not there (a false alarm). What are the consequences of each? A miss could lead to disaster. Reporting a false alarm would waste some interceptor missiles. The relative weight of each error will influence an operator's decision. An operator who establishes a lenient criterion will produce many false alarms. A strict criterion will minimize false alarms but will risk the possibility that an incoming missile or airplane will not be reported and consequently not intercepted.

Signal detection theory provided a mathematical technique to sort out the observer's sensitivity from his decision criterion. In addition, it conceptualized humans as information processors and decision makers, basic constructs in the newly emerging cognitive orientation.

Contributions of Other Disciplines to Cognitive Psychology

A reasonable case can be made that cognitive psychology, or what some prefer to call *cognitive science,* is more a product of engineering, linguistics, and computer science than it is of psychology. These disciplines provided fundamental ideas that

molded the development of cognitive psychology, particularly in the research area designated as information processing.

Communications Engineering.

Modern technology demands numerous kinds of communication: telephone, television, radio, and so forth. Can all forms of communication be analyzed within a common framework? Claude Shannon (1948), a mathematician in the employ of Bell Telephone Laboratories thought so, and presented a general theory of communication for inanimate systems such as the telephone that took account of all the changes that occurred within the system from the physical input to the physical output. The basic structure of this general communication system is illustrated in Figure 1. Several psychologists applied Shannon's ideas to human communication, both to the cognitive processes within an individual, and to communication between individuals.

Consider the relevance of Shannon's general communication system to the case of a student in a classroom listening to a professor's lecture. The professor is the *source* of the *message* which is *transmitted* by both auditory signals (the lecture) and visual *signals* (diagrams on blackboard) to the auditory and visual *channels.* The signals in a channel can be degraded by *noise.* For example, a neighboring conversation can prevent a student from hearing the professor clearly. The concept of noise in communication theory, however, is not simply limited to interfering sound. Noise refers to all events, outside or within a receiver, that degrade a signal. Just as static reduces the clarity of a radio signal, so do the fantasies of a student degrade the signals emitted by the professor.

The signals *received* by the student are transformed (encoded) into a message that is remembered and later decoded into information that can be utilized during an examination; test performance is determined by the quality of the message at its *destination* (examination). Numerous events throughout the general communication system can influence the quality of that message. For example, the professor's too-rapid lecturing style could overload the auditory channel and prevent the student from encoding the entire message.

Communication engineering had an important influence on the development of cognitive psychol-

Figure 1

The Basic Structure of Shannon's General Communication System

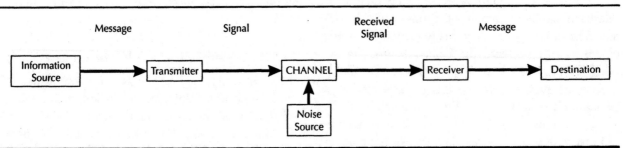

The text describes the operating characteristics of this system.

ogy, not because its theory could be simply superimposed on human cognition, but instead because it offered a fruitful analogy for interpreting cognitive processes. Of basic importance was the concept of *information* which, in Shannon's theory, referred to physical changes (e.g., electrical changes in a telephone line) in an inanimate communication system. Shannon offered a mathematically precise interpretation of information that proved extremely useful in designing computers and communication systems but was discovered to be inadequate for representing human knowledge. Nevertheless, the notion that information is a basic component in human cognition was encouraged, and numerous structures and processes were suggested by communication theory which provided direction, as well as hypotheses, for the experimental analysis of the mind. Examples include *encoding, decoding, information processing, communication channels, channel capacity, noise,* and so forth. Finally, communication engineering suggested the idea of a flowchart of the sort that appears in Figure 1. The flowchart is a diagrammatic representation of a sequence of successive events within an integrated system. Cognitive theorists found flowcharts useful for analyzing cognitive activities into their basic components.

Chomsky's Linguistic Theory.

Since the time of Wundt, psychologists have sought to understand language. Skinner (1957) offered an interpretation of verbal behavior that assumed that contingencies of reinforcement govern linguistic actions. Implicit in this assumption are several important corollaries: (1) Verbal behavior is concep-

tualized in terms of its adaptive characteristics; (2) Human language is continuous with animal behavior; (3) Verbal behavior is primarily learned behavior; and (4) Theories, particularly mentalistic ones, are not required for understanding human language.

Noam Chomsky played a major role in stimulating the development of cognitive psychology by vigorously opposing all of Skinner's basic assumptions at the time that Skinner reigned as the dominant behaviorist. Chomsky argues that the understanding of language is not to be found in the contingencies of reinforcement but instead in the innate biological structure of human beings. Every child is born with a general notion of a universal syntax that enables her to communicate, in her native language, at an early age in a grammatically appropriate form. Even though the child cannot state the grammatical rules, and at times makes errors, linguistic usage is nevertheless guided by the innate syntactical rules, as demonstrated by the fact that she intuitively distinguishes between a correct sentence like, *Jimmy ate the apple,* and ungrammatical strings of words like, *Ate Jimmy the apple.*

Chomsky also argues that linguistic behavior is a creative enterprise; it cannot be reduced to a simple mechanical chaining conception in which a sentence is formed by each successive word triggering the next one. Two reasons are offered for rejecting this associative chaining hypothesis. One is that an enormous amount of time would be required to learn grammatically correct sentences, much too long for children to be able to speak grammatically. Second, each person is capable of uttering and understanding an *infinite* number of sentences, sentences that are different (e.g., *the unicorn jumped over the satellite*) from those previously uttered or heard. The principle of associative chaining could not possibly explain such novelty. Because of these two criticisms, Chomsky was led to the position that "rules in the head" generated sentences, not an associative network of words.

Chomsky distinguishes between *linguistic performance* and *linguistic competence,* a distinction that bears some similarity to the *learning-performance* distinction of Tolman and Hull. Linguistic performance involves sentences uttered or comprehended. Linguistic competence is the knowledge of language that enables a person to determine whether a sentence is syntactically correct.

A sentence consists of two components: *surface structure* and *deep structure.* Surface structure refers to the syntactical organization of a sentence. *The girl throws the ball* and *The ball is thrown by the girl* have two different phrase structures; the first being a simple active sentence while the second is a simple passive sentence. Both sentences express the common notion that a girl is throwing a ball, but each expresses it with a different surface structure. To account for their shared meaning, Chomsky formulates the construct *deep structure,* the crucial element of his original theory. Deep structure is a theoretical construct that represents a basic syntactical structure within the mind from which a series of sentences such as *The girl throws the ball, The ball is thrown by the girl, Is the ball thrown by the girl?* and so forth are generated into their surface form.

Supporting the distinction between deep structure and surface structure are cases of ambiguous sentences. *The shooting of the hunters was terrible* can mean either that *The hunters were poor marksmen* or *The hunters were targets.* Chomsky concludes that the ambiguity occurs when the same surface structure emerges from different deep structures. Such differences cannot be understood, Chomsky argues, if language is analyzed simply in terms of an associative chaining mechanism.

This brief description of a complicated linguistic theory stresses several of Chomsky's important attitudes and ideas that encouraged the development of cognitive psychology. First, Chomsky's concerns shifted attention away from the functional properties of verbal behavior to the organization of language, which is responsible for its endless novelty and diversity: "The central fact to which any sig-

nificant theory must address itself is this: a mature speaker can produce a new sentence of his language on the appropriate occasion, and other speakers can understand it immediately, though it is equally new to them" (Chomsky, 1964). Second, Chomsky insisted that a theoretical effort was necessary to explain language, one in which postulating mental structures (e.g., deep structure) and cognitive processes (e.g., transformation of deep structure into surface structure) were demanded. Third, by emphasizing genetic factors, Chomsky alerted psychologists to theoretical distortions resulting from ignoring genetic preprogramming. Fourth, Chomsky's theory conceptualized human language behavior as species-specific, thus encouraging the view that the higher mental processes could only be understood by studying humans. By accepting this position, Chomsky was essentially bucking the Darwinian trend in American psychology which assumed that all forms of human behavior were continuous with the behavior of lower animals.

Computer Science.

Computer science is a loosely organized collection of related disciplines that have emerged from the development of computers. Computers, with which most students are now familiar, are electronic machines capable of accepting, processing, and communicating information. These activities correspond to the three functional units of the typical computer: *input, information processing,* and *output* (Figure 2). The input unit of the computer receives the information, which is then encoded and transferred in its coded state into the information-processing unit, where the information is stored in a simple magnetic code on a disk, tape, or drum. The arithmetic-logic component performs arithmetical and logical operations on the information that is stored in memory. The control component interprets and executes the commands of the *program,* a set of instructions that is stored in memory. The computer will do exactly what it is instructed to do—nothing more, nothing less. To illustrate: at one college campus, a computer was programmed to select partners for blind dates on the basis of students' interests, attitudes, likes, and dislikes. The results were rather successful except for a brother and sister who were paired together. No one had bothered to program the instruction that siblings should not be paired.

The output unit communicates the processed information to the user of the computer in a particular form desired (e.g., printer, cathode ray oscilloscope, etc.). Computers, as you know, can be programmed to furnish immediate information about available seatings for all flights of an airline or to steer a spacecraft to a rendezvous in space. The ability of computers to *behave* intelligently has been referred to as *artificial intelligence,* a term that can be most clearly defined as "the art of creating machines that perform tasks considered to require intelligence when performed by humans" (attributed to Minsky by Kurzweil, 1985). It is important to recognize that this definition of artificial intelligence is neutral as to whether or not a particular example of artificial intelligence simulates human cognition.

While the computer, with its capacity for artificial intelligence, was revolutionizing society, two computer scientists, Alan Newell (born 1927) and Herbert Simon (born 1916), who was awarded a Nobel Prize in economics in 1978, offered an idea that revolutionized psychology, namely, that *computers can be programmed to simulate human thinking.* The justification for this strategy is that the human mind, according to Newell and Simon, can be conceptualized as a symbol manipulating system, and *so can the computer.* Both the mind and the computer are instances of the same kind of system; they both process information. This assumption led to an important research program that was designed to unravel the mysteries of the mind—the principles of human cognition—with the assistance of the digital computer.

THE EMERGENCE OF COGNITIVE PSYCHOLOGY

The historical roots of cognitive psychology all, in some way or another, are related to how the mind is functionally organized and operates. These general ideas were perceived by a large segment of the psychological community in the 1960s as being in direct opposition to the views of radical behaviorism, which had become the preeminent stimulus-response psychology. In fact, radical behaviorism's status had become so dominant that it was frequently, and erroneously, taken to be equivalent to

Figure 2 ⎯⎯⎯⎯⎯⎯⎯⎯⎯⎯⎯⎯⎯⎯⎯⎯⎯

Schematic Diagram of the Main Functional Units of a Computer

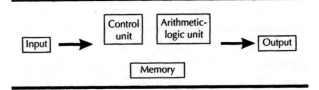

all of behaviorism. The result of this historical error was to ignore evolutionary changes that were occurring in stimulus-response psychology from its early beginnings.

Robert S. Woodworth (1869–1962), who helped establish the Functionalist school at Columbia University, noted that:

> The objections raised to S-R formula [to describe behavior] means that it is too limited. It seems to imply that nothing important occurs between the stimulus and motor response. Or it seems to imply that the sensory stimulus is the only causative factor in the arousal of a response. These limitations can be avoided by the addition of another symbol to stand for the organism (the S-O-R formula). The O inserted between S and R makes explicit the obvious role of the living and active organism in the process; O receives the stimulus and makes the response. This formula suggests that psychologists should not limit their investigations to the input of stimuli and output of motor responses. They should ask how the input of stimuli can possibly give rise to the output; they should observe intervening processes if possible or at least hypothesize them and devise experiments for testing the hypothesis (Woodworth, 1958, p. 31).

This general S-O-R orientation was adopted by many neofunctionalists to investigate a variety of problem-solving phenomena that was later to interest cognitive psychologists. The general approach to these research problems by neofunctionalists and cognitivists differed. Influenced by the antimentalism of behaviorism, neofunctionalists minimized, if not eliminated, any mentalistic processes in their interpretation of thinking while subsequent cognitive psychologists felt no such inhibitions.

Woodworth: S-O-R conception anticipated the efforts of S-R mediational psychologists, who sought to interpret cognitive phenomena by postulating intervening processes between stimulus input and the response output within the general orientation of Hull and Spence. Osgood: (1957) offered an elaborate mediational analysis of perception and language while Kuenne (1946) and Kendler and Kendler (1962) emphasized the importance of representation in developmental changes that occur in the discriminative behavior of young children. Spence (1950) acknowledged that different mechanisms were required to explain the cognitive behavior of humans than were needed to interpret animal behavior. In analyzing human cognitive behavior, Spence proposed a flowchart that anticipated later information-processing conceptions, and that radically departed from his own analysis of the discrimination learning of the rat (Spence, 1936). In his flow diagram, he employed concepts (e.g., sense reception, signification, verbal meaning) that referred to the innate organization of the brain, cognitive expectations, and linguistic meaning. These higher level processes "badly need the attention of all psychologists, cognition, S-R, or whatever else" (Spence, 1950).

Thus, the stimulus-response psychology of Hull and his disciples, which had its roots in the theoretical analysis of animal learning, was gradually expanding to the cognitive process of humans. Why did psychology have to experience a *cognitive revolution* instead of gradual evolutionary development of stimulus-response learning theories to encompass human cognition?

Four interrelated historical forces operated to encourage a cognitive revolution instead of a gradual evolutionary extension of stimulus-response psychology. First, because Hull's general theory fell far short of its stated objectives, little interest was expressed in employing the Hullian framework as a launching pad for the investigation of human cognition. Second, a disenchantment was spreading with the general strategy of basing a theory of human cognition, even partly, on the analysis of animal behavior. Many psychologists perceived human cognition as unique in the animal kingdom and, therefore, any theory of animal behavior was considered irrelevant to the task of understanding cognitive psychology, a position that S-R mediational theorists strongly rejected. Third, and probably of paramount importance, was the emerging intuition that the mind could not be ignored when interpreting human cognition. Even though the idea that the direct examination of consciousness could yield

valid theoretical principles was generally rejected, the conception of a psychology free of the mind, as Hull proposed, was considered inadequate to the task of interpreting human cognition. A satisfactory theory demanded a conception of the mind, which in turn required an appropriate descriptive language. The idea that a stimulus-response language, even when enlarged by mediational mechanisms, could describe cognition seemed unrealistic. Stimulus-response language, with its antimentalistic bias, seemed too sterile and restrictive to represent the full richness of human cognition. Cognitively oriented psychologists decided it would be more strategic to start with a new language than to continue with an impoverished stimulus-response idiom. Fourth, the need for a revolution in psychology was encouraged by Thomas Kuhn's *The Structure of Scientific Revolutions* (1962), a book that described the history of physics from the time of Copernicus. Kuhn's major thesis is that scientific progress is not based on the accumulation of individual discoveries and theoretical refinements, but instead results from a repetitive historical cycle that consists of two markedly different enterprises, *normal science* and *revolution.* Normal science refers to the accumulation of knowledge within a widely adopted global orientation known as a *paradigm,* a "strong network of commitments—conceptual, theoretical, instrumental, and methodological, and quasimetaphysical" (Kuhn, 1962), that shapes the kind of research that is conducted and the type of theoretical interpretation that is offered. During this period of normal science, facts are discovered that cannot be easily incorporated into the prevailing paradigm. This initiates the second state of historical development, during which time a prevailing paradigm is overthrown by a new one. *The Structure of Scientific Revolutions* enjoyed instant popularity and its historical conception was perceived to be applicable to psychology. Many psychologists became convinced that a paradigmatic shift from stimulus-response behaviorism to cognitive psychology was demanded. Because Kuhn's historical analysis appeared so compelling, the cognitive revolution was encouraged.

REFERENCES

Angell, J. R. (1904). *Psychology.* New York: Holt, Rinehart & Winston.

Bartlett, F. C. (1932). *Remembering: A study in experimental and social psychology.* Cambridge: Cambridge University Press.

Blumenthal, A. L. (1977). *The process of cognition.* Englewood Cliffs, NJ: Prentice-Hall.

Bruner, J. S. (1980). Jerome S. Bruner. In G. Lindzey (Ed.), *A history of psychology in autobiography.* Vol. 7, San Francisco: W. A. Freeman.

Bruner, J. S., Goodnow, J. J., & Austin, G. A. (1956). *A study of thinking.* New York: John Wiley & Sons.

Chapanis, A., Garner, W. R. & Morgan, C. T. (1949). *Applied experimental psychology.* New York: John Wiley & Sons.

Chomsky, N. (1964) *Current issues in linguistic theory.* The Hague: Mouton.

Green, D. M. & Swets, J. A. (1966). *Signal detection theory and psychophysics.* New York: John Wiley & Sons.

Kendler, H. H. & Kendler, T. S. (1962). Vertical and horizontal processes in problem solving. *Psychological Review,* 69, 1–16.

Kuenne, M. R. (1946). Experimental investigation of the relation of language to transposition behavior in young children. *Journal of Experimental Psychology, 36,* 471–490.

Kuhn, T. S. (1962). *The structure of scientific revolutions.* Chicago: University of Chicago Press.

Miller, G. A., Galanter, E. & Pribram, K. H. (1960). *Plans and the structure of behavior.* New York: Holt, Rinehart & Winston.

Neisser, U. (1966). *Cognitive psychology.* New York: Appleton-Century-Crofts.

Osgood, C. E. (1957). A behavioristic analysis of perception and language as cognitive phenomena. *Contemporary approaches to cognition: A symposium held at the University of Colorado.* Cambridge, MA: Harvard University Press.

Shannon, C. E. (1948). A mathematical theory of communication. *Bell Systems Technical Journal, 27,* 379–423, 623–656.

Skinner, B. F. (1957). *Verbal behavior.* New York: Appleton-Century-Crofts.

Spence, K. W. (1950). Cognitive versus stimulus-response theories of learning. *Psychological Review,* 57, 159–172.

Woodworth, R. S. (1958). *Dynamics of behavior.* New York: Holt, Rinehart & Winston.

2

Walter Schneider

Connectionism: Is It a Paradigm Shift for Psychology?

Connectionism is a method of modeling cognition as the interaction of neuron-like units. Connectionism has received a great deal of interest and may represent a paradigm shift for psychology. The nature of a paradigm shift (Kuhn, 1970) is reviewed with respect to connectionism. The reader is provided an overview on connectionism including: an introduction to connectionist modeling, new issues it emphasizes, a brief history, its developing sociopolitical impact, theoretical impact, and empirical impact. Cautions, concerns, and enthusiasm for connectionism are expressed.

In recent years there has been an explosive interest in modeling cognition within a connectionist framework. The connectionist framework assumes that cognition is carried out via the mutual interaction of neuron-like elements. The theoretical interest in this approach probably represents the most dramatic shift in theoretical orientation in psychology in the last 20 years. This modeling is still in its infancy. We are currently in a period of exciting development. In this presidential address, I review some of the basics of connectionist modeling and describe the reasons for the enthusiasm and some reasons for caution. I also encourage the reader to try to decide for himself/herself whether or not this represents a paradigm shift in the sense of Kuhn (1970).

Throughout the history of psychology, we have generally tried to describe the brain in terms of the most complex systems we understand. In this century the brain has been described in terms of a telephone network, a homeostatic system, a computer system, a semantic net, and a production system. Connectionism is different: it seeks to model cognition in terms of something we do not understand, that is, how the brain operates. It utilizes very simplistic features of the brain's physiology to attempt to model cog-

From Walter Schneider, "Connectionism: Is It a Paradigm Shift for Psychology?" *Behavior Research Methods, Instruments, and Computers,* vol. 19, no. 2 (1987), pp. 73–83. Copyright © 1987 by Walter Schneider. Reprinted by permission of The Psychonomic Society, Inc.

nitive processes. Connectionism examines computation based on the assumption of many parallel processing elements. Each element combines simple analog inputs weighted by the strength of the connection to produce analog or digital outputs. Connectionism does not incorporate either the microstructure (e.g., differential polarization, depending on whether the synapse contacts the cell body or the dendrite) or macrostructure (e.g., very specific neuroanatomical connections between regions of the cortex) of neurophysiology (see Sejnowski, 1986). However, the simplifications do make the models tractable and allow us to begin looking at what neural-like systems could compute. As a result of dissatisfaction with previous modeling frameworks and an availability of computer resources, a number of researchers have begun a movement toward modeling connectionist systems.

CHARACTERISTICS OF A PARADIGM SHIFT

It is useful to review some of the characteristics of a paradigm shift according to Kuhn (1970). Four characteristics of a paradigm shift seem to be present in the current movement toward connectionism. Kuhn commented that "all crises begin with a blurring of the paradigm and a consequent loosening of the rules for normal research" (p. 84). This loosening typically occurs partially because few practitioners agree on what the paradigm is. In the 1970s there was a clear movement away from box models of information processing to a variety of representations (e.g., levels of processing, schemata, semantic networks, and production systems). One of the examples of this loosening is that a number of psychologists are now studying learning in computer models rather than explicitly examining learning in humans. Kuhn commented that anomalies appear that do not fit the traditional view (pp. 82–91). In psychology, due to our relatively weak theories, there are many phenomena that we poorly predict. Two phenomena that are particularly important from the connectionist perspective are our abilities to learn without instruction and to perform procedural tasks very well even when we are unable to specify the rules of that performance. The difficulty of obtaining knowledge from experts to build expert systems illustrates the problems of rule-based descriptions.

Kuhn (1970) suggested that a new paradigm must provide the hope that it is possible to march forward (p. 158). The connectionist framework suggests that we might be able to connect the computational, cognitive, and physiological levels of analysis and to do so with a conceptually very simple system. During a paradigm shift "communication across the revolutionary divide is inevitably partial" (p. 149). Connectionism is introducing new vocabulary (e.g., vectors, weight spaces), new mathematics (e.g., eigenvectors, gradient descent), and even new rules of evidence in psychology (e.g., posing simulation experiments about small-scale learning systems to illustrate what can be learned by such systems). Finally, Kuhn stated that "during the transition period there will be a large but never complete overlap between the problems that can be solved by the old and the new paradigm" (p. 85). For example, connectionism and production systems both examine learning. However, connectionism focuses on slow learning, such as learning the correspondence between text and speech, which may require 40,000 trials of training (e.g., Sejnowski & Rosenberg, 1986). Product system learning typically examines learning that occurs in under 10 trials (e.g., J. R. Anderson, 1983).

DEFINING FEATURES OF CONNECTIONIST MODELS

Four defining features are common to all connectionist models. First, processing is assumed to occur in populations of simple elements. The letter H, for example, may be encoded as a set of eight elements that have binary values for features, such as vertically symmetric, horizontally symmetric, diagonally symmetric, not rounded, no diagonal, not closed, and without descender. Although some information may be encoded by a single element being on, most information is coded by a set of elements being on or a vector of activation.

The second, and perhaps prototypical, characteristic is that all knowledge is stored in the connectionist weights between the elements. Knowledge is stored in the associations or strength of connections between neural-like elements. The knowledge is stored in a small number of association matrices that represent the addition of all the stimulus response patterns the system has learned. This results in making the knowledge very context sensitive. For example, it may be more difficult to learn the past tense of *go* as being *went* because for most words the past tense of words is formed by adding *ed* (see Rumelhart & McClelland, 1986a).

The third characteristic is that all the units perform a simple combination of their inputs (e.g., addition or multiplication) and perform a simple nonlinear transformation on those inputs (e.g., a logistic function). There is generally no complex matching of a particular set of inputs to a unit to some internal pattern (e.g., as might occur in a symbol-processing–based comparison). Rather, a unit generally simply adds or multiplies all the inputs. The nonlinear transformation is sometimes represented as a simple saturation effect (e.g., a neuron can fire at a frequency of no less than 0 and no more than 1,000 times per second). This nonlinearity is critical in that it gives the models the ability to categorize information (J. A. Anderson & Mozer, 1981).

The fourth characteristic is that learning occurs via simple learning rules that are based on local information available within the unit. Learning involves modifying the connections to enable a later input pattern to evoke a new output pattern. There are a variety of learning rules that have been employed (see Rumelhart & McClelland, 1986b). In order to associate an input to an output, the weights between the input and output units are modified so that the input unit will evoke the output. If two units were on in the input layer and two units were on in the output layer, the connection strength between the input and output units would be increased to a level of a desired output of one divided by the number of input neurons that were on. This results in the input pattern becoming able to evoke the output pattern. In order to reduce the interference between different input patterns in the same association network, a variety of more sophisticated learning rules (e.g., delta rule, Boltzmann learning, back propagation algorithm; see Rumelhart, Hinton, & Williams, 1986) are utilized.

EXAMPLE OF CONNECTIONIST LEARNING

There are six basic steps in conducting a connectionist simulation. First, the input and output units and codes for the model must be specified. Second, the connection architecture specifying the number of units at the input, output, and any intermediate layers of processing must be established. Third, the initial weights must be set to small random values. Fourth, the input and the desired output must be presented for all the input and output relations to be learned. Fifth, some learning rule must be applied such that the weights are updated so that the input comes to activate the output. The simulation may present the presentation and learning steps hundreds of thousands of times. Sixth, diagnostic experiments (e.g., presenting degraded stimuli, cutting out connections, examining transfer to related patterns) must be run to determine the robustness and generalizability of the knowledge.

Probably the flashiest demonstration of connectionist learning is embodied in NET-TALK by Sejnowski and Rosenberg (1986) (see Figure 1). They taught a network to learn to associate English text to the appropriate English phonology. There were seven groups of letter positions of visual input. Each position could be encoded as one of 29 characters including punctuation. There were 26

Figure 1 ————————

Schematic Drawing of the Sejnowski and Rosenberg (1986) NET-TALK Connection Architecture

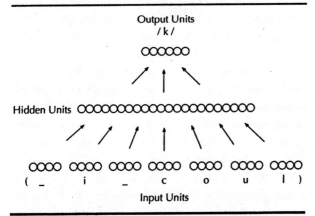

Input units are shown on the bottom of the pyramid, with seven groups for sequential letter positions. Each hidden unit in the intermediate layer receives inputs from all of the input units on the bottom layer, and in turn sends its outputs to all 26 phonemic feature units in the output layer. An example of an input string of letters is shown below the input groups, and the correct output phoneme for the middle letter is shown above the output layer. The network was presented letter strings and phonemic patterns. The connection weights were altered using back propagation. Sejnowski, T. J. and Rosenberg, C. R., Parallel networks that learn to pronounce English text, Complex Systems 1, 145–168 (1987).

output feature units coding one of 53 potential phonemes. The intermediate or hidden units recoded the input to produce the desired output. The model was presented successive passes over the text and the phonology of a corpus of 1,024 words of continuous informal speech produced by a child. After 10,000 presentations of words, the network was about 85% accurate at specifying the phonemes for the text input. An accuracy of 90% was reached by 20,000 trials and of 95% by 50,000 trials. The demonstration is particularly memorable because one can listen to the network speak. The output of the network controls a synthetic speech production system. During the initial learning, the system babbles, continuously outputting a few vowels. It gradually learns to distinguish between vowels and consonants, and then it learns to identify the space as a pause. The system begins to babble in pseudospeech form and gradually acquires some words. After 40,000 trials, it produces words that sound intuitively like those you might expect to hear from a 2-year-old child. This demonstration is very intriguing, and the auditory tape produced by the network has been played many times, including once on network television on the "Today Show."

With a working connectionist model in hand, there are a variety of experiments that can be performed. First, one can look at the type of units developed to perform the task. This is done by examining the input and output weights for each of the units. The units each specialize in performing some complex functional transformation of the input to the output. It is generally very difficult to interpret the form of the units. The units operate in very high-dimensional spaces (e.g., 80 dimensions). Examining any one unit in isolation provides one with little information about what the network is doing as a whole. The information is distributed across all of the units in the network. After the network has learned to map a particular input to an output, one can examine how well this learning generalizes to novel words. NET-TALK reproduced correctly 78% of the novel words it was presented. One can also examine how the network reacts to damage to the network. These systems are typically quite robust to substantial amounts of damage in the network (e.g., J. A. Anderson, 1983). NET-TALK illustrated that relearning after damage to the network can be substantially faster (i.e., 10 times faster) than the original learning. One can

also explore such issues as how learning changes as a function of the number of units in the intermediate layers.

A PARADIGM SHIFT EXPOSES NEW ISSUES

A paradigm shift emphasizes new issues. These are often issues that existed in the field before but now are brought to center stage for close examination. Four issues are particularly important in the connectionist paradigm. The issue of representation, the hidden units problem and learning rules, the problem of sequencing, and the nature of teaching.

The representational issue involves coding information so that connectionist networks can perform nontrivial information processing tasks. For example, if one wants a model to perceive words exhibiting behaviors that humans produce, should the model have levels for visual features, letters, and word units (e.g., see McClelland & Rumelhart, 1981)? What are the semantic features of nouns (McClelland & Kawamoto, 1986)? How are family relationships coded in a network (Hinton, 1986)? In order to produce a workable model, people have to become very explicit as to what information is stored in a network. Rumelhart and McClelland (1986a) were unable to have their simulation accurately associate word phonemes to the phonemes for the past tense of words using a number of coding schemes. They then tried coding words in terms of Wickelphones (a scheme proposed by Wickelgren [1969] to code a phoneme in the context of its preceding and following phoneme). With this coding scheme the networks could learn to associate words with the past tense sound of the words. Producing representations that are learnable in realistic time periods provides a serious constraint on connectionist models. These constraints allow the use of learnability constraints to evaluate representations.

Connectionism has given considerable emphasis to the "hidden unit problem" (Hinton & Sejnowski, 1986). In order to learn complex responses to a given input pattern, one cannot simply connect the inputs to the output units. If one directly connects the input units to the output units, only first-order relationships can be learned. For example, if two inputs are connected to one output, the network can learn to perform either an AND or an OR operation. However, it cannot learn to perform an exclusive XOR operation (i.e, "on" if either of the inputs are on; "off" either if both of the inputs are off or if both of the inputs are "on"). A network cannot learn such second-order information with only pair-wise weights between the visible units (i.e., the input and output units). In order to learn such input/output relationships, a set of hidden units are needed that receive connections from the input unit and make connections to the output units. However, the hidden units themselves are not set directly by either the input or the output. Changes in the connection strength in the hidden units reorganize the input pattern to allow the learning of more complex input/output patterns (Rumelhart, Hinton, & Williams, 1986). Algorithms that enable hidden unit learning develop truly emergent properties. For example, networks with hidden units can solve the XOR problem (Ackley, Hinton, & Sejnowski, 1985). NET-TALK reached only an 80% accuracy in a network without hidden units, whereas it reached a 95% accuracy with hidden units. The study of the hidden unit problem has emphasized the need to understand the nature of higher order similarity. Human learning is very much influenced by similarity. Traditional approaches to learning have had relatively poor techniques for interpreting and predicting these similarity effects.

The third issue emphasized in connectionist simulations is the problem sequencing. For example, should training proceed by first showing the prototypes of a category and then showing the more distant exemplars? As networks are presented examples, they perform a search through a weight space (i.e., the strengths of all the connections), trying to come up with the best combination of weights. Depending upon whether practice is distributed or massed, differential learning is observed that looks similar to that seen in humans (see Rosenberg & Sejnowski, 1986). Connectionism emphasizes learning rules that can rapidly modify weights so that the hidden units can perform complex computations (e.g., Boltzmann learning, back propagation; see Rumelhart, Hinton, & Williams, 1986).

The fourth issue in connectionism is an explicit concern for various levels of teaching. Connectionist networks can learn in one of three types of learning or supervision environments. The first class is *supervised learning,* in which a teacher explicitly indicates to the network what the correct output state is for any input state. In this sense, the teacher is a supervisor. The network then compares the output produced by the input to the desired output and uses that difference in activation to modify the weights in the network. The NET-TALK example is an instance of supervised learning. Supervised learning is slow initially, but the network can very quickly acquire new associations that are similar to previous associations.

The second class of learning involves a yes-no teacher and is referred to as *reinforcement learning.* In such a situation the teacher provides the learner feedback only at the end of a trial, after the student has executed many operations. Barto and Anandan (1985) taught a connectionist network to perform a pole-balancing operation on a moving cart. The network would push the stick left or right, trying to balance it on the cart as long as possible. Eventually, after many stick movements, the cart would run into a barrier on the left or right side. This running into the barrier was the only feedback the network received. The network then had to learn when to push the pole to the left or right to try to balance it so that the cart would stay between the two barriers. The stick might be moved a hundred times before the cart would hit one of the barriers. The system learned to perform this task by dividing the learning into two components. The controlled network controlled the stick and performed operations similar to supervised learning. However, the supervision was provided by a second teacher network. This network used the input from the controller to try to predict whether or not a "yes" or a "no" would come from the teacher (i.e., whether it would hit a barrier). The teacher network developed the ability to predict error signals that the supervised learning teacher would provide during the time preceding the "yes/no" reinforcement. The teacher network used this information to give feedback to the controller network. The controller network then learned via supervised-like learning procedures and eventually acquired the skill. It should be noted that learning under this procedure is far slower than learning via supervised learning procedures.

The third class of learning is *unsupervised learning,* or learning without any teacher at all. Under this type of learning, the system tries to predict its own behavior through a small number of hidden units. For example, Elman and Zipser (1987) used unsupervised learning to have a network learn the basic features of speech phonetic perception. In their model they used 50 input units for portions of the speech spectrogram, 20 hidden units, and 50 output units that predicted the speech spectrogram. The input pattern activated the hidden units, and the hidden units activated output units that paralleled the input units. The network was able to compare the input to what it produced from that coded version of the input. Since the hidden unit level contained far fewer units than the input or output level, the hidden units had to develop some type of generalized scheme for coding the information. The hidden units captured the major higher order invariances of the input. Elman and Zipser (1987) presented the acoustic stimulus, "this is the voice of the neural network," to the network 100,000 times. Then the hidden units captured sufficient features of the input so that the network could reproduce the speech quite intelligibly. More importantly, the network captured generalizations of the inputs. The hidden units were, in essence, encoding the stimulus in phoneme-like feature codes that could be used for higher levels of processing. Using unsupervised learning, a network can develop representations of higher-order invariances of the external world as a result of mere exposure. This type of unsupervised learning suggests how the Suzuki method of teaching violin might be effective. A student who repeatedly hears certain acoustic patterns learns to encode those features of the pattern. This encoding can be used later to verify whether the student can produce the desired acoustic code. More generally, this unsupervised learning provides an interpretation of how listening to speech might help a child learn the phonemes of the target language in the absence of corrective feedback.

BRIEF HISTORY OF CONNECTIONISM

In the short history of connectionism in psychology, it has already had a birth, a death, and a rebirth (see Rumelhart & McClelland, 1986b, for detailed account). In the late 1950s the perceptron was a basic connectionist network with no hidden units. This system was proposed as a neurally feasible mechanism that could accomplish complex learning (Rosenblatt, 1962). In 1969, Minsky and Papert provided a very severe and influential critique that suggested that the study of perceptrons would be "sterile" because it could not deal with the hidden unit problem. The field was fairly dormant for about 10 years. By 1981 there was a substantial rebirth of interest in perceptron-type models as illustrated by the publication of the book *Parallel Models of Associative Memory* by Hinton and J. A. Anderson (1981). By 1985 the Minsky and Papert critique was finally confronted and overcome with the solution of the hidden unit problem by Ackley et al. (1985). Shortly thereafter, Rumelhart, Hinton, and Williams (1986) developed the back propagation algorithm that allowed very rapid computer simulation of learning for networks with hidden units. With NET-TALK, Sejnowski and Rosenberg (1986) provided a very imaginative and enthusiastic demonstration of connectionist learning processes. In 1986 Rumelhart and McClelland and McClelland and Rumelhart provided a two-volume textbook entitled *Parallel Distributed Processing: Explorations in the Microstructures of Cognition.* These volumes provide a 1,158-page compendium of the techniques and simulations of connectionism. The books provide a wealth of new connectionist modeling simulations and concepts. The volumes are likely to be classics and are the basis for many courses in connectionism throughout the country.

SOCIOPOLITICAL IMPACT OF THE SHIFT

A paradigm shift has a substantial social and political impact on a field. Connectionism is certainly having such an impact. First, there is a great deal of excitement and interest in the topic. Many young and older researchers are exploring such modeling. Connectionists seminars are probably occurring in a hundred universities in the country this year. Established researchers, such as Walter Kinsch, Earl Hunt, Danny Kahneman, and Gordon Bower, are examining or applying connectionist models to their work. The sales of the *Parallel Distributed Processing* books have been phenomenal. The books literally sold out (6,000 copies) before they went to press. One wonders if psychology has ever before had a two-volume advanced textbook sellout. The rapid growth of connectionist talks at the Cognitive Science Society meetings illustrates this exciting interest: in the years 1984, 1985, and 1986, the percentage of connectionist talks were 17%, 23%, and 31%, respectively. In a period of about 5 years, connectionism went from being nearly nonexistent to being one third of the program of the Cognitive Science Society.

Granting agencies have also shifted toward connectionism. The Sloan Foundation, the National Science Foundation, the Office of Naval Research, the Defense Advanced Research Project Agency, and the Air Force Office of Scientific Research all have initiated programs to fund this type of modeling. This modeling has caught the interest of basic researchers who wish to understand cognition and biological computing, as well as of applied researchers who want to build better weapon systems. Note this shift in cognitive science has in some cases reduced funds available for experimental research. Thus there is a shift in the research base for the future.

In the summer of 1986 there was a connectionist summer camp. Under Sloan Foundation sponsorship, Sejnowski, Hinton, and Touretzky brought together 50 graduate students for an 11-day workshop on connectionism. The goal was explicitly to seed the world with connectionists. The workshop brought these researchers together so they could exchange techniques and develop substantial enthusiasm for changing the field.

More important than changing the social climate, connectionism is altering the conceptual environment. McClelland, for example, describes sentence processing as not being grammar processing, but rather as being the unitization of a set of clues to interpret meaning. Rumelhart describes "representations as being built not specified." The ability to use large quantities of information in an interactive manner allows conceptualization of processing in a manner very different from that of serial computers.

The impact of connectionism is likely to go well beyond the psychological laboratory. Hammerstrom (1986), a computer architect, predicts that "it will be possible within 5–10 years to build a silicon-based system that emulates a network of a billion connections between millions of nodes," and these systems "will be relatively cheap" (approximately $300 for production costs) and compact (size of a floppy disk), simulating neural systems at roughly two orders of magnitude faster than real time. Think of the implications, perhaps in 20 years, of having the processing capacity of our speech processing available for a $300 device that can be connected to a personal computer. If these learning systems can perform perceptual and learning activities that we currently associate with humans, this connectionism movement will cause a second computer revolution that would be more significant than the first.

THEORETICAL IMPACT

The theoretical impact of connectionism on psychology is strong and likely to be great. Connectionism is making theories of learning much more explicit. For these models one must describe the number of elements of each level, the internal codes, the problem sequencing rules, and the learning algorithms.

Connectionism allows new types of studies. Most connectionist modelers are examining the psychology of nonhuman intelligence systems. The typical procedure is to build a network-type robot to see what it learns on its own. This is an engineering approach with simulation providing existence proofs. It should be noted that this method of existence proofs has been very productive in computer science by developing a basis of algorithms and procedures. It may help the psychology of cognition to become a more cumulative endeavor.

Connectionism has introduced a variety of new (improved) concepts and language. We can now discuss representations in terms of vector spaces. Learning is described as a method of gradient descent or learning by approximation. We can categorize the type of supervision of the learning process and how the problems should be sequenced to maximize learning. All of these issues can now be tested with simulations providing quantitative data.

Connectionism has provided a new emphasis to a number of psychological phenomena. McClelland and Rumelhart (1981) emphasized the importance of top-down influences in the word superiority effect. Ackley, Hinton, and Sejnowski (1985) described mechanisms that enable unsupervised learning to acquire complex relationships. Hinton and Plaut (in press) illustrated how relearning can be much faster than original learning and can even transfer to material that was not explicitly taught. For example, if one has not used a foreign language for many years, learning to use a subset of the words of that language can show substantial transfer to words that were not explicitly relearned. Hinton refers to this process as compensating for the defocusing of memory across time. Hinton and Nowlan (in press) recently described how a learning mechanism can greatly speed evolution. In this system, genes can either be in one of two states or be in a modifiable/learnable state. He shows that with learnable states, individual learning trials can be substituted for generations. Given that learning trials are very cheap compared with spawning a new generation, this learning mechanism can greatly speed evolution.

CONNECTIONIST REFORMULATION OF PSYCHOLOGICAL CONCEPTS

There are three formulations of psychological concepts provided by connectionism that I find particularly interesting and exciting. All of these concepts existed before connectionism, but the concepts have become more concrete and elegant within the connectionist framework.

The concept of a semantic network can be recast within a connectionist framework. In a semantic network one typically has "Is-A" links between nodes in a network. For example, in a semantic network of family relationships, one might have the names of family members connected with "Is-A son," "Is-A father," "Is-A daughter," and so forth. One of the problems of the semantic network is that if the network is taught only a subset of the links, it must use some complex strategies to find new relationships. For example, if the system is taught that Jim is the son of Jack and that Sue is the daughter of Jack, the system does not directly generalize that Jim and Sue are siblings. This can be done with complex postretrieval processing where various alternative link combinations are examined to infer whether the sibling relationship holds. Hinton (1986) taught a connectionist network to learn family relationships. The system was required to learn 100 relationships among 24 names

from two families. There were 24 input names, 12 family relationships, and 24 output names. In addition there were 12 hidden units representing the input family, 12 hidden units representing the output family, 6 hidden units for the relationship, and 12 central representational units. The system was taught 100 of the 104 instances of relationships (e.g., father, mother, husband, wife, son, daughter, etc.). The 12-name hidden units learned to code relationships. The hidden units recoded input names in terms of their generation level and family type. Note that this recoding rule was developed by the network as a result of presenting family relationships and the network applying a simple (i.e., back propagation) learning rule to change the weights of the hidden units. The hidden units encode individual names in terms of family relationships (e.g., generation, sex). If the system is taught that Jim is the son of Jack and that Sue is the daughter of Jack, the system will infer (via generation and relational coding) that Jim is the brother of Sue. This is done without any complex postprocessing, but rather is a side effect of building an internal representation for the family codes. This kind of coding might explain why a parent may make the verbal slip of calling a child by the name of one of his or her siblings. Connectionism provides a very simple interpretation of these phenomena and how both the encoding and retrieval processes can be accomplished with a simple parallel distributed operation.

Connectionism enables recasting schemata within the concrete representational framework. The concept of schemata has been around for a long time and is felt by some researchers to be a major building block of recognition (Rumelhart, 1980). Generally the representations of schemata have been vague specifications of a grouping of elements that co-occur in some expected fashion. In the connectionist framework, schema theory can have an explicit form that can predict the interrelationships of objects (Rumelhart, Smolensky, McClelland, & Hinton, 1986). The elements of the schema can be represented as individual units in a connectionist network. The strengths of the connection between the units are determined by the co-occurrence frequency of the various objects of the schema. For example, Rumelhart had subjects list the objects that one would typically find in a living room, bathroom, study, etc. The strengths of connections between the elements were determined by the co-occurrence frequency of the elements. Accordingly, *bookshelf* and *desk* would have a very strong co-occurrence frequency, whereas *bookshelf* and *oven* would not. The connections between the units for *bookshelf* and *desk* would have a strong weight; *bookshelf* and *oven* would not. In a simulation, two of the 40 units would be activated, and the activation of the others would be measured. This activation represented the filling in of the schema elements. For example, the activation of *desk* and *ceiling* would activate the terms *computer, books, bookshelf, typewriter, doors,* and *walls.* In contrast, activating *bathtub* and *ceiling* would result in the activation of *scale, toilet, very small,* and *walls.* If such unexpected combinations as *sofa, bed,* and *ceiling* were activated, novel configurations of rooms would be activated including *television, dresser, drapes, fireplace, books,* and *large.* This connectionist network illustrates how schemata can be built up and can fill in missing information, as well as misinterpret information, to make it more consistent with the current schema. All of the current operations occur through the simple mechanism of the parallel distributed activation of the elements that might occur in a room.

The third example of connectionism's recasting of a vague concept into an explicit form is one of my own. In 1977 Shiffrin and Schneider described a dual processing model in which the two forms of processing were called automatic and controlled. . . . Automatic processing was viewed as fast, parallel, and fairly effortless. In contrast, controlled processing was viewed as a slow, typically serial, and effortful form of processing. At that time we could not provide a mechanism of these two qualitatively different forms of processing. Recently, Schneider and Mumme (1987) recast the concept of automatic and controlled processing within a connectionist architecture. Controlled processing involves an external source that modulates the output of all of the elements from a module. Automatic processing involves a local circuit (through the priority report cell), which enables the output of a module in the absence of an external attentional input. Within each module there is a connectionist association of the input patterns to a priority tag for that message. If that message is of high enough priority, the message is automatically transmitted in the absence of controlled processing input. The priority mechanism produces the four phenomena of automatic

processing as emergent properties. That is, as automatic processing develops, performance becomes fast, effortless, and difficult to control, and it results in reduced ability to modify memory (see Schneider & Mumme, 1987; Schneider & Detweiler, 1987). The connectionist model predicts how performance shifts from a serial to a parallel processor as practice continues in a consistent search paradigm. The simulation also illustrates that even though the mechanisms of controlled and automatic processing are qualitatively different, the transition is a continuous process.

The connectionist simulation of automatic processing learns to perform visual search tasks. First, the model makes a few errors as it sets its performance criterion, then executes a slow serial search. As practice proceeds, it gradually acquires a fast parallel search. Connectionist autoassociative processing allows the network to generalize learning to similar patterns and provides an interpretation for why consistency is an important factor. The simulation of the model illustrates how a process can be both automatic and controlled and how the processes interact. It also has produced some novel predictions about cortical thalamic neural activity that are being examined physiologically.

EMPIRICAL IMPACT OF CONNECTIONISM

Although the theoretical impact of connectionism has been large, the empirical impact has been minimal and may remain limited. There is a very serious problem of the nonuniqueness of connectionist predictions. This problem is well illustrated by the modeling of the word superiority effect. McClelland and Rumelhart (1981) provided the archetype of a connectionist model that had three levels (a visual feature, a letter level, and a word level) to predict the word superiority effect. This model suggests that as an empiricist, one might try to perform experiments to examine the existence of each of these stages. However, Golden (1986) presented a model for the word superiority effect that had only a single level. In essence, he could predict the word superiority effect assuming only a visual feature level. The model did not even require a visual letter level, much less a word level. The second connectionist model substantially countered the take-home message of the first connectionist model. The first model suggested that we should think in terms of top-down influences from the word level to the letter and visual feature level. The Golden model shows that we can have much the same effect, assuming there is nothing but a visual feature level of processing.

It is likely that within 5 years we will have a proliferation of connectionist models with very different architectures predicting the same empirical phenomena. Massaro (1986) presented a connectionist model that could predict a variety of effects in speech perception. Given the input and expected output, this system found connection weights that produced human-like data. Unfortunately, given slightly different output patterns, this system produces data that have never been observed in humans. It is critical to *remember that connectionist models use very powerful curve fitting procedures to map the input to the output.* Typically these models search in a several-thousand–parameter space of connections. These are powerful search techniques, and it is not surprising that they find solutions. This may be great for computer science, but causes a real problem for psychology. In general, psychologists seek to understand how humans perform processing. If 10 very different connectionist architectures can be built to model the same phenomenon, it is difficult to have much confidence in any one of the architectures. As connectionism matures, it will be critical to examine how it deals with this multiple-model problem. Mathematical psychology somewhat lost its enthusiasm because of its inability to resolve issues between models. In Norman's (1970) Models of Human Memory there were at least 12 different models for the recall curve. After the book was published, most of the contributors went on to perform different types of research, never coming to a consensus on the true underlying cause for the free recall effect.

When a connectionist model fails, there are many interpretations or outs for why it failed. Connectionist models are sensitive to the initial state, structure, number of elements, specific problems, learning sequence, learning rule, and coding patterns of the initial model. Given so many degrees of freedom and a very powerful learning rule, it is difficult to identify the limits of connectionist modeling. If the system fails to learn, there is always the possibility that given more units and more it-

erations, the system would have learned. Clear disconfirmation of a particular class of connectionist models is very hard to achieve.

WILL CONNECTIONISM FIZZLE?

It is important to note that perceptrons did fizzle. There was a great deal of early excitement, but after extensive analysis it was found that the learning systems were, in fact, far too limited. Connectionism is currently enjoying a very explosive growth, and it is hard to be rational during this period. To be viable, connectionism must deal with the problem of scaling well. The problem of scale is the bane of artificial intelligence. Many learning rules learn very well with small or toy problems but fail, due to a combinatoric explosion, with more complex problems. The scaling of connectionist models is not understood. Hinton indicates that they appear to scale by a factor of about N^3 to the number of connections. If it takes 10^4 learning trials to fill up a 100-connection network (as in NET-TALK), it would take 10^7 trials (or 14 man years of effort at 10 sec/trial) for a thousand-connection network. Cortical connection inputs can easily reach a million connections in a region. Connectionism must deal with procedures that allow problems to be decomposed so that the learning can occur in realistic time scales. Artificial intelligence started by generating great enthusiasm about general problem-solving methods. During this stage of artificial intelligence research, the mind was viewed as a tabula rasa. However, this approach quickly fell off a combinatoric cliff, making it untenable. Artificial intelligence started to solve real-world problems once it began trying to represent limited task domains via expert systems approaches. Some practitioners of connectionism feel that connectionism can solve the tabula rasa learning issue. My view is that eventually we will see some compromise between the position of restricted domain knowledge as an expert system and that of connectionism modeling to remove the brittleness of those systems. Norman (1986) comments that connectionism must deal with sequential processing, which is typical in human problem solving. To some extent, connectionist modeling can be viewed as modeling of events that typically occur in less than 1 sec. Much production system modeling (e.g., J. R. Anderson, 1983) looks at processing well above the 1-sec period. There is presently a great deal of interest in connectionism; however, one must be cautious that part of this enthusiasm may be coming from being tired of old concepts. Psychology dropped box models for semantic networks and production systems. It is now dropping those perhaps to embrace connectionism.

IS IT GOOD FOR THE FIELD?

Yes, but it may be another field. I generally think of psychology as being the study of human or animal systems. Connectionism studies learning systems that can be simulated in computers and may occur in animals. Human learning systems are a small sample of the possible learning systems that could exist. To make an analogy, think of the study of aerodynamics. To some extent, the study of aerodynamics began with the study of natural flight. Birds provided an existence proof of how an object could fly through the air under its own power. However, as the principles of aerodynamics began to be understood, researchers studied artificial man-made systems of flight. In cognitive science something similar may occur. Connectionist models may prove to be very effective learning systems that greatly advance the computation of learning. However, they may not perform those operations in a manner analogous to human learning.

CAUTIONS ON CONNECTIONISM

In a presidential address it is appropriate to comment about the status of the field. Although I view the connectionist movement with great enthusiasm, there are some factors that give me pause. Connectionism will produce some loss of the empirical tradition of psychology and perhaps promote an animosity toward other views. It is now acceptable to test learning concepts by running computer models as opposed to human subjects. This loosening of the paradigm is important and good for the field. However, I see developing signs of animosity between the modelers and the empirical researchers. If we are going to experience a paradigm shift, I hope that we can do it without the animosity that

occurred as a result of Chomsky's linguistic theories. Chomsky's influential work caused many linguists to abandon the empirical study of linguistic processing in favor of the purely theoretical representation of that processing. The established connectionist modelers clearly have a strong regard for empirical data. I am, however, concerned by the younger generation of modelers, many of whom have only a passing interest in empirical data. I feel that if we wish to model human cognition, it is critical that we generate testable predictions so that we can limit the set of models that we search for.

HOW BIG A PARADIGM SHIFT?

I believe connectionist modeling does represent a significant paradigm shift in psychology. It is certainly beyond the level of a shift of the transition from box models to semantic nets in the early 1970s. Perhaps it is a shift approaching that of the shift from behaviorism to information processing in the late 1950s. It may be on a scale comparable to transformational grammar in linguistics. The current enthusiasm and exciting developments suggest that it may be the largest paradigm shift that most psychologists will see during their careers.

Connectionism is certainly changing the perspective that psychology has of human cognition. I end with a quote by Kuhn (1970, p. 121): "though the world does not change with a change in paradigm, the scientist afterward works in a different world."

REFERENCES

Ackley, D. H., Hinton, G. E., & Sejnowski, T. J. (1985). A learning algorithm for Boltzmann machines. *Cognitive Science, 9,* 147–169.

Anderson, J. A. (1983). Cognitive and psychological computation with neural models. *IEEE Transactions on Systems, Man, & Cybernetics, 13,* 799–815.

Anderson, J. A., & Mozer, M. C. (1981). Categorization and selective neurons. In G. E. Hinton & J. A. Anderson (Eds), *Parallel models of associative memory* (pp. 213–236). Hillsdale, NJ: Erlbaum.

Anderson, J. R. (1983). *The architecture of cognition.* Cambridge, MA: Harvard University Press.

Barto, A. G., & Anandan, P. (1985). Pattern recognizing stochastic learning automata. *IEEE Transactions on Systems, Man, & Cybernetics, 15,* 360–375.

Elman, J., & Zipser, D. (1987). *Learning the hidden structure of speech* (Tech. Rep. No. ICS 8701). Institute for Cognitive Science, University of California, San Diego, CA.

Golden, R. M. (1986). A developmental neural model of visual word perception. *Cognitive Science, 10,* 241–276.

Hammerstrom, D. (1986, August). *Neural computing: A new paradigm for LLSI computer architecture.* Paper given at the Attention and Brain Communication Workshop, Jackson, Wyoming.

Hinton, G. E. (1986). Learning distributed representations of concepts. *The eighth annual conference of the cognitive science society* (pp. 1–12). Hillsdale, NJ: Erlbaum.

Hinton, G. E., & Anderson, J. A. (Eds). (1981). *Parallel models of associative memory.* Hillsdale, NJ: Erlbaum.

Hinton, G. E., & Nowlan, S. J. (in press). *How learning can guide evolution* (Tech. Rep.). Carnegie-Mellon University, Pittsburgh, PA.

Hinton, G. E., & Plaut, O. C. (in press). *Using fast weights to deblur old memories and assimilate new ones* (Tech. Rep.). Carnegie-Mellon University, Pittsburgh, PA.

Hinton, G. E., & Sejnowski, T. J. (1986). Learning and relearning in Boltzmann Machines. In D. E. Rumelhart & J. L. McClelland (Eds.), *Parallel distributed processing: Explorations in the microstructure of cognition. Volume 1: Foundations* (pp. 282–317). Cambridge, MA: MIT Press.

Kuhn, T. S. (1970). *The structure of scientific revolutions.* Chicago: University of Chicago Press.

Massaro, D. W. (1986, November). *Connectionist models of the mind.* Paper presented at Psychonomic Society meeting, New Orleans, LA.

McClelland, J. L. (1986). Resource requirements of standard and programmable nets. In D. E. Rumelhart & J. L. McClelland (Eds.), *Parallel distributed processing: Explorations in the microstructures of cognition. Volume 1: Foundations* (pp. 460–487). Cambridge, MA: MIT Press.

McClelland, J. L., & Kawamoto, A. H. (1986). Mechanisms of sentence processing: Assigning roles to constituents. In J. L. McClelland & D. E. Rumelhart (Eds.), *Parallel distributed processing; Explorations in the microstructure of cognition. Volume 2: Psychological and biological models* (pp. 272–325). Cambridge, MA: MIT press.

McClelland, J. L., & Rumelhart, D. E. (1981). An interactive activation model of context effects in letter perception: Part 1. An account of basic findings. *Psychological Review, 88,* 375–407.

McClelland, J. L., & Rumelhart, D. E. (1986). *Parallel distributed processing: Explorations in the microstructure of cognition. Volume 2: Psychological and biological models.* Cambridge, MA: MIT Press.

Minsky, M., & Papert, S. (1969). *Perceptrons.* Cambridge, MA: MIT Press.

Norman, D. A. (Ed). (1970). *Models of human memory.* London: Academic Press.

Norman, D. A. (1986). Reflections on cognition and parallel distributed processing. In J. L. McClelland, & D. E. Rumelhart (Eds.), *Parallel distributed processing: Explorations in the microstructure of cognition. Volume 2, Psychological and biological models* (pp. 531–546). Cambridge, MA: MIT Press.

Rosenberg, C. R., & Sejnowski, T. J. (1986). The spacing effect on NETtalk, a massively-parallel network. *The Eighth Annual Conference of the Cognitive Science Society* (pp. 72–89). Hillsdale, NJ: Erlbaum.

Rosenblatt, F. (1962). *Principles of neurodynamics.* New York: Spartan.

Rumelhart, D. E. (1980). Schemata: The building blocks of cognition. In R. Spiro, B. Bruce, & W. Brewer (Eds.), *Theoretical issues in reading comprehension* (pp. 33–58). Hillsdale, NJ: Erlbaum.

Rumelhart, D. E., Hinton, G. E., & Williams, R. J. (1986). Learning internal representations by error propagation. In D. E. Rumelhart & J. L. McClelland (Eds), *Parallel distributed processing: Explorations in the microstructure of cognition. Volume 1: Foundations* (pp. 318–362). Cambridge, MA: MIT Press.

Rumelhart, D. E., & McClelland, J. L. (1986a). On learning the past tenses of English verbs. In J. L. McClelland & D. E. Rumelhart (Eds), *Parallel distributed processing: Explorations in the microstructure of cognition. Volume 2: Psychological and biological models* (pp. 216–271). Cambridge, MA: MIT Press.

Rumelhart, D. E., & McClelland, J. L. (1986b). *Parallel distributed processing: Explorations in the microstructure of cognition. Volume 1: Foundations.* Cambridge, MA: MIT Press.

Rumelhart, D. E., Smolensky, P., McClelland, J. L., & Hinton, G. E. (1986). Schemata and sequential thought processes in PDP models. In J. L. McClelland & D. E. Rumelhart (Eds), *Parallel distributed processing: Explorations in the microstructure of cognition. Volume 2: Psychological and biological models* (pp. 7–57). Cambridge: MA: MIT Press.

Schneider, W., & Detweiler, M. (1987). A connectionist/control architecture for working memory. In G. H. Bower (Ed.), *The psychology of learning and motivation* (Vol. 21). New York: Academic Press.

Schneider, W., & Mumme, D. (1987). *Attention, automaticity and the capturing of knowledge: A two-level cognitive architecture.* Manuscript submitted for publication.

Sejnowski, T. J. (1986). Open questions about computation in cerebral cortex. In J. L. McClelland & D. E. Rumelhart (Eds.), *Parallel distributed processing: Explorations in the microstructure of cognition: Volume 2: Psychological and biological models* (pp. 372–389). Cambridge, MA: MIT Press.

Sejnowski, T. J., & Rosenberg, C. R. (1986). NETtalk: *A parallel network that learns to read aloud.* (Tech. Rep. No. JHU/EECS-86/01). The Johns Hopkins University Electrical Engineering and Computer Science, Baltimore, MD.

Shiffrin, R. M., & Schneider, W. (1977). Controlled and automatic human information processing. II: Perceptual learning, automatic attending, and a general theory. *Psychological Review, 84,* 127–190.

Wickelgren, W. A. (1969). Context-sensitive coding, associative memory, and serial order in (speech) behavior. *Psychological Review, 76,* 1–15.

3

Earl Hunt

Pulls and Pushes on Cognitive Psychology: The View Toward 2001

THE PROBLEM OF PREDICTION

The purpose of this [selection] is to predict the future of a science. Of course, the most likely thing to happen in any science in the next twenty years is something unexpected. Nevertheless, I will try.

It is possible to make reasonable predictions about scientific progress if the focus of the prediction is fairly narrow—for example, a prediction about the hot topics in episodic memory, visual attention, or analogical reasoning. A competent reviewer can usually extrapolate progress a few years ahead, by using a reasonable amount of tunnel vision. An implicit assumption in such predictions is that progress in a field is continuous; we build on what has gone on before. Since, of course, we do, the predictions usually work. Intellectual revolutions will not be predicted this way, but revolutions are not that common.

Another way to make a prediction that is not entirely wrong is to be very wide ranging. If there are enough subpredictions, one of them is bound to be right. This is what I shall do.

Instead of focusing on developments within psychology that affect our ideas, I am going to focus on developments outside psychology that influence our opportunities. Figure 1 illustrates my argument. There are two types of influence that psychology (or any other science) will have to deal with. One is a push; developments in one field permit progress in another. A spectacular example is the way in which developments in the physics of superconductivity have influenced medical imaging, by making it possible to sense fantastically small electrical fields generated by neural events.

Outside influences can also exert a pull. They selectively encourage those bits of potential scientific progress that the society as a whole wants to develop. Whatever history's ultimate verdict on the Cold War is, it is

Figure 1

Pulls and Pushes on Cognitive Psychology

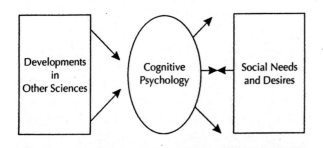

Developments in other areas of science produce capabilities within cognitive psychology. Social needs and desires selectively encourage the development of some of these capabilities.

certainly true that a perceived need for a superb military machine led to major advances in many of the sciences. By the same token, perceived needs in the health field have pulled results from one scientific field, while perhaps holding back results from others.

Cognitive psychology is not exempt from such influences. Developments in the scientific study of thought depend on doors being opened for us by progress in other fields. Society then pulls us through these metaphorical doors because our services are needed in the next room. This essay is a guess about how the pushes and pulls will play themselves out in the next quarter-century. Going further would move us from cognitive science to cognitive science fiction.

THE FIRST PUSH: ADVANCES IN THE BIOLOGICAL AND PHYSICAL SCIENCES

Progress in any science is based on the available technology and on contemporary ideas about how that technology should be used. Technological advances make it possible to gather data that then has to be explained. Scientific advances occur when we develop new ways of looking at the data. Technology and science often go hand in hand, but on occasion, technology will lead. Astronomy provides a good example. The first humans (and for that matter, their ancestors) had sufficient visual acuity to see both clouds and stars. The first major conceptual advance in astronomy appears to have oc-

curred over 3000 years ago, when the Babylonians realized that the atmosphere and the heavens are separate systems (Boorstin, 1983). Various theories were then proposed to explain astral observations, culminating in Ptolemy's theory of an Earth-centric universe, about A.D. 150, and its replacement, the Copernican theory, more than a thousand years later. These great advancements in theory took place without a corresponding improvement in the technology of observation.

The next step did require instrumentation. Copernicus saw the Sun at the center of the universe. We now think that humanity occupies a smallish planet, revolving around a slightly below average sized star, at the tail of a distant galaxy that is very far from the center of the universe. These conclusions depend on a technology of observation well beyond anything Galileo ever dreamed of.

At the end of the twentieth century, advances in three areas of the physical sciences—solid-state electronics, biophysics, and superconductivity—created a new technology of medical imaging that may well have as profound effects for cognitive psychology as the telescope had for astronomy. We now have a noninvasive way of looking at the normal brain. Positron emission tomography (PET) and magnetic resonance imaging (MRI) studies are increasingly reported in our journals.

Developments in electronic computing have enabled us to make a quantum leap forward using another recording technique that is, itself, fairly old. For over fifty years, we have been able to record electrical potentials (EEGs) arising from neural activity. It was quickly learned that these potentials change in response to stimuli. The alteration may be controlled either by the physical form of the stimulation or by its meaning in the context in which it appears. These findings have led to an elaborate technology for analyzing EEG wave forms and associating them with psychological states, varying from surprise to responses to syntactically anomalous sentences (Osterhout & Holcomb, 1992). Thanks to miniaturization and superior computing facilities, it is now possible to locate the brain events that produce the EEG with ever-increasing accuracy.

This is not the point to explain how all these techniques work (nor am I the person to offer the explanation). The point is that our ability to observe brain events directly has increased to an almost un-imaginable degree.

It has been suggested that this ability will wipe out a field closely related to cognitive psychology, the study of intelligence, because the intelligence test will shortly be replaced by biological meas-ures (Matarazzo, 1992). I think this is optimistic. However, we certainly can anticipate tremendous differences in the way that we do information-proc-essing psychology.

At present, we infer psychological states, such as attended and unattended processing, by measur-ing behaviors, such as variations in reaction times. Psychologists have developed impressive analytic techniques to allow us to infer such things as serial or parallel processing from the examination of the behavioral measures. These analyses serve as sur-rogates for the direct observation of brain proc-esses. Sometime before the middle of the next century, such surrogates will become unnecessary. We should be able to use noninvasive techniques to answer, directly, questions about, say, the extent to which verbal and visuospatial, short-term memo-ries are supported by the same brain structures.

We shall not just identify brain structures, we shall also learn how they work as physical devices. Great progress is being made in the identification of neurotransmitters. For medical reasons, such progress has been paralleled by studies of the phar-macology of cognition and affect. I am sure that this work will also have a profound influence on cognitive psychology, especially when we seek to determine the interaction between affect and thought.

These startling advances in the neurosciences are going to affect information-processing psychol-ogy in two very different ways. One is a way that we can all applaud. There will be an increasing demand for research paradigms that isolate psycho-logical functions, so that their biological correlates can be similarly isolated. We can see an excellent example already, in the work of Posner, Petersen, Fox, and Raichle (1988). These investigators used PET imaging to locate different areas of metabolic activity as they progressively complicated the task, moving from looking at lines to looking at words, and then to doing some sort of semantic or syntac-tic task. This enabled them to identify the brain regions involved in various stages of linguistic processing.

The biological techniques that Posner et al. used depended strongly on an implicit psychologi-cal theory. The areas associated with word reading, for instance, were located by subtracting the activ-ity throughout the brain when a person reads a word from the same activity when looking at a nonsense collection of letters. This procedure implicitly im-plies a stage model of the reading process, where activity moves discretely from one area to another. Since the temporal resolution of the PET scan is (today) on the order of tens of milliseconds, the stage assumption may not be too bad. However, one can imagine a future study in which imaging tech-niques with a temporal resolution of a few milli-seconds will be used to distinguish between a stage model, in which information processing in one place must be completed before the second stage has begun, and a cascade model (McClelland, 1979), in which information is gradually leaked from lower to higher levels of semantic complexity.

The distinction between the two models is cru-cial, because it addresses the extent to which the mind (and the brain) is broken into modules that receive input from other modules, but whose inter-nal actions are independent of the actions of the other modules. Stage theories assume that such in-dependence is maintained; cascade theories assume that it is not. It is very difficult to distinguish be-tween such models on the basis of behavioral ob-servations (Townsend & Ashby, 1983). It may be much easier to make the distinction by direct bio-logical observations. This assumes a very different experiment than the one conventionally conducted in the psychological laboratory.

Every knowledgeable person agrees that ad-vances in biological measurement will have a pro-found effect on psychology, partly because this particular revolution is already fairly well along. There is a second biological revolution whose im-plications are less clear.

Neuroscientists are soon going to have a much better idea of who the individual is, at the level of molecular biology. The human genome project will undoubtedly result in a close map of the relation between a person's genotype (which will be meas-urable) and the performance of his or her brain. Look then at what we have. Owing to advances in our ability to observe brain processes, we shall know how elementary information-processing ac-tions are produced by the brain. Because of advances in molecular biology, we shall know how the brain structures got the way they are, on an individual basis. It follows that we shall certainly advance our knowledge of how a person's biological makeup influences his or her thought processes. Biological makeup, here, should be construed very broadly. Of course, it includes genetic makeup. It also includes an understanding of how cognitive capabilities are likely to change in response to induced structural changes in the brain, such as the changes induced by alcoholism, disease, or advanced age.

These trends have major implications for the way in which we construct psychological theories. Since 1950, most papers in cognitive psychology, and especially those papers that fall under the rubric "information processing," have taken a functionalist view of thought. Information-processing psychologists have asked questions about the functional organization of the mind, without being concerned about the material roots of that organization in the brain. Reviews of the field have documented considerable progress, within the limits of the philosophical orientation (e.g., Massaro & Cowan, 1993). Much of the motivation for accepting these limits has been pragmatic; given our technology, we could do nothing else. As the technologies advance, we can anticipate, and look forward to, a decline of information-processing psychology of the sort reviewed by Massaro and Cowan, and an increase in the sort of direct ties between information processing and biology that are exemplified by the Posner et al. approach.

Although the rapprochement between information-processing models and direct observation of brain processes is certainly dramatic, it has major limitations. Suppose that all the biologically based approaches that I have cited are successful. This would mean that we would have identified the location of the anatomical structures that carry out the many elementary information-processing actions required for thinking. If the biologically based approaches are very successful, we would know how each of these anatomical structures worked. What next?

We still would not have explained thinking. The complex topics that cognitive psychologists are really interested in, such as text comprehension and scene interpretation, are not hardwired into the brain. They are emergent properties of the informa-

tion-processing properties of the brain, and can no more be explained by listing the brain structures involved than the architecture of the Cathedral of Notre Dame can be explained by listing the equipment on a medieval mason's workbench. We have to explain how higher-order cognition emerges from lower-order capabilities.

THE SECOND PUSH: ADVANCES IN MATHEMATICS AND COMPUTER SCIENCE

Cognitive psychology will not be complete without a model of how complex phenomena emerge from simple systems. Developing such a model is a major theoretical problem. It has defeated us for over a century because we keep stating our theories in natural language. This has placed us very much in the same position that mathematicians were before the development of modern algebraic notations. The statement of the theory becomes so complicated that we oversimplify the issue or we become incomprehensible. Citations could be given for both responses.

Here we may get help from another allied science: the continued development of digital computers and, most important, the developments in mathematical conceptualization associated with increases in computational capabilities.

Saying that computer programs will become the language of psychological theory is nothing new; this was said at mid-century (Newell, Shaw, & Simon, 1958). In retrospect, most of the efforts at computer simulation from the 1950s to the 1990s were useful, precise descriptions of thinking at the phenomenological level. This can be said of the early simulations based around the General Problem Solver (Newell & Simon, 1972) and of recent simulations, such as Carpenter, Just, and Shell's (1990) work on the Raven Matrix test of intelligence.

This work, which undoubtedly will continue, produced useful concepts, such as the distinctions between working memory and long-term memory, the use of production systems as psychological models, and the distinction between procedural and declarative knowledge (Baars, 1986; Hunt, in press-a). What this work did not produce was a clear link between general brain processes and cognitive phenomena. Nor was it intended to do so. But that is the theoretical challenge facing us today.

Basically, what we shall need is a way of describing how the properties of the mind emerge from the processing capabilities of the brain. We cannot create such a theory by introducing a few special terms, such as "spreading activation," into everyday language. The resulting verbal statement is, as I have said, either unacceptably vague or unacceptably incomprehensible. Therefore, what some psychologists, the *connectionists,* have done is to turn to investigating computer programs that are supposed to be based on models of the brain, but to display computing capabilities equivalent to properties of the mind. In Rumelhart's (1989) terms, we use the computer to explore the brain as a model for the mind.

Before looking at this idea in more detail, let me point out that it is another example of how technology can fuel scientific progress. Whatever you think of the connectionist approach, you have to admit that it would not be possible without modern developments in computer science. Most of these "massively parallel" models of computation, which look at what happens when lots of brain events occur at the same time, are in fact being studied on very fast, conventionally designed serial computers.

Since the connectionist movement is so prominent, and since it represents a major attempt to link the brain to the mind, I shall take the time to describe it in a bit of detail.

Figure 2 illustrates the argument. The connectionists begin with a truism: that behavior is the result of (1) presenting a stimulus to the sensors, (2) passing the resulting neural activation through a maze of connections in the brain, and eventually (3) activating the effectors. Common sense (and today, some direct observations of neural events) tells us that the connections in the brain can be reconfigured, so that animals can learn to achieve a very wide range of stimulus–response connections.

This process can be mimicked mathematically. We can create mathematical objects, called "nodes," that carry with them associated levels of activation. The activation can be passed from node to node via links, where each link has a weight that, in effect, tells how much activation can be passed along it. Some of the nodes can be designated as input nodes and others as output nodes, analogous to sensors and effectors. Internal nodes

Figure 2

The Connectionist Analogy to Thought

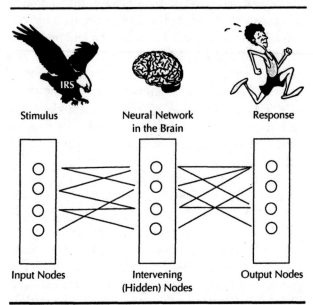

Stimulus — Neural Network in the Brain — Response

Input Nodes — Intervening (Hidden) Nodes — Output Nodes

Features of the external stimulus and responses are represented by the activation of input and output nodes. Complex pathways of sensor–effector connections in the brain are represented by pathways from input to output nodes, through a complex of intervening (hidden) nodes.

that intervene between input and output play the role of the neural pathways in the brain. *Voilà!* We can mimic stimulus–response connections. And to make the analogy still more complete, there are algorithms that can be used to readjust the weights on each link, thus mimicking learning.

It can be shown that if one carries on the analysis as just described, connectionism will always work, in the sense that some arrangement of input, output, and intermediate nodes can be found to mimic any stimulus–response system. In other words, an unrestricted connectionist devise is a universal (Turing) computing machine. This is a good outcome for computer science, since it shows how computers can program themselves by observing examples, instead of having to be programmed by having a human make an analysis of the function to be computed. However, the universality of connectionist models is a bad outcome for psychological science, since we believe that a theory that can be tweaked to account for any outcome is no theory at all.

If connectionism is going to provide the link between brain and mind, two conditions are going to have to be fulfilled. First, it is going to have to be shown that networks that are constrained by biologically plausible limitations (i.e., using only certain learning algorithms, or using restricted sets of pathways) are capable of the emergent behaviors we associate with the mind. While establishing the appropriate biologically justified constraints is a formidable task, it is not, in principle, impossible. Second, we are going to have to understand how the constraints achieve their effects. Too little attention has been paid to this problem.

In most interesting situations, connectionism does not yield to conventional pencil-and-paper mathematical analysis. Instead, connectionists experiment, using computers, to determine whether different models can adjust themselves to display the required behaviors. The brain models proposed depend on involved, nonlinear matrix manipulations and can involve thousands of parameters. If you want to understand X by making an analogy to Y, you have to understand Y. The pessimistic view is that the connectionist approach can lead to the development of nonunderstandable models, so the demonstration that these mysterious mathematical objects mimic psychological phenomenon is not enlightening (McCloskey, 1991).

The answer may lie in mathematics. Computer scientists and mathematicians are developing new and interesting branches of mathematics in order to understand the principles that drive the emergence of complicated behavior in networks of simple elements. In speaking about connectionism, Hintzman (1990) said that if it took hold all our currently practicing scientists would have to "[t]ake tensor calculus or take early retirement." That may not turn out to be a joke, and tensor calculus will not be enough. If mathematical annealing, catastrophic progressions over time, and chaotic functions turn out to be necessary tools for describing models of psychological processes, then the graduate training programs for experimental psychologists will have to be vastly altered.

The likely resurgence of mathematics in the explanation of cognition does not depend solely on the success or failure of the connectionist effort. It is a general consequence of developments in the neurosciences. In computing terms, the neuroscience approach can, at best, lay out the architecture of a distributed processing system of elements of known capabilities. Distributed processing here does not refer to distributed processing in the connectionist sense of distributed processing on the elements of a representation. It is more analogous to the distributed processing of a variety of special-purpose computers, linked together in a network. Computing proceeds asynchronously and in parallel, sometimes, but at other times the units must link together with lock-step precision.

The computer scientist Marvin Minsky has speculated that such networks form a "society of the mind" that is a more appropriate metaphor for psychology than the connectionist's idealized brain metaphor (Minsky, 1986). There is presently a mathematical language for describing distributed networks, derived from graph-theoretic concepts developed originally for scheduling industrial activities. Although psychological models have been stated in this language (Townsend & Ashby, 1983; Schweikert, Fisher, & Goldstein, 1992), in all honesty it must be said that the mathematics are so formidable that most cognitive psychologists cannot deal with them.

This raises a very serious issue. Until the 1970s, many students in experimental psychology programs were recruited from the biological and physical sciences. In the 1970s and 1980s, as psychology became more of a social-science discipline with an increasingly stronger push for immediate societal relevance, recruitment began to be increasingly from students with social science and humanities backgrounds. With the exception of applied statistics, emphasis on mathematical training decreased. In response to the legitimate needs of the new students, statistics training itself increasingly was applied and procedural rather than emphasizing the mathematical grounding of statistics. It is not my purpose to criticize this movement, which was probably inevitable. It did have the important side effect of decreasing the amount of mathematical training offered in many psychology programs to something well beyond the levels offered in the 1950s and 1960s. As a result, psychologists were, on the average, not well prepared to deal with mathematics as a formal language for theory. This effect was exacerbated as relatively fewer undergraduates took mathematics courses in the 1980s. This has a serious implication for the role of scientific psychology in the future.

Because of the advances in the brain sciences, and because of the need to understand brain–mind interactions in order to solve pressing problems in health care, society is going to demand (and fund) someone to produce the required theories. If psychologists are not adequately trained to deal with these issues, someone else will deal with them. A discipline of computational neuroscience could easily develop quite outside psychology departments. If this happens, cognitive psychology will be the poorer, both intellectually and, more crassly, in our funding opportunities.

THE PULL FROM WITHOUT

Just as cognitive psychology is pushed by developments within other sciences, it is pulled by developments in the general society. The reason for the pull is simple; science takes money. Society will pay only for those products for which there is a perceived need. This does not mean that every scientific project is weighted for its short-term economic contribution. At the level of the granting agency and review board, most basic research proposals are indeed reviewed primarily for scientific merit. The political and economic review occurs at a higher level, when the agency or subagency itself competes for funds. The decision to put finds into Defense, the National Science Foundation, Commerce, or the National Institutes of Health, and to distribute funds to the major subdivisions of those agencies is, and should be, a political act. While pork-barrel politics is certainly not unknown, by and large funding for particular branches of science represents an attempt to fund those agencies that can respond to perceived social needs. In turn, this means that, given equal intellectual preparation, those branches of a science that are seen as responding to a societal need are more likely to be developed than branches that are seen as an intellectual ornament.

Influences of this sort are so pervasive that the laboratory scientist may be quite unaware of them. Nevertheless, they exist, and historically they have been very important to cognitive psychology. The period from 1950 to 1980 was the heyday of information-processing psychology. The reason was in part the fact that psychological theory had laid the groundwork for an explosion of effort in that field, as opposed, for instance, to the study of higher-order problem solving or motor responding, fields

that grew at a much slower rate. Another reason was, however, that information-processing studies could be funded.

The 1950 to 1980 period can also be thought of as the culmination of the Industrial Age. Muscular effort became obsolete, to the point that the lack was itself a national health problem. But perceptual effort did not become obsolete. Human beings acted as the eyes and ears for aircraft, read radar scopes, and guided landers onto the moon. In many cases, it turned out that the bottleneck in human-machine system performance was a person's ability to make rapid perceptual and minor cognitive decisions—that is, decisions requiring less than two or three seconds. In a sensible response, society funded that branch of science that had something to contribute.

Times are changing. Developments in computer and sensor technology are rapidly removing humans from the perceptual loop, just as developments in the nineteenth century removed humans from the energy generation loop (Hunt, 1995). If this trend is completed, a good part of our field—information-processing psychology—will not be needed. Outside of psychology, no one will care what it means to say that a person has "fixated on this or that part of the visual field" because the sort of millisecond difference this makes in responding will be of interest only to pure scientists.

Of course, it would be too extreme to expect that studies of visual attention, short-term memory scanning, and the role of the icon will end overnight. They will not, and they should not. Low-level research in these fields will undoubtedly continue, for two reasons. First, it is interesting science in itself, and our society does place some value on the advancement of pure knowledge. Second, this research may assist us in relating behavioral observations to physiological and anatomical observation, as discussed in the preceding section. Although I do not think information-processing psychology will be eradicated, it will assume a far less dominant role in cognitive psychology than it has today.

The situation is quite different for studies of higher-order problem solving: analogical reasoning, the learning of very complex skills, such as computer programming, mathematics, and even social problem solving. In the workplace there are more and more situations in which humans deal with the world indirectly, through the medium of a computer model. For instance, that is the way that your travel agent deals with commercial aviation. Surprisingly often, it is also the way in which commercial aviation pilots deal with their aircraft. Such a workplace can be characterized in two ways.

The good jobs will require a great deal of flexibility, because people will need to know when to trust the model and when not to trust it. This assertion requires a specific example.

For the last fifty years, business analysts and economists have pushed the development of decision-theoretic models for analyzing policies. It can be shown, on highly rational grounds, that decision trees are the appropriate way to choose policies. It is also well known that real-life managers do not proceed that way. Most people's management style is much better explained by the psychological concept of schematic reasoning than by a decision-theoretic model (Beach, 1990; Wagner, 1991).

Future enterprises are increasingly going to be run by a combination of human-management and computer-based decision-making. The computers will be faster and faster, have access to more and more data, and compute ever more detailed decision trees. The result of all this computation will be reported to human managers who reason with a brain left over from the Pleistocene. How are we going to develop a match between these two very different types of reasoners?

This is potentially an issue for cognitive psychologists. However, what is needed here is not a theory of how the brain produces mental action. What is needed is a theory of how education and experience interact to produce a reasonable human being, who controls computer systems instead of being controlled by them.

The rosy view of things is that cognitive psychology will contribute by developing theories of human problem solving, rooted in our understanding of the information-processing capabilities that underlie it. Unfortunately, though, we do not have such a theory. What we do have, with our various studies of expert problem solving and cognitive developmental psychology, is a very good "guild literature" about how to analyze problems involving human thought. Within the next ten years, our major "doable" project may be systematizing this literature. The result will not be a theory of problem solving driven by models of information

processing, in the sense that theories of visual perception might be driven by models at the neuroscience level. It will be a pretheoretical (and hopefully increasingly orderly) way of looking at an important slice of the world. Although we shall not have a general theory of how people develop problem representations, we can develop a methodology for analyzing a wide range of problem-solving situations. This may be just what society needs.

In this sort of endeavor one keeps sharp by having competitors. If we do not establish good ways of thinking about complex thought, others will. The "knowledge engineering" subspecialty of computer psychology or the industrial-organizational specialists in the business schools will compete with us in the marketplace.

My comments thus far have referred to the way that technological changes in the workplace will change the market for cognitive psychology. I now want to turn to a very different sort of change in society—social diversity.

When most academics hear the words "social diversity," they read it as a code word for the increasing number of "people of color" in the student body. The trend toward ethnic diversity is certainly a fact, and it must be dealt with. However, there is a much larger trend.

The workforce is aging. During the next two decades, the fastest growing segments of the workforce are going to be workers over 45 years of age (Johnston & Packard, 1987). There are some reasons to regard this as a benefit. Historically, older workers have traded job knowledge for wages, in a beneficial arrangement for all concerned. As the workplace changes, job knowledge becomes less valuable. How do we introduce major technological changes into the workplace without dislocating major segments of the workforce?[1]

This is partly a problem for cognitive psychology. Studies of aging, which are based largely on intelligence test data, have shown that the variance in intellectual abilities generally increases over the adult life-span. Can we obtain a clearer picture of this phenomenon? What do we mean by "the ability to learn"? And what determines both acquisition and retention of this ability? These are very interesting theoretical questions, which have applied implications. Cognitive psychologists should leap to the chance to make a contribution.

Since there are certainly information-processing correlates to aging, it is worth noting that a good theory relating information processing to higher-order cognition would be especially useful in this field.

There is a flip side to the emphasis on aging. Unless there are major changes in birth trends—and all the pressures are in the other direction—children will be an increasingly smaller percentage of the population. Obviously, people will not cease to have children, and developmental cognitive psychology will not cease. However, studies in developmental psychology may become relatively less important than they are today.

This is something of a heresy, since there is, today, a great hue and cry about how we need "better prepared students" for the workforce of tomorrow. Therefore, I bring up a discouraging fact. No one doubts that the workplace is going to be computerized. The only arguments are over how quickly this will occur. Computer-controlled systems have an interesting by-product; they multiply the number of smart people. A good spread-sheet programmer can unemploy vast numbers of bookkeepers. On a societal basis, we shall have a great need for a few very smart people. Translated to the marketplace for cognitive psychology, there may be social reasons to emphasize identification and training of the very talented. There may, however, be less societal need to move the lower-middle range of cognitive capability to the upper-middle range. If this is what is going to happen to the workplace (and others disagree with me!), it will have profound implications for the sociology of education. It certainly will not create a market for cognitive developmental psychology.

While this reasoning suggests a diminution of interest in cognitive development, there is another trend that suggests an increase in interest in the field—changes in family structure. The evidence for changes in American family structure are quite clear. These cannot be easily summarized in a few sentences, especially because the trends seem to be different for different segments of our society. For instance, in classic upper-middle-class society, there is a trend toward smaller families, with greater interaction between children and adults. In other social groups, adult–child interactions are being reduced. I leave it to social commentators to explain what these trends are. My point is what these trends mean for cognitive psychology.

There will be an increasingly greater need to understand how adult–child interaction and peer-group practices influence cognitive development. In particular, we need to know how post-infant family and peer-group social structures influence children's cognitive development, especially their receptivity for the sort of abstract thinking that the technological world demands.

So what can we see for the future of developmental cognitive psychology? I hazard two predictions. First, there will be much less interest in the study of the "immutable facts" of how cognition unfolds. Old copies of Piaget's books will be less in demand. So will studies of the development of working memory, attention, and the like. On the other hand, there may be an increase of interest in the interaction between social and cognitive development.

Now, let us move away from life-span psychology to another issue. The highly publicized diversification due to changes in the ethnic composition of the country is worth comment. This is not solely a social trend. It also has implications for cognitive psychology.

So long as cognitive psychology is synonymous with information processing, we can simply ignore the trend. I believe that priming works the same way in Spanish and Swahili as it does in English. The acultural aspects of our field are even more true when we tie ourselves to biology. The relationship between short-term memory and the hippocampus is well documented in Canadians, and I am sure, quite without documentation, that the same relationship occurs among the Kurds.

As we move to the study of problem solving and reasoning, we cannot be so cavalier about cultural effects. Of course, we can always account for cultural differences in reasoning by saying, "Those people have different schema than we do," but this is hardly a scientific explanation of anything. We need to know what cultural experiences produce particular schema, and how those schema interact with the schema required to operate in a common meeting ground—the workplace—where one social group will often design systems to be used by another.

Once again, let me provide some content. Western European society places great stress on the use of abstract knowledge that does not depend on direct personal experience. This has proven to be a very useful tool; most of modern technology depends on it. There are other societies in which much more stress is placed on personal knowledge. Our textbooks usually cite relatively exotic groups—for example, central Asian peasants in the 1920s—who, if they still exist, have little economic impact. What about intermediate cases? Anyone can be controlled by modern technology. In order to control it, a person must welcome a chance to do some abstract thinking. What are the appropriate ways of teaching abstract thinking to both adults and children from the various immigrant groups that are increasingly part of our society? For instance, is bilingual education a good or a bad idea? Or, as is more likely, is it good at some points and bad at others?

In this section I have tried to list a few places where the society needs to pull results out of cognitive psychology; the problems I have listed are the ones that appear, to me, to be most important. Others may have other lists. However, I think that all of us who think very much about how cognitive psychology fits into the grand scheme of things would agree with my next two points.

Although many social problems cannot be solved without research on cognition, very few social problems can be solved just by research on cognition. Put more pithily, problems are where you find them; they do not belong exclusively to one or another academic discipline. Furthermore, as cognitive psychology itself moves away from the study of information processing and toward the study of problem solving, it becomes more and more important, from an academic viewpoint, to understand the interactions between individual capabilities and social settings.

Social problems have to be solved. How they are solved may have a tremendous impact on society, but a solution will be found. There are many places where cognitive psychology can make a contribution and, in doing so, can influence society. But there are competent thinkers in education, sociology, computer science, social work, and many other fields whose solutions are, in some sense, competitive with the contribution of cognitive psychology. For instance, the computer science field of "knowledge engineering," which involves the transfer of knowledge from people to machines, is developing virtually independently of input from cognitive psychology. Once again, if we do not answer society's call, someone else will. Financial opportunities for further scientific advances will be arranged appropriately.

WHAT WILL THE SYNTHESIS LOOK LIKE?

Future developments in scientific cognitive psychology will depend on two things: what scientific capabilities are offered to us, by developments in other fields, and what economic support is offered to us, by a society that, quite reasonably, wants to purchase solutions to its problems. How shall we organize ourselves to respond to these opportunities? A few long-term predictions will now be attempted.

Pure information-processing models, for the sake of building models, are probably on the way out. They made an honorable contribution to science, but they have had their day. There is, however, a major exception to this statement. Where information-processing models can be tied to biological observations, they will prosper. Where they cannot, they will not.

One of the hardest trends to predict is the role of formal mathematics in psychology. If connectionism proves to be a key part of future theories, theoretical cognitive psychology will become much more mathematical than it is today. This could happen, but it is not at all certain that it will. Similarly, if it becomes increasingly important to tie cognition to formal models of human-machine systems, there will be a greater need for mathematical models of human cognitive performance.

Somewhat ominously, while mathematics may become more important in studying *cognition*, this could have the effect of diminishing *cognitive psychology*. The reason is that our graduate education programs are becoming increasingly less mathematical, as we are less and less able to compete for the shrinking pool of talented, mathematically able undergraduates. The worst of this trend is that it feeds back on itself. Once the nonmathematicians get into the faculty, it becomes harder and harder to introduce further mathematical training to the entering students. If this trend continues, psychology will have to yield the mathematical modeling of cognition to human-oriented computer scientists and industrial engineers.

There is a social need to develop an understanding of higher order cognition: problem solving, learning to learn, and lifelong reasoning. Several aspects of this endeavor could have profound implications for cognitive psychology.

Intellectually, society does not need a scientifically testable grand theory of human problem solving. That is good, because we do not have one. What society needs is a set of intellectual tools that can be used to provide useful guides in social engineering. These we can provide. However, we must remember that these tools will not be used in isolation. The study of applied problem solving is inherently multidisciplinary. Psychologists will not have the luxury of superspecialization. Many of the problems cannot be solved by observing bored undergraduates, working "to obtain extra class credit." The needed research will require long-term observation of groups as diverse as neuropsychological patients and air traffic controllers. Laboratory research will still have its place, but we shall have to think a good deal more than we have about what that place is.

Of course, the comments in the last paragraph apply as much to studies of the information processing–biology connection as to studies of the problem solving–social setting connection. The problems can be solved only by the simultaneous application of multiple types of expertise. In virtually every field of psychology, the superspecialized principal investigator, working in his or her own little laboratory, is about to become an endangered species. There will be no protection for a being whose niche has disappeared as ideas and demands evolve.

The evolutionary analogy is a good place to close. If I am correct, both scientific advances and changes in social needs are about to have profound influences on cognitive psychology. As these changes snow down upon us, a few of our species are going to die out. (Would "Go the way of the behaviorists" be appropriate?) But will the genus survive? Looking about at the latest meetings of the Psychonomic Society, one certainly sees dinosaurs.[2] And yet, there are probably enough furry creatures underfoot to ensure against a total extinction.

NOTES

1. Two newspaper articles that were published as this article was being written illustrate my point. On December 18, 1992, the *New York Times* reported that General Motors was moving 450 million dollars from a fund for retraining to a fund to induce early retirement. The company wished to retool its factories and clearly did not see their older workforce as an asset. On December 20, the *New York Times* reported serious underfunding of pension programs in the United States. The two articles were disturbing alone, and far more disturbing when seen together.

2. Names withheld to protect the guilty

REFERENCES

Baars, B. J. (1986). *The cognitive revolution in psychology.* New York: Guilford.

Beach, L. R. (1990). *Image theory: Decision making in personal and organizational contexts.* New York: Wiley.

Boorstin, D. J. (1983). *The discoverers.* New York: Random House.

Carpenter, P. A., Just, M. A., & Shell, P. (1990). What one intelligence test measures: A theoretical account of processing in the Raven Progressive Matrix Test. *Psychological Review, 97,* 404–431.

Hintzman, D. L. (1990). Human learning and memory: Connections and dissociations. *Annual Review of Psychology, 41,* 109–140.

Hunt, E. (in press-a). *Thoughts on thought: A discussion of basic issues in cognitive psychology.* Hillsdale, NJ: Erlbaum.

Hunt, E. (1995). *Will we be smart enough? A psychological analysis of the coming workplace and workforce.* New York: Russell Sage Foundation.

Johnston, W. B., & Packard, A. H. (1987). *Workforce 2000: Work and workers for the 21st century.* Indianapolis: The Hudson Institute.

Massaro, D., & Cowan, N. (1993). Information processing models: Microscopes of the mind. *Annual Review of Psychology, 44,* 383–425.

Matarazzo, J. D. (1992). Psychological testing and assessment in the 21st century. *American Psychologist, 47,* 1007–1018.

McClelland, J. L. (1979). On the time-relations of mental processes: An examination of systems of processes in cascade. *Psychological Review, 86,* 287–330.

McCloskey, M. (1991). Networks and theories: The place of connectionism in cognitive science. *Psychological Science, 2,* 387–395.

Minsky, M. (1986). *The society of mind.* New York: Simon & Schuster.

Newell, A., Shaw, J. C., & Simon, H.A. (1958). Elements of a theory of human problem solving. *Psychological Review, 65,* 151–156.

Newell, A., & Simon, H. A. (1972). *Human problem solving.* Englewood Cliffs, N.J.: Prentice-Hall.

Osterhout, L., & Holcomb, P. J. (1992). Event-related brain potentials elicited by syntactic anomaly. *Journal of Memory and Language, 31,* 785–806.

Pylyshyn, Z. W. (1989). Computing in cognitive science. In M. I. Posner (Ed.), *Foundations of cognitive science* (pp. 51–91). Cambridge, Mass.: MIT Press.

Posner, M. I., Petersen, S. E., Fox, P. T., & Raichle, M. E. (1988). Localization of cognitive operations in the human brain. *Science, 240,* 1627–1631.

Rumelhart, D. E. (1989). The architecture of mind: A connectionist approach. In M. I. Posner (Ed.), *Foundations of cognitive science* (pp. 133–160). Cambridge, Mass.: MIT Press.

Schweikert, R., Fisher, D. L., & Goldstein, W. M. (1992). General latent network theory: Structural and quantitative analysis of networks of cognitive processes. Privately circulated paper. Purdue University, Department of Psychological Sciences. Lafayette, Ind.

Townsend, J. T., & Ashby, F. G. (1983). *Stochastic modeling of elementary psychological processes.* Cambridge: Cambridge University Press.

Wagner, R. K. (1991). Managerial problem solving. In R. J. Sternberg & P. A. Frentsch (Eds.), *Complex problem solving: Principles and mechanisms* (pp. 159–184). Hillsdale, N.J.: Erlbaum.

On the Internet . . .

Basic Neural Processes

This is a highly interactive site tutorial on brain structures by Dr. John H. Krantz, Hanover College.
http://psych.hanover.edu/Krantz/neurotut.html

David Landrigan's Gallery of Illusions

David Landrigan, University of Massachusetts–Lowell, presents a series of visual illusions as a basis to learn about sensation and perception and about research methods in psychology.
http://aspen.uml.edu/~landrigad/ILLUSION.HTML

Hall of Illusions

This site offers interactive demonstrations of visual illusions, including impossible objects and figures, ambiguous illusions, distortion illusions, aftereffects and afterimages, auditory illusions, and camouflage.
http://www.illusionworks.com/jump01.htm#Impossible

Part❖2

Perception and Neurocognition

Sally P. Springer and Georg Deutsch

❖

Christine M. Temple

❖

Mark H. Ashcraft

❖

Keith Rayner

Perception and Neurocognition

Neuropsychology has linked up with cognitive psychology to create cognitive neuropsychology. This new discipline attempts to understand the mind by assessing cognitive function in the face of brain damage. This section presents some selections on neurocognition and some intriguing recent research on the perceptual aspects of reading.

Cognitive neuropsychology brings a different set of concepts and methods to traditional cognitive psychology. Of course there is the focus on the brain but, more than this, there is a focus on *neurological specificity*. The view that there is localization of function in the brain has been in vogue since the middle of the nineteenth century. Neurological specificity is a modern version of localization that attempts to locate specific mental functions at particular regions of the brain. The concept of *modularity* extends the neurological specificity concept in that brain modules are seen as dedicated to processing specific kinds of information (e.g., syntax, face recognition) while being self-contained and relatively unaffected by other kinds of information. An analogy might help to elucidate this: An automobile has an electrical system, a fuel system, a suspension system, and so on. Each system "does its own thing," with some interaction between the systems. The final desireable end product, which is a fully functional automobile, is ultimately dependent on the integrity of the various systems.

An important logical technique that is used to evaluate neurological specificity is called *double dissociation*. If one patient performs adequately on one task but inadequately on another, whereas a different patient shows the reverse pattern, then the tasks are doubly dissociated. If the patients also show different patterns of brain damage, then there is good reason to associate certain functions with specific brain areas. In practice, however, this condition is rarely met in its pure form.

Nevertheless, there are numerous findings that are consistent with the concepts of neurological specificity and modularity. For example, some individuals exhibit *blindsight*, in which certain visual perceptual abilities remain intact but the individual shows little awareness of these abilities and may even deny them. In some cases of *visual agnosia*, an individual can discern some features of a common object without being able to identify the object. Some individuals may be *prosopagnosic*; that is, unable to recognize familiar faces, yet able to recognize nonfaces. Some patients may neglect one-half of the visual field but not the other, which may be manifest in their drawings, for example. In some cases of *dyslexia*, an individual can read real words but have difficulty reading nonsense words (e.g., *blirk*); other dyslexic individuals can read regular words (e.g., *painter*) but have difficulty reading irregular words (e.g., *colonel*). In general, there is a great deal of evidence for neurological specificity and for modularity, although the latter is more open to interpretation.

The emergence of cognitive neuropsychology has fostered the use of different methodologies. In general, studies in the area are conducted with smaller samples than those used for more traditional experiments in cognitive psychology, largely because of obvious limitations in finding patients who share similar brain deficits. In fact, single-case studies are common. Moreover, recently developed neuroimaging techniques (CT, PET, MRI) are being used to pinpoint the brain regions that subserve particular cognitive functions.

THE FIRST THREE SELECTIONS IN PART 2 PROVIDE AN interesting sample of research on neurocognition. In an extended excerpt from their book *Left Brain/ Right Brain*, Sally P. Springer and Georg Deutsch discuss research done on people who had severe cases of epilepsy. These individuals underwent a surgical procedure in which the corpus callosum, the major neural conduit between the two cerebral hemispheres, was cut. Springer and Deutsch present some of the history of research on the corpus callosum and split-brain operations and then describe some of the typical findings that have emerged from various tests. For example, a brief stimulus presented to the right visual field (to the right of the visual fixation point) could be verbally described, but a stimulus presented to the left visual field (to the left of the visual fixation point) could not, the reason being that the right visual field projects information to the left hemisphere, which for most people contains Broca's area, the speech center. However, these surgical subjects could respond appropriately, if nonverbally, to left visual field presentations—nude figures elicited a smile, for example—and they could select objects, sight unseen, with their left hand (controlled primarily by the right hemisphere) in correspondence with the stimuli presented in the left visual field. Springer and Deutsch also describe the *cross cuing* phenomenon, in which one hemisphere would cue the other about a stimulus when only one hemisphere had the information. The authors also report some of the everyday experiences of split-brain patients, including incidences of temporary muteness, neglect of the left side of the body, and more long-term prob-

lems in learning associations between names and faces.

SPLIT-BRAIN RESEARCH HAD A MAJOR IMPACT ON PSYchology. It helped to effect a rapprochement between psychology and neurology, it motivated psychologists to study cerebral asymmetries, and it led to some interesting speculation about consciousness and personal identity: Is consciousness a unitary phenomenon because introspection makes it seem that way, or are there separate aspects to consciousness that work together to produce an illusion of integrated consciousness? Is consciousness of self something that is more than the sum of its (neurophysiological) parts?

The view that the mind contains specialized mechanisms or modules receives support in Christine M. Temple's article "Developmental Memory Impairment: Faces and Patterns." In it, Temple tells the fascinating saga of Dr S, a highly intelligent woman (a medical doctor by training) who had a lifelong problem recognizing faces. Problems in facial recognition are a form of visual agnosia known as *prosopagnosia*. Temple reports the results of various tests that were given to Dr S in an attempt to pin down the precise nature of her problem. For example, Dr S performed quite well on the Weschler Adult Intelligence Scale test; indeed, she showed exceptional verbal abilities. She also performed well on perceptual tests that required her to match the angles of lines, mental rotation tests, tests of common object recognition, and even face recognition tests for which testing was done after a very short retention interval. However, Dr S performed poorly on tests of visual memory for designs, and she had problems recognizing the faces of famous people. Temple concludes that there are "brain mechanisms that are specific to face recognition."

DR S HAS HAD A LIFELONG DEFICIENCY IN A RESTRICTED aspect of visual perception. In the next selection, we encounter a temporary deficiency in a higher-order cognitive function—the ability to name things. The author, Mark H. Ashcraft, a professor of cognitive psychology, presents his own case history and experience with *transient anomia* in "A Personal Case History of Transient Anomia."

Professor Ashcraft describes an episode in which he found he could not verbally label objects and concepts that were extremely common to him and his work, such as *printout, data, experiments,* and *results.* He also could not remember the command to log off from his computer, even though he used the command frequently. The entire episode lasted only about 45 minutes and was later diagnosed as due to an arteriovenous malformation in the left temporal lobe of the brain.

After detailing his episode, Ashcraft muses about his emotional reactions and train of thought and about the nature of language-thought interactions. Emotionally, he was initially amused that he could not retrieve routine words or even substitutes for them. He felt more puzzled than panicky, however. Ashcraft states that his train of thought was clear, conscious, and directed, if possibly irrational at times. In his opinion, various processes, including motor, short-term memory, and most of long-term memory (e.g., problem solving) were left intact, indicating that these processes were not dependent on fluid verbal retrieval. The important point is that Ashcraft's problem solving and thought were nonlinguistic. He reports that meanings and concepts were clear and conscious but that, theoretically, the step of accessing a word for the concept had broken down. As Ashcraft himself puts it, "The most powerful realization I had during the episode, and the most intriguing aspect to me since then, was the dissociation between a thought and the word or phrase that expresses the thought. The subjective experience consisted of knowing with complete certainty the idea or concept that I was trying to express and being completely unable to find and utter the word that expressed the idea or concept." Of course, the noninteraction of language and thought that Ashcraft describes is only one logical possibility—there can also be language without thought, as well as constant interaction between the two.

IN "EYE MOVEMENTS IN READING: RECENT DEVELOPMENTS," by Keith Rayner, we return to more familiar terrain in cognitive psychology—experiments rather than case studies, larger sample sizes, undamaged brains, and conclusions based on complex statistical analyses. In this case the topic is perceptual aspects of reading as indexed by some sophisticated techniques for measuring eye movements.

Rayner first presents some basic facts about perceptual aspects of reading. Information is taken in, for example, only during eye fixations, not during eye movements (or *saccades*). Rayner focuses on perceptual and cognitive processes that occur during reading, as inferred from the characteristics of eye movements. These movements are tracked by a complex system in which a computer controls the display of text on a screen and, depending on the location of the reader's eyes, changes are made in the text. This is called the *eye-contingent display change* paradigm. Using this paradigm it becomes possible to replace text that is outside the "moving-window" of fixation. That is, when the reader moves his or her eyes, the text is changed outside the fixation area. This technique indicates that the perceptual span of reading is lopsided, in that readers of English (who read left to right) see at most 15 letters to the right of fixation and 4 letters to the left. Other techniques indicate that readers benefit from previewing letters to the right of a fixation. Rayner also reports that reading takes place within a small, fixated region, involving perhaps only a single word, that the word is processed in about 50 milliseconds, and that eye movements are programmed primarily on the basis of word length and processing complexity. A final, important conclusion is that the *eye-mind span*—the time between first fixating on text and mentally processing it—is quite short.

The research on eye movements in reading is opening up some exciting inroads into text processing in general. This is because it is a relatively unobtrusive means of measuring processing while it is actually occurring (i.e., online). The data that this technique yields will undoubtedly help decide theoretical questions and could lead to techniques for improving reading skills.

4

Sally P. Springer and Georg Deutsch

The Human Split Brain: Surgical Separation of the Hemispheres

In 1940, an article appeared in a scientific journal describing experiments on the spread of epileptic discharge from one hemisphere to the other in the brains of monkeys.[1] The author concluded that the spread occurred largely or entirely by way of the corpus callosum, the largest of several *commissures,* or bands of nerve fiber connecting regions of the left brain with similar areas of the right brain. Earlier, other investigators had observed that damage to the corpus callosum from a tumor or other problem sometimes reduced the incidence of seizures in human epileptics.[2] Together, these findings paved the wave for a new treatment for patients with epilepsy that could not be controlled in other ways: the split-brain operation.

Split-brain surgery, or *commissurotomy,* involves surgically cutting some of the fibers that connect the two cerebral hemispheres. The first such operations to relieve epilepsy were performed in the early 1940s on approximately two dozen patients. The patients subsequently gave scientists their first opportunity to study systematically the role of the corpus callosum in humans, a role that had been speculated on for decades.

The corpus callosum was a puzzle for researchers who expected to find functions commensurate with its large size and strategic location within the brain. Animal research had shown the consequences of split-brain surgery on a healthy organism to be minimal. The behavior of split-brain monkeys, for example, appeared indistinguishable from what it was before the operation. The apparent absence of any noticeable changes following commissurotomy led some scientists to suggest facetiously that the corpus callosum's only function was to hold the halves of the brain together and keep them from sagging.

Speculations on the philosophical implications of split-brain surgery go back to the nineteenth century and the writings of Gustav Fechner, considered by many to be the father of experimental psychology. Fechner considered consciousness to be an attribute of the cerebral hemispheres, and he believed that continuity of the brain was an essential condition for unity of consciousness. If it were possible to divide the brain through the middle, he speculated, something like the duplication of a human being would result. "The two cerebral hemispheres," he wrote, "while beginning with the same moods, predispositions, knowledge, and memories, indeed the same consciousness generally, will thereafter develop differently according to the external relations into which each enter."[3] Fechner considered this "thought experiment" involving separation of the hemispheres impossible to achieve in reality.

Fechner's views concerning the nature of consciousness did not go unchallenged. William McDougall, a founder of the British Psychological Society, argued strongly against the position that unity of consciousness depends on the continuity of the nervous system. To make his point, McDougall volunteered to have his corpus callosum cut if he ever got an incurable disease. He apparently wanted to show that his personality would not be split and that his consciousness would remain unitary.

McDougall never got the opportunity to put his ideas to the test, but the surgery Fechner thought an impossibility took place for the first time almost a century later. The issues these men raised have been among those explored by scientists seeking a fuller understanding of the corpus callosum through the study of split-brain patients.

CUTTING 200 MILLION NERVE FIBERS: A SEARCH FOR CONSEQUENCES

The First Split-Brain Operations on Humans

William Van Wagenen, a neurosurgeon from Rochester, New York, performed the first split-brain operations on humans in the early 1940s. Postsurgical testing by an investigator named Andrew Akelaitis showed surprisingly little in the way of deficits in perceptual and motor abilities.[4] The operation seemed to have had no effect on everyday behavior. Unfortunately, for some patients the surgery also seemed to do little to alleviate the condition respon-

sible for the surgery in the first place. Success in relieving seizures seemed to vary greatly from patient to patient.

In retrospect, this variability seems attributable to two causes: (1) individual differences in the nature of the epilepsy in the patients and (2) variations in the actual surgical procedures used with each patient. Figure 1 shows the corpus callosum and the adjacent smaller commissures. Van Wagenen's operations varied considerably but usually included sectioning of the forward (anterior) half of the corpus callosum. In two patients, he also sectioned a separate fiber band known as the anterior commissure.

At the time, the importance of these factors was not known, and Van Wagenen soon discontinued the commissurotomy procedure in cases of intractable epilepsy. Clearly, it was not producing the dramatic results he had hoped for. Despite these discouraging findings, other investigators continued to study the functions of the corpus callosum in animals. A decade later, in the early 1950s, Ronald Myers and Roger Sperry made some remarkable discoveries that marked a turning point in efforts to study this enigmatic structure.

Myers and Sperry showed that visual information presented to one hemisphere in a cat with its corpus callosum cut would not be available to the other hemisphere.[5] In most higher animals, the visual system is arranged so that each eye normally projects to both hemispheres. But by cutting into the optic-nerve crossing, the *chiasm*, experimenters can limit where each eye sends its information. When this cut is made, the remaining fibers in the optic nerve transmit information to the hemisphere on the same side. Visual input to the left eye is sent only to the left hemisphere, and input to the right eye projects only to the right hemisphere.

Myers performed this operation on cats and subsequently taught each animal a visual-discrimination task with one of its eyes patched. A discrimination task involves, for example, an animal's pressing a lever when it sees a circle but not pressing it when it sees a square. Even if this training is done with one eye covered, a normal cat can later perform the task using either eye. Myers found that cats with the optic chiasm cut were also able to perform the task using either eye when tested after the one-eyed training. However, when he cut

Figure 1

The Major Interhemispheric Commissures

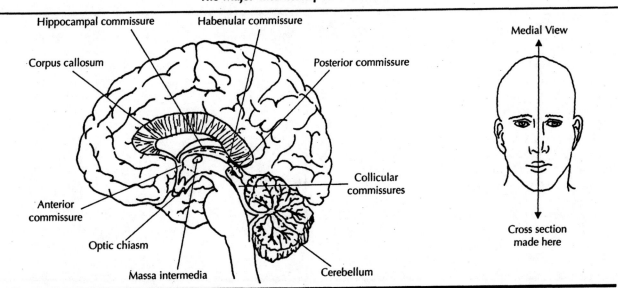

the corpus callosum in addition to the optic chiasm, the results were dramatically different.

The cat trained with one eye open and one eye patched would learn to do a task well; but when the patch was switched to the other eye, the cat was unable to do the task at all. In fact, it had to be taught the same task over again, taking just as long to learn it as it had the first time. Myers and Sperry concluded that cutting the corpus callosum had kept information going into one hemisphere isolated from the other hemisphere. They had, in effect, trained only half of a brain. Figure 2 schematically illustrates the different conditions of their experiment.

These findings, as well as some further studies, led two neurosurgeons working near the California Institute of Technology, in Pasadena, to reconsider the use of split-brain surgery as a treatment for intractable epilepsy in human beings. The surgeons, Philip Vogel and Joseph Bogen, reasoned that some of the earlier work with human patients had failed because the disconnection between the cerebral hemispheres was not complete. As we have mentioned, Van Wagenen's operations varied considerably from patient to patient. Some parts of the corpus callosum as well as several smaller commissures were usually not included in his operations, and these remaining fibers may have connected the

hemispheres sufficiently to mask the effects of the fibers that were cut. On the basis of this logic, coupled with new animal data showing no ill effects from the surgery, Bogen and Vogel performed a complete commissurotomy on the first of what was to be a new series of two dozen patients suffering from intractable epilepsy.

Bogen and Vogel's reasoning proved to be correct. In some of the cases, the medical benefits of the surgery even appeared to exceed expectations. In striking contrast to its consequences for seizure activity, the operation appeared to leave patients unchanged in personality, intelligence, and behavior in general, just as had been the case with Van Wagenen's patients. More extensive and ingenious testing conducted in Roger Sperry's California Institute of Technology laboratory, however, soon revealed a more complex story, for which Sperry was awarded the 1981 Nobel Prize in Physiology or Medicine.

Testing for the Effects of Disconnecting Left from Right

Split-brain patient N. G., a California housewife, sits in front of a screen with a small black dot in the center. She is asked to look directly at the dot.

Figure 2

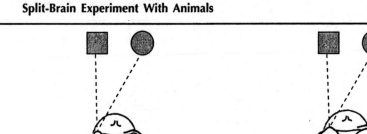
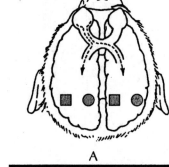
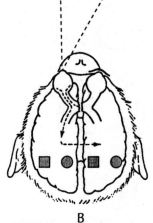
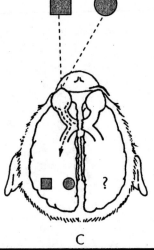

Split-Brain Experiment With Animals

A   B   C

In a control situation, both eyes and both hemispheres see the stimuli. Experimental conditions alter this in the following ways: A. When one eye is patched, the other eye continues to send information to both hemispheres. B. When one eye is patched and the optic chiasm is cut, the visual information is transmitted to both hemispheres by way of the corpus callosum. C. When one eye is patched and both the optic chiasm and corpus callosum are cut, only one hemisphere receives visual information.

When the experimenter is sure she is doing so, a picture of a cup is flashed briefly to the right of the dot. N. G. reports that she has seen a cup. Again, she is asked to fix her gaze on the dot. This time, a picture of a spoon is flashed to the left of the dot. She is asked what she saw. She replies, "No, nothing." She is then asked to reach under the screen with her left hand and to select, by touch only, from among several items the one that is the same as the one she has just seen. Her left hand palpates each object and then holds up the spoon. When asked what she is holding, she says, "Pencil."

Once again the patient is asked to fixate on the dot on the screen. A picture of a nude woman is flashed to the left of the dot. N. G.'s face blushes a little, and she begins to giggle. She is asked what she saw. She says, "Nothing, just a flash of light," and giggles again, covering her mouth with her hand. "Why are you laughing, then?" the investigator inquires. "Oh, doctor, you have some machine!" she replies.

The procedure just described is frequently used in studies with split-brain patients and is illustrated in Figure 3. The patient sits in front of a tachistoscope, a device that allows the investigator to control precisely the duration for which a picture or pattern is presented on a screen. The presentations are kept brief, about one- or two-tenths of a

second (100 to 200 milliseconds), so that the patient does not have time to move his or her eyes away from the fixation point while the picture is still on the screen.* This procedure is necessary to ensure that visual information is presented initially to only one hemisphere. Stimuli presented to only one hemisphere are said to be *lateralized.*

The design of the human nervous system is such that each cerebral hemisphere receives information primarily from the opposite half of the body. This contralateral rule applies to vision and hearing as well as to body movement and touch (somatosensory) sensation, although the situation in vision and hearing is more complex.

In vision, the contralateral rule applies to the right and left sides of one's field of view (visual field), rather than to the right and left eyes per se. When both eyes are fixating on a single point, stimuli to the right of fixation are registered in the left half of the brain, while the right half of the brain processes everything occurring to the left of fixation. This split and crossover of visual information results from the manner in which the nerve fibers

*the rapid eye movements that occur when gaze is shifted from one point to another are known as *saccadic eye movements* or saccades. Although once started, saccades are extremely rapid, they take about 200 milliseconds to initiate with the eye at rest. If a stimulus is presented for less than 200 milliseconds, the stimulus is no longer present by the time an eye movement can occur.

Figure 3

The Basic Testing Arrangement Used to Lateralize Visual and Tactile Information and Allow Tactile Responses

from corresponding regions of both eyes are divided between the cerebral hemispheres. Figure 4 shows both the optics and the neural wiring involved.

In animal studies, as we have seen, visual information can be directed to one hemisphere by cutting the optic chiasm so that the remaining fibers in the optic nerve are those transmitting information to the hemisphere on the same side as the eye. This allows experimenters to present a stimulus easily to either hemisphere alone by simply presenting the stimulus to the appropriate eye. The procedure is used only with animals, however, because cutting the chiasm substantially reduces peripheral vision, eliminates binocular depth perception, and plays no part in the rationale for the split-brain operation on humans. For these reasons, investigators wishing to transmit visual information to one hemisphere at a time in a human split-brain patient must do so through a combination of controlling the patient's fixation and presenting information to one side of space.

With this as background, let's return to an analysis of the tests administered to patient N.G. In those tests, the patient saw the left half of the screen (everything to the left of the fixation point) with the right side of her brain and everything to the right with her left hemisphere. The split in her brain prevented the normal interchange of information between the two sides that would have occurred before her surgery. In effect, each side of her brain was blind to what the other side was seeing, a state of affairs dramatically brought out by the knowledge that only one hemisphere controls speech.

As a consequence, the patient reported perfectly well any stimuli falling in the right visual field (projecting to the verbal left hemisphere), although she was unable to tell anything about what was flashed in her left visual field (sent to the mute right hemisphere). The fact that she "saw" stimuli in the left visual field is amply demonstrated by the ability of her left hand (basically controlled by the right brain) to select the spoon from among several objects hidden

Figure 4 ───────────────

Visual Pathways to the Hemispheres

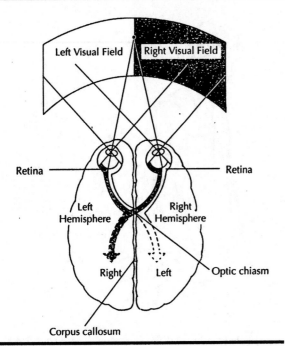

When fixating on a point, each eye sees both visual fields but sends information about the right visual field only to the left hemisphere and information about the left visual field only to the right hemisphere. This crossover and split is a result of the manner in which the nerve fibers leading from the retina divide at the back of each eye. The visual areas of the left and right hemisphere normally communicate through the corpus callosum. If the callosum is cut and the eyes and head are kept from moving, each hemisphere can see only half of the visual world.

from view. It is also demonstrated by her emotional reaction to the nude picture, despite her claim not to have seen anything.[6]

The patient's response to the nude picture is particularly interesting. She seemed puzzled by her own reactions to what had appeared. Her right hemisphere saw the picture and processed it sufficiently to evoke a general, nonverbal reaction—the giggling and the blushing. The left hemisphere, meanwhile, did not "know" what the right had seen, although its comment about "some machine" seems to be a sign that it was aware of the bodily reactions induced by the right hemisphere. It is very common for the verbal left hemisphere to try to make sense of what has occurred in testing situations where information is presented to the right hemisphere. As a result, the left brain sometimes comes out with erroneous and often elaborate rationalizations based on partial cues.

EVERYDAY BEHAVIOR AFTER SPLIT-BRAIN SURGERY

It is natural to wonder what evidence of disconnection effects there is in the everyday behavior of split-brain patients. Some instances of bizarre behavior have been described by both patients and onlookers and are frequently mentioned in popular articles on split-brain research. One patient, for example, described the time he found his left hand struggling against his right when he tried to put his pants on in the morning: one hand was pulling them up while the other hand was pulling them down. In another incident, the same patient was angry and forcibly reached for his wife with his left hand while his right hand grabbed the left in an attempt to stop it.[7]

The frequency with which such stories are mentioned would lead one to believe that they are commonplace events. In fact, the frequency of such events is low in most patients. However, there are exceptions. One example is P. O. V., a female patient operated on by Dr. Mark Rayport of the Medical College of Ohio. The patient reported frequent dramatic signs of interhemispheric competition for at least three years after surgery. "I open the closet door. I know what I want to wear. As I reach for something with my right hand, my left comes up and takes something different. I can't put it down if it's in my left hand. I have to call my daughter."[8]

Another case is a young man in Georgia who continued to show some profound problems two years after his operation.[9] In working at his father's grocery store he had tremendous difficulty performing stocking and shelving tasks. For example, in stocking canned goods, one hand would place a can in its proper spot on a shelf and the other hand would remove it. These conflicting hand movements persisted even when he thought he was "really" concentrating on the task. His physical and occupational therapists tried many times to practice similar tasks with him, but were unable to stop the problem in real life contexts.

Cases such as these support the concept that the cerebral commissures transmit a good deal of information that is inhibitory in nature—that is, activity in one hemisphere leads to callosal transmissions that serve to moderate, decrease, or stop certain activity in the other. Creating efficient new function through the balance of competitive or "opponent" processes is very common in biological systems. All locomotion, for instance, is based on the action of opposing muscle groups, and all postures depend on a careful balance of such muscle groups. In the central nervous system, opponent processes seem to underlie, for example, geometric illusions where the same drawing can be viewed in two different ways and appears to alternate dramatically between them.

With respect to hemispheric interaction, research with animals has indicated that the cerebral commissures pass information that can either excite or inhibit activity.[10] Colwin Trevarthen reported that split-brain baboons at times reached for an object with both forelimbs at the same time, presumably because no inhibitory processes were available to establish unilateral control over the action.[11] Other work demonstrated that monkeys whose corpus callosum was cut reached to grasp presumably hallucinated objects when the occipital region of one hemisphere was electrically stimulated.[12] This did not occur in animals with the commissures intact, suggesting that in normal animals the unstimulated hemisphere would "disconfirm" the hallucination through inhibitory information passed via the callosum.

It seems likely, thus, that inhibition mediated by the corpus callosum is an important process in maximizing efficiency in behavioral performance and perhaps even in producing new kinds of functions. It is very apparent, however, that these functions are quickly masked by some compensatory mechanisms in most split-brain patients. In fact, in a large majority of cases the two sides of the body appear to work in a coordinated fashion. Perhaps the rarity of patients with persistent disconnection effects indicates that more than callosal damage is necessary in order for the patient to be unable to adjust to the commissurotomy.

For the most part, a battery of sophisticated tests specifically designed to identify a commissurotomy patient would be needed for anyone to know the operation had occurred. Much more common, however, are reports of subtle changes in behavior or ability after surgery. Although some of the reported changes have not held up when carefully studied, others do appear to be verifiable consequences of the operation.

Subtle Deficits Following Surgery

Several patients have reported great difficulty learning to associate names with faces after surgery. Verification of this came from a study in which subjects had to learn first names for each of three pictures of young men.[13] This procedure was only incidental to the main purpose of the study, but it proved to be a major stumbling block for the subjects. The investigators reported that subjects eventually learned the name–face associations by isolating some unique feature in each picture (for example, "Dick has glasses") rather than by associating the name with the face as a whole. This suggests that the deficit in the ability to associate names and faces may be due to the disconnection of the verbal naming functions of the left side of the brain from the facial-recognition abilities of the right side.

Deficits in the ability to solve geometrical problems have been anecdotally linked to the absence of the corpus callosum. Patient L. B., a high school student with an IQ considerably above average, was transferred out of geometry into a class in general math after he experienced inordinate difficulty with the course. Another report told of a college student who had exceptional difficulty with geometry despite average grades in other courses. Research with split-brain patients studying the ability of each hemisphere to match two- and three-dimensional forms on the basis of common geometrical features showed the right hemisphere to be markedly superior, especially on the most difficult matches.[14] Thus, as in the preceding example, the patient's deficits may be the result of the disconnection of the speaking left hemisphere from the right-hemisphere regions specialized for such tasks.

Another complaint of some split-brain patients is that they no longer dream. Because dreaming is primarily a visual-imaging process, investigators have speculated that it might be the responsibility of the right half of the brain. The operation would serve to disconnect this aspect of the patient's mental life from the speaking left hemisphere and would result in verbal reports that the patient does not dream.

This idea, however, has not been confirmed by further research. Split-brain patients were monitored for brain-wave activity while sleeping and were awakened whenever the recordings indicated they were dreaming. They were then asked to describe the dreams they had just been having. In contrast to the prediction that they would be unable to do so, the patients provided the experimenters with descriptions of their dreams.[15]

Other anecdotal evidence has pointed to poorer memory after surgery. These reports were apparently supported by a study of memory abilities in which several split-brain patients were compared with other epilepsy patients and were found to have poorer scores on a variety of memory tests.[16] A major problem with this type of study, though, is that we really do not know much about split-brain patients' preoperative memory abilities. We can compare their performance after surgery with that of epileptic control subjects who have not had surgery, but we have no way of knowing if the memory skills of the split-brain patients before their surgery were really comparable to the memory skills of the control group. Perhaps they had poorer memories to begin with! *haha !*

The best approach is to compare memory abilities before and after surgery in the same patient. This was done informally in five patients in the Rayport series. When tested for attention, memory, and sequencing abilities, four showed noticeably impaired performance when tested five to 38 months after surgery. A male patient, J. A. C., reportedly prepared for a shower by removing his clothes, only to put them on again without getting wet. P. O. V., the female patient mentioned earlier, became forgetful to the point of being unable to keep track of her own medication or remember simple directions and arrangements even for a few hours.[17]

This pattern apparently is not found in all or even most patients, however. In the case of patient D. H. operated on by Dr. Donald Wilson of the Dartmouth Medical School, memory performance improved considerably after surgery.[18]

The most likely explanation for this finding is that D. H.'s true abilities were suppressed by drugs and his general condition before surgery. The operation did not miraculously improve his memory; instead, it allowed his true abilities to emerge. In any case, this single-subject study shows that memory deficits do not *necessarily* follow split-brain surgery, and it indicates that further work will be needed to answer the question of whether the operation affects memory and, if so, in which way. It also points to the importance of appropriate controls in studies looking for changes in split-brain patients.

Overall, it is not clear why a few patients seem to show persistent patterns of deficit after commissurotomy, whereas the majority of patients do not. Important differences among patients in their preoperative condition and surgical treatment probably exist, although we do not yet know what they are. There are some consequences of commissurotomy, however, that are dramatic and quite consistent across patients but are short lived.

Acute Disconnection Syndrome

The *acute disconnection syndrome* is probably due to the surgical division of the commissures as well as to the general trauma resulting from the surgeon's having to squeeze or compress the right hemisphere to gain access to the nerve tracts between the hemispheres.

Patients are often mute for a time after surgery and sometimes they have difficulty controlling the left side of the body, which may at first seem almost paralyzed and then work very awkwardly. As the patient recovers use of the left hand, competitive movements between the left and right hands sometimes occur. This problem usually passes quickly.

After recovering from the initial shock of major brain surgery, most patients report an improved feeling of well-being. Less than two days after surgery, one young patient was well enough to quip that he had a "splitting headache." Within a few weeks, the symptoms of the acute disconnection syndrome subside, making it necessary to use carefully contrived laboratory tests to reveal what had taken place earlier in the operation.

CROSS CUING

As the study of split-brain patients continued, certain inconsistencies in the findings began to occur with greater frequency. Patients previously unable to identify verbally objects held out of sight in the left hand began to name some items. Some pictures flashed in the left visual field (to the right hemisphere) were also correctly identified verbally. One interpretation of these results is that over time, the right hemispheres of the patients acquired the ability to talk. Another is that information being transmitted between the hemispheres by way of pathways other than those that were cut.

Although these were interesting and exciting possibilities, Michael Gazzaniga and Steven Hillyard were able to pinpoint a much simpler explanation for their findings.[19] They coined the term *cross cuing* to refer to patients' attempts to use whatever cues are available to make information accessible to both hemispheres. Cross cuing is most obvious in the case where a patient is given an object to hold and identify with his or her left hand, which is out of the line of vision and thus disconnected from the verbal left hemisphere. If, for example, the left hand is given a comb or a toothbrush to feel, the patient will often stroke the brush or the surface of the comb. The patient will then immediately identify the object because the left hemisphere hears the tell-tale sounds.

Cross cuing provides a way for one hemisphere to provide the other with information about what it is experiencing. The direct channels of information transfer are eliminated by the surgery in most instances leaving the patient with indirect cues as the only means of interhemispheric communication. Cross cuing can often be quite subtle, testing the ingenuity of investigators seeking to eliminate it from the experimental situation.

A good example of this is the patient who was able to indicate verbally whether a 0 or a 1 had been flashed to either hemisphere. The same patient was unable to identify verbally pictures of objects flashed to the right hemisphere, nor was he able to identify most objects held in his left hand. This suggested that he lacked the ability to speak from the right hemisphere. Instead, the investigators proposed that cross cuing was involved when the patient reported the numbers flashed to the right hemisphere. They hypothesized that the left hemisphere would begin counting "subvocally" after a presentation to the left visual field and that these signals were picked up by the right hemisphere. When the correct number was reached, the right hemisphere would signal the left to stop and report that digit out loud.

To test this idea, the patient was presented with an expanded version of the task: the digits 2, 3, 5, and 8 were added without his knowledge. At first the subject was very surprised when a new number was presented. His response to the first unexpected number presented to the right hemisphere was, "I beg your pardon." With a little practice, however, he was able to give the correct answer for all the numbers presented to the right hemisphere, but with hesitation when the number was high. In contrast, responses to the same digits presented in the right visual field (to the left hemisphere) were quite prompt.

These findings fit well with the idea that the left hemisphere began counting subvocally after a digit was presented to the right hemisphere. The larger the number of potential digits, the longer the list of numbers the left hemisphere had to go through before reaching the correct one.

Cross cuing generally is not a conscious attempt by the patient to trick the investigator. Instead, it is a natural tendency by an organism to use whatever information it has to make sense of what is going on. This tendency, in fact, contributes further insight into why the common, everyday behavior of split-brain patients seems so unaffected by the surgery.

Careful testing procedures that prevent cross cuing, however, can lead to striking "disconnection" effects, such as those described in the case of patient N. G. In these situations, the patient is unable to tell what picture was flashed to the right hemisphere, although the left hand can point to the correct object. If blindfolded, the patient cannot verbally identify an object held in the left hand but can select with that hand other objects related to it (for example, selecting a book of matches after having held a cigarette).

To an observer unfamiliar with the patient's surgical history, these findings give the impression that the left arm has a mind of its own. They are less mysterious when we realize that the split-brain operation has disconnected the patient's right hemisphere from the centers in the left hemisphere that control speech. The left hand, thus, is the primary means through which the right hemisphere can communicate with the outside world.

NOTES

1. T. C. Erikson, "Spread of Epileptic Discharge," *Archives of Neurology and Psychiatry* 43 (1940): 429–452.

2. W. Van Wagenen and R. Herren, "Surgical Division of Commissural Pathways in the Corpus Callosum," *Archives of Neurology and Psychiatry* 44 (1940): 740–759.

3. G. Fechner (1860), cited in O. Zangwill, "Consciousness and the Cerebral Hemispheres," in *Hemispheric Function in the Human Brain,* ed. S. Dimond and G. Beaumont (New York: Halsted Press, 1974).

4. J. Akelaitis, "Studies on the Corpus Callosum. II: The Higher Visual Functions in Each Homonymous Field Following Complete Section of the Corpus Callosum," *Archives of Neurology and Psychiatry* 45 (1941): 789–796.

5. A. J. Akelaitis, "The Study of Gnosis, Praxis and Language Following Section of the Corpus Callosum and Anterior Commissure," *Journal of Neurosurgery* 1 (1944): 94–102.

6. R. E. Myers, "Function of Corpus Callosum in Interocular Transfer," *Brain* 79 (1956): 358–363.

7. R. E. Myers and R. W. Sperry, "Interhemispheric Communication Through the Corpus Callosum. Mnemonic Carry-Over Between the Hemispheres," *Archives of Neurology and Psychiatry* 80 (1958): 298–303.

8. R. W. Sperry, "Hemisphere Deconnection and Unity in Conscious Awareness," *American Psychologist* 23 (1968): 723–733.

9. M. S. Gazzaniga, *The Bisected Brain* (New York: Appleton-Century-Crofts, 1970).

10. S. M. Ferguson, M. Rayport, and W. S. Corrie, "Neuropsychiatric Observations on Behavioral Consequences of Corpus Callosum Section for Seizure Control," in *Epilepsy and the Corpus Callosum,* ed. A. G. Reeves (New York: Plenum Press, 1985).

11. M. White, Personal Communication.

12. F. Bremer, "An Aspect of the Physiology of Corpus Callosum," *Journal of Electroencephalography and Clinical Neurophysiology* 22 (1967): 391.

13. C. B. Trevarthen, "Manipulative Strategies of Baboons, and the Origins of Cerebral Asymmetry," in *Hemispheric Asymmetry of Function,* ed. M. Kinsbourne (London: Tavistock, 1974).

14. R. W. Doty, "Electrical Stimulation of the Brain in Behavioral Cortex," *Annual Review of Psychology* 20 (1969): 289–320.

15. J. Levy, C. Trevarthen, and R. W. Sperry, "Perception of Bilateral Chimeric Figures Following Hemispheric Disconnection," *Brain* 95 (1972): 61–78.

16. L. Franco and R. W. Sperry, "Hemisphere Lateralization for Cognitive Processing of Geometry," *Neuropsychologia* 15 (1977): 107–114.

17. P. Greenwood, D. H. Wilson, and M. S. Gazzaniga, "Dream Report Following Commissurotomy," *Cortex* 13 (1977): 311–316.

18. E. Zaidel and R. W. Sperry, "Memory Impairment Following Commissurotomy in Man," *Brain* 97 (1974): 263–272.

19. Ferguson, Rayport, and Corrie, "Neuropsychiatric Observations on Behavioral Consequences of Corpus Callosum Section for Seizure Control."

5

Christine M. Temple

Developmental Memory Impairment: Faces and Patterns

Children with developmental dyslexia have selective difficulty in learning to read despite normal intelligence. It could be something unusual about reading itself, which makes it particularly problematic, but it is also possible that these reading difficulties are only one of a range of different types of selective learning problems. Our attention may be particularly attracted to reading difficulties because of their obvious educational implications. Can fluent and articulate people who read well, and pass exams easily, nevertheless have other cognitive weaknesses? The answer to this question is important in understanding the extent to which different systems in the brain are dependent upon each other as the child develops. Is it possible for one system in the brain to function poorly whilst the rest functions well? If different systems are independent this provides information about the brain's underlying organization.

The traditional view is that there can be 'plasticity' in brain development, which means that if a system is not working well the developing brain may have the capacity to reorganize and compensate for the problem. According to this view, selective problems in cognitive skills should not occur in otherwise normal and healthy children and adults. The common existence of developmental dyslexia (see Snowling and Goulandris, chapter 6) suggests that plasticity and compensation fail to correct for potential reading difficulty. Are there comparable non-verbal disorders which show similar resistance to compensation?

Dr S came to our attention because of the life-long difficulty she reported in recognizing people's faces. When I first met her this, of course, was not obvious, as I did not expect her to recognize me. Instead, two other characteristics were instantly apparent. First, she became completely lost trying to find me. Given the complexity of the university buildings, this in itself might have been unsurprising but, as we moved between offices and laboratories, it became apparent that she was quite unable to find her way around. Even relatively simple routes appeared to be a mystery, and at the end of the day when I left her by the station I had to ensure that she had actually noted the entrance or she would walk the wrong way down the street, away from the station itself. Secondly, I was struck by the speed and quantity of her speech. She remains the most fluent talker I have ever encountered. So rapid is her speech output, that at times it becomes a challenge to decipher the individual words. The continuous flow of speech, as Dr S herself knows, is tiring for the listener and, because of her capacity to inflict headaches, she carries aspirin with her to hand out in cases of need!

On my second encounter with Dr S, and as I continued to see her, the face recognition problem became obvious. She failed to recognize me as I went to meet her, looking blankly through me until I said her name. She would also report that as she knew I had blond hair, she had moved expectantly towards several other people before I arrived, thinking them to be me.

Face recognition impairment is documented in the neurological literature; it was given the name *prosopagnosia* by Bodamer in 1947. Prosopagnosia is one of a range of recognition disorders for visually presented material termed visual agnosias. However, in the case of Dr S the difficulty does not result from any neurological injury but has been present since birth.

An intelligent and perceptive lady, Dr S has clear insight about the nature of her difficulties as her own description illustrates:

> There are two problems. I meet somebody who I totally feel I have never seen before, like I told you happened with you, after one or two encounters with you. I had absolutely no idea what you look like and yet know that you are a lovely person, and have the embarrassment of the feeling that I have never seen you before. Also sometimes, I know I have met this person but I do not know where.
>
> I do this game with people to whom I try to explain ... I say 'Close your eyes', and then I ask them can you see (visualize) my face, and 99 per cent of them say they can. When I close my eyes, I see virtually nothing. In your case, I know that you have blonde hair because I have fixed that verbally. But if asked what do you wear, I haven't got the faintest idea ... I know that

you have lovely blonde hair but the rest I wouldn't have known at all.

Dr S is also aware of her rapid speech:

> I may be overfluent ... I talk too much. I overexplain, and all this I'm conscious of. I find it difficult to get out of ... Most people complain about me. The most striking thing is she talks too much and too fast.

Dr S was happy to be our guinea-pig and we decided particularly to investigate her face recognition problems but also to explore her intelligence, her verbal fluency and her memory. Before discussing the way in which the studies developed, I shall give a little of Dr S's personal history.

BIOGRAPHICAL HISTORY

Dr S is now in her sixties and lives in London. She was born in Germany, into a prosperous Jewish family, and lived there and in Austria as a child, coming to the UK at the age of fifteen. In the UK she qualified as a doctor of medicine, in 1945, from the London School of Medicine for Women, at the Royal Free Hospital. Further qualifications included training as a pathologist; a diploma in tropical medicine and hygiene; a diploma in family planning; and a BA in psychology. The latter was taken in evening classes at Birkbeck College, London. For many years, Dr S worked as a family planning specialist in Mauritius. She has also travelled widely.

Dr S speaks fluent German, English, French and some Danish. She reports that she was very good at Latin at school. She has had difficulty in mastering both Russian and Greek, possibly relating to problems in mastering the Cyrillic alphabet. She is highly motivated to learn Hebrew but continues to have difficulty with the script.

Dr S has been married twice. Her first husband was a university professor. Her second husband was a medical doctor. She has four children, three boys and a girl, all of whom have university degrees. None of the children is left-handed. All of the boys are colour blind. Dr S has a first cousin who also has difficulty in recognizing faces.

Dr S is in good health. She has had no major illnesses, has never had an accident with loss of consciousness and has had no seizures. In addition to the difficulties discussed here, Dr S complains of clumsiness; difficulty with figures; excessive anxiety about using machines and appliances; and that she is tone deaf.

INTELLIGENCE AND VERBAL FLUENCY

Dr S was obviously intelligent because of the formal qualifications she had attained, and her sharp, alert and thoughtful mind was also apparent in conversation. To assess her intelligence more formally, we used the Weschler Adult Intelligence Scale, in its revised format, and the scores she attained are given in table 1. The Weschler contains a range of verbal sub-tests and also non-verbal sub-tests involving puzzles, designs and pictures, which are called performance tests. We were interested in whether Dr S would have much better verbal than non-verbal intelligence. However, the scores revealed that her non-verbal abilities were just as good as her verbal abilities. Thus, any difficulty in face recognition can be attributed neither to a general intellectual problem, nor to a general problem in dealing with pictorial or visual material. Dr S had an exceptionally high IQ. Her scores would be attained by fewer than 1 in a 1000 women in their sixties.

Another feature which struck us about her performance was the exceptionally high score which she attained on the vocabulary sub-test. In fact, her ability to give definitions of words was perfect for all those which we gave to her. This was particularly impressive given that English was not Dr S's first language. However, it was consistent with our

Table 1 ━━━━━━━━━━━━━━━━━━━━━━

Scores on the Intelligence Test

Verbal sub-tests		Performance sub-tests	
Information	14	Picture completion	12
Digit span	12	Picture arrangement	13
Vocabulary	19	Block design	10
Arithmetic	13	Object assembly	13
Similarities	16	Digit symbol	17

10 is an average sub-test score. Possible scores are 1–19. The standard deviation is 3, which means that about two-thirds of people score between 7 and 13 on sub-tests

Verbal IQ	136	Performance IQ	147
Full-scale IQ	147		

100 is an average IQ. Two-thirds of people have an IQ between 85 and 115. Only one in a thousand has an IQ as high as 147.

Table 2 ━━━━━━━━━━━━━━━━━━━━━━

Animals Generated in the Fluency Tasks

Subject	Named animals
Typical control	cat dog horse goat sheep elephant leopard lion monkey parrot donkey snake mouse
Dr S	monkey bear walrus whale dog cat hen mouse rat lion tiger leopard wolf hyena eagle owl swan duck goose chicken elephant buffalo cow ox sheep lamb horse donkey sparrow ram dove heron pelican ostrich polar bear

informal observations of her extensive speech production.

Another way in which verbal production skills can be measured is to look at the ease with which words in the vocabulary can be found. A standard clinical measure is a fluency task. The subject is asked to generate as many words as possible in one-minute time slots for particular categories. Here we used animals, household objects, words beginning with 'f' and words beginning with 's'. We compared Dr S's performance with that of six other healthy women in their sixties, who acted as normal 'controls'. Results were consistent on all the categories. Dr S generated significantly more items than the other women. For example, the other women generated on average 14 animals in a minute; Dr S generated 35 on one occasion and 42 on another. The animals that she and a typical control subject named are given in table 2.

From these investigations, we conclude that Dr S is of exceptionally high intellectual ability and that her vocabulary and verbal fluency are also exceptionally highly developed. If abnormality is defined in terms of distance from the average, then Dr S's fluency is abnormal in its extreme quality. Later, we will examine the difficulty which this extremely highly developed skill creates for Dr S in everyday life. It is not simply impairments which create problems. However, first we will discuss the way in which we explored her face recognition problems.

NORMAL MODELS OF VISUAL PERCEPTION AND FACE RECOGNITION

Cognitive neuropsychologists have discussed the recognition disorders, both visual agnosias and prosopagnosias, in relation to information-processing models of object and face recognition. Such models incorporate elements of Marr's theory of visual perception. According to Marr (1976, 1980, 1982), there are at least three levels of description involved in the recognition of objects. The first level is the primal sketch in which texture, gradations of light and discontinuities are coded. The second level is called the '2½-D level'. This incorporates descriptions of the structures of objects but these are said to be *viewer-centred,* in that they are entirely dependent upon the angle of sight of the observer. Thus, if you are looking at a chair from one angle and you get up and move and look at it from a different angle the 2½-D representation changes completely. At the third level in Marr's model, there is a 3-D representation which is said to be *object-centred,* in that it is independent of the view of the observer. At the 3-D level there must be stored descriptions of the variable appearances of objects. The 3-D level is essential for object constancy and in order for us to deal effectively with unusual or partially obscured views of objects.

A functional model for face processing, against which subjects can be interpreted has been proposed by Bruce and Young (1986) (see figure 1). This model does not make explicit the distinction between initial representations, viewer-centred representations and object-centred representations. Instead, it describes a general process of *structural encoding,* which includes these processes and which can gain access to *face recognition units.* Each face recognition unit corresponds to a particular person's face and these units are established in the course of our daily life and encounters. In a way analogous to the biologist's discussion of the 'firing' of a nerve cell, face recognition units are said to have thresholds of activation. When a face is seen, there will be an increase in activity in all the units representing faces which resemble it but only the unit which corresponds to the viewed face will be fully activated. This unit will reach threshold and will 'fire'.

Following the structural encoding of a face's appearance, several types of information are extracted simultaneously. Expression is analysed, providing information about the mood and affect of the speaker or his/her message. Facial speech analysis monitors the mouth and tongue movements involved in producing speech. Lip-readers exploit this system which also reduces ambiguity in normal

Figure 1 ───────────────────

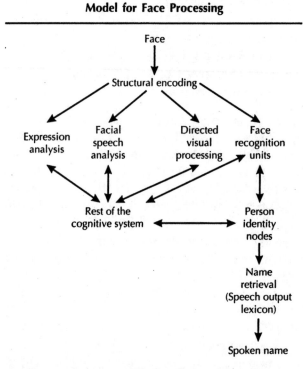

Model for Face Processing

Adapted from Bruce and Young, 1986, and reproduced with permission.

processes of speech comprehension. Directed visual processing is used, for example, to see the similarities and differences between the faces of unfamiliar people. These inputs all feed into a semantically structured cognitive system. When a face recognition unit fires, it will trigger a corresponding *person identity node* which contains information which specifically identifies an individual, for example, their occupation and their personal characteristics.

In order to retrieve a person's name, it is necessary to first activate a person identity node. Thus, it is an explicit prediction of this model that one should never be able to name a person from their appearance unless one also knows something about the person (i.e. their profession or partner). But one can know something about the person without being able to name him/her.

Face recognition disorders may arise from impairments at several different levels within the face recognition system, and a number of these have been described in patients following neurological injury. In Bodamer's original paper (1947), one patient had a deficit in structural encoding. He appeared to have difficulty perceiving faces and even considered that a dog's face was an unusually hairy human being. Most forms of prosopagnosia in neurological patients will result in difficulties in gaining access to or utilizing face recognition units.

Patients with amnesia, who have generalized memory loss, may have lost or be unable to gain access to the person identity nodes themselves. Patients with language problems may have intact person identity nodes but may have difficulty in generating names.

The model of Bruce and Young (1986) clearly implies that faces are 'special' in the sense that there are specialized brain mechanisms for processing them. This would make sense in terms of the importance of both face recognition and expression analysis in our social interaction.

In our investigation of Dr S we wished to determine whether there was a difficulty with her basic visual perceptual or spatial skills or whether there was a difficulty with a particular component of the face recognition system.

VISUAL PERCEPTION

To assess Dr S's basic perceptual skills and her capacity to make judgements about simple components of the visual scene, we tested her ability to make judgements about the orientations of lines. We modified the Benton et al. (1978) line orientation task. Subjects are presented with an array of 31 lines displayed on the lower part of a booklet. On the upper part are two lines of different orientations and varying lengths. The subject must select from the response array, the two lines whose angles match those of the stimulus pair (see figure 2).

The performance of Dr S was compared with that of 12 other healthy women in their sixties, who acted as controls. Unless mentioned otherwise, these women acted as controls for all tests. This line orientation task is not easy, as figure 2 may indicate. The control subjects averaged ten correct. Dr S got 12 correct. Thus her performance was normal. She also performed normally on a tactile version of this task. Thus there is no unusual difficulty in making basic perceptual judgements about orientations of lines.

As mentioned above, Marr's model emphasizes the importance of being able to integrate different viewpoints and recognize things from different angles. We tested Dr S's ability mentally to rotate an abstract shape and recognize it in a different angle. The Mental Rotation task used was a shortened version of a task (Vandenburg and Kuse, 1978) requiring the internalized spatial rotation of 3-D structures depicted by 2-D drawings. The drawings appear to represent 3-D structures composed of multiple cubes (see figure 3). The subjects are told that they may mentally rotate the structure in any direction and they must then select, two identical structures from an array of four. The score out of 20, represents the number of correct selections.

Once again Dr S's performance was compared with the controls. They averaged nine correct and Dr S averaged 14 correct. Thus Dr S can perform this complex spatial manipulation. She can recognize shapes from different angles. In these tests and others we gave we could find no problem with basic perceptual processes and no reason for difficulty in

Figure 2

Line Orientation Test

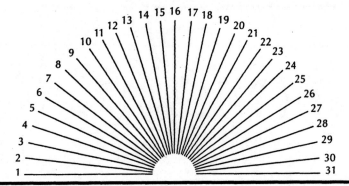

Marr's terms in establishing either viewer-centred or object-centred representations.

FACE PROCESSING

In order to recognize that a face is a face it is necessary to integrate its features. Sometimes this must be done in conditions of poor lighting or when the face is partially obscured. Dr S says that she does realize that a face is a face but could she have difficulty with the 'gestalt' processes involved in integrating features? To assess this we tested her with Mooney faces. The Mooney faces (Lansdell, 1968) present patterns of light and shadow in black and white, depicting faces for which sex and appropriate age are judged. The subject is told that all the pictures are faces but she will only be able to assess the face correctly if she can integrate the blocks of black and white (see figure 4). Dr S was able to make these judgements as easily as the control subjects. Thus she has intact gestalt integrative skills and she is also able to make correct judgements of age and sex about faces.

We had established that Dr S could match an unfamiliar structure in different rotations but we wanted to see if she could do the same things with faces. We also wanted to see if she could match identical pictures of faces. To test these skills we used Benton's Facial Recognition task (Benton et al., 1983). This involves matching a target face with an identical face in the same or a differing orientation. The faces are black and white and are photographed partially in shadow. Both in comparison to the controls and in comparison to the published test norms Dr S performed normally on these tasks. Although she has difficulty in recognizing faces in real life, she is able to match unfamiliar faces seen at different angles. The results of the Mooney faces and the Benton task indicate that Dr S's structural encoding of faces and directed visual processing (see figure 1) have developed normally. Difficulties in face recognition have a basis elsewhere in the face-processing system.

We decided to investigate Dr S's ability initially to register face recognition units by teaching her some new faces. For this we used the Warrington Recognition Memory Battery (Warrington, 1984). The test is in two matched sections. In the first section, the subject is shown a pack of 50 words. Each word is exposed for three seconds and the subject is required to make a judgement of whether or not the associations of the word are pleasant. This encourages some degree of encoding of meaning or semantics. Immediately after the stimulus cards have all been exposed, the subject is required to make a forced choice judgement between pairs of words, one of which has appeared in the stimulus pack and one of which is novel. The faces section is identical except that the stimulus cards consist of unfamiliar faces of men. The forced choice responses are made to pairs of faces, one of which has been shown in the stimulus pack.

Unsurprisingly, on the word section, Dr S had a perfect score. On the faces section, she was correct on 43/50 items which was slightly better than the controls. Thus Dr S is able to set new face recognition units and gain access to these in a choice situation a few minutes later. Her problems must therefore either lie in a failure of these units to become permanently established in memory or in difficulty in using the units to gain access to person identity information and names.

By this stage we were beginning to wonder what Dr S would be unable to do with faces. She seemed to be able to do all our face tasks yet she

Figure 3

Mental Rotation

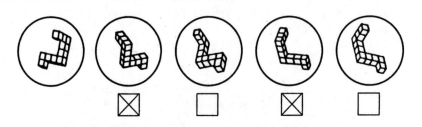

Figure 4

Mooney Face

still failed to recognize us. We wanted to get another measure of these recognition problems so we tested her on her recognition of famous faces. This would indicate her ability to gain access to person identity information (see figure 1) and names.

We showed her two sets of pictures of famous people. There were 45 pictures in total, though a few people appeared on both picture sets. Dr S was able to identify 14 pictures (31 per cent). She was significantly poorer than the six healthy women in their sixties with whom we compared her. It appears that she has difficulty in accessing person identity information from faces. One uninteresting interpretation of these results would be that, although these people seem famous, Dr S simply does not know them. We were particularly concerned about this possibility since she had spent time overseas and some of the figures were British. In order to see whether she knew the people and whether there was a genuine difficulty in identifying people from their faces, we gave her the names of 37 of the people who had appeared in the picture sets. For each name, we asked who they were and what was their occupation to determine whether Dr S had person identity information for these people which was accessible from their spoken name. Dr S could give identifying information for 27 of the

37 people (73 per cent). Thus there were many people whom she knew but whom she had been unable to identify from their faces.

However, we then wondered whether giving somebody's occupation was a less specific task than naming them. You could, after all, identify someone as a politician without knowing exactly who they are. We therefore decided to do a more balanced experiment, with another set of faces. Here we took 40 faces and asked Dr S to give us the occupation of each person from their face. Then, much later, we took the 40 names of these people and spoke them aloud, again asking her to give us their occupations. Dr S could give the occupations for 12 of the faces but 28 of the names. Thus she can gain access to person identity information more easily from spoken names than faces. Many faces failed to elicit the person identity information which we know Dr S possesses.

In terms of the model in figure 1, it would appear that there is intact structural encoding and that the initial registration of face recognition units is normal, but we have found that there is a significant impairment in accessing person identity information from faces in order to recognize the face. Either the face recognition units have failed to consolidate and despite their initial registration they are lost over time or there is difficulty in using the units to activate the person identity information.

RECOGNIZING OTHER PICTURES

As mentioned above, there is a theoretical debate about whether faces are 'special' and have special brain mechanisms devoted to them or whether they are very complex visual stimuli when it comes to identifying individuals. We believed that despite Dr S's difficulty in recognizing faces she did not have generalized recognition difficulties for other visually presented stimuli but we wanted to test this more formally. We therefore gave her the Boston naming test which is a standardized test of object recognition. It consists of a graded set of line drawings of objects: the earlier items are common, e.g. toothbrush, whistle, octopus; the later items are more unusual, e.g. palette, trellis, sphinx. Dr S performed normally on this task.

As another test of object recognition, in comparison to face recognition, we gave her a test constructed by Edward De Haan. It consists of three sets of photographs: familiar (famous) and unfamiliar (novel) faces; familiar (real) and unfamiliar (novel) objects; and familiar and unfamiliar names of people. The novel objects are actually real but rare objects like specialist hardware tools, unfamiliar to any one except an expert. In each group the subject must indicate whether the items are familiar or not. Thus this test permits a direct comparison of recognition skills for faces, objects and names. There are 16 familiar and 16 unfamiliar items in each set. Results are given in table 3. Only with the familiar faces was performance abnormal. Yet on all other sections, performance was good. Dr S can discriminate between familiar and unfamiliar objects. She can also correctly categorize the names of the famous people whose faces she cannot recognize. The deficit is thus specific to faces of people. This supports the view that there are brain mechanisms which are specific to face recognition.

VISUAL MEMORY

We had established that the face recognition problems did not generalize to problems in recognizing objects. However, in view of Dr S's difficulty with topographical orientation we decided to explore whether she had other visual memory problems.

We therefore gave her the Weschler Memory battery which contains a range of different types of memory tasks, including both verbal and visual memory. Her overall score gave a memory quotient of 132, which is in line with her IQ. This result indicated that there was no generalized memory impairment. We did not have control data on the subtests from the controls used above, but we had control data from another study we had been doing, which came from 15–16-year-olds. The performance of Dr S is compared to the teenagers in table 4. Her logical memory, which involves the recall of stories, is somewhat better than the teenagers, as is her ability to learn new associations between words in the paired associates sub-test. On other tasks her performance is at approximately the control level except for the visual memory items. On both immediate and delayed recall of simple designs she is significantly impaired. This difficulty in drawing the designs from memory cannot be attributed to any difficulty with the motor control of drawing as her copying is at a normal level.

This impairment in visual memory for designs was confirmed using another, more complex, figure, known as the Figure of Rey. Here, Dr S's recall of the figure was at a 4-year-old level. Thus visual memory is poor.

Table 4

Scores on the Weschler Memory Battery

	Dr S	Controls (mean ± s.d.)
Personal and current information	6	5.7 ± 0.48
Orientation	5	5.0 ± 0.0
Mental control	7	6.5 ± 2.55
Logical memory (story recall)		
Immediate recall	13.5	9.5 ± 3.08
		[age-matched controls 8.4 ± 2.7]
Delayed recall	10	8.15 ± 2.64
Digits forward and back	10	9.6 ± 1.96
Associate learning (of pairs of words)		
Immediate recall	20	16.9 ± 2.95
Delayed recall	9	9.5 ± 1.08
Visual memory (for designs)[1]		
Immediate recall	4	10.5 ± 1.9
Delayed recall	3	9.9 ± 1.9
Copy of designs	13	12.5 ± 1.27
Overall Memory Quotient	132	

[1]Significant impairment.

MEMORY FOR FACES AND PATTERNS

When Dr S had seen something many, many times she may learn to recognize it. She is able to recognize her family and familiar friends and she recognizes the faces of Margaret Thatcher and Princess Anne. She is also able to recognize everyday objects. However, she seems to be unable to register,

Table 3

Scores on Familiarity Decision

	%
Familiar faces	44
Unfamiliar faces	100
Familiar objects	100
Unfamiliar objects	88
Familiar names	82
Unfamiliar names	94

and gain access to after a few minutes, memories for complex visual information which is novel. Just as she fails to recognize me, she fails to recall designs, and fails to recognize the house in which she lives, which is identified only by number, despite familiarity with the building for several years. In relation to our model of face recognition (see figure 1), she cannot gain access to person identity information from faces.

LIVING WITH THESE PROBLEMS

Dr S has had a career with professional success, has four healthy children and many friends. Nevertheless, her life has often been difficult and her pattern of cognitive strengths and weaknesses have contributed to her problems. In excerpts from our conversations with her she gives these examples from her life.

On faces
There was a very striking example in America [Dr S had just returned from a lengthy visit] of a lady who took me home, when I was trying to find my way home, and I had noticed her in the synagogue every Saturday. I met her in an unexpected place. If I had met her in the synagogue I would have made a probably word-based recognition ... but by meeting her in the unexpected place I have the feeling dimly that I have seen her a few years ago when I was in the same town and I asked her 'Excuse me, have we met?' which is what I tend to do. I then fish from the conversation. And she couldn't believe it, because the week before she had shown me the way and we had had an intense conversation several times in the synagogue. And I was absolutely totally unable to know who she is. The moment she said 'But we walked home together' I remembered the conversation, I remembered how many children she had, I remembered details which sometimes surprise people, based on verbal memory ... I have a kind of photographic memory for conversations ... but as to the visual I was sure that I had perhaps seen her when I was there a year ago and was absolutely unaware that I had seen her every Saturday ... She thought I was peculiar ...

... In Cambridge now, I kept on getting lost, and ... it's very embarrassing because I kept on getting lots of lifts and I met lots of people. I had very intense conversations and I didn't recognize them, even though they had been helpful by giving me lifts ... I look, but the only person I recognize is a lady with a big wart on her nose, that is very

striking. It is very embarrassing because they say, you know the fellow with the glasses or whatever they say, I have no idea if they have got glasses. It just doesn't register. People don't like not to be remembered. So I always say, 'You beautiful ladies, I don't recognize you, excuse me, have we met before?'

I warn people now. If we have a wonderful exchange and are going to be friends for life. I say, look if we meet again outside ... and I wouldn't recognize you, just give me the code word. The code word is something we talked about and then I would recall what we talked of.

People complain, I don't greet them. So I warn them beforehand. It is very embarrassing. I live in this active community ... and I ask now after four years in the community, 'Who is this?' Now people, cannot understand it. I ask friends of mine who do not know that I have this problem, 'Who is this?' They are amazed. 'Of course, she is so and so.'

On houses
My own house, I can't recall what it looks like. If I had to draw it, I'm not even sure if it's three storeys. I'm on top so it must be three storeys.
[CMT: You can't conjure up a picture in your own mind of what your own house looks like?]

No, no. I only know it's got three storeys because I am in the attic.
[CMT: How long have you known this house?]

Four and a half years, I've been there. First, I lived in the house next door. I rather think it looks similar. It may not be similar.

On talking
I have extremely low self-confidence. I feel very concerned about mutual thoughtfulness. And I feel very upset that I make a lot of effort hoping, wishing, trying, to talk less and even tell people 'give me feedback'. The amazing thing is that people I do talk a lot to don't complain. But the vast majority of people who know me, do complain that I talk too much. They mostly say I am quite interesting but I talk too much. I give more than they want. I overexplain, and all this I'm conscious of. I find it difficult to get out of ... Most people complain about me. 'The most striking thing is she talks too much and too fast'. I am deeply hurt, not offended because of this valid comment, but I am hurt that I do this to people because I have such a love for people and I want to be mutually constructive and mutually helpful. I don't give others enough chance to get their word in edgeways and I say please interrupt me. I go on too much. I am now talking to you like a psychologist, a psychotherapist, but it is a problem ... The Jews are a fast-speaking people but I am in the front line of the Jews, I think.

Dr S is eager that problems such as hers should be investigated further and that people should have greater awareness of these types of developmental difficulty. Lack of awareness, in her view, increases the difficulty which people have in tolerating her behaviour. To this end, she has requested from us a written document explaining her problems which she can show to those who become exasperated with her. To her, both this and a copy of this chapter have been of benefit.

ACKNOWLEDGEMENTS

This research was supported by a research award from the Wolfson Foundation. On sections of data, research assistance was given by Kim Cornish, Joanne Ilsley and Metke Shawe-Taylor.

FURTHER READING

Bruce, V. (1988) *Recognising Faces*. London: Lawrence Erlbaum.

Stiles-Davis, J., Kritchevsky and Bellugi, U. (ed.) (1988) *Spatial Cognition: Brain Bases and Development*. London: Erlbaum.

Temple, C. M. (1992) Developmental pathologies and developmental disorders. In I. Rapin and S.J. Segalowitz (eds) *Handbook of Neuropsychology: Child Psychology*. Amsterdam: Elsevier.

REFERENCES

Benton, A. L., Hamsher, K. des, Varney, N. R. and Spreen, O. (1983) *Facial Recognition*. New York: Oxford University Press.

Benton, A. L., Varney, N. R. and Hamsher, K. des (1978) Visuospatial judgement: a clinical test. *Archives of Neurology, 35*, 364–7.

Bodamer, J. (1947) Die Prosopagnosie. *Archiv für Psychiatrie und Nervenkrankbeiten, 179*, 6–53.

Bruce, V. and Young, A. (1986) Understanding face recognition. *British Journal of Psychology, 77*, 305–27.

Ellis, A. W. and Young, A. W. (1988) *Human Cognitive Neuropsychology*. Hove, East Sussex: Lawrence Erlbaum.

Lansdell, H. (1968) Effect and extent of temporal lobe ablation on two lateralised deficits. *Physiology and Behaviour, 3*, 271–3.

Marr, D. (1976) Early processing of visual information. *Philosophical Transactions of the Royal Society (London), 275B*, 483–524.

Marr, D. (1980) Visual information processing: the structure and creation of visual representations. *Philosophical Transactions of the Royal Society (London), 290B*, 199–218.

Marr, D. (1982) *Vision*. San Francisco: W. H. Freeman.

Vandenburg, S. G. and Kuse, A. R. (1978) Mental rotation, a group test of three dimensional spatial visualization. *Perceptual and Motor Skills, 47*, 599–604.

Warrington, E. K. (1984) *Recognition Memory Battery*. Windsor: NFER-Nelson.

6

Mark H. Ashcraft

A Personal Case History of Transient Anomia

The article presents a first-person account of a transient anomia or word-finding deficit; the assumption is that such an account, reported by someone with a professional background in memory, cognition, and language processes, may shed additional light on the nature of an anomic episode and on the subjective experience of memory and language disruption due to brain-related abnormalities. During the 45-min episode, I was unable to retrieve and use specific content words and terms ("data," "experiment," "printout") in overt speech. I was completely conscious of these target concepts, although not of their names, and was aware of my inability to find the words. Neither word finding for "everyday" words nor ongoing thought processes were particularly disrupted. The nature and quality of my thoughts during the episode indicate no loss of awareness of circumstances or "presence of mind," but no genuine awareness of the seriousness of the episode. I briefly consider the implications of my experience and the similarities to another published case history.

What is it like to lose one's language abilities? What is the inner experience, both cognitive and emotional, of an individual whose language or memory abilities are disrupted? Research on aphasic and amnesic syndromes has provided an impressive catalog of evidence about the behavioral consequences of brain abnormalities and damage, and there is no need to repeat or review these consequences here. But what of the mental consequences, as experienced subjectively by the affected individual?

Two reasons for inquiring into the subjective experience of language dysfunction may be offered. The first is basic curiosity about the nature and extent of an individual's disruption. For example, a neuropsychologist may attempt to draw inferences about a patient's subjective experience based on whatever evidence is available, often the fragmented language a patient can generate or the apparent emotional reaction displayed by the patient. Second, it is not uncommon to marshall additional evidence about a patient's cognitive status from the individual's apparent subjective state or emotional reaction; for example, Kertesz (1982) described the neologisms of a Wernicke's aphasic by adding "There is a rather curious cool and calm manner about her speech as if she did not realize her deficit . . . a very characteristic feature of this disturbance" (p. 42). However difficult it is to devise thorough assessments in such a case, the patient suffers a double disadvantage, being unable to communicate fluently or precisely and naive about the cognitive and linguistic processes that have been disrupted. Our inferences about preserved and disrupted functions, therefore, generally remain somewhat uncertain and tentative.

In this paper, I offer a detailed recollection of inner mental experience during an episode characterized by anomia or word-finding difficulty. Because my recollection is not subject to the typical double disadvantage, the analysis may shed some light on the nature of thought in the absence of fluent language ability. While I do not claim that my experience is to be taken as universally true for all such language disruptions, it is quite similar to at least one reported case (Kay & Ellis, 1987; see Part 3 below). As such, it may be useful in corroborating inferences drawn by these investigators and in devising assessments in future research.

For organizational purposes, I have divided this case history into three parts. The first part is background, which describes relevant demographic, setting, and diagnostic information. In the second part, I relate the several events that occurred during the 45-min episode, including my thoughts and reactions to those events. The two individuals I spoke with during the episode have corroborated the observable events and behaviors I describe in this account. My assistant and I independently wrote diary-like accounts of the episode, hers within 2 weeks, mine within a month. These agree with my current recollections, which can still be described as indelible. Finally, in the third part I attempt to identify general characteristics of the episode that may be of interest to the study of cognition and the neurosciences.

PART 1—BACKGROUND

At the time of the seizure, 14 September, 1988, I was 38 years old, an Associate Professor of Psychology, with a 1975 Ph.D. in Experimental Psy-

chology. My specialty is cognitive psychology, and my research is in the area of cognitive arithmetic. I had taught Cognitive Psychology for approximately 12 years, and Psychology of Language for 3 years. The only noteworthy exception to general good health was a single grand mal seizure at age 18, my sophomore year in college, diagnosed at the time as due to overwork and fatigue.

On the date of the episode, some 2 weeks before the beginning of Fall term classes, my research assistant, Machelle, and I had spent several hours at professional "housekeeping," selecting which printouts, many of which were at least 10 years old, to keep for archival purposes and which to discard. While my assistant continued this activity, I spent the last few hours of the day reading and doing paperwork, sitting at the desk in my office. The episode began at approximately 4:45 PM, and was over at 5:30 PM.

The episode was tentatively diagnosed by the attending emergency room physician that evening as a transient ischemic attack, with instructions to see my regular doctor the following day. Eight days later, angiography revealed an arterio-venous malformation (AVM) in the anterior left temporal lobe. Two neurosurgeons independently diagnosed the 45-min episode as a seizure caused by the "steal effect;" i.e., blood is "stolen" from brain tissue by the AVM, triggering a seizure. There was no evidence of prior hemorrhage in any diagnostic test. Some 10 weeks later, the AVM was surgically removed with no complications and no short- or long-term sequelae.

PART 2—THE EPISODE

For clarity, I adopt the following notational conventions in Part 2. Explanatory information about the setting and activities surrounding the six events of the episode appears in normal typeface. My verbatim overt speech appears in double quotations. I note paraphrases of overt speech, mine as well as Machelle's and my wife Mary's, in single quotations; not surprisingly, I cannot quote these two people verbatim, nor myself in the lengthy conversations of events 5 and 6.

My thoughts during the 45-min episode are described in italics and set off in brackets [*as shown here.*] It is critical to this account that the following point be clear. My inner thoughts, stated in the present tense to convey the stream of consciousness, are described as if they consisted of straightforward, syntactically and semantically fluent sentences. They were not simply inner or subvocal speech, however. The most powerful realization I had during the episode, and the most intriguing aspect to me since then, was the dissociation between a thought and the word or phrase that expresses the thought. The subjective experience consisted of knowing with complete certainty the idea or concept that I was trying to express and being completely unable to find and utter the word that expressed the idea or concept. The thoughts can only be described in sentence-like form, because they were as complex, detailed, and lengthy as a typical sentence. They were not sentences, however. The experience was not one of merely being unable to articulate a word currently held in consciousness. Instead, it was one of being fully aware of the target *idea* yet totally unable to accomplish what normally feels like the single act of finding-and-saying-the-word.

Event 1, 4:45 PM

I was looking at a printout from a study on math anxiety, unable to tell if it was one of the old analyses, in which we analyzed three levels of anxiety, or a newer one, with four levels. It vaguely seemed like too much trouble to figure out which analysis I was examining, although looking at the degrees of freedom would have answered this question. Machelle came into my office with a computer printout, put it in front of me on my desk, and said 'I don't know if you want to keep this one or not, or what label to put on it if you do want to keep it.'

[*This is the ANOVA printout from Ben's experiment, the study on 3rd, 4th, and 6th graders. We always call it DevCogArith.*]

I said "Oh, that's . . . uh . . ." After a few seconds, I tried again. "It's the . . ." [*That's sort of funny; I can't remember DevCogArith, or the words printout or experiment.*]

I recognized the printout immediately. The abbreviation stood for Developmental Cognitive Arithmetic, since it was the first developmental study on arithmetic that we had conducted, in school year 1978–1979 (Ashcraft & Fierman, 1982). Handwrit-

ten on the printout was G-3 4 6, indicating that the factor labeled G was for those three grades.

I chuckled audibly at my inability to label the printout, then said "We'll have to do this tomorrow." Machelle returned to her office and I remained at my desk. Her written recollection 2 weeks later says: "He seemed distracted. He said something about not being able to find the words, laughed a little, and continued to stare at the printouts." She later explained that she assumed I had been engrossed in what I was doing and was unable or unwilling to shift to a different topic.

Event 2, 4:55 PM

Machelle came into my office again. [*I've been sitting at my desk for about 10 min, staring at the desk lamp, with nothing on my mind; I'm not even daydreaming.*] Machelle asked me another question about some printouts, and I was again unable to respond with anything more than sentence fragments. [*I know exactly what I'm trying to say, why won't the words come to me?*]

Event 3, 4:56 PM

As Machelle left, I turned to the computer on the table opposite my desk. The message on the screen indicated that I was still logged onto the mainframe computer. [*It's late, I have to log off so I can go home.*] As I positioned my hands at the keyboard, I realized I could not remember the command to log off—the command, of course, is simply *logoff,* a command I issue with great regularity. I stared at the screen for a few moments, still could not remember the command, and at that point realized that something unusual was happening.

Event 4, 5:00 PM

[*This is weird, something is wrong. I wonder if I'm ok. I'll test myself, I'll walk to the restroom and see if I'm weaving down the hall, or if my vision is distorted.*] I had no difficulties walking to the restroom and returned to my office satisfied that I was physically all right.

Event 5, 5:10 PM

Although it was not unusually late for me to be at the office, I decided to phone home anyway to say I'd be leaving shortly. I was sitting at the computer again, still unable to remember the logoff command. I reached for the phone next to the computer, pressed the line button for a dial tone, pressed 8 for an outside line, and dialed my home phone number with no difficulty or hesitation.

Mary answered, and I said "I'm coming home." Mary was immediately aware that something was wrong, given that I was speaking quite hesitantly, and said "Are you all right—you sound funny." I responded "I guess I'm confused." "Confused about what?" Mary asked. [*Well, we were cleaning out the cabinets, going through printouts of old experiments, and I couldn't remember the words printout or experiment—but I still can't remember those words. I can't even remember the word cabinet. How can I explain what I'm confused about when I still can't think of the words to say it?*]

I attempted several times to start a sentence that explained my inability to remember these words, but each one trailed off after 'well, we were' and the like. Mary said, roughly, 'Stay there, I'm calling Steve to come get you.' I knew, however, that this colleague had already left for the day, having seen his darkened office during Event 4. I said "No, I'll just come home." Mary insisted 'Something is wrong, and you have to go to the emergency room.' I became very stubborn about driving myself home. [*I have to sound very calm and firm; I don't want to leave my car here overnight, so I have to persuade Mary I can drive home.*] Mary said "Stay there" and then hung up. The line was busy when I phoned again.

Machelle came into the office again, and I told her 'Mary is worried about me.' I do not recall mentioning the computer problems, but Machelle's written record indicates that I also mentioned that I could not remember how to logoff from the computer.

Event 6, 5:20 PM

I reached my wife by phone again and once again insisted that I drive myself home. I said 'I'm leaving for home now. If I'm not there in half an hour, or if I have problems, I'll stop at a phone booth

and call you.' [*I just want to get home. And I don't want to leave my car here overnight.*] Mary insisted that I not drive and then asked to speak to Machelle, asking her to drive me to the hospital; I gave up on driving myself home. Machelle hung up, said she was going to get her car and would be back in 5 minutes. She left the office.

At approximately 5:25, I looked at my computer again and with no difficulty at all remembered the logoff command; I typed the command, logged off successfully, and turned off the computer. As I waited for Machelle, I remembered the words I had had difficulty with and said them out loud to myself; "printout, data, experiment, results." When Machelle returned, I said 'I'm fine now. I can drive myself, but I'd like you to follow me just in case.' She agreed reluctantly, and we left the office. As we walked down the hall, I looked at my watch—it was 5:30—and I realized that whatever had happened was now over. I repeated this to Machelle. I forced myself to concentrate on driving, not letting myself think about what had just happened.

PART 3—ISSUES

There are several interesting facets of his experience that deserve mention. Given my involvement, however, I would offer only three; even now, these seem completely certain to me.

(a) Emotional Reaction

It seemed mildly amusing to me, to the point of chuckling, that I was unable to think of those words, for the most part my ordinary and routine "professional vocabulary" (but I was also unable to retrieve "cabinet," which is not plausibly described as part of "professional vocabulary"). The feeling was similar to a tip-of-the-tongue (TOT) experience, except that no synonyms, word initial letters or sounds, or alternate ways of expressing the idea came to me either. I responded to the retrieval difficulty by slowing my rate of speech, hesitating, and stopping when the next word was unavailable ("fumbling for words," in my wife's description). Stated differently, I did not substitute general words (e.g., "thing," "stuff"), i.e., did not invent the circumlocutions typical of more permanent anomia. Event 3, however, represented a memory failure that made me aware of a genuine disorder. In response, I tested myself by walking down the hall, careful to note physical balance, vision, and so forth.

There was never a sense of panic or desperation during the episode, which I attribute to the nature of the disruption. I imagine that sudden pain or physical inability might easily generate panic; see, for instance, Kolb's (1990) reaction upon discovering that his visual field defect was binocular, hence central rather than retinal. Furthermore, my reaction would very likely have changed to concern or desperation if the episode had lasted substantially longer. But the largely mental nature of my disruption seems to have yielded a slightly bemused and puzzled reaction. Normally, we do not become overly concerned if we momentarily "block" on remembering a word, the name of a film, etc., and this is how the experience seemed to me at the time.

(b) "Train of Thought"

Event 4 is a clear demonstration, in my opinion, of how a relatively complex sequence of thought proceeded without disruption during the seizure. I realized that something was wrong, devised an assessment of my coordination and perception, collected data by self-observation, and then drew a conclusion from those data; the sequence seems quite similar to Kolb's (1990) self-test of visual functioning. In my interpretation, this activity represents a straightforward instance of conscious (i.e., not automatic) cognitive processing and problem solving, which was conceived, devised, and accomplished during the seizure itself. (Note also that it was during Event 4 when I noticed that my colleague Steve had left for the day, a fact I then retrieved during Event 5.)

Nonetheless, I cannot say how the undeniable stubbornness at Events 5 and 6 should be judged, a disruption of logical thought or an overriding (yet subdued) emotional reaction. I clearly felt competent to drive, wanted to be at home, and tried to be persuasive enough to win the argument. On the one hand, the motivation for this, not leaving my car in a downtown University parking lot, strikes me as understandable, and the ensuing 'phone booth plan'

was rather complex. On the other hand, it also seems irrational; objectively, people should not drive during a seizure (but of course I did not self-diagnose the seizure). In some ways, there was no gross disruption of ongoing thought. Being unaware of the potential gravity of the episode, however, may be evidence of a greater disruption of thought than I suspect, or of the overruling of rational thought by emotional reaction.

Ironically, it did not occur to me to test any other mental capacities during the seizure; as the "subject" in an unplanned study of temporary brain dysfunction, I failed to act as an "experimenter" in testing other mental functioning. Awareness of the word-finding problem could have prompted me to determine if other nonprofessional words besides "cabinet" were also blocked. I could have tested my ability to do arithmetic or math problems, given my involvement in a project on acalculia among brain-damaged children. In retrospect, a major disappointment is that my assistant did not refer to the printouts by name; my guess is that I would have correctly recognized that word even though it was blocked from retrieval (see below).

I infer that sensory-motor processes, short-term memory, and a good deal of long-term memory were unaffected by the seizure (e.g., vision, physical balance, etc. were intact; I maintained the topic in the conversations with my wife, I recognized the need to logoff in Event 3, and I retrieved my home phone number in Events 5 and 6). I conclude that attention/awareness, short-term memory, and problem solving processes requiring a sustained "train of thought" were relatively unaffected by the seizure. Based on preserved functions, the language retrieval deficit that was apparent, and the location of the AVM, I assume that the seizure was restricted largely to the left temporal lobe and those nearby regions that could have been affected by the steal effect. If this assumption is correct, then the preserved cognitive functions apparently do not depend in any major way on these left temporal regions, or, alternatively, they can be accomplished by other regions if need be. In either case, and regardless of the localization of the seizure, the preserved cognitive processes and functions do not seem to depend on fluent and undisrupted word retrieval.

(c) Thought and Language

I reiterate the conclusion—problem solving and cognition accomplished during the seizure—with one addition; the problem solving and cognition were *thoughts without language*. I was not saying sentences to myself mentally as I planned to assess my coordination and perception, or as I attempted to converse with my wife. The idea, expressed in Event 4 as [*I'll test myself; I'll walk to the restroom . . .*] was as complete and full as any idea one might have normally, but was not an unspoken mental sentence.

James (1890, p. 651) described the experience of recalling a memory as occurring "in one integral pulse of consciousness." I understand this to refer to an immediacy of awareness, the sense that an idea comes into awareness *right now,* as it were. Such a description is a completely apt expression of my experience during the seizure, in terms of accessing concepts and ideas. It is also an introspectively appealing description of the normal operation of memory and recall. When a student asks a question during my lecture, I know—in a seeming instant—what idea to express in answering the question. I then proceed to verbalize my answer, occasionally laboring over a word or phrase, but more usually generating the sentence quite automatically. It was the unusual "gap" in this usually seamless process, a process taken completely for granted in normal circumstances, that amazes me and requires expression here.

Throughout the seizure, I was completely aware of the concepts and meanings I wished to express. This was not merely awareness of a general meaning or some vague approximate idea. It was, to use standard terminology, complete and successful semantic access to (retrieval of) the precise target concept. In several cases (e.g., the specific experiment in Event 1), there was also successful retrieval of exact episodic concepts or memories. But for those "professional" words, *no words or labels accompanied the retrieval.*

I think of the events that occurred in terms of three sequential steps, with a disruption in the second step of the normal sequence; see the Post Script below, where a strikingly similar explanation by Kay and Ellis (1987) is described. Step 1 is semantic retrieval, which yields access to and awareness of the idea to be expressed. Step 2 is the process of accessing the word or phrase that names this retrieved idea, essentially lexical access. Finally, the fluent articulation of the retrieved word name is Step 3. Typically, the three steps occur quite rapidly and automatically, as in James' "integral pulse." And needless to say, we are not introspectively aware of the three-part separation. During my seizure, however, the seamless operation of the sequence broke down, because of a disruption in Step 2.

Note three points about the proposed Step 2. First, it was not tied uniquely to articulation; beyond the inaccessible words "printout," "experiment," "cabinet," etc., I could not access the logoff command to be typed at the computer keyboard. Second, word retrieval was not totally disrupted, in that retrieval and articulation of "confused" and "phone booth," along with more common, everyday words, was successful. It is tempting to cast my distinction between "professional" and everyday vocabulary in other terms, for instance the abstract/concrete dimension, or in terms of word frequency (e.g., Ellis, 1985), and to claim that the mental lexicon or the process that accesses the lexicon is sensitive to that dimension. On the other hand, my claim about "professional" words may simply be the result of not having attempted to converse about other substantive topics.

Third, the specific retrieval failures in Step 2, although possibly not surprising in anomia, are peculiar from the perspective of memory and cognition. There is a wealth of information concerning retrieval cues, context, and the effects of encoding specificity (e.g., Schacter, 1989; Tulving, 1983, chap. 9). As a rule, the more similar a retrieval attempt is to original encoding of information, the more successful retrieval will be. As such, it is odd that those particular words were inaccessible in the very location where they are normally most common, my office.

Post Script

Since drafting this paper, I have discovered a fascinating report by Kay and Ellis (1987), discussing patient EST's permanent anomia. In most respects, and with the obvious exception of the permanence of the anomia, the cases seem quite similar, even down to EST's awareness of his deficit, apparent in several of his verbatim remarks (e.g., "I should know this," "I jumped at the wrong thing"). I comment here on two points raised in that paper.

First, EST's performance led Kay and Ellis to conclude that EST suffered little or no semantic impairment, but instead that he suffered a phonologically based anomia. In particular, their explanation of EST's anomia suggests a partial disconnection between the semantic system and the phonological lexicon, realized as "weak or fluctuating levels of activation between corresponding representations" in the two systems. If my failure to retrieve the logoff command for *motor* output can be attributed to the same phonological lexicon that failed for "printout," "data," and so forth, then the explanation fits my anomia extremely well. Alternatively, the lexicon may be described as phonological merely because its output is normally in spoken form, as is output in our typical assessments.

Second, Kay and Ellis discuss the observation that "anomic patients, in some sense, 'know' the word that they are trying to find" (p. 614), i.e., that semantic access may be preserved in some anomias. Two citations they provide, however, have apparently argued against this TOT view (Geschwind, 1967; Goodglass, Kaplan, Weintraub, & Ackerman, 1976). In those reports, patients did not show the classic TOT pattern to pictures they were unable to name to confrontation, i.e., they were unable to demonstrate even partial access to phonological and morphological information about the lexical target (respectively, word initial sounds and number of syllables). My experience suggests that classic, partial access to the target may be only a coincidental part of the TOT experience. If the typical TOT state can be described as *informed* by partial access, then my anomic TOT state was *uninformed*. I had no sense at all of knowing word length or initial sounds, nor did I retrieve similar sounding words. Yet I "knew" the words I was looking for at the time and said them aloud after the seizure was over. I am confident that I would have recognized "printout" as the target word in Event 1 if my assistant had said "printout" instead of "this one" and "it," just as patient EST correctly recognized picture names with 94% accuracy (Kay & Ellis, 1987).

An outside investigator might have mistaken my word finding problems, and my lack of knowledge for word length and initial sounds, as evidence for a semantic based anomia. Instead, I argue that the pattern described by Kay and Ellis, complete semantic retrieval *and* partial, word-specific blocking of lexical access, is indeed possible in anomia. The feeling is difficult even for me to describe and is no doubt more difficult for someone to imagine without having experienced it. The description that anomics "in some sense, 'know' the word" may be to blame. I did not "know" the word, at least in its articulation or output sense. I did 'know' the word in its semantic, "idea" or "concept" sense, without a hint as to the verbal name for the idea.

REFERENCES

Ashcraft, M. H., & Fierman, B. A. 1982. Mental addition in third, fourth, and sixth graders. *Journal of Experimental Child Psychology,* **33,** 216–235.

Ellis, A. W. 1985. The production of spoken words: A cognitive neuropsychological perspective. In A. W. Ellis (Ed.), *Progress in the psychology of language.* London: Erlbaum. Vol. 2.

Geschwind, N. 1967. The varieties of naming errors. *Cortex,* **3,** 97–112.

Goodglass, H., Kaplan, E., Weintraub, S., & Ackerman, N. 1976. The 'tip-of-the-tongue' phenomenon in aphasia. *Cortex,* **12,** 145–153.

James, W. 1890. *The principles of psychology.* New York: Dover.

Kay, J., & Ellis, A. 1987. A cognitive neuropsychological case study of anomia: Implications for psychological models of word retrieval. *Brain,* **110,** 613–629.

Kertesz, A. 1982. Two case studies: Broca's and Wernicke's aphasia. In M. A. Arbib, D. Caplin, & J. C. Marshall (Eds.), *Neural models of language processes.* New York: Academic Press. Pp. 25–44.

Kolb, B. 1990. Recovery from occipital stroke: A self-report and an inquiry into visual processes. *Canadian Journal of Psychology,* **44,** 130–147.

Schacter, D. L. 1989. Memory. In M. I. Posner (Ed.), *Foundations of cognitive science.* Cambridge, MA: MIT Press. Pp. 683–725.

Tulving, E. 1983. *Elements of episodic memory.* New York: Oxford Univ. Press.

7

Keith Rayner

Eye Movements in Reading: Recent Developments

When we read, our eyes do not move smoothly across the page of text as our phenomenological impressions imply. Rather, we make a series of eye movements (referred to as *saccades*) separated by periods of time when the eyes are relatively still (*fixations*). Eye movements are necessary during reading because of acuity limitations in the visual system. A line of text extending around the point of fixation can be divided into three regions: foveal, parafoveal, and peripheral. The foveal region is the center of vision (extending 1° of visual angle to the left and right of fixation), where acuity is sharpest, enabling us to resolve the letters in the text easily. In the parafoveal region (extending out to 5° of visual angle on either side of fixation) and the peripheral region (everything on the line beyond the parafoveal region), acuity drops off markedly so that our ability to identify letters is not very good even in the near parafovea. The purpose of eye movements in reading is therefore to place the foveal region on that part of the text we wish to process next.

The basic facts about eye movements during reading have been known for some time. The typical saccade is about eight to nine letter spaces; this value is not affected by the size of the print as long as it is not too small or too large. The appropriate metric to use when discussing eye movements during reading is therefore letter spaces, and not visual angle; generally, three to four letter spaces is equivalent to 1° of visual angle. Because of the high velocity of the saccade, no useful information is acquired while the eyes are moving; readers acquire information from the text during fixations. The average fixation duration is about a quarter of a second (250 ms). The other primary characteristic of eye movements during reading is that about 10% to 15% of the time, we move our eyes back in the text (*regressions*) to look at material that we have already read.

From Keith Rayner, "Eye Movements in Reading: Recent Developments," *Current Directions in Psychological Science,* vol. 2, no. 3 (June 1993). Copyright © 1993 by The American Psychological Society. Reprinted by permission of Cambridge University Press.

It is also important to note that as text difficulty increases, fixation duration increases, saccade length decreases, and regression frequency increases. More important, the values just presented are averages, and there is considerable variability in the measures, both between and within readers. Thus, although the average fixation duration for a given reader might be 250 ms, for others it could be on the order of 200, 235, 280, or 300 ms. The average saccade length and regression frequency also vary across readers. As far as within-subject variability is concerned, although a reader's average fixation duration might be 250 ms, the range could be from under 100 ms to over 500 ms within a passage of text. Likewise, although the average saccade length for a given reader might be 8 letter spaces, the range could be from 1 letter to over 15 (though such long saccades typically follow regressions). A great deal of recent research has documented that the variability in these measures is related to the ease or difficulty associated with processing the text.

Since the mid-1970s, there has been a resurgence of interest in using eye movement data to study the reading process.[1] Researchers have typically been interested in eye movements during reading for two reasons: (1) to describe the characteristics of the eye movements per se and (2) to use eye movement data to infer something about perceptual and cognitive processes during reading. Because most of the work in my laboratory has focused on the latter issue, the major focus of this article is on processing during reading.

THE EYE-CONTINGENT PARADIGM

A major breakthrough in studying the reading process has been due to the development of the *eye-contingent display change* paradigm.[2] In this paradigm, a reader's eye movements are monitored (generally every millisecond) via an accurate eye-tracking system. The eye-tracker is interfaced with a computer, which, in turn, controls a display monitor (which has a rapidly decaying phosphor) from which the subject reads. Changes in the text are made at precise times contingent on the location of the reader's eyes; sometimes the changes are made during a saccade (so that they are not perceived by the reader), and sometimes the changes are made during a fixation.

Moving-Window Technique

The moving-window technique was developed to investigate the size of the span of effective vision during an eye fixation. With this technique, on each fixation, a portion of the text around the fixation is available to the reader. Outside this window area, the text is replaced by other letters or by Xs (see Fig. 1). When the reader moves his or her eyes, the window moves with the eyes. Thus, wherever the reader looks, there is readable text within the window and altered text outside the window. The rationale is that when the window is as large as the region from which a reader can normally obtain information, reading will not differ from when there is no window present.

A number of studies using the moving-window technique have found that the span of effective vision extends about 14 to 15 letter spaces to the right of fixation. However, the span is asymmetric, extending no more than about 4 letters to the left of fixation for readers of English. For readers of right-to-left orthographies, such as Hebrew, the span is asymmetric in the other direction (extending further to the left than to the right). Characteristics of the orthography also influence the size of the span: More densely packed orthographies, such as Chinese and Japanese, yield smaller spans.[3] Another interesting finding is that beginning readers have a smaller span than skilled readers; the span extends only about 11 letters to the right of fixation for children at the end of first grade, but it is asymmetric. Finally, skilled readers do not obtain useful information from below the fixated line, though if the task is visual search, some information is acquired.[4]

Boundary Technique

The boundary technique was developed to determine what type of information is integrated across eye movements in reading. In this technique, a boundary location is specified in the text; when the reader's eye movement crosses the invisible boundary, an originally displayed word or letter string is

Figure 1 ───

Examples of the Moving-Window Paradigm

eyes do not move smoothly across the page of text	Normal
XXXX XX XXX move smoothly acXXXX XXX XXXX XX XXXX	Moving Window
XXXX XX XXX XXXX XXXothly across the XXXX XX XXXX	
XXXX XX XXX XXXX smoothly acXXXX XXX XXXX XX XXXX	Asymmetric
cqcr bc maf move smoothly acsarr fbc qoyc at fcvf	Similar-Letters
XXXXXXXXXXXXmove smoothly acXXXXXXXXXXXXXXXXXXXXXXX	No-Spaces
XXXX XX XXX XXXX smoothly XXXXXX XXX XXXX XX XXXX	One-Word
XXXX XX XXX XXXX smoothly across XXX XXXX XX XXXX	Two-Word

The first line shows a normal line of text with the fixation location marked by an asterisk. The next two lines show an example of two successive fixations with a window of 17 letter spaces. The remaining lines show examples of other types of experimental conditions. In the asymmetric example, the window extends 3 letters to the left of fixation and 8 to the right; in the similar-letters condition, the letters outside the window are replaced by similar letters rather than Xs; in the no-spaces example, all of the spaces between words are filled in outside the window; in the one-word example, only the fixated word is within the window; and in the two-word example, the fixated word plus the word to the right of fixation is available.

replaced by a target word (see Fig. 2). The amount of time that the reader looks at the target word is computed both as a function of the relationship between the initially displayed stimulus and the target word and as a function of the distance that the reader was from the target word prior to launching the saccade that crossed the boundary.

Experiments using both the moving-window and the boundary techniques have demonstrated a *preview benefit* from the word to the right of fixation. That is, information obtained about the parafoveal word on fixation *n* is combined with information on fixation *n* + 1 to speed the identification of the word when it is subsequently fixated.

In a number of different experiments, orthographic, phonological, morphological, and semantic similarity between the initially displayed stimulus and the target word have been varied to determine the basis of the preview effect.[5] The results of these experiments indicate that there is facilitation due to orthographic similarity, so that *chest* facilitates the processing of *chart*. However, the facilitation is not strictly due to visual similarity because changing the case of letters from fixation to fixation (so that *cHaRt* on one fixation would be *ChArT* on the next) has little effect on reading behavior. Thus, the facilitation is due to abstract letter codes associated with the first few letters of an unidentified parafoveal word to the right of fixation.[6] There is also facilitation due to phonological similarity, so that *beech* facilitates *beach* and *chute* facilitates *shoot*, but there is less facilitation in the latter than in the former case. Although morphological factors can influence fixation time on a word, they are not the source of the preview benefit. Finally, there is no facilitation due to semantic similarity: song as the initial stimulus does not facilitate the processing of *tune* (though such words yield semantic priming under typical priming conditions).

Figure 2

An Example of the Boundary Paradigm

---

eyes do not move smoothly across the date of text   Prechange

eyes do not move smoothly across the page of text   Postchange

---

The first line shows a line of text prior to a display change with fixation locations marked by asterisks. When the reader's eye movement crosses an invisible boundary (the letter *e* in *the*), an initially displayed word (*date*) is replaced by the target word (*page*). The change occurs during the saccade so that the reader does not see the change.

Masking Technique

The foveal masking technique is quite similar to the moving-window technique, except that a mask moves with the eyes (see Fig. 3). When the mask is larger than seven letters, this situation results in an artificial foveal scotoma for normal readers. Skilled readers find it very difficult, if not impossible, to read when foveal vision is masked.

The results of experiments using the masking technique and the boundary technique suggest that word identification takes place within a rather restricted region during each eye fixation. Readers typically identify the word that they are fixated on. However, when the word to the right of fixation is short, they often identify it as well, and skip over it with the ensuing saccade.

By delaying the onset of the mask, it has also been possible to determine how quickly information is extracted from the text within a fixation. The results of these experiments indicate that if the reader has 50 ms to process the text prior to the onset of a mask, reading proceeds quite normally; earlier masking disturbs reading. Although readers may typically acquire the visual information needed for reading during the first 50 ms of a fixation, other experiments have demonstrated that readers can extract information at other times during the fixation as needed.[7]

Finally, the masking technique has been used to examine eye movement control during reading.[8] For example, by filling in spaces between words at certain points during each eye fixation or by delaying the onset of the text by first presenting a mask, it has been possible to learn a lot about the programming of eye movements. The results of such studies indicate that decisions about where to move

the eyes next and when to move are computed separately: Where to move next is based primarily on word length information, and when to move is based on the ease or difficulty associated with processing the fixated word.

Fast Priming Technique

In the fast priming technique, a target word location is identified in the text. The technique is similar to the boundary technique in that a letter string initially occupies the target location to prevent parafoveal preview. When the reader's eyes cross the boundary, a prime word is first presented for a very brief period. During the fixation, the prime is replaced by the target word (see Fig. 4). To date, only one set of studies has been completed using this technique, and semantic priming effects were observed.[9] The technique is now being used to investigate the extent to which phonological codes are automatically activated during eye fixations in reading and to investigate the resolution of lexically ambiguous words during reading.

PERCEPTUAL PROCESSES

Studies using the eye-contingent display change techniques have led to a number of important observations concerning perceptual processes in reading: The region of effective or useful vision in reading is quite small, the span of word identification is such that on most fixations only the fixated word is identified, information is generally acquired within the first 50 ms of a fixation, and decisions

Figure 3 _____

An Example of the Foveal-Mask Paradigm

eyes do not move smoothly across the page of text   Normal
                              *

_____

eyes do not moveXXXXXXXly across the page of text
                         *   Foveal
                                                      Mask
eyes do not move smoothXXXXXXXss the page of text
                              *

The lower two lines show two successive fixations with a mask of 7 letter spaces. As in the moving-window paradigm, the mask moves in synchrony with the eyes.

about where to move the eyes and when to move the eyes are computed independently.

The fact that the area from which readers get useful information is small is undoubtedly related to acuity limitations. However, acuity limitations cannot account for this entirely. In particular, it has been demonstrated that how much information a reader gets to the right of fixation is related to the processing difficulty associated with the fixated word: When it is difficult to process (because, e.g., it is a low-frequency word), readers get less information to the right of fixation.[10] It has also been demonstrated that when the parafoveal word is highly predictable, readers obtain more information from the parafovea.[11]

Although the eye-contingent paradigm has yielded a great deal of information about reading, other studies in which eye movements are monitored (without display changes) have also yielded a number of insights. Research examining where readers fixate in words has demonstrated that fixation location in a word is not random: Readers tend to fixate about halfway between the beginning and the middle of the word.[12] Extensive research efforts on this effect have examined the consequences of being fixated at locations other than this optimal viewing location.[13] The general finding has been that the consequences are more serious when words are presented in isolation than when they are in text. This result suggests either that contextual information overrides low-level visual-processing constraints or that readers are somewhat flexible about where they can acquire information around fixation.

COGNITIVE PROCESSES

An important conclusion that has emerged from eye movement research is that the eye–mind span, or

Figure 4 _____

An Example of the Fast Priming Paradigm

eyes do not move smoothly across the qcpf of text   Prechange
  *   *   *   *

eyes do not move smoothly across the book of text   Prime
                                      *

eyes do not move smoothly across the page of text   Postchange
                                      *

The first line shows a line of text prior to a display change with fixation locations marked by asterisks. When the reader's eye crosses the invisible boundary location (the letter *e* in *the*), the prime word (*book*) is presented for a brief duration (30 ms) and is in turn replaced by the target word (*page*) for the remainder of the trial. The duration of the prime can be varied, and subjects are usually not aware of its presence if the exposure is less than 50 ms.

the lag between what the eye is fixating and what the mind is processing, is quite tight. For example, effects due to eye-contingent display changes show up immediately on the fixation following a display change, and are not delayed in the eye movement record for a couple of fixations. It has also been demonstrated that low-frequency words yield longer fixation times than high-frequency words, and words that are highly constrained or predictable within a given context are fixated for less time than words that are not so constrained. The point is that increased fixation times show up on the low-frequency word and the unconstrained word. If there were an appreciable eye–mind lag, the effect would not appear until a couple of fixations later.

The general finding that the area of effective vision and the word identification span are small (so that readers typically identify only the fixated word) coupled with the conclusion that there is no appreciable eye–mind span has led to considerable optimism concerning the use of eye movement data in investigating cognitive processes during reading. In the past 10 years, there has been considerable research using eye movement data to investigate (1) word recognition processes during reading, including the processing of lexically ambiguous words; (2) how readers parse sentences containing temporary syntactic ambiguities; and (3) inferences during reading.

It is beyond the scope of the present article to review all these lines of research.[14] The point that would simply like to make is that eye movement data have revealed a great deal of important information about moment-to-moment cognitive processes during the reading process. Variations in how long readers look at certain target words or phrases in text have been shown to be due to the ease or difficulty associated with processing those words. Many paradigms used to study the reading process either disrupt the normal processing or are artificial in some way. Because eye movements are a natural part of the reading process, one does not have to worry if task-induced strategies are influencing the pattern of results obtained in an experiment. Indeed, eye movement data have often ended up being the primary source of evidence for adjudicating between alternative theoretical positions. My guess is that this will continue to be the case as more and more researchers find the record left by the movements of the eyes to be an appealing source of experimental data.

ACKNOWLEDGMENTS

The research from the author's laboratory described in this article has been supported by grants from the National Science Foundation (currently Grant DBS-9121375) and the National Institutes of Health (currently Grant HD26765).

NOTES

1. For overviews, see M. A. Just and P. A. Carpenter, *The Psychology of Reading and Language Processing* (Allyn & Bacon, Boston, 1987) and K. Rayner and A. Pollatsek, *The Psychology of Reading* (Prentice Hall, Englewood Cliffs, NJ, 1989).

2. The eye-contingent display change paradigm was developed in the mid-1970s by George McConkie and myself. Around the same time, Steve Reder and Kevin O'Regan developed similar techniques. The paradigm was developed further in my laboratory in collaboration with Alexander Pollatsek, Charles Clifton, and James Bertera. For a comprehensive review of research using this paradigm, see Rayner and Pollatsek, note 1.

3. N. Osaka, Size of saccade and fixation duration of eye movements during reading: Psycho-physics of Japanese text processing, *Journal of the Optical Society of America A, 9,* 5–13 (1992).

4. A. Pollatsek, G. E. Raney, L. LaGasse, and K. Rayner. The use of information below fixation in reading and in visual search, *Canadian Journal of Psychology* (in press).

5. For a recent article summarizing this work, see A. Pollatsek, M. Lesch, R. K. Morris, and K. Rayner, Phonological codes are used in integrating information across saccades in word identification and reading, *Journal of Experimental Psychology: Human Perception and Performance, 18,* 148–162 (1992).

6. Albrecht Inhoff has conducted a number of studies that show that some information is obtained from other parts of the word to the right of fixation besides the beginning letters; see A. W. Inhoff and S. Tousman, Lexical priming from partial-word previews, *Journal of Experimental Psychology: Human Perception and Performance, 16,* 825–836 (1990). However, it is clear that the bulk of the preview effect comes from the beginning letters. In-

hoff's research also shows that the effect is not simply due to spatial proximity because there is facilitation from the beginning letters of words when readers are asked to read sentences from right to left, but with letters within words printed from left to right.

7. H. E. Blanchard, G. W. McConkie, D. Zola, and G. S. Wolverton, Time course of visual information utilization during fixations in reading, *Journal of Experimental Psychology: Human Perception and Performance, 10,* 75–89 (1984).

8. R. K. Morris, K. Rayner, and A. Pollatsek, Eye movement guidance in reading: The role of parafoveal letter and space information, *Journal of Experimental Psychology: Human Perception and Performance, 16,* 268–281 (1990).

9. S. C. Sereno and K. Rayner, Fast priming during eye fixations in reading, *Journal of Experimental Psychology: Human Perception and Performance, 18,* 173–184 (1992).

10. J. M. Henderson and F. Ferreira, Effects of foveal processing difficulty on the perceptual span in reading: Implications for attention and eye movement control, *Journal of Experimental Psychology: Learning, Memory, and Cognition, 16,* 417–429 (1990); A. W. Inhoff, A. Pollatsek, M. I. Posner, and K. Rayner, Covert attention and eye movements in reading, *Quarterly Journal of Experimental Psychology, 41A,* 63–89 (1989).

11. D. A. Balota, A. Pollatsek, and K. Rayner, The interaction of contextual constraints and parafoveal visual information in reading, *Cognitive Psychology, 17,* 364–390 (1985).

12. K. Rayner and R. K. Morris, Eye movement control in reading: Evidence against semantic pre-processing, *Journal of Experimental Psychology: Human Perception and Performance, 18,* 163–172 (1992).

13. G. W. McConkie, P. W. Kerr, M. D. Reddix, and D. Zola. Eye movement control during reading: I. The location of initial fixations on words, *Vision Research, 28,* 1107–1118 (1988); F. Vitu, J. K. O'Regan. and M. Mittau, Optimal landing position in reading isolated words and continuous text, *Perception & Psychophysics, 47,* 583–600 (1990).

14. For a summary of this research, see K. Rayner. S. C. Sereno, R. K. Morris, A. R. Schmauder, and C. Clifton, Eye movements and on-line language comprehension processes, *Language and Cognitive Processes, 4* (Special Issue), 21–50 (1989).

On the Internet...

The Whole Brain Atlas

This site contains a comprehensive collection of brain slice images with labels.
http://www.med.harvard.edu/AANLIB/home.html

Your Mind's Eye

This site is a multimedia museum exhibit on illusions, which is a natural teaching device that will inform and delight the user about something that is most central to us: how we think and perceive.
http://illusionworks.com/YME001.htm

Part❖3

Memory: Real, False, and Broken

Endel Tulving

❖

Elaine Funnell

❖

Fergus I. M. Craik

❖

Katherine Nelson

❖

Elizabeth F. Loftus

❖

Des Power

❖

K. Anders Ericsson, William G. Chase, and Steve Faloon

Memory: Real, False, and Broken

The study of memory is at the core of psychology. The reason, of course, is that memory is fundamental to mental life. In some deep way, we are our memories. Memory is necessary for essentially all of our behavior and thought. Bereft of memory, we could not type, eat, fantasize, read, watch TV, listen to a friend's story, or boil some rice. Furthermore, there is no known limit to memory. By contrast, no computer comes close to having the memory capacity and flexibility of humans.

VARIOUS QUESTIONS CAN BE ASKED ABOUT MEMORY: WHAT IS IT? ARE THERE different kinds? How does it develop? How is it controlled? and so on. The first article in this section, "What is Episodic Memory?" by Endel Tulving, begins with a distinction between *episodic*, *semantic*, and *procedural* memory. Episodic memory consists of personal memories that are time-dated, tied to a particular circumstance, subjectively unique, and personally significant. Presumably, one's sense of self and of the temporal continuity of one's life is heavily dependent on episodic memory. Episodic memory entails *autonoetic* awareness of incidents of remembering. In contrast, semantic memory involves knowledge about the world, word meanings, and abstract schemas, information that is probably not time-dated, tied to a particular circumstance, or subjectively unique. For example, we know what trees are, that 6 times 6 is 36, and that Earth has one moon, but it is hard to say exactly when and where we learned these things, and they are hardly significant or personally unique memories. Semantic memory entails *noetic* awareness of incidents of knowing. Procedural memory involves knowing how to do things, such as riding a bicycle, adding numbers, and reading. It entails *anoetic* awareness of these activities, inasmuch as people perform them in an automatic way.

Tulving provides a lengthy discussion of the now-classic case of K. C., a young man who suffered brain damage as the result of a motorcycle accident. In general, K. C. has intact semantic knowledge but poor episodic memory. He can play chess, read, write, converse, and learn new facts. He seems to be intellectually normal. He can even recall some personal facts from the past, for example, that he had once owned a car. However, he cannot remember ever driving it. In general, he is amnesic for all prior personal, episodic events once they are more than a few minutes old. Tulving claims that K. C. has lost autonoetic awareness of personal experiences, in that he cannot mentally re-create a single thing that he has done or experienced. In contrast, he is aware of himself, and he knows things about the world. Tulving goes on to hypothesize a difference between *remembering* and *knowing*, based, respectively, on autonoetic and noetic awareness.

IF SOMEONE CAN LOSE MOST OF THEIR EPISODIC MEMORY, can this happen for semantic memory as well? In "A Case of Forgotten Knowledge," Elaine Funnell answers yes. She presents a cognitive neuropsychological case study of Mrs. P, an elderly woman who seems to be losing knowledge of the concepts that underlie words. For this reason her syndrome is called *semantic dementia*. For example, when asked, she did not know what a kitten or a beak was or who wrote *Hamlet*, or even what the word *Hamlet* referred to. Funnell implies that Mrs. P's problem could be traced to focal atrophy in the left cerebral hemisphere. In exploring the problem, Funnell asked several general questions about Mrs. P's broken memory. First, what knowledge had she forgotten? Based on tests that required the subject to provide word meanings or to name pictures, it became clear that less familiar concepts caused more problems than familiar ones. For example, Mrs. P could define common words such as *short* but had difficulty defining less common words such as *stale*. The next question was, exactly what sort of information was being lost? Prior research suggested that individuals such as Mrs. P might be losing information about the features or properties of things rather than their category membership. Mrs. P was asked questions that tapped these factors, but a different conclusion emerged: while Mrs. P could often understand a concept, she could not point to its defining features in a picture. Familiarity was again the crucial variable. Funnell speculated that dementia may lead to an inability to distinguish concepts that are part of the same semantic field. The next question was whether or not the same concepts were always problematic. Performance on several tasks, including word-to-picture matching and picture naming, indicated that there was indeed consistency. It also was clear that while Mrs. P forgot the meanings of some words and failed to identify some objects, she nevertheless retained some knowledge of the surface character of objects. For example, she could distinguish real words from nonsense words and real objects from nonsense objects, although her performance was not perfect. Finally, Funnell demonstrated that Mrs. P could

relearn some words, although unfamiliar items were again troublesome.

MRS. P'S PROBLEM IS RATHER UNIQUE TO SEMANTIC memory and possibly due to brain atrophy. Of course, the elderly's experience with memory problems are well known—names for things are harder to retrieve, intentions to get something from a room are lost by the time the individual enters the room, sustained lines of thought become harder, and so on. Is there something general going on as we age? In "Memory Changes in Normal Aging," Fergus I. M. Craik asserts that there is. Craik argues that, in general, memory loss in the elderly has more to do with the type of processing that is required than with structural aspects of memory. If these mental processes are effortful and require self-initiation, then the elderly will show a memory loss. However, to the extent that there are clues and cues in the environment that are relevant to a target memory, then the memory will remain intact. Thus, the elderly generally do less well than younger adults on tasks that require self-initiation, including free recall, working memory, prospective memory, and source memory. Prospective memory refers to having to remember to do something in the future, such as turning off an oven one hour from now. Source memory refers to memory for the origin of some event, such as remembering that it was a neighbor who told us that they saw a fox in the street. The elderly do much better on less effortful tasks, such as priming, implicit memory, and forward digit span.

Craik illustrates his cognitive effort hypothesis with an experiment involving three groups of elderly people and one group of young adults. All groups performed four tasks, representing the various combinations of cued or free learning and cued or free recall of words. The young adults were superior on the free learning–free recall task, the most effortful, least environmentally supported task, but the group of socially active, better-educated elderly with a high socioeconomic status performed as well as the young adults on the other three tasks. To some extent, environmental cuing could compensate for lack of cognitive effort. Craik therefore suggests that the elderly be provided good environmental clues for remembering.

Craik's article suggests that memory is not just a biological phenomenon but one that involves the whole person and the larger social situation in which the person lives. People's educational and work backgrounds, their general intelligence and motivation, and the circumstances of their lives will all have an effect on their ability to remember and, per Craik's cognitive effort hypothesis, especially on memories for which it is hard to marshal environmental support.

CRAIK'S LARGER CONCEPTION OF MEMORY RAISES THE question of how people develop memories about themselves; that is, how an *autobiographical memory* develops. The concept of episodic memory is a springboard for Katherine Nelson's article "The Psychological and Social Origins of Autobiographical Memory." Nelson views autobiographical memory as a more complex and personally significant form of episodic memory, one that differentiates from general episodic memory in early childhood. One question for Nelson is why 2- to 3-year-old children often have particular episodic memories that they cannot remember as adults—so-called infantile amnesia. The answer for Nelson lies in the larger issue of how autobiographical memory differentiates from generic episodic memory (general memories about repeated, similar events). In pursuit of this issue, Nelson reasons that children learn "memory talk" through verbal interaction with adults. That is, adults teach children, albeit unconsciously, how to formulate their personal memories. This is accomplished through a narrative format. Thus, certain episodic events become part of the story line of a child's life. In Nelson's terms, "Children gradually learn the forms of how to talk about memories with others, and thereby also how to formulate their own memories as narratives." In this regard, Nelson points to some research showing that if an "elaborative" mother couches her child's experiences in a story line, then the child is likely to remember the experiences better than if the mother is more "pragmatic" and focuses on the here-and-now categorical and instrumental character of events. By this social interaction hypothesis, language mediates the development of the story narratives. The language and story-based character of autobiographical memory contains the seeds for further reactivation of this memory. Infantile amnesia therefore occurs because early, less verbalized childhood experiences were never entered into the schema of narrated stories about the self, so they are less accessible.

THE NEXT TOPIC ADDRESSED IN THIS SECTION IS THE ACcuracy of memory. It is one thing to say that we have episodic memories and perhaps a distinct autobiographical memory, but the accuracy of these memories is another matter. Once these memories are laid down, do they remain in their original literal state forever? That is, is information in long-term memory in a permanent, unalterable, pristine form? Does it just remain there, like a hammer in one's basement, unchanged and waiting to be used again? Some people, including some psychologists, hold this view. They might point to results from studies involving electrical stimulation of the brain, hypnosis, or psychoanalysis that suggest that memories can be retrieved in untainted form. The problem for the permanence view is that these results have been discredited, largely through the research efforts of Elizabeth F. Loftus and her associates. In prior papers, she has argued that patients whose brains were stimulated during surgery rarely remembered long-forgotten experiences in verbatim form and that many of these memories were affected by inferences. Similarly, she argues, hypnosis may produce many fabrications and an uncritical willingness to report, and psychoanalysis may lead people to report a variety of fantasies, hunches, etc., that are hard to distinguish from original memories.

Loftus's major experimental attack on the permanence hypothesis has been to show that memory can be "tricked by revised data." In "When a Lie Becomes Memory's Truth: Memory Distortion After Exposure to Misinformation," she elaborates on the *misinformation effect*, by which people experience some event and are later exposed to new but false information about the event that becomes part of the original memory. The experimental paradigm for studying this effect is simple—expose people to a complex event, then provide new, misleading information to an experimental group while leaving a control group alone. Then ask the two groups to recall or to recognize the original event. A typical result is that the experimental group performs 30–40 percent less well on tests involving the misleading information, which suggests that their memory for the original event has been changed by this information.

Loftus looks at four questions about the misinformation effect. Research on the first indicates that susceptibility is increased when there is a time delay in remembering the event, when the misleading information is subtle, and when the discrepancy between the original event and the new information is not immediately detected. However, warnings about the false nature of the new information help to reduce the effect. Second, it appears that children and the elderly are more susceptible to the effect than are young adults. Third, as to what happens to the memory trace for the original event, Loftus hypothesizes that the trace changes and becomes impaired and that people lose details about the original event. This effect is not a simple matter of impairment or bias in reporting the memory. Finally, Loftus asserts that people believe in their false memories, inasmuch as they are confident in them, even when they are told that the misleading information was wrong. Loftus concludes that "misleading information can turn a lie into memory's truth."

Loftus's research and that of others has clear implications for everyday life, including the recent controversy surrounding the return of so-called repressed memories in the context of psychotherapy (see the article by Stephen J. Ceci and Loftus in Part 6).

LOFTUS'S RESEARCH ON THE FALLIBILITY OF MEMORY focuses on episodic memory. Are all episodic memories capable of being tainted? What of other forms of memory, such as memory for skills or for procedural skills in general? It is apparent, for example, that people can remember how to swim even if they have not swum in years. But does this hold up in other domains? For example, memory for Spanish that was acquired in school may decline somewhat in the first several years after school but show little decline over the next 25 years. Harry Bahrick, who was the primary investigator for this and similar studies, states that such information resides in a kind of "permastore."

In "Very Long-Term Retention of a First Language Without Rehearsal: A Case Study," Des Power uses a case study approach to delve into the long-term retention of American Sign Language (ASL) by a congenitally deaf woman. The woman, aged 72 at the time of the study, was born in 1920. From age 7 to age 19 she went to a school for the deaf, where she became fluent in ASL through her extra-classroom contacts with other ASL users. In 1940, when she left the school, she could write English but could not speak it. She then went to live with her parents, who were illiterate and did not know ASL but who used fabricated "home signs" with her. From 1940 to 1960 she had essentially no contact with ASL users but received a few visits from a deaf signing couple between 1960 and 1977 (amounting to less than 1 hour once a year). Thus, for 37 years this woman had almost no chance to use ASL with other people. An interview conducted in ASL with the woman established that, during the 37-year period in question, her syntax was fluent and her vocabulary was good. Power argues that she did not use ASL to talk to herself, although this point is debatable and somewhat hard to believe. In closing, Power stresses Bahrick's conclusion that rehearsal seems unimportant in retaining some memories and that, when needed, they are simply accessed rather than reconstructed. In some sense, these memories remain in their original literal form. The difference between this kind of memory and the more alterable form studied by Loftus and others seems to hang on the procedural-versus-episodic distinction.

IN THE FINAL ARTICLE IN THIS SECTION, "ACQUISITION OF a Memory Skill," K. Anders Ericsson, William G. Chase, and Steve Faloon consider whether or not short-term memory performance can be expanded. The usual finding with normal adults is that short-term memory span is about 7 items, plus or minus 2. Over the course of a year and a half, Ericsson et al. gave the subject (S.F.) 230 hours of practice at recalling digits. His memory span went from an initial 7 digits to an incredible 80 digits, an accomplishment equivalent to some of the feats performed by the best-known mnemonists. Ericsson et al. provide evidence that S.F. used his expert knowledge of runners' times (he was a track-and-field enthusiast) to organize the digits and that he used a stategy of grouping the chunks of digits into bigger groups and adding more subgroups to the higher-level groups. The authors argue that S.F. did not actually increase his short-term memory capacity—his recall of letters was normal. Rather, he was able to recruit long-term memory knowledge and strategies to improve his short-term memory skill.

8

Endel Tulving

What Is Episodic Memory?

Few problems in science are as difficult as those of working out the precise relation between two complex concepts that are deceptively similar. The relation between episodic and semantic memory belongs in this category. Intuition and rational thought reveal many similarities between these two kinds of memory and tempt us to think of the two as one. Yet, closer scrutiny reveals a number of fundamental differences. In this article, I discuss one such difference, namely, the nature of conscious awareness that characterizes retrieval of episodic and semantic information.

Not everyone accepts the general idea of multiple memory systems, and among those who do, not everyone accepts the same scheme of classification.[1] What follows represents my views on the issue.

The distinction between episodic and semantic memory has changed considerably since my 1972 essay in which I argued for the heuristic usefulness of a taxonomic distinction between episodic and semantic memory, conceived of as parallel, partially overlapping information processing systems. At that time, I could think of only five (hypothetical) differences between the two kinds of memory. Some 10 years later, in 1983, I suggested that, despite the scarcity of the data, it seemed reasonable to hypothesize that episodic and semantic memories represented different functional systems. At that time, it was possible to list some 28 diagnostic features of the distinction. After that, further progress was made in evaluating these ideas, and in revising and modifying the nature of the distinction. Thus, I elaborated on the concept of a memory system, suggesting that different systems deal with different kinds of information, operate according to different principles, and are represented in the brain by different neural structures and mechanisms. I further proposed that (a) episodic memory is a unique extension of semantic memory, rather than a separate, parallel system, (b) episodic and semantic memory differ with respect to the kind of conscious awareness that accompanies their operations, and (c) the distinction is related to the broader problem of classification of learning and memory.[2]

As a result of these developments, one now finds in the literature two different, albeit related, uses of the term episodic memory, one referring to a type of information and type of experiment, and another to a hypothetical

From Endel Tulving, "What is Episodic Memory?" *Current Directions in Psychological Science,* vol. 2, no. 3 (June 1993). Copyright © 1993 by The American Psychological Society. Reprinted by permission of Cambridge University Press.

neurocognitive system that fits into a more comprehensive theory of organization of memory. This article is about the theory of episodic memory.

EPISODIC AND SEMANTIC MEMORY SYSTEMS

In a nutshell, the theory holds that episodic and semantic memory are two of the five major human memory systems for which reasonably adequate evidence is now available. The other three systems are procedural, perceptual representation, and short-term memory.[3] Although each system serves particular functions that other systems cannot serve (the so-called criterion of functional incompatibility[4]), several systems usually interact in the performance of tasks in everyday life as well as in the memory laboratory.

Semantic memory registers and stores knowledge about the world in the broadest sense and makes it available for retrieval. If a person knows something that is in principle describable in the propositional form, that something belongs to the domain of semantic memory. Semantic memory enables individuals to represent and mentally operate on situations, objects, and relations in the world that are not present to the senses: The owner of a semantic memory system can think about things that are not here now.

Episodic memory enables a person to remember personally experienced events as such. That is, it makes it possible for a person to be consciously aware of an earlier experience in a certain situation at a certain time. Thus, the information of episodic memory could be said to concern the self's experiences in subjective space and time. In contrast, the information of semantic memory processes concerns objects and their relations in the world at large. The owner of an episodic memory system is not only capable of remembering the temporal organization of otherwise unrelated events, but is also capable of mental time travel: Such a person can transport at will into the personal past, as well as into the future, a feat not possible for other kinds of memory.

The relation between episodic and semantic memory is hierarchical: Episodic memory has evolved out of, but many of its operations have remained dependent on, semantic memory. A corollary is that semantic memory can operate (store and retrieve information) independently of episodic memory, but not vice versa. Episodic memory is not necessary for encoding and storing of information into semantic memory, although it may modulate such encoding and storage. Semantic memory develops earlier in childhood than episodic memory: Children are capable of learning facts of the world before they remember their own past experiences. Finally, whereas medical temporal lobe and diencephalic structures, among others, play a critical role in semantic memory, frontal lobe structures seem to be involved in subserving episodic memory.[5]

CONSCIOUS AWARENESS IN REMEMBERING

One idea that was not clearly articulated in the *Elements of Episodic Memory* concerned the nature of conscious awareness that accompanies the act of retrieval of information from the two systems. At that time, there was little objective evidence relevant to that problem. Some progress on this front has now been made, and I summarize some of it here.

The working hypothesis is that episodic and semantic memory differ fundamentally with respect to the nature of conscious awareness that accompanies retrieval of information. The act of remembering a personally experienced event, that is, consciously recollecting it, is characterized by a distinctive, unique awareness of reexperiencing here and now something that happened before, at another time and in another place. The awareness and its feeling-tone are intimately familiar to every normal human being. One seldom mistakes remembering for any other kind of experience—perceiving, imagining, dreaming, daydreaming, or just thinking about things one knows about the world.

I refer to the kind of conscious awareness that characterizes remembering one's past as *autonoetic* awareness, contrasting it with *noetic* awareness, which characterizes retrieval of information from semantic memory, and *anoetic* awareness, which accompanies expression of procedural knowledge.[6]

The relation between autonoetic and noetic awareness, on the one hand, and episodic and semantic memory, on the other hand, can be illustrated with material derived from observations of a densely amnesic individual. K. C. is a 40-year-old man who at the age of 30 had a motorcycle accident that damaged his brain highly selectively. His intellectual functions other than memory are quite normal: He has a large vocabulary and a vast store of factual information, he can read and write, he can identify pictures of objects and photographs of people he knows, he can play bridge and chess, and he can do most other things that any normal person does. At any time, he also remembers things that have happened to him in the last few minutes or so. He can describe his minutes-old recollections, and he is aware that he is remembering the very recent past. But he cannot remember, in the sense of bringing back to autonoetic awareness, a single thing that he did or experienced more than a few minutes before the present moment. He claims to have no recollections of happenings even when given detailed descriptions of some of the rather traumatic events from his life before or after he became amnesic (such as his brother's accidental death, the derailment of a train carrying deadly chemicals near his house, or a traffic accident that caused his jaw to be wired shut for a week).[7]

K. C. is fully conscious, noetically aware of the world and of himself. But he has no autonoetic consciousness, and no autonoetic awareness of any past happening. He can recall facts from his own past, and in that sense can be said to know them. For instance, he knows that he owned a car, and he knows its make and color. But he cannot remember a single trip he took in his car, in anyone else's car, or by any other means. We can say that his episodic memory system is wholly dysfunctional, and that this fact is reflected in his inability to consciously reexperience any of his earlier experiences in subjective space and time.

Despite his total inability to remember any happenings from his past, and his inability to remember any ongoing events for a period longer than a few minutes, K. C. is capable of learning some new factual information. This learning is spotty and unreliable, but it does occur. For instance, when we drive by the structure known to the whole world, or at least to the whole baseball world, as Toronto's Sky Dome—a structure built after K. C. became amnesic—he is familiar with it in the sense that he knows what it is and what its name is. Of course, when I ask him whether he has ever been inside, he says that he does not know; when I ask him, "When did you drive by here last time," he does not know;

when I ask him whether he's ever seen it before, he says, "I guess so," and when I ask him to explain why he guesses so, he says, "Otherwise I would not know its name."

K. C.'s knowledge of things that he has learned, and his retention of newly learned semantic facts, has been documented more formally and objectively in several extensive studies in which he has been taught new (experimentally manufactured) "facts." Thus, he can answer questions that few other people can, such as "Who is so tall that he cannot see his own shoelaces?" The answer, "giraffe," is an unknown "fact of the world" that he was taught in one of our experiments. K. C.'s learning is much slower and more laborious than that of normal subjects, but it does occur. Moreover, once he has learned a new fact, he retains it over many months, indistinguishably from normal subjects. In contrast to the retention of learned facts, he remembers nothing. The assertion that a person cannot remember any happening from his past, if remembering is defined narrowly, as it is in this article, can be proved wrong by identifying a single instance of the person remembering a happening. So far, attempts to identify such an instance with K. C. have failed.

The conclusion drawn from these formal experiments accords with the Sky Dome anecdote. Although K. C. cannot recollect anything autonoetically, his semantic memory capabilities, and his noetic awareness, are reasonably intact, and therefore he can recover information about the world acquired on particular occasions through his at least partly intact semantic memory system.

If K. C.'s semantic memory is reasonably intact, why does he learn new facts so much more slowly than do normal subjects? One plausible answer is that his semantic system is also damaged, although not as severely as his episodic system. Another idea that fits into the theory of episodic and semantic memory is that K. C. does not learn particularly slowly, but that normal people, because of their fully intact episodic memory systems, learn much more quickly. One possible reason for such facilitation is that episodic memory minimizes the effects of proactive and retroactive interference.[8] Future research will show which of these hypotheses, or which other hypothesis, is closest to the truth.

"REMEMBER" AND "KNOW" JUDGMENTS

If amnesics can learn new facts and subsequently know them, in the absence of any autonoetic recollection of the sources of the facts, is it possible that normal people, too, know facts without remembering where or how they acquired them? Of course, it happens all the time. Every person knows hundreds and thousands of facts, without remembering the circumstances of their acquisition. This *source amnesia* that characterizes the learning in hypnotized people and amnesics, as well as older people, is well known to all of us. The phenomenon is simply more extreme in some of these special cases than in normal adults.

Gardiner and his collaborators have reported a number of studies on remembering versus knowing newly learned information in normal people.[9] The interesting feature of these studies is that the information in question is something that is usually associated with episodic memory, namely, occurrence of familiar words in a to-be-remembered list tested by recognition. In a typical experiment, subjects see a list of unrelated words, presented one at a time, on a single study trial, and then take a two-step test. In the test, they are shown both studied and nonstudied words and are asked to make a judgment about each word's presence in or absence from the study list and to indicate the basis of each positive recognition judgment.

Subjects are instructed that there are two ways in which they can tell that a word was in the study list: They either "remember" the event of the word's presentation in the study list or simply "know" on some basis that the item had appeared in the list, without remembering its occurrence.

In one experiment, for example, subjects studied a list of words under the conditions of either full or divided attention and were then tested as described. Division of attention reduced the proportion of "remembered" words (.50 vs. .38) but did not affect the proportion of words "known" to have been in the list (.21 vs. .20). Other experiments have examined the effect of other variables, such as levels of processing, generating versus reading the word at study, retention interval, word frequency, and age of subjects. These too have produced dissociations between the "remember" and "know" components of recognition memory. Yet other studies—done on brain-damaged subjects, or using psychoactive drugs, or recording event-related potentials—have begun to identify some of the neural correlates of "remember" and "know" judgments.[10]

There are other approaches to the study of awareness of source of information,[11] and correspondingly different ways of interpreting these experiments and their results. I prefer the hypothesis that "remember" judgments, based on autonoetic awareness, reflect the operation of the episodic system, whereas "know" judgments, based on noetic awareness, reflect the operation of the semantic system. Thus, subjects have two sources of information concerning the membership of words in a study list—episodic and semantic memory. When they retrieve this information from semantic memory, they appear to suffer source amnesia: They do not remember the particular event of encountering the word. In amnesic patients, such as K. C., the source amnesia is more extensive, covering not just encounters with individual words, but personal encounters of all kinds.

CONCLUSION

Episodic memory is a neurocognitive memory system that enables people to remember past happenings. The remembering in this proposition is not a generic term designating all kinds of retrieval of stored information, but rather a specific concept that designates retrieval from episodic memory. For a rememberer to remember something means that he or she is autonoetically aware of a past happening in which he or she has participated. For an experimenter or theorist to study episodic memory means to study autonoetic awareness of past experiences, separately from noetic retrieval of the semantic contents of the remembered episodes. This is a 1993 view of episodic memory. It is different from but related to the earlier ideas expressed in 1972 and 1983. It reflects the progress in our understanding of the human brain-mind, based on methods, approaches, paradigms, findings, and insights we did not yet have 10 or 20 years ago.

ACKNOWLEDGMENTS

The author's research is supported by the Natural Sciences and Engineering Research Council of Canada, Grant A8632.

NOTES

1. H. L. Roediger, III, M. S. Weldon, and B. H. Challis, Explaining dissociations between implicit and explicit measures of retention: A processing account, in *Varieties of Memory and Consciousness: Essays in Honour of Endel Tulving,* H. L. Roediger, III, and F. I. M. Craik, Eds. (Erlbaum, Hillsdale, NJ, 1989); M. S. Humphreys, J. D. Bain, and R. Pike, Different ways to cue a coherent memory system: A theory for episodic, semantic, and procedural tasks, *Psychological Review, 96,* 208–233 (1989).

2. E. Tulving, Episodic and semantic memory, in *Organization of Memory,* E. Tulving and W. Donaldson, Eds. (Academic Press, New York, 1972); E. Tulving, *Elements of Episodic Memory* (Clarendon Press, Oxford, 1983); E. Tulving, Multiple learning and memory systems, in *Psychology in the 1990's,* K. M. J. Lagerspetz and P. Niemi, Eds. (Elsevier Science Publishers, North Holland, 1984); E. Tulving, How many memory systems are there? *American Psychologist, 40,* 385–398 (1985).

3. E. Tulving, Concepts of human memory, in *Memory: Organization and Locus of Change,* L. R. Squire, N. M. Weinberger, G. Lynch, and J. L. McGaugh, Eds. (Oxford University Press, New York, 1991).

4. D. F. Sherry and D. L. Schacter, The evolution of multiple memory systems, *Psychological Review, 94,* 439–454 (1987).

5. E. Tulving, Memory: Performance, knowledge, and experience, *European Journal of Cognitive Psychology, 1,* 3–26 (1989); A. P. Shimamura, J. J. Janowsky, and L. R. Squire, Memory for the temporal order of events in patients with frontal lobe lesions and amnesic patients, *Neuropsychologia, 28,* 803–813 (1990).

6. E. Tulving, Varieties of consciousness and levels of awareness in memory, in *Attention: Selection, Awareness and Control: A Tribute to Donald Broadbent,* A. Baddeley and L. Weiskrantz, Eds. (Oxford University Press, London, in press).

7. E. Tulving, C. A. G. Hayman, and C. A. Macdonald, Long-lasting perceptual priming and semantic learning in amnesia: A case experiment, *Journal of Experimental Psychology: Learning, Memory, and Cognition, 17,* 595–617 (1991); C. A. G. Hayman, C. A. Macdonald, and E. Tulving, *The role of repetition and associative interference in new semantic learning in amnesia,* manuscript submitted for publication (1993).

8. A. P. Shimamura and L. R. Squire, A neuropsychological study of fact memory and source amnesia, *Journal of Experimental Psychology: Learning, Memory, and Cognition, 13,* 464–473 (1987); F. I. M. Craik, L. W. Morris, R. G. Morris, and E. R. Loewen, Relations between source amnesia and frontal lobe functioning in older adults, *Psychology and Aging, 5,* 148–151 (1990).

9. J. M. Gardiner and R. I. Java, Recognizing and remembering, in *Theories of Memory,* A. Collins, M. Conway, S. Gathercole, and P. Morris, Eds. (Erlbaum, Hillsdale, NJ, in press).

10. H. V. Curran, J. M. Gardiner, R. I. Java, and D. Allen, Effects of lorazepam upon recollective experience in recognition memory, *Psychopharmacology, 110,* 374–378 (1993); M. E. Smith, Neurophysiological manifestations of recollective experience during recognition memory judgments, *Journal of Cognitive Neuroscience, 5,* 1–13 (1993); T. A. Blaxton, *The role of temporal lobes in remembering visuospatial materials: Remembering and knowing,* manuscript submitted for publication (1993).

11. G. Mandler, P. Graf, and D. Kraft, Activation and elaboration effects in recognition and word priming, *The Quarterly Journal of Experimental Psychology, 38A,* 645–662 (1986); L. L. Jacoby, A process dissociation framework: Separating automatic from intentional uses of memory, *Journal of Memory and Language, 30,* 513–541 (1991); M. K. Johnson and W. Hirst, MEM: Memory subsystems as processes, in *Theories of Memory,* A. Collins, M. Conway, S. Gathercole, and P. Morris, Eds. (Erlbaum, Hillsdale, NJ, in press).

9

Elaine Funnell

A Case of Forgotten Knowledge

INTRODUCTION

If you were to meet Mrs P, she would tell you that she has a memory problem and that it is getting worse. This however, would be only partly true: Mrs P has a memory problem, but only for a particular sort of knowledge.

What Mrs P has forgotten are the concepts underlying word meanings. For example, when she was asked: 'Who wrote Hamlet?', she replied: 'Who's Hamlet?'; when she was asked: 'Is a kitten young?', she replied: 'What on earth is a kitten?'; and to the question: 'Does a mouse have a beak?', she answered: 'If I knew what a beak was I could tell you.' But, in spite of this very marked memory problem for concepts, she has not forgotten her life history; what she has been doing recently; or what she has planned to do tomorrow.

So, while Mrs P seems to have lost knowledge about concepts, she has not forgotten the episodes or events of her life. Tulving (1972) first made the distinction between memory for knowledge about words, word meanings and the relationships between words, which he called *semantic memory*, and memory for personal events or episodes, which he called *episodic memory*. Mrs P's memory problem seems to affect semantic memory only, and gives some support to Tulving's suggestion that there may be distinct types of memory representations.

I first met Mrs P in January 1990. She was then 62 years old, and had retired two years previously from a teaching job where she had been head of department for maths in a middle school (teaching children aged from 8 to 12 years). Her husband had noticed that, twelve months previously, she had begun to have difficulty in finding unusual words and the names of people. She was referred to the Radcliffe Infirmary in Oxford for neurological investigation; a CT scan of her brain carried out there in November 1989 showed focal atrophy of the left temporal lobe. Hodges et al. (1992) have since diagnosed Mrs P's condition as a case of semantic dementia, a condition first identified by Snowden et al. (1989).

When I assessed Mrs P's disorder, there was no doubt that her comprehension was very poor, for she scored at the level of a child of five and a half years on the British Picture Vocabulary Test designed by Dunn et al. (1982). She could point to the correct picture for some words, for example 'teacher', 'disagreement', 'wrist', 'surprise', but made mistakes on words such as 'link', 'tusk', 'snarling', 'locket', 'bloom', and 'weasel'. There can be no doubt that, as a school teacher, she would have understood these words in the past. In spite of these difficulties, Mrs P did very well indeed on other cognitive tests. She could repeat lists of seven numbers and understand complex grammatical constructions such as 'The pencil is on the book that is yellow' and semantically reversible sentences such as 'The elephant is pushed by the boy', taken from the Test for the Reception of Grammar, compiled by Bishop (1982). She was also excellent at the nonverbal Colour Matrices Test (Raven, 1965) on which she scored in the top band for her age.

In her daily life, Mrs P's semantic memory problem has fairly limited effect. She drives, and can map-read her way to new places. She is a keen country-dancer and takes her turn at calling the dances. She is a skilled dress-maker and can alter clothes and make up complicated patterns, and she continues to cook and manage the house. However, reading and spelling cause problems, particularly when the words have an irregular spelling-to-sound correspondence. For example, she reads the words 'yacht' and 'pint' as if they rhymed with 'hatched' and 'mint' respectively, and spells these words as 'yot' and 'pynt'. Her mistakes, which are typical of cases of surface dyslexia and dysgraphia, suggest that she reads and spells many of these words on the basis of phonic rules. The only other characteristics which set her apart from others are a rather childlike exaggeration of emphasis and intonation in speech, and a somewhat concrete approach to thinking and planning.

WHAT SORT OF KNOWLEDGE IS FORGOTTEN?

I decided to investigate Mrs P's lost knowledge. In particular, I wanted to know whether there was any pattern to the loss of knowledge, or whether the concepts that caused problems were a random sample of the full set. I also wanted to know whether particular concepts always caused problems, or whether knowledge came and went across different

occasions. I set about this task, using a number of different sorts of tests, including object naming, defining object names and matching spoken words to pictures.

The first test investigated the effect of differences in word frequency and familiarity upon her ability to define words. Word frequency counts, such as those produced by Kucera and Francis (1967), measure the incidence of words in the language, in this case in the written language. Common words, such as 'man', obviously occur very much more frequently than uncommon words such as 'goose'. Oldfield and Wingfield (1965) found that common names were produced faster by normal subjects in picture naming tasks, and Newcombe et al. (1965) showed that aphasic patients were better at naming pictures with common names than uncommon names. However, it is perhaps worth noting that Morrison et al. (1991) have suggested recently that word frequency measures reflect the age at which words are acquired—more common words being learned earlier—rather than the frequency with which a word is used.

Concepts, also, may be more or less familiar. Snodgrass and Vanderwart (1980) asked subjects to rate 260 line drawings according to how often they came into contact or thought about the concept illustrated in the drawing. They found only modest correlations between the familiarity of the concept and the frequency of the picture names in the language, and argued that familiarity and name frequency are independent attributes. Differences in familiarity can also affect object naming and defining. Funnell and Sheridan (1992) found that a young woman who had suffered brain damage as a result of a road traffic accident had forgotten many concepts and, perhaps not surprisingly, the ones she had forgotten were the least familiar. Mrs P's husband had also observed that the names she was forgetting seemed to be the less-common, less-familiar words.

I selected 24 nouns and adjectives which were highly familiar and frequent, words such as 'table', 'book', 'people', 'good', 'short', 'hot', and 24 less-familiar nouns and adjectives that occur less frequently in the language, words such as 'feather', 'axe', 'peg', 'tame', 'nasty', 'stale'. The names were spoken to her and she was asked to give the meaning of each word. The test was presented to Mrs P in 1990 and 1992, and as table 1 shows, she

Table 1 ————————————————

Proportion of Spoken Nouns and Adjectives Correctly Defined by Mrs P

	N	1990	1992
High frequency/High familiarity	(24)	1.00	0.83
Low frequency/Low familiarity	(24)	0.38	0.04

was able to give significantly more meanings of common familiar words than of less-common, less-familiar words. These differences were significantly above chance: 1990, $z = 4.31$, $p < 0.001$; 1992, $z = 5.18$, $p < 0.001$.

When Mrs P knew the meaning of a word, her definitions were clear and fairly precise, but when she failed, she usually said she didn't know, or that she had forgotten. For example, she defined 'station' as 'A place where trains go from here to London'; 'fat' as 'What a person may look like: bigger and heavier than usual', and 'narrow' as 'Not very wide'. In contrast she answered 'Don't know' or 'Forgotten' to the words 'peg', 'tulip', 'cart', and 'stale'.

Mrs P had the same difficulty when she was given pictures to name. She was asked to name 24 pictures and to define the 24 names of the pictured objects, all of which had low-frequency names occurring fewer than ten times in every million spoken words. Half were more familiar items, for example 'apple', and 'thumb', with a mean rating for familiarity of 4.32 (range 3.98–4.72), and half were less-familiar items, such as 'goat' and 'cigar', with a mean rating for familiarity of 2.50 (range 1.92–2.95). The pictures and names were split into half and presented in an ABBA design. As table 2 shows, Mrs P was better at naming and defining the more familiar items. The difference is significant: $z = 3.15$, $p < 0.001$. Dr Kathi Hirsh has carried out some regression analyses on Mrs P's naming data and has shown that the important factor is how familiar the concept is, not how common is the name, nor indeed how early in life the name is learned (Hirsh and Funnell, 1994).

WHAT IS LOST WHEN KNOWLEDGE BREAKS DOWN?

Warrington (1975) has suggested that when knowledge of a concept breaks down, information about the defining properties or features of the concept are lost before knowledge of the category to which

the item belongs. When Warrington asked patients questions about properties of the lost concepts, she found that the patients were generally poor at deciding whether items were bigger or smaller than a cat, were foreign or English, were black or white. However, they could generally decide whether the item was an animal or an object. Studies by other research groups, for example, Chertkow et al. (1989), have also reported that patients appear to know more about the general category to which an item belongs than anything about the properties of the items.

Warrington argued that object concepts (such as 'dog') are collections of properties, arranged in a hierarchy in which the most general property ('animal') is placed at the highest level, and the most specific, defining properties ('*barks*') are placed at the lowest level, much like the model of semantic memory suggested by Collins and Quillian (1969). However, Warrington's view differed from Collins and Quillian's view in one important respect: in Warrington's theory, the hierarchy can only be entered from the highest level, at which the most general properties are stored.

While Warrington's idea would fit with the fact that patients often appear to know about the general category to which an item belongs, and little else, it would not fit with other evidence. Collins and Quillian found that normal subjects are faster to answer basic-level questions about typical members of a category, such as 'Is a canary a bird?' than category questions such as 'Is a canary an animal?', and Rosch et al. (1976) showed that subjects use basic-level names rather than category names to name pictures. Rosch et al. also found that young children sort objects into basic level-categories (for example, cats versus dogs) before they learn to sort into categories (for example, cats and dogs versus types of cars). These findings suggest that, if semantic memory is indeed organized as a hierarchy, the information stored in it must be accessible from

Table 2 ————————————————

Proportion of Pictures Correctly Named and Picture Names Correctly Defined by Mrs P, According to the Familiarity of the Object

	N	Named	Defined
Familiar concepts	(12)	0.67	0.75
Less familiar concepts	(12)	0.08	0.25

Table 3

Numbers of Questions Correctly Answered by Mrs P About Category Membership and Semantic Properties

| | Questions | | |
	Category 1990	1991	Property 1990
High familiar	20/20	17/20	41/48
	Is a rose a flower?		Does a salmon have eyes?
Low familiar	12/20	10/20	33/48
	Is a dahlia a flower?		Does a salmon have fins?

Note: In the category questions, the items vary in familiarity and in the property questions the properties vary in familiarity.

other levels besides the superordinate category level, as Collins and Quillian proposed.

Bayles et al. (1990) pointed out that the questions about object properties, for example 'Is it heavier than a telephone directory?', 'Is it used to cut wood or stone?', tend to be more complex than questions about category membership: 'Is it an animal?', and this difference may be the reason why patients do better with category questions. It is also likely that the vocabulary that is used in category questions—'Is it an animal/building/clothing?'—is generally more familiar than the vocabulary used in questions about properties, for example 'Is it made of metal?' 'Is it foreign?'. If patients are less likely to understand the words in questions about properties, they will be less likely to answer property questions correctly. They will also be less likely to produce such words when defining object names.

With these points in mind, I composed two sets of questions, one about the category membership of items and one about the properties of items. The same category question was posed for items which varied in familiarity and word frequency. For example, Mrs P was asked: 'Is an apple a fruit?', and later; 'Is a guava a fruit?', or 'Is a buzzard a bird?'; and later again, 'Is a sparrow a bird?'. 'Apple' and 'sparrow' are higher in familiarity, than 'guava' and buzzard', but the hierarchical model would not predict any difference in performance for these two sets of items, for if knowledge about category membership (such as fruit) can be accessed for the familiar items (such as apple), it should also be accessible for the low-familiarity items (such as guava).

However, Mrs P's performance was strongly affected by the familiarity of the item. The test was presented twice, once in March 1990 and again in January 1991. As table 3 shows, she answered the category questions about more-familiar items significantly more successfully than the same category questions asked about less-familiar items: 1990: $\chi^2 = 7.66$, $p < 0.01$; 1991: $\chi^2 = 4.10$, $p < 0.05$.

Questions were asked about properties too. These questions varied the familiarity (F) of the property, while keeping the item unchanged; for example, 'Does a chicken have legs?' (high F property) and 'Does a chicken have a beak?' (low F property); or 'Does a rabbit have a nose?' (high F property) and 'Does a rabbit have paws?' (low F property). Sixty-two questions were about correct pairings (for example, 'Does a bicycle have wheels?') and 34 were about incorrect pairings (for example, 'Does a bicycle have an engine?'). Twenty-four additional negative questions to six further items drawn from the same categories were included to balance yes and no questions more evenly.

The test was presented in October 1990. As table 3 shows, Mrs P's ability to answer the property questions was *not* significantly affected by the familiarity of the property name ($\chi^2 = 2.89$; $p > 0.05$), suggesting that the familiarity of the object name is the important factor. Overall, there is no evidence that Mrs P knows more about the category membership of items and less about their properties. When the scores for 1990 were summed, Mrs P was found to have answered 32/40 (80 per cent) questions about category membership and 74/96 (77 per cent) about properties. The results do not support the theory that when semantic knowledge breaks down, knowledge about properties is lost before knowledge of the category. Nor do the results fit with the idea that knowledge about category membership is accessed before knowledge of features.

What is more, it soon became clear that even when Mrs P clearly understood a concept, she was nevertheless often unable to point to the critical defining features given in a typical coloured picture of the item. For example, she defined fish in the following way: 'Something that lives in the water, that you can eat when you cook it. Its supposed to be good for your memory too. They breathe in the water, I suppose they get some air from somewhere.' She pointed correctly to the highly familiar properties 'head', 'eye' and 'tail' when these were named, but she failed to point correctly to any less-familiar properties: for 'scales' she pointed to fins, for 'gills' she pointed to the fin nearest to the gills; and for 'fins' she pointed to the gills. Similarly, she correctly defined 'bird' as 'Something which flies, outside, which has babies fairly early in the year. Some come from foreign places to this country', and pointed correctly to the head and the tail, but to the word 'feathers' she pointed to the wings; to the word 'wings' she pointed to the fluffy breast feathers, and to the word 'beak' she made no response, saying only 'What on earth is a beak?'. These less familiar features—fins, gills, scales, feathers, beak, wings—which Mrs P cannot identify, happen to be the so-called defining features of the concepts 'fish' and 'bird' which Mrs P can accurately define. It is clear that knowing or not knowing the defining features of a concept indicates nothing about a person's knowledge of the concept itself. I have suggested elsewhere that, as comprehension worsens, semantic features are not lost but, instead, concepts become increasingly difficult to separate from associated concepts within the same semantic field (Funnell, 1992).

DO THE SAME CONCEPTS ALWAYS CAUSE PROBLEMS?

I was also interested to discover whether Mrs P's problems with particular concepts occurred every time a concept was tested, or whether she could retrieve the answer correctly on some occasions but not on others.

I gave Mrs P three tasks, which were repeated at regular intervals. One task was the word-to-picture matching task taken from the Psycholinguistic Battery (PALPA) developed by Kay et al. (1992). This test asks the patient to match a spoken or written name to one of five pictures: the picture named by the word; two semantically related pictures (one close, one more distant); a visually similar picture; and an unrelated picture.

The second test used the target pictures from the PALPA test and Mrs P was asked to name them. In the third test, she was asked to define the spoken names of these target pictures. The matching tests were interleaved between tests of naming and defining. Each type of test was presented in a different testing session and tests were spaced no less than

Table 4

Numbers of Items That Produce Consistent and Inconsistent Answers from Mrs P Across Repeated Tests of Word–Picture Matching, Naming and Defining

	Matching 1990/1992	Naming 1991/1992	Defining 1991/1992
Both correct	24	6	10
Both incorrect	7	26	21
Correct → incorrect	8	8	8
Incorrect → correct	1	0	1
Consistency (*c*)	0.41	0.46	0.45
Probability (*p*)	<0.01	<0.01	<0.01

two weeks apart and, more usually, two to three months apart. Table 4 shows that Mrs P gave the same responses to the same items across testing occasions, and that her performance declined across all three tasks. In each case, eight items she had formerly answered correctly were answered incorrectly the second time tested, but only very rarely were items answered incorrectly the first time and correctly the second time. For example, when I compared her performance on word–picture matching tests, spaced two years apart (February 1990 and February 1992), I found that 31/40 items in the set had produced either two correct answers or two incorrect answers; eight items had been correctly identified on the first test, but not on the second (reflecting a decline in overall performance over two years) and only one item was wrong the first time and correct on the second. It is clear that Mrs P either knows an item or does not and that, apart from some worsening in overall performance over time, this pattern is stable across tests.

It is also obvious that there are many items that Mrs P can match between word and picture that she can neither name nor define. Why is this? My first thought was that matching is an easier task; a match between a word and its referent picture has only to be recognized, whereas a name or definition has to be recalled. So if Mrs P knows the item, this may show up in a recognition task and not in a recall task. However, further investigation suggested that word–picture matching may be a less stringent test of picture and name comprehension than either naming or defining, and some correct responses may occur because alternative items in the set are not close enough in meaning.

Table 5

Number of Mistakes Made by Mrs P in Recognizing Pictures of Real and Nonsense Objects

	1990	1991	1992
Real objects (N = 62)	11	12	10
Nonsense objects (N = 55)	2	4	5

Matching tests are made more or less easy, by the nature of the semantic relationship between the distractor pictures and the target picture. In the PALPA word–picture matching test, some semantic distractors are close semantic co-ordinates of the target; for example, 'lobster and crab'; 'cat and dog'; 'fence and wall'; while others are associative and thus more distant in meaning: for example, 'pram and baby'; 'cobweb and spider'; 'stamp and envelope'. I divided the stimuli into those with a semantic co-ordinator distractor and those with an associative distractor. I then looked to see how many times Mrs P matched the items correctly *after she had failed to both name and define them.* I found that she matched only 56/84 (40 per cent) of the targets paired with a close semantic co-ordinate, but 27/39 (69 percent) of the targets paired with a semantic associative item. This difference was highly significant: $\chi^2 = 9.34$ $p < 0.01$. So at least part of the reason why she was more successful at matching than naming or defining was that the semantic distinction between the target and distractors was not always difficult enough to test subtle difficulties in comprehension.

However, if Mrs P could name the picture, she could reliably match the word to the picture on the following matching test. Over five repeats of the naming test, she named a total of 38 pictures, and matched 37/38 (97 per cent) of these correctly on the matching test which followed the naming test (by an interval of at least one month). These results indicate that, of the three tests used here, picture naming is the most sensitive test of the ability to comprehend an object. I looked in vain for evidence that Mrs P could name the picture but not match it. Such evidence would have supported the idea, first put forward by Ratcliff and Newcombe (1982), that pictures can be named without knowledge of their meaning: a theory which has received preliminary confirmatory evidence in a study reported by Kremin (1988). Although this idea seems plausible,

especially for items that are very distinctive in structure (such as scissors), Mrs P's performance provided no support for this theory.

RECOGNIZING WITHOUT IDENTIFYING?

Although Mrs P was forgetting the meaning of words and failing to identify objects, she did not lose her sense of familiarity with the surface forms of objects and words. For example, she could distinguish 23/24 of the spoken words of low familiarity that she defined very poorly (see table 1) from 24/24 nonsense words of similar structure. Similarly, she failed to identify real objects, but could distinguish pictures of real objects and nonsense objects pretty well (in a test developed by Riddoch and Humphreys in 1987). Table 5 shows her scores on this test over three years. She made most mistakes with real objects, but there were less than 20 per cent of such errors, and most of these seemed to be connected to the quality of the picture. For example, she would comment that the picture 'looked wrong', saying of the picture of the accordion: 'You play it, but it looks wrong'; and of the motor bike: 'It doesn't look right where you have to put your hands'. In most cases, there was something odd about the drawing, for example the lines did not quite meet up, or the proportions were distorted.

The only nonsense pictures that caused her problems were those where parts from semantically related objects were subtly combined. For example she decided that a pig with a rabbit's head, a cow with a camel's head, and a duck with a dog's head were real animals, but she made no mistakes with more obviously bizarre combinations, such as a kangaroo with a human foot in place of its tail. Warrington was the first person to observe that a patient with a disorder of comprehension was able to recognize an object as familiar without being able to identify it. She suggested that there was a perceptual process for recognizing objects that was separate from semantic knowledge about the identity of the object (Warrington, 1975). While Mrs P's semantic knowledge is shrinking, her knowledge of the visual forms and spoken names of these objects remains almost unchanged, lending support to Warrington's theory that perceptual and semantic records are distinct.

CAN CONCEPTS AND NAMES BE RELEARNED?

Mrs P's husband tells of one autumn day when he dug the first leeks of the season and took them into the kitchen to be cooked for lunch. Apparently Mrs P took one look and said: 'What are they? And what do I do with them?' If you asked Mrs P now what a leek is, she would tell you, in a rather stereotyped manner (as if these are lines that she has learned by rote) that they are long things that you have to cut down from the top, wash carefully, and then slice. She has learned to recognize and name leeks again.

Although Mrs P was losing her knowledge of concepts, and this was a continuing process, she nevertheless appeared to learn new words. New words, seemingly connected to new events, would suddenly appear in her vocabulary. For example, she told me the name of the village in Italy where she had recently stayed for a few days on holiday; she learned my name—and how to spell it—and she referred to 'Himalayan balsam', an unusual wild flower that she and her husband had found on a recent walk. Paradoxically, even while she was forgetting information, she was learning new facts, and these examples of what seemed to be new learning of concepts and names suggested that she might be able to relearn concepts and names that she had forgotten.

I decided to try to reteach her some names and concepts. But choosing the concepts to reteach was not an easy matter. It was important to choose a related set of concepts to show that she could learn not only the 'sort of thing' but also that she could learn to distinguish one specific thing from other, similar, things. Thus it seemed important to select similar items belonging to one particular semantic category. If she could identify particular members of the category, it would show that she had relearned specific concepts and names. Vegetables are quite an important part of Mrs P's life: her husband has a flourishing vegetable garden and she herself cooks vegetables every day for lunch. For this reason, when I searched for a category of items to reteach to Mrs. P, I chose vegetables.

In January 1991, I took to Mrs P's house 22 fresh vegetables, which varied from very common items such as potato, cabbage and onion, to unusual items such as aubergine, courgette and fennel. I asked her to name each vegetable in turn, and then, when this test was completed, I spoke each vegetable name to her and asked her to describe it from memory. It became clear very quickly that she did not recognize many vegetables or their names, and that this was particularly true for the less-familiar items. She could neither name nor define 'asparagus', 'courgette', 'chicory', 'broccoli', 'aubergine', 'pepper', 'chili' and 'fennel', saying 'I don't know' in every case. Some of these vegetables may never have been familiar to her, although the cookery books in her kitchen are modern and would certainly include recipes for these vegetables.

She could name and define the most common vegetables, 'potato', 'onion', 'carrot', 'lettuce', 'sprouts', 'cabbage' and 'leek', correctly, but there was a further set of fairly common vegetables which she either failed to name and define or for which she showed only partial knowledge. She failed to name and define 'turnip' and 'cauliflower' but could define (but not name) 'parsnip', 'celery' and 'cucumber', and could give the initial letter only of 'mushroom'. It was this set of six vegetables (turnip, cauliflower, parsnip, celery, cucumber and mushroom), for which she had some remaining knowledge or which should have been known well in the past, that I decided to reteach.

Mrs P was taught to name the vegetables by showing her each object and telling her the name. The vegetables were then shown again, one at a time, for her to name. She was corrected or reminded if she failed. The testing was repeated ten times, with the vegetables being presented in different sequences. She had to be reminded of the name of the cucumber in the first test, but after that she needed no reminding or correcting in any test. She learned quickly and in total got 9/10 of these naming tests correct.

At the end of this session, I left the six 'treated' vegetables with Mrs P together with a set of written names and descriptions, and suggested that she practised testing herself on naming and describing the vegetables. When I returned a week later, she could name and describe all six vegetables correctly, but failed to name or describe any of the six unusual vegetables in the control set. Tests a week

Table 6

Number of Vegetables Named Correctly by Mrs P Over Repeated Tests

	Pretest	Retests				
		Jan.	Feb.	Mar.	Apr.	Sept.
7 common untreated veg	7	7	6	7	7	2
6 fairly common treated veg	0	6	6	5	5	3
6 unusual untreated veg	0	0	0	0	NT	NT

Notes: NT = Not tested
Vegetables were either named correctly on the pretest; not named and then retaught; or not named and not retaught.

later showed that the relearning had been completely retained.

After that, I retested her on an irregular basis so that she would not expect a test each time I visited her. Table 6 shows that she continued to name the vegetables through March and April, with only the occasional mistake. The winter vegetables then disappeared from the shops, and the next test was delayed until the following September. By then, she had forgotten the names of 3/6 vegetables she had relearned, but she had also forgotten the names of 5/7 vegetables she had previously known well. Time and a period during which many of the vegetables were not available seem to have weakened her memory for winter vegetables in general; not just those that she had relearned. It is of interest that since this study was carried out, Swales and Johnson (1992) have reported similar relearning of forgotten concepts in a patient whose semantic loss followed herpes encephalitis.

POSTSCRIPT

Although Mrs P can learn new names and concepts and relearn old information, her semantic memory has worsened gradually over the three years that I have been working with her. As her memory has declined, her vocabulary has become increasingly restricted to her own activities and interests, and seems to reflect how recently she has thought about or named a concept. Topical words may appear for a time and then disappear. Schwartz et al. (1979) have described a patient who, as her condition worsened, spent increasing amounts of time walking to the local shopping centre and back. At the same time, her vocabulary diminished to just one

specific naming word—'shopping centre'—which she used as both a noun and a verb. It is to be hoped that this will not happen to Mrs P.

FURTHER READING

1. Funnell, E. (1992) 'Progressive loss of semantic memory in a case of Alzheimer's disease,' *Proceedings of the Royal Society of London,* **B.249**: 287–91.
2. Funnell, E. (1995) 'Objects and properties: a study of the breakdown of semantic memory', *Memory: Special Issue on Semantic Memory* (in press, Spring 1995).
3. Hodges, J. R., Patterson, K., Tyler, L. K. (1994) 'Loss of semantic memory: implications for the modularity of mind', *Cognitive Neuropsychology,* **11**: 505–42.
4. Patterson, K. E. and Hodges, J. R. (1994) 'Disorders of semantic memory', in A. Baddeley, B. A. Wilson and F. Watts (eds), *Handbook of Memory Disorders* (Chichester, W. Sussex: John Wiley).

REFERENCES

Bayles, K. A., Tomeoeda, C. K. and Trosset, M. W. (1990) 'Naming and categorical knowledge in Alzheimer's disease: the process of semantic memory deterioration', *Brain and Language,* **39**: 498–510.

Bishop, D. (1982) *TROG Test for the Reception of Grammar* (London: Medical Research Council).

Chertkow, H., Bub, D. and Seidenberg, M. (1989) 'Priming and semantic memory in Alzheimer's disease', *Brain and Language,* **36**: 420–46.

Collins, A. M. and Quillian, M. R. (1969) 'The comparison of word meanings', *Journal of Experimental Psychology,* **86**: 343–6.

Dunn, M. D., Dunn, L. M., Whetton, C. and Pintile, D. (1982) *British Picture Vocabulary Scale* (Windsor, Berks.: NFER-Nelson).

Funnell, E. (1992) 'Progressive loss of semantic memory in a case of Alzheimer's disease', *Proceedings of the Royal Society of London,* **B.249**: 287–91.

Funnell, E. and Sheridan, J. (1992) 'Categories of knowledge? Unfamiliar aspects of living and non-living things', *Cognitive Neuropsychology,* **9**: 135–54.

Hirsh, K. and Funnell, E. (1994) 'Age of acquisition of names and concept familiarity: evidence for differing locus of effects in progressive aphasia', paper presented to the Experimental Psychology Society, University College London.

Hodges, J. R., Patterson, K., Oxbury, S. and Funnell, E. (1992) 'Semantic dementia', *Brain,* **115**: 1783–1806.

Kay, J., Lesser, R. and Coltheart, M. (1992) *PALPA* (London and Hove: Lawrence Erlbaum Associates).

Kremin, H. (1988) 'Independence of access to meaning and phonology: arguments for direct nonsemantic pathways for the naming written words and pictures', in G. Denes, C. Semenza and P. Bisiacchi (eds), *Perspectives on Cognitive, Neuropsychology* (Hove: Lawrence Erlbaum).

Kucera, H. and Francis, W. N. (1967) *Computational Analysis of Present-day American English* (Providence, R.I.: Brown University Press).

Morrison, C. M., Ellis, A. W. and Quinlan, P. T. (1991) 'Age of acquisition, not word frequency, affects object naming, not object recognition', *Memory and Cognition,* **20**: 705–14.

Newcombe, F., Oldfield, R. C. and Wingfield, A. (1965) 'Object naming by dysphasic patients', *Nature (London),* **207**: 1217–18.

Oldfield, R. C. and Wingfield, A. (1965) 'Response latencies in naming objects', *Quarterly Journal of Experimental Psychology,* **17**: 273–81.

Ratcliff, G. and Newcombe, F. (1982) 'Object recognition: some deductions from the clinical evidence', in A. W. Ellis (ed.), *Normality and Pathology and Cognitive Functions* (London: Academic Press).

Raven, J. C. (1965) *Guide to Using the Coloured Progressive Matrices* (London: H. K. Lewis).

Riddoch, M. J. and Humphreys, G. W. (1987) 'Visual object processing in optic aphasia: a case of semantic access agnosia', *Cognitive Neuropsychology,* **4**: 131–86.

Rosch, E., Mervis, C. B., Gray, W., Johnson, D. and Boyes-Braem, P. (1976) 'Basic objects in natural categories', *Cognitive Psychology,* **7**: 573–605.

Schwartz, M., Marin, O. S. M. and Saffran, E. M. (1979) 'Dissociations of language function in dementia: a case study', *Brain and Language,* **7**: 277–306.

Snodgrass, J. G. and Vanderwart, M. (1980) 'A standardized set of 260 pictures: norms for name agreement, image agreement, familiarity, and visual complexity', *Journal of Experimental Psychology: Human Memory and Learning,* **6**: 174–215.

Snowden, J. S., Goulding, P. J. and Neary, D. (1989) 'Semantic dementia: a form of circumscribed cerebral atrophy', *Behavioural Neurology,* **2**: 167–182.

Swales, M. and Johnson, R. (1992) 'Patients with semantic memory loss: can they relearn lost concepts?', *Neuropsychological Rehabilitation,* **2**: 295–306.

Tulving, E. (1972) 'Episodic and semantic memory', in E. Tulving and W. Donaldson (eds), *Organisation of Memory* (London: Academic Press).

Warrington, E. K. (1975) 'The selective impairment of semantic memory', *Quarterly Journal of Experimental Psychology,* **27**: 635–7.

10

Fergus I. M. Craik

Memory Changes in Normal Aging

Does memory decline as we get older? It certainly seems as if it does: People in their 60s and 70s have greater difficulty remembering names and finding words than they did in their teens and 20s; they also report an increasing liability to everyday forgetfulness—where they left their glasses or a book—or a failure to carry out some action that they had decided on only moments before. Several questionnaire studies[1] have shown that older adults report these and other memory problems in their everyday lives; so it does not seem that age-related losses in memory are attributable simply to negative stereotypes of the elderly held by younger people, or to the results of artificial laboratory tests of memory, which older people might find boring and irrelevant. On the contrary, it appears that age-related declines in memory are real, and that they cause concern in many older people. The purpose of the present article is to give an overview of some theoretical ideas and experimental findings that bear on the phenomenon of age-related memory loss. Given the space restrictions, the article focuses largely on my own point of view; readers will find reviews that are more comprehensive, and less partisan. in the recent literature.[2]

PATTERNS OF RESULTS

One of the most striking aspects of the experimental psychological literature on memory and aging is that age-related changes in performance are extremely variable. Some tasks show substantial losses with age, whereas performance on others is essentially unimpaired. Presumably, this pattern of findings should yield clues to the underlying causes of the deficits and perhaps also clues to the nature and organization of memory itself. Examples of tasks that show losses with age are free recall of lists of unrelated words, paired-associate learning of unrelated word pairs, working memory tasks, memory for context or for the original source of some remembered fact, recall of pictures, and memory for spatial location. Tasks that show little or no age-related decline include implicit memory, or priming, tasks (such as perceptual identification of recently presented words in a tachistoscope and word-fragment completion), forward digit span, recall of the last few words in a free-recall list (the recency effect), recognition memory, and memory for well-learned facts and pieces of knowledge.

What common principles can be induced from this very varied collection of strengths and weaknesses? One attractive possibility is that certain memory structures or systems may be more vulnerable than others to the effects of aging, and that the observed pattern of behavioral deficits reflects this differential vulnerability. However, structural accounts do not generally provide satisfactory accounts of the findings. For example, the findings that digit span performance and the recency effect in free recall are largely unaffected by aging suggest that short-term memory is unimpaired. But when the short-term memory task involves two simultaneous inputs (as in dichotic listening), or necessitates reorganization of the material held in mind (as in backward digit span), the age-related losses are substantial. If the task involves the relatively passive reproduction of small amounts of material, then older people can perform as well as their younger counterparts; but when the task requires more active reorganization of the material, or a need to both hold some material and perceive further inputs, then the older person is at a disadvantage. This latter type of short-term memory task, involving storage, active processing, and often updating of the material held, is nowadays referred to as reflecting working memory, and it is well documented that such working memory tasks are vulnerable to the effects of aging.[3] It is apparently not the involvement of short-term memory as a structure but rather the type of processing operation required that correlates with the degree of age-related loss.

Another possible account is in terms of memory systems, especially perhaps Tulving's[4] "mono-hierarchical" view, in which procedural memory is seen as the most primitive in both evolutionary and developmental terms, representational memory for facts and acquired knowledge (semantic memory) is embedded within procedural memory, and memory for personally experienced events (episodic memory) is embedded in turn within semantic memory, and is the latest form of memory to develop. This account is attractive in several ways. First, many priming effects may be attributed to (relatively) early and primitive procedural sensorimotor systems, which are in turn relatively immune to the effects of aging and other types of brain insult. Second, general knowledge remains intact and accessible in the elderly, for the most part, in contrast to episodic memory for recent events, which is typically impaired. It makes sense that the most recent form of memory (in evolutionary and developmental terms) should also be the most vulnerable when brain processes lose their efficiency. On the other side of the argument, however, is the point that an inability to remember names (from semantic memory) is perhaps the most commonly reported memory failure of older people, whereas recognition memory for recently presented events (an episodic memory task) is usually well maintained in the elderly. Again, it seems that it is the type of mental operation required that is crucial, not the memory system in which the processing takes place.

A PROCESSING VIEW OF REMEMBERING

Rather than thinking of memory in structural terms—as a set of fixed memory traces, for example—my own preference (shared with many other current researchers) is to think of remembering as a pattern of mental activity. In my version of a processing account, I have argued that remembering may be regarded as being very similar to perceiving. Just as perceiving is determined by the interaction of incoming sensory information with the mental machinery representing accumulated past experience, so remembering may be viewed as the interaction of incoming stimuli (now termed retrieval cues or context) with stored past experience in varying degrees of generality and specificity. By this view, "memory" is therefore not some characteristic of the organism alone, but (like perception) necessarily reflects the interaction of external environmental stimuli and constraints with internal mental operations. A further point is that it is obviously not very sensible to talk about the percept in the absence of perceiving—perception is an activity, produced reliably by the interaction of stimuli with stored perceptual experience. But it may be equally misleading to talk about the memory trace (the engram) in the absence of recollecting—again, remembering is a pattern of mental activity constructed from the interaction of stimuli and stored experience.

By this account, encoding is simply the set of processes involved in the perception and interpretation of the original event (plus their consequential effects on brain mechanisms, presumably), and retrieval is the attempted recapitulation of the original pattern of encoding activity. Remembering will obviously be more effective and successful to the extent that the external stimuli and context are similar to those present during encoding; that is, remembering is helped by environmental support. However, people can also remember events when the present context is very different from the encoding context; in this case, environmental support is minimal, and the rememberer must invoke effortful "self-initiated" processing in order to recapitulate the original pattern of mental activity. Environmental support and self-initiated processing are thus complementary sets of processes; the person must rely on self-initiated processing to the extent that environmental support is lacking.

With regard to aging, my suggestion is that age-related decrements are found in memory tasks to the extent that self-initiated processing is necessary. Older people have comparatively few problems with recognition memory tasks (in which past experience is used passively) or primary memory tasks (in which recently presented information is given back in an unmodified form). They *do* have problems with free recall, with memory for source, and with working memory tasks—all of which require substantial amounts of effortful self-initiated processing. The suggestion is therefore that age-related memory decrements are associated with the type of processing operations required by the task rather than with specific stores or systems. This viewpoint is obviously related to other accounts of age-related changes, most notably to the arguments of Hasher and Zacks.[5]

EMPIRICAL EVIDENCE

The results of a number of studies provide good support for the ideas just sketched, although other results make it clear that more theoretical elabora-

Table 1

Characteristics of the Four Groups of Subjects in Craik, Byrd, and Swanson[6]

Characteristic	Group			
	Old 3	Old 2	Old 1	Young
Mean age	76.2	73.5	73.3	19.7
Socioeconomic status	Low	Low	High	Moderate
Vocabulary score[a]	31.2	35.0	52.2	48.1
Activity level	Low	High	High	High

[a]Mean Vocabulary score on the Wechsler Adult Intelligence Scale-Revised. Each score indicates the mean number correct out of 70.

tion is necessary before a fully satisfactory account is achieved. Byrd, Swanson, and I[6] contrasted the recall performance of four groups of subjects under various degrees of environmental support. Three of the groups were elderly (mean age = 74 years), and the fourth was a group of young college undergraduates (mean age = 20 years). The three older groups varied in their socioeconomic level, their level of verbal intelligence, and their level of social activity within the community. As shown in Table 1, the group referred to as Old 3 was relatively low in all three characteristics. Old 2 members were not well off financially and had relatively low verbal intelligence scores, but were socially active (they were volunteers in a local Foster Grandparents program). The Old 1 subjects were comparatively affluent, had high verbal intelligence scores, and were also socially active. Finally, the Young subjects were moderately well off, had high verbal intelligence scores, and were socially active.

The subjects were given four recall tasks under different conditions of environmental support. In one condition (free learning–free recall), a list of 10 words was presented and subjects then attempted to recall the words without cues. In a second condition, cues were presented for each word, both during the learning phase (e.g., "a type of bird–LARK") and at retrieval ("What was the type of bird?"); this second condition offered greater support at encoding and retrieval, and might therefore be expected to help the older groups differentially. The two intermediate conditions involved cues at encoding only and cues at retrieval only, respectively. Figure 1 shows the pattern of results; scores within the same performance range are shaded to make the point more clearly.

The critical finding is the interaction between group and experimental condition. One way of

Figure 1

Recall Scores for the Four Groups of Subjects in Craik, Byrd, and Swanson[6]

Condition	Group			
	Old 3	Old 2	Old 1	Young
Cued learning–cued recall	5.5	7.3	8.1	7.8
Cued learning–free recall	2.2	5.4	5.8	5.6
Free learning–cued recall	2.2	4.5	5.3	5.8
Free learning–free recall	2.4	4.6	4.7	6.0

Note: See Table 1 for data on the groups' characteristics. Each score indicates mean number correct out of 10 words. Scores within the same shaded area are within the same performance range.

looking at this result is that task support can compensate for the negative effects of aging, to some extent at least. For example, the recall scores of the Old 1 and Old 2 groups are poorer than those of the Young group under the free-learning–free-recall condition, but virtually equivalent under the cued-learning–cued-recall condition. Even the comparatively disadvantaged Old 3 group performs quite well when both learning and recall are cued.

McDowd and I[7] contrasted cued-recall and recognition performance in younger and older subjects. The typical result in such studies is that age differences are less in recognition than in recall tests, a result in line with the environmental-support notion. But recognition tests are also easier as a rule. Is it possible that age-related decrements simply increase as the task becomes more difficult? One purpose of our study was to examine age differences when the difficulty of the tests was equated; we attempted to do this by testing recall immediately after each list and recognition after all lists had been presented and the recall tests performed. A second purpose was to check whether recall was indeed more effortful; this point was explored by having subjects perform a continuous reaction time (RT) task concurrently with each of the two retrieval tasks. The RT task consisted of responding to each of a series of lights by pressing an appropriate key; each correct response illuminated the next stimulus light.

The main results are shown in Figure 2. In this experiment, cued recall was actually easier than recognition; however, there was an age-related dec-

rement in recall performance but no age difference in recognition. It seems that older people are more penalized when less support is provided. The right-hand panel of Figure 2 shows the additional RT required (above the base-line value when no concurrent task was present) to respond to each light stimulus during the two retrieval tasks. The results show that recall was associated with longer RTs than was recognition, and that this effect was greatly exaggerated in the older group. One implication is that recall is more effortful than recognition and thus diverts more processing resources from efficient performance of the RT task; another implication is that both retrieval tasks (especially recall) are more "costly" to carry out for older subjects. These results are at least in line with the view that aging is associated with a decline in processing capacity (or in available attentional resources) and that this decline is reflected in lower performance on those memory and other cognitive tasks that involve a heavy expenditure of processing resources.

Two other memory tasks that show age-related declines are memory for context or the source of some learned fact and prospective memory—remembering to carry out some task at a future time. A failure of memory for source can show itself as an inability to remember where or when you met a person whose face is quite familiar, or as a failure to remember that you have told the present listener that same story before. In the latter case, a rapid glazing of the listener's eyes may provide some environmental support to aid recollection! Prospective memory is an interesting case. Einstein, McDaniel, and their colleagues[8] have recently suggested that some intentions to carry out future actions may be well supported by cues and reminders; in these cases, the older person performs well. But if the task is time based ("remember to call home at 3 p.m.") as opposed to event based ("when you see John, tell him about the tickets"), then age-related decrements are typically observed. It is at least plausible that substantial attentional resources are required for successfully integrating events with their source or context, and are also required to remember to carry out future actions in the absence of reminders.

The notion of declining resources in the elderly is given further credibility by the observation that other conditions that plausibly involve a reduction in available processing resources (e.g., sleep depri-

Figure 2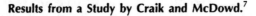

Results from a Study by Craik and McDowd.[7]

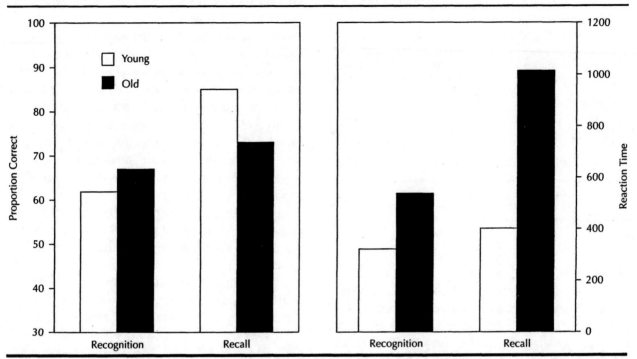

The left panel shows recognition scores (hits minus false alarms) and cued-recall scores (proportion correct) as a function of age. The right panel shows reaction time (RT) costs (mean dual-task RT minus mean baseline RT, in milliseconds) as a function of age and retrieval task.

vation, fatigue, intoxication, and division of attention in young subjects) are all associated with the same pattern of impaired memory performance as that observed in normal aging.[9] The positive and somewhat optimistic aspect of the present analysis is that all of these examples are losses associated with functional as opposed to structural changes. Although aging is unfortunately not reversible in the same sense as is fatigue or sleep deprivation, there is nevertheless reasonable evidence that the negative effects of aging can be somewhat ameliorated by the provision of appropriate environmental support. The challenge is therefore to restructure the older person's environment so that such support is available, and to let older people know what they are capable of accomplishing so that they are not inhibited from helping themselves.

NOTES

1. E. M. Zelinski, M. J. Gilewski, and L. W. Thompson, Do laboratory tests relate to self-assessment of memory ability in the young and old? in *New Directions in Memory and Aging: Proceedings of the George A. Talland Memorial Conference,* L. W. Poon, J. L. Fozard, L. S. Cermak, D. Arenberg, and L. W. Thompson, Eds. (Erlbaum, Hillsdale, NJ, 1980).

2. F. I. M. Craik and J. M. Jennings, Human memory, in *The Handbook of Aging and Cognition,* F. I. M. Craik and T. A. Salthouse, Eds. (Erlbaum, Hillsdale, NJ, 1992); L. L. Light, Memory and aging: Four hypotheses in search of data, *Annual Review of Psychology, 43,* 333–376 (1991).

3. F. I. M. Craik, R. G. Moris, and M. L. Gick, Adult age differences in working memory, in *Neuropsychological Impairments of Short-Term Memory,* G. Vallar and T. Shallice, Eds. (Cambridge University Press, Cambridge, England, 1990).

4. E. Tulving, How many memory systems are there? *American Psychologist, 40,* 395–398 (1985).

5. L. Hasher and R. T. Zacks, Automatic and effortful processes in memory, *Journal of Experimental Psychology: General, 108,* 356–388 (1979).

6. F. I. M. Craik, M. Byrd, and J. M. Swanson, Patterns of memory loss in three elderly samples, *Psychology and Aging, 2,* 79–86 (1987).

7. F. I. M. Craik and J. M. McDowd, Age differences in recall and recognition, *Journal of Experimental Psychology: Learning, Memory, and Cognition, 13,* 474–479 (1987).

8. M. A. McDaniel and G. O. Einstein, Aging and prospective memory: Basic findings and practical applications, *Advances in Learning and Behavioral Disabilities, 7,* 87–105 (1992).

9. L. G. Nilsson, L. Bäckman, and T. Karlsson, Priming and cued recall in elderly, alcohol intoxicated and sleep deprived subjects: A case of functionally similar memory deficits, *Psychological Medicine, 19,* 423–433 (1989).

11

Katherine Nelson

The Psychological and Social Origins of Autobiographical Memory

Recent research on young children's memory for personal episodes provides new insights into the phenomenon of infantile amnesia, first identified by Freud. New research indicates that children learn to share memories with others that they acquire the narrative forms of memory recounting, and that such recounts are effective in reinstating experienced memories only after the children can utilize another person's representation of an experience in language as a reinstatement of their own experience. This competence requires a level of mastery of the representational function of language that appears at the earliest in the mid to late preschool years.

> Remembering past events is a universally familiar experience. It is also a uniquely human one. As far as we know, members of no other species possess quite the same ability to experience again now, in a different situation and perhaps in a different form, happenings from the past, and know that the experience refers to an event that occurred in another time and in another place. Other members of the animal kingdom . . . cannot travel back into the past in their own minds. (Tulving, 1983, p. 1)

This passage introducing Tulving's book on episodic memory makes a strong claim, similar to the more familiar claim of the uniqueness of human language. If remembering past events is uniquely human, as Tulving claims, the point calls out for further investigation. What is the significance of this ability for human social and psychological functioning? How and why does it arise phylogenetically and ontogenetically? Is it related to other uniquely human functions such as language, symbolic cognitive processing, and the establishment of complex cultures?

Tulving's claim is controversial, and has been argued extensively (see commentators on Tulving, 1984). For the purposes of this article, I take it as an assumption to be examined, but I confine the assumption only to the

From Katherine Nelson, "The Psychological and Social Origins of Autobiographical Memory," *Psychological Science,* vol. 4, no. 1 (January 1993). Copyright © 1993 by The American Psychological Society. Reprinted by permission of Cambridge University Press.

late-developing type of episodic memory that humans possess, namely, autobiographical memory. And I examine the assumption in the course of addressing the question of why a specific kind of episodic memory—autobiographical memory—may develop in human childhood.

For the developmental account outlined here, it is important to distinguish not only between semantic and episodic memory, as Tulving has, but also between generic event memory, episodic memory, and autobiographical memory, taking autobiographical memory as a subtype of episodic. *Generic event memory* (not specifically considered by Tulving) provides a schema derived from experience that sketches the general outline of a familiar event without providing details of the specific time or place when such an event happened, whether once or many times. A basic type of this kind of general schema is the *script* (Schank & Abelson, 1977) that specifies the sequence of actions and empty slots for roles and props that may be filled in with default values, in the absence of specifications. Generic event memory may also be considered for some purposes a type of semantic memory in that it crosscuts the distinctions that Tulving set forth.

Both of Tulving's memory types (and those considered in this article) fall under the *declarative* memory system distinguished by Squire (1992) or the *explicit* memory system described by Schacter (1992), which involve conscious recollection of previous experiences. The present distinctions among memory types are adopted primarily for the purpose of interpreting the developmental research and providing an explanation for the establishment of a "life history" memory.

In contrast to generic event memory, an *episodic* memory has the phenomenal characteristic of referring to something that happened once at a specific time and place. But the specific identification of time and place does not seem to be necessarily part of episodic recall, although adults can often reconstruct an episodic memory from different types of cues, and find a way of identifying a specific time and place at which a specific event was experienced, even if the location is not available in declarative form. All that seems to truly distinguish episodic recall from generic event memory is the sense that "something happened *one* time" in contrast to the generic "things happen this way." Yet it is not at all clear that this somewhat vague impression (of "one time") will bear the weight of Tulving's claim of human uniqueness. We simply do not know whether other animals, or even human infants, experience a phenomenal difference between remembering and knowing, differentiating between one-time happenings and usual happenings. They very well might.

Equally important, not all episodic memory is *autobiographical memory*. This point is critical to the theoretical and empirical explication of the development of autobiographical memory. To take a simple example, what I ate for lunch yesterday is today part of my episodic memory, but being unremarkable in any way, it will not, I am quite sure, become part of my autobiographical memory. It has no significance to my life story beyond the general schema of lunch. In contrast, the first time I presented a paper at a conference is part of my autobiographical memory: I remember the time, place, and details of the program and participants, and I have a sense of how that experience fits into the rest of my personal life story. It is important to make this distinction at the outset, because, as recent research has established, very young children do have episodic memories, but do not yet have autobiographical memory of this kind.

Autobiographical memory as used here is specific, personal, long-lasting, and (usually) of significance to the self-system. Phenomenally, it forms one's personal life history. Prior to the development of this system, memories do not become part of a personally known life history, although of course they may be important in other ways to one's life, and one may derive a strong sense of one's early history from hearing about it from other people.

Autobiographical memory has its onset during the early childhood years. Surprisingly, it is only recently that this onset has been thought of in developmental terms. In the past, it has usually been conceived of in terms of childhood (or infantile) amnesia, the phenomenon, first identified by Freud (1963) and familiar to all who reflect on it, that memories for events from the early years of our lives—before about 3 to 4 years—are not available to adult consciousness, although many memories from later childhood usually are easily called up.

The onset of autobiographical memory is simply the inverse of infantile amnesia. In the present framework, the critical questions are when and why an autobiographical system—in which some memories are retained for a lifetime—becomes differentiated from a general episodic system.

Most of the research on childhood amnesia—the period of life before the onset of autobiographical memory—has come from studies of adults' recall of childhood memories, beginning with a questionnaire study by Henri and Henri in 1897 (see review by Dudycha & Dudycha, 1941). As in many studies that followed, they asked adults (N = 120) to recall their earliest memories from childhood and reported the data in terms of the number of childhood memories from a given age range. No memories were reported from before 2 years, but 71% of the subjects had some memories from the period between 2 and 4 years of age. Summarizing over a large number of such studies, Pillemer and White (1989) found that the earliest memory is reported on average at about 3½ years. They noted that there are actually two phases of childhood amnesia, the first a total blocking of memories, usually prior to about 3 years, and the second, between 3 and 6 years, a significant drop-off of accessible memories relative to later memories. Such a pattern has been verified by the analysis of the forgetting curve for adult recall of childhood memories (Wetzler & Sweeney, 1986). However, it is important to note also that there is considerable variability both in age of earliest memory—from 2 years to 8 years or even later—and in number of memories reported from early childhood. In the early empirical literature on the topic, the age of earliest memory has been negatively correlated with IQ, language ability, and social class, and females tend to have earlier memories than males.

It is commonly objected that the data on early childhood memories are unreliable and unverifiable, but for the following reasons these objections do not invalidate the conclusions drawn. First, those who can reliably date their memories—because they experienced moves or other disruptions during early childhood—or whose parents can verify events (Usher & Neisser, 1991) exhibit the same general age relations as those suggested by the overall research. For example, it is rare to find anyone who claims to remember a specific incident from before the age of 2 years. Moreover, a study of memory for the birth of a sibling, which could be definitively dated, showed the same age relation as the questionnaire data: Children could remember the event if it occurred when they were 3 years or older, but not before that age (Sheingold & Tenney, 1982).

The validity of any given memory is not relevant within the present theoretical framework. Although the validity of a memory may be of concern if one is interested in such issues as whether children are reliable witnesses, it is of less concern if one is interested in when they begin to retain memories in the autobiographical memory system. Memories do not need to be true or correct to be part of that system.

The term childhood amnesia implies that something was there and is lost. This in turn implies that we need to find an explanation either in terms of loss or in terms of some force that interferes with retrieval of memories that still exist, as Freud proposed. The alternative possibility explored here is that something develops that leads to a new organization of memory or the establishment of a new memory system or function. These possibilities can be evaluated only in terms of the study of memory during the period prior to and subsequent to the emergence of autobiographical memory. The adult research, on the basis of which so much of the discussion has been based, can tell us only that the phenomenon is real; it cannot reveal anything about its development.

EVIDENCE FROM DEVELOPMENTAL RESEARCH

Research on memory in very early childhood is very recent, coming mostly from the past 15 years. My colleagues and I began investigations of children's event memory in the mid-1970s, and our early studies revealed that 3-year-olds are quite good at telling what happens in general in a familiar event such as having lunch at the preschool or going to McDonald's, but they are relatively poor at telling what happened on one particular occasion (Nelson, 1978; Nelson & Gruendel, 1981). These early findings suggested to us an explanation for infantile amnesia, namely, that children do not preserve episodic memories, although they may remember bits of information from specific events in their schematic event memory. In early childhood, we believed, all information retained from experience is absorbed by the generic memory system. Recently, Gopnik and Graf (1988) and Perner (1991) have suggested similar "overwrite" mechanisms.

However, this hypothesis—that young children have generic memory only—has not stood up to empirical test. Subsequent research indicated that very young children do remember novel events, within limits, and sometimes quite readily report episodes that they find interesting (Hudson, 1986; Ratner, 1980). When asked about routine events, they simply give routine answers, but when asked about novel events, they are sometimes able to respond with details even when as young as 2½ years. More recent research has verified that children do have specific episodic memories and can remember them for extensive periods—sometimes as long as 2 years—prior to the age of the earliest autobiographical memories reported by adults (see Fivush & Hudson, 1990, for reviews). Why do these memories not persist into later childhood and adulthood?

Not only does this research invalidate the proposal that memory is at first completely generic, but it calls into question some other theoretical proposals as well. For example, there is nothing in this recent evidence to support the idea that young children's memories are especially threatening, either positively or negatively affect laden, as Freud's theory would suggest.

Schachtel (1947) and Neisser (1962) suggested that autobiographical memories are the outcome of a reconstructive process based on schemas or frames of reference, along the lines suggested by Bartlett (1932). Remembering, then, involves *reconstructing* past events using presently existing schemas, and the claim is that adult schemas are not "suitable receptacles" for early childhood experience; "adults cannot think like children" and thus cannot make use of whatever fragments of memories they may retain. In this view, socialization and the impact of language force a drastic change in the child's schemas at age 6.

The recent developmental data cast doubt on this proposal as well. Although very young children often need extensive probing to elicit their memories, suggesting that they may retain only random and unschematized fragments, there is also evidence of specific episodic memories that have the same form as we might find in older children. A fragment from a 2½-year-old girl talking to herself when alone in her room is illustrative:

> We *bought* a baby, cause, the well because, when she, well, we *thought* it was for Christmas, but *when* we went to the s-s-store we

didn't have our jacket on, but I saw some dolly, and I *yelled* at my mother and said I want one of those dolly. So after we were finished with the store, we went over to the dolly and she *bought* me one. So I have one.

In this example, Emily was recounting to herself what apparently was a significant episode in her life (she had not rehearsed this recent episode with her parents or others; see Nelson, 1989, for further details). This recount is well organized, with clear and concise temporal and causal sequencing. It—and others like it—does not suggest that the preschool child's schemas are dramatically different from those of the older child and adult.

Indeed, recent reports of young children's free recall of salient episodic memories (Engel, 1986; Hudson, 1990; Tessler, 1991) support the conclusion that the basic ways of structuring, representing, and interpreting reality are consistent from early childhood into adulthood. These studies indicate that young children, in both their script recounts and their specific memory recounts, typically tell their stories in a sequence that accurately reflects the sequence of the experience itself and that has the same boundaries that seem natural to adult listeners (Nelson, 1986).

Of course, there may be other differences between adult and child memories, including what is noticed and remembered of an event. The extensive cuing and probing often required to elicit details from a young child suggest that adult and child may have different memories of the same event. An analysis of the content of crib talk (talk to self alone before sleep) by the child Emily, recorded from 21 to 36 months, supports the suggestion that adult and child may focus on different events and different aspects of events. Emily's memories were concerned mostly with the quotidian, unremarkable, routines of her life. They were not concerned with the truly novel events of her life (from the adult's point of view), such as the birth of her baby brother or her airplane trips to visit relatives (Nelson, 1989). Thus, interest in—and therefore memory for—aspects of experience that seem unremarkable to adults, and indifference to what adults find interesting, as well as lack of facility with language and differences in the knowledge base, may account for why children sometimes seem to have organized their knowledge in a different form or have remembered only fragments from an episode that adults consider memorable.

In summary, recent research on episodic memory in early childhood indicates that children have at least some well-organized specific and general event memories, similar to those of adults; thus, the suggestion that a schematic reorganization may account for infantile amnesia is not supported. However, recent research that has shown that children learn to talk about their past experiences in specific ways does provide some clues as to what may be developing and how.

NARRATIVE CONSTRUCTION OF MEMORY

Over the past decade, a number of researchers have studied the ways in which parents engage in talking about the past with their very young children. These studies, some focused on the specific language forms used, others on the content of talk, and still others on narrative forms and differences in communicative styles, have revealed the active role that parents play in framing and guiding their children's formulation of "what happened."

Hudson (1990) concluded from a study of her own daughter's memory talk between 21 and 27 months that eventually Rachel began to "interpret the conversations not as a series of questions to be answered but as an *activity of remembering*" (p. 183). Hudson endorses a *social interaction model* of the development of autobiographical memory, a model that Pillemer and White (1989) and Fivush and Reese (1991) have also invoked. In this view, children gradually learn the forms of how to talk about memories with others, and thereby also how to formulate their own memories as narratives. The social interaction model differs from the schematic change model in that it claims that children learn *how* to formulate their memories and thus retain them in recoverable form.

Several studies at the City University of New York (and elsewhere) have found that parents not only engage in memory talk but also differ among themselves in the number of memory-relevant questions they ask, the kind of memory they attempt to elicit, and the ways in which they frame the talk, Engel (1986) studied mother–child conversations about past episodes with children from 18 months to 2 years and identified two styles of mother talk, one described as *elaborative,* the other more *pragmatic.* The elaborative mothers tended to talk about episodes in narrative terms of what happened when, where, and with whom. Pragmatic mothers referred to memory primarily in instrumental terms, such as "where did you put your mittens?" For pragmatic mothers, memory is useful for retrieving information relevant to ongoing activities. For elaborative mothers, memory provides the basis for storytelling, constructing narratives about what mother and child did together in the there and then. Engel found that children of elaborative mothers contributed more information to the memory talk at 2 years than children of pragmatic mothers.

Tessler (1986, 1991) studied the effect of adult talk during an experience on children's subsequent memory for the experience in two naturalistically designed experiments. She observed differences in mother's style of interaction similar to those identified by Engel, and found that children of narrative (or elaborative) mothers remembered more from a trip to a natural history museum a week later, when probed with a standard set of questions, than did children of pragmatic-type mothers. Most strikingly, none of the children remembered any of the objects that they viewed in the museum if they had not talked about them together with their mothers. In a second study, Tessler found that there was no difference between children experiencing different types of interaction with mothers during an event in recognizing elements of the experience, but there were differences in the amount of information recalled from the experience, with the children of narrative mothers recalling significantly more. Again, things that were not talked about were not recalled. These findings indicate not only that talk about the past is effective in aiding the child to establish a narrative memory about the past, but that talk during a present activity serves a similar purpose. In both cases, adults who present the activity in a narrative format, in contrast to a focus on identification and categorization, appear to be more effective in establishing and eliciting memories with their young children. Could this be important in establishing an autobiographical memory system? The social interaction hypothesis would certainly suggest so.

EFFECTS OF LANGUAGE ON MEMORY

What is it that talking about events—past and present—contributes to memory? The social interaction hypothesis emphasizes learning to structure memories in narrative form. Another suggestion might be the effects of rehearsal. However, there are two indications that rehearsal is not the major contributor. First, children are frequently unresponsive to maternal probing (Fivush & Fromhoff, 1988), suggesting that often the event being talked about was not what the child remembered but what the adult remembered. Second, available evidence suggests that events that do seem rehearsed are not subsequently remembered. For example, Emily sometimes recounted an event many times during an evening's session of crib talk but did not apparently remember the event months later (Nelson, 1989) or when probed years later (Nelson, unpublished data). Emily seemed to be attempting to understand the events she took part in, and to use them in her representation of her world, but not for holding on to memories of specific episodes. Longterm follow-up studies of memories rehearsed in early childhood are obviously important but are very rare. In one instance, similar to the findings from Emily, J. A. Hudson (personal communication, April 1992) has indicated that her daughter at 8 years remembers nothing of the events they rehearsed together when she was 2.

In a unique follow-up study, Hudson and Fivush (1991) reported on the long-term memories of sixth graders for a class trip they took as kindergartners. Some memories of the trip could be retrieved when the children were probed and viewed pictures taken at the time, but none of the children spontaneously recalled the event. These children would have been on the edge of the amnesia barrier at age 5 or 6 when they experienced the event; however, the trip may not have seemed personally significant, or may have been absorbed into the generic memory of class trips as years went by.

A possible function of memory talk distinct from rehearsal is that of reinstatement. Reinstatement is a concept that has been invoked in infant memory studies by Rovee-Collier and Hayne (1987). The idea is that a learned response (e.g., kicking to make a mobile move) that would otherwise be lost over time may be reinstated and thus preserved if a part of the context is re-presented within a given time period. A study by Fivush and Hamond (1989) with 2-year-old children found a similar effect; specific memories that tended to be lost over a period of weeks could be retained if they were reinstated by providing an experience similar to the original event at least once within a specific period of time—in this case, 2 weeks. In a memory test 3 months later, children whose memory had been reinstated remembered significantly more than children who had not had this experience. Equally important, the reinstated group remembered as much at 3 months as they had at 2 weeks; that is, there was no subsequent loss.

FUNCTIONS OF EARLY MEMORY

At this point, it may be possible to construct an integrated picture of the development of memory in early childhood and the establishment of an autobiographical memory system. The proposal rests on the assumption that the basic episodic memory system is part of a general mammalian learning-memory adaptive function for guiding present action and predicting future outcomes. The most useful memory for this function is generic memory for routines that fit recurrent situations, that is, a general event schema (or script) memory system. Memory for a specific episode presumably becomes part of that system when a new situation is encountered, and thus it becomes apparent that a new schema must be established. A new experience alerts the organism (person, animal) to set up a new schema, which at first may be equivalent to an episodic memory, but with further experience with events of the same kind comes to be more and more scriptlike. Indeed, research on novel and repeated events with preschool children found that this was precisely what happened (Hudson & Nelson, 1986). The more frequently an event (such as going to the beach or the zoo) had been experienced, the more scriptlike the child's account became. Events experienced five or more times tended to be formulated in general present-tense terms and to confuse slot-fillers (e.g., animals seen) for different episodes of the event.

This general scheme leaves us with a problem, however: How is the basic memory system to know whether a novel event is the first of a recurrent series of events that should therefore be remembered (i.e., schematized for future reference) or is an aberration that is of no functional significance? (Of course, if the aberration is life-threatening, it is likely to be entered into the general memory and knowledge system as important information for that reason alone.) The point is, the system cannot know on the basis of one encounter what significance the event might have with respect to future encounters.

The solution for a limited memory system is either to integrate the new information as part of the generic system or to keep the novel memory in a separate, temporary, episodic memory for a given amount of time to determine if it is the first of a series of recurrent events and thus should become part of the generic system. Then, if the event reoccurs, the memory may be transferred to the more permanent generic memory system. If a similar event does not recur during that test period, the episode is dropped from memory as of no adaptive significance.

Reinstatement would play an important part in this proposal. Reinstatement signals that the episode is not a one-time occurrence and thus the memory should be retained for future reference. Reinstatement would extend the amount of time that a memory is held in the episodic system, as found by Rovee-Collier and Hayne (1987) and by Fivush and Hamond (1989). In the basic functionally based system being described here, all memory is either generic knowledge—scriptlike—or temporarily episodic. The basic episodic system is claimed to be a *holding pattern,* not a permanent memory system. I suggest that this basic system characterizes human infants and young children and probably our close primate relatives as well, and perhaps other mammals.

Thus far then, the proposed system can account for the good generic event memory found in early childhood, as well as the availability of episodic memories that may persist for 6 months, or longer if there are conditions of reinstatement. But this proposal does not account for the establishment of an autobiographical memory system in which some specific memories may persist for a lifetime. This raises the question as to what function the autobiographical system serves beyond that of the long-lasting generic plus temporary episodic system just described.

The claim here is that the initial functional significance of autobiographical memory is that of sharing memory with other people, a function that language makes possible. Memories become valued in their own right—not because they predict the future and guide present action, but because they are shareable with others and thus serve a social solidarity function. I suggest that this is a universal human function, although one with variable, culturally specific rules. In this respect, it is analogous to human language itself, uniquely and universally human but culturally—and individually—variable. I suggest further that this social function of memory underlies all of our storytelling, history-making narrative activities, and ultimately all of our accumulated knowledge systems.

The research briefly reviewed here supports these speculations. Children learn to engage in talk about the past, guided at first by parents who construct a narrative around the bits and pieces contributed by the child (Eisenberg, 1985; Engel, 1986; Hudson, 1990). The timing of this learning (beginning at about $2\frac{1}{2}$ years and continuing through the preschool years) is consistent with the age at which autobiographical memory begins to emerge. The fact that the adult data suggest a two-phase process, as noted earlier, including the absence of memories in the first 2 to 3 years, followed by a sparse but increasing number of memories in the later preschool years, supports the supposition that the establishment of these memories is related to the experience of talking to other people about them. Also, the variability in age of onset of autobiographical memory (from 2 to 8 years or later) and its relation to language facility is consistent with the idea that children's experiences in sharing memories of the right kind and in the right form contribute to the establishment of autobiographical memory.

The social interaction hypothesis outlined earlier clearly fits these data well. This proposal is not simply one of cultural transmission or socialization, but rather a dialectical or Vygotskian model in which the child takes over the forms of adult thought through transactions with adults in activity contexts where those forms are employed—in this case, in the activities where memories are formed and shared. The problem that the child faces in taking on new forms and functions is to coordinate earlier memory functions with those that the adult displays incorporating adult values about what is important to remember, and the narrative formats for remembering, into his or her own existing functional system.

This, then, is the functional part of the proposal, suggesting that sharing memories with other people performs a significant social-cultural function, the acquisition of which means that the child can enter into the social and cultural history of the family and community. However, identifying this function, and some of the social-linguistic experiences that support it, does not in itself explain why personal autobiographical memories continue to persist. For that explanation we must call on an additional function of language.

Recall that reinstatement through action was shown to be effective in establishing the persistence of a memory of an event. I hypothesize that an important development takes place when the process of sharing memories with others through language becomes available as a means of reinstating memory. (See also Hudson, 1990.) Further, I suggest that language as a medium of reinstatement is not immediately available when mothers and their young children first begin to exchange talk about a remembered experience.

Rather, reinstatement through language requires a certain level of facility with language, and especially the ability to use the verbal representation of another person to set up a representation in one's own mental representation system, thus recognizing the verbal account as a reinstatement of one's prior experience. Using another person's verbal representation of an event as a partial reinstatement of one's own representation (memory) depends on the achievement of language as a representational system in its own right, and not only as either an organizing tool or a communication tool. This achievement is, I believe, a development of the late preschool years (Nelson, 1990).

In summary, the theoretical claim here is that language opens up possibilities for sharing and retaining memories in a culturally shared format for both personal and social functions. Sharing memory narratives is important to establish the new social function of autobiographical memory, as well as to make reinstatement through language possible. Following Vygotsky's (1978) model of internalization, after overt recounting becomes established, covert recounting or reexperiencing to oneself

may take place, and take on the function of reinstatement.

If memory is not talked about, to oneself or to others, should it persist? Once an autobiographical memory system is established, it takes on a personal as well as a social value in defining the self, as other scholars (e.g., Fivush, 1988) have recently argued. Thus, replaying a memory, even without talking about it specifically, overtly or covertly, might well reinstate it and cause it to persist, once the autobiographical system is set in motion.

A number of lines of research are suggested by this proposal. For example, a shift in linguistic communities should disrupt autobiographical memory, because of its dependence on linguistic representations, and there is some evidence from D. Pillemer's (personal communication, March 1990) work that such is the case. Also, the number of recounting opportunities should be important, and this might be variable across families and communities. Deaf children of hearing parents might be expected to be delayed in establishing early memories because of their lack of opportunities to engage in talk about past experiences. Cultural differences in discourse practices might be expected to lead to differences in autobiographical memory. Most of our present evidence is from middle-class Western children. In other cultures, for example, cultures that discourage children's participation in adult talk, such as the Mayan (Rogoff & Mistry, 1990), autobiographical memory might be a very late development, or take on different cultural forms such as shared myths.

To conclude, autobiographical memory may be thought of as a function that comes into play at a certain point in human childhood when the social conditions foster it and the child's representational system is accessible to the linguistic formulations presented by other people.

Finally, to return to Tulving's claim, memory, that is, autobiographical memory, "is a universally familiar experience. It is also a uniquely human one." It is uniquely human because of its dependence on linguistic representations of events, and because human language itself is uniquely human. As Miller (1990) has recently stressed, human language is unique in serving the dual function of mental representation and communication. These dual functions make possible its use in establishing the autobiographical memory system. And because such memory is at once both personal and social, it enables us not only to cherish our private memories, but also to share them with others, and to construct shared histories as well as imagined stories, in analogy with reconstructed true episodes. Once the child has begun to share memories with others, he or she is well on the way to sharing all of the accumulated cultural knowledge offered at home, in school, or in the larger world.

ACKNOWLEDGMENTS

This article is based on a paper presented at the International Conference on Memory at the University of Lancaster, July 1991. I thank Marcia Johnson, Robyn Fivush, and Judith Hudson for their helpful comments and ideas, and Minda Tessler for permitting me to report her unpublished research and for goading me over the years to reconsider the central importance of socially shared memory.

REFERENCES

Bartlett, F. C. (1932). *Remembering: A study in experimental and social psychology.* Cambridge, England: Cambridge University Press.

Dudycha, G. J., & Dudycha, M. M. (1941). Childhood memories: A review of the literature. *Psychological Bulletin, 38,* 668–182.

Eisenberg, A. R. (1985). Learning to describe past experiences in conversation. *Discourse Processes, 8,* 177–204.

Engel, S. (1986). *Learning to reminisce: A developmental study of how young children talk about the pass.* Unpublished doctoral dissertation, City University of New York Graduate Center, New York.

Fivush, R. (1988). The functions of event memory: Some comments on Nelson and Barsalou. In U. Neisser & E. Winograd (Eds.), *Remembering reconsidered: Ecological and traditional approaches to the study of memory* (pp. 277–282). New York: Cambridge University Press.

Fivush, R., & Fromhoff, F. A. (1988). Style and structure in mother–child conversations about the past. *Discourse Processes, 11,* 337–355.

Fivush, R., & Hamond, N. R. (1989). Time and again: Effects of repetition and retention interval on two year olds' event recall. *Journal of Experimental Child Psychology, 47,* 259–273.

Fivush, R. & Hudson, J. A. (Eds.). (1990). *Knowing and remembering in young children.* New York: Cambridge University Press.

Fivush, R., & Reese, E. (1991, July). *Parental styles for talking about the past.* Paper presented at the International Conference on Memory, Lancaster, England.

Freud, S. (1963). Three essays on the theory of sexuality. In J. Strachey (Ed.). *The standard edition of the complete works of Freud* (Vol. 7). London: Hogarth Press.

Gopnik, A., & Graf, P. (1988). Knowing how you know: Young children's ability to identify and remember the sources of their beliefs. *Child Development, 59,* 1366–1371.

Hudson, J. A. (1986). Memories are made of this: General event knowledge and the development of autobiogriphic memory. In K. Nelson. *Event knowledge: Structure and function in development* (pp. 97–118). Hillsdale, NJ: Erlbaum.

Hudson, J. A. (1990). The emergence of autobiographic memory in mother–child conversation. In R. Fivush & J. A. Hudson (Eds.), *Knowing and remembering in young children* (pp. 166–196). New York: Cambridge University Press.

Hudson, J. A. & Fivush, R. (1991). As time goes by: Sixth graders remember a kindergarten experience. *Applied Cognitive Psychology, 5,* 347–360.

Hudson, J. A., & Nelson, K. (1986). Repeated encounters of a similar kind: Effects of familiarity on children's autobiographical memory. *Cognitive Development, 1,* 253–271.

Miller, G. A. (1990). The place of language in a scientific psychology. *Psychological Science, 1,* 7–14.

Neisser. U. (1962). Cultural and cognitive discontinuity. In T. E. Gladwin & W. Sturtevant (Eds.). *Anthropology and human behavior* (pp. 54–71). Washington, DC: Anthropological Society of Washington.

Nelson, K. (1978). How young children represent knowledge of their world in and out of language. In R. S. Siegler (Ed.), *Children's thinking: What develops?* (pp. 225–273). Hillsdale, NJ: Erlbaum.

Nelson, K. (1986). *Event knowledge: Structure and function in development.* Hillsdale, NJ: Erlbaum.

Nelson, K. (Ed.). *(1989). Narratives from the crib.* Cambridge, MA: Harvard University Press.

Nelson, K. (1990). Event knowledge and the development of language functions. In J. Miller (Ed.), *Research on child language disorders* (pp. 125–141). New York: Little, Brown & Co.

Nelson, K., & Gruendel, J. (1981). Generalized event representations: Basic building blocks of cognitive development. In M. Lamb & A. Brown (Eds.), *Advances in developmental psychology* (Vol. 1, pp. 131–158). Hillsdale, NJ: Erlbaum.

Perner, J. (1991). *Understanding the representational mind.* Cambridge, MA: MIT Press.

Pillemer, D. B., & White, S. H. (1989). Childhood events recalled by children and adults. In H. W. Reese (Ed.), *Advances in child development and behavior* (Vol. 21, pp. 297–340). New York: Academic Press.

Ratner, H. H. (1980). The role of social context in memory development. In M. Perlmutter (Ed.), *Children's memory: New directions for the child development* (Vol. 10, pp. 49–68). San Francisco: Jossey-Bass.

Rogoff, B., & Mistry, J. (1990). The social and functional context of children's remembering. In R. Fivush and J. A. Hudson (Eds.), *Knowing and remembering in young children* (pp. 197–223). New York: Cambridge University Press.

Rovee-Collier, C., & Hayne, H. (1987). Reactivation of infant memory: Implications for cognitive development. In H. W. Reese (Ed.), *Advances in child development and behavior* (Vol. 20, pp. 185–283). New York: Academic Press.

Schachtel, E. (1947) On memory and childhood amnesia. *Psychiatry, 10,* 1–26.

Schacter, D. L. (1992). Understanding implicit memory, *American Psychologist, 47,* 559–569.

Schank, R. C., & Abelson, R. P. (1977). *Scripts, plans, goals, and understanding.* Hillsdale, NJ: Erlbaum.

Sheingold, K., & Tenney, Y. J. (1982). Memory for a salient childhood event. In U. Neisser (Ed.), *Memory observed* (pp. 201–212). San Francisco: W. H. Freeman.

Squire, L. R. (1992). Memory and the hippocampus. A synthesis from findings with rats, monkeys, and humans. *Psychological Review, 99,* 195–231.

Tessler, M. (1986). *Mother–child talk in a museum: The socialization of a memory.* Unpublished manuscript. City University of New York Graduate Center, New York.

Tessler, M. (1991). *Making memories together: The influence of mother–child joint encoding on the development of autobiographical memory style.* Unpublished doctoral dissertation. City University of New York Graduate Center, New York.

Tulving, E. (1983). *Elements of episodic memory.* New York: Oxford University Press.

Tulving, E. (1984). Precis of *Elements of episodic memory* with open peer commentary, *Behavioral Brain Sciences, 7,* 223–268.

Usher, J. A., & Neisser, U. (1991). *Childhood amnesia in the recall of four target events* (Emory Cognition Project Report No. 20). Atlanta: Emory University, Department of Psychology.

Vygotsky, L. S. (1978). *Mind in society: The development of higher psychological processes.* Cambridge, MA: Harvard University Press.

Wetzler, S. E., & Sweeney, J. A. (1986). Childhood amnesia: An empirical demonstration. In D. C. Rubin (Ed.), *Autobiographical memory* (pp. 191–201). New York: Cambridge University Press.

12

Elizabeth F. Loftus

When a Lie Becomes Memory's Truth

What happens when people witness an event, say, a crime or accident, and are later exposed to new information about that event? Two decades of research have been devoted to the influence of new information on the recollections of such witnesses. An all-too-common finding is that after receipt of new information that is misleading in some way, people make errors when they report what they saw. New, postevent information often becomes incorporated into a recollection, supplementing or altering it, sometimes in dramatic ways. New information invades us, like a Trojan horse, precisely because we do not detect its influence. Understanding how we become tricked by revised data about a witnessed event is a central goal of this research.

Current research showing how memory can become skewed when people assimilate new data utilizes a simple paradigm. Participants first witness a complex event, such as a simulated violent crime or automobile accident. Subsequently, half the participants receive new, misleading information about the event. The other half do not get any misinformation. Finally, all participants attempt to recall the original event. In a typical example of a study using this paradigm, participants saw a simulated traffic accident. They then received written information about the accident, but some people were misled about what they saw. A stop sign, for instance, was referred to as a yield sign. When asked whether they originally saw a stop or a yield sign, participants given the phony information tended to adopt it as their memory; they said they saw a yield sign.[1] In these and many other experiments, people who had not received the phony information had much more accurate memories. In some experiments, the deficits in memory performance following receipt of misinformation have been dramatic, with performance differences as large as 30% or 40%.

This degree of distorted reporting has been found in scores of studies, involving a wide variety of materials. People have recalled seeing nonexistent items, such as broken glass, tape recorders, and even something as large and conspicuous as a barn (in a bucolic scene that contained no buildings at all), and have recalled incorrect traits for items they did see, such that a clean-shaven man developed a mustache, straight hair became curly, a stop sign became a yield sign, and a hammer became a screwdriver. In short, misleading postevent information can alter a person's recollection in a powerful, even predictable, manner.

The change in report arising after receipt of misinformation is often referred to as the *misinformation effect*.[2] Four questions about the misinformation effect have occupied the attention of researchers:

1. When are people particularly susceptible to the damaging influence on recollection of misleading information, and when are people particularly resistant?
2. What groups of people are particularly prone to having their recollections be modified, and what groups are resistant?
3. Does misinformation actually impair a person's ability to remember details of an event? Put another way, what happens to the original memory after exposure to misinformation?
4. Do people genuinely believe in the misinformation?

WHEN ARE PEOPLE SUSCEPTIBLE TO MISINFORMATION?

A growing body of studies reveals the conditions that make people particularly susceptible to the influence of misinformation. For example, people are particularly prone to having their memories modified when the passage of time allows the original memory to fade. Put another way, with a long interval between the event and the misinformation, the injection of misinformation becomes relatively easy. In its weakened condition, memory—like the disease-ridden body—becomes especially vulnerable to repeated assaults on its very essence. This finding leads us to a principle, the *discrepancy detection principle,* for determining when changes in recollection will occur:

> Recollections are more likely to change if a person does not immediately detect discrepancies between postevent information and memory for the original event.

Other lines of research fit well with the discrepancy detection principle. For example, if people are exposed to misinformation that is subtle, they are more likely to be influenced than if the misinformation is not subtle. Consider the simple interrogative sentence "Was the mustache worn by the tall intruder light or dark brown?" This sentence not so subtly suggests the existence of a mustache. By comparison, "Did the intruder who was tall and had a mustache say anything to the professor?" is more subtle in its suggestion of the mustache, having embedded this idea in a relative clause. People are more likely to falsely claim that they saw a mustache when exposed to the more subtle version.

Another line of research that fits well with the discrepancy detection principle involves explicit warnings. If people are warned prior to a postevent narrative that the narrative may be misleading, they are better able to resist its influence than if they are not warned. In these various lines of research, the subject's detection of discrepancies between the original memory and the postevent passage (or failure to detect discrepancies) appears to be crucial. With a long interval between event and misinformation, and with misinformation that is subtly embedded, the ability of subjects to detect a discrepancy is minimized. In contrast, when subjects are warned about the likelihood of incorrect information, they scrutinize the postevent information, and the likelihood of detection of a discrepancy is enhanced. It is also true that people are particularly susceptible if they can be induced to repeat the misinformation as fact.

WHO IS SUSCEPTIBLE TO MISINFORMATION?

The majority of the studies of the misinformation effect have been conducted with college students, and few individual difference variables have emerged. Where group differences do emerge is in misinformation studies using children as subjects. It is common (although not universal) to find that young children are especially susceptible to these manipulations.[3]

The largest study of individual differences was recently conducted with nearly 2,000 people who were attending a science museum in San Francisco.[4] The experiment was one of the interactive exhibits at the museum, which means that subjects provided data for the experiment while learning form the exhibit. All subjects watched a short film clip and later answered a series of questions about it. Some subjects were exposed to misleading questions but others were not, so that the impact of misinformation could be assessed. The most important demographic variable was the age of the subject, which varied between 5 and 75. Memory performance rose as a function of age up to the 20s, leveled off, and then fell sharply for subjects over 65. Moreover, the youngest and the oldest groups showed large misinformation effects. Put another way, the very young and the elderly were significantly more accurate when not misinformed than when misinformed, a result that is consistent with other age effects in the literature on episodic memory. The article describing the study also reviews relevant literature on individual differences in susceptibility to misinformation.[4]

WHAT HAPPENS TO THE ORIGINAL MEMORY?

An important issue that has been debated is whether misinformation actually impairs a person's ability to remember details of an event. Put another way, are memory traces altered by postevent misinformation? There are several ways in which misinformation could impair memory. First, misinformation could cause *trace impairment;* that is, it could update or alter the previously formed memory. New information could combine with earlier traces to change the representation. Second, misinformation could cause *retrieval impairment;* that is, misinformation could make the original memory trace less accessible without altering it.[5] Impairment of some sort is implied by either the trace impairment or the retrieval impairment mechanism.

Some theorists have rejected the notion that misinformation impairs memory. McCloskey and Zaragoza[6] disagreed with the idea that the misinformation effect is due to recoding processes or updating of previously stored memories or arises because inhibition or suppression renders the older memory less accessible. McCloskey and Zaragoza argued instead that the misinformation does not affect memory at all, but merely influences the reports of subjects who have never encoded (or do not recall) the original event. Instead of guessing

blindly, these subjects use the misinformation to decide what to report as their memory. Misinformation effects could also be obtained if subjects remember both sources of information but select the misleading information because they conclude it must be correct.

Several lines of evidence support the notion that misinformation occasionally does impair the ability to remember original details, however. One kind of evidence involves studies using tests that do not permit the misinformation option. Say a subject originally saw a stop sign, but it was later referred to as a yield sign. Suppose we now give the subject a test that does not permit the selection of the yield sign (e.g., the choice is between a stop sign and a no-parking sign). If the misinformation has impaired memory for the stop sign, then the misinformed subjects would be less likely to remember the stop sign than the control subjects. If there has been no memory impairment due to misinformation, then misled subjects would be expected to be as accurate as control subjects on a test of this type. Although some studies do show equal performance, there are several published demonstrations of deficits in performance with this restrictive type of test. One study[3] presented preschool children with stories and found impairment following misinformation. Another study[7] presented adult subjects with visual scenes (e.g., nature scenes including ponds, flowers, mountains) and then provided similar visual scenes as postevent information. Subjects who received misinformation were less able than control subjects to discriminate the original scenes from novel distractors.

A second line of work supporting a memory impairment interpretation involves the use of a yes-no test.[8] Belli showed subjects a simulated crime via slides and then fed them some misinformation via postevent narrative that they read under a pretense. Finally, subjects were presented with a series of statements, each dealing with a critical item from the crime. Subjects said "yes" if they saw the item in the slides and "no" otherwise. Compared with memories for control items, there was a large reduction in accurate memory for the items about which subjects had received misinformation. The large reduction was not offset by the small improvement in memory for completely novel items.

Other lines of research that are consistent with memory impairment involve implicit memory testing[9] and logic-of-opposition procedures (described in the next section). Although any of these findings might be readily explained by alternative interpretations, taken together, these studies support the idea that misinformation can impair a subject's ability to remember original details.

DO PEOPLE GENUINELY BELIEVE IN THE MISINFORMATION?

One reason to think that subjects truly believe in their misinformation memories is that they often express these memories with a great deal of confidence. But how can we rule out the possibility that subjects report misinformation memories to appear observant or prove they are "good" subjects?

The logic-of-opposition paradigm, developed by Jacoby and applied to the study of misleading suggestions by Lindsay,[10] provides an ideal means of assessing what subjects really believe. By instructing his subjects that any information contained in the postevent narrative was wrong and should not be reported on the test, Lindsay set the tendency to report suggested details in opposition to the ability to remember the details from the postevent narrative. Put another way, he tried to offset subjects' tendency to want to report an item they remembered reading by harshly warning the subjects not to report anything they remembered from the reading. If subjects continued to base their test responses on suggested items, despite explicit instructions against doing so, Lindsay could conclude that misled subjects truly believe that they saw the suggested details at the time of the initial event. In fact, Lindsay obtained such results. He first showed an event via slides, and later provided misinformation about some items. Misinformed subjects who saw the slides and read the narrative in the same session claimed to have seen the misinformation in the slides 27% of the time, compared with 9% for subjects who had not been misinformed.

CONCLUDING REMARKS

Misleading information can turn a lie into memory's truth. It can cause people to believe that they saw things that never really existed, or that they saw things differently from the way things actually were. It can make people confident about these false memories and also, apparently, impair earlier recollections. Once adopted, the newly created memories can be believed as strongly as genuine memories. If handled skillfully, the power of misinformation is so enormous and sufficiently controllable that a colleague and I recently postulated a not-too-distant "brave new world" in which misinformation researchers would be able to proclaim: " 'Give us a dozen healthy memories . . . and our own specified world to handle them in. And we'll guarantee to take any one at random and train it to become any type of memory that we might select . . . regardless of its origin or the brain that holds it.' "[11] The implications of these findings for the legal field, for advertising, for political persuasion, and for clinical settings are far-reaching.

The author's research described in this article was supported by grants from the National Institute of Mental Health, the National Science Foundation, and the U.S. Department of Transportation.

NOTES

1. E. F. Loftus, *Eyewitness Testimony* (Harvard University Press, Cambridge, MA, 1979).

2. E. F. Loftus and H. G. Hoffman, Misinformation and memory: The creation of new memories, *Journal of Experimental Psychology: General, 118,* 100–104 (1989).

3. S. J. Ceci, D. F. Ross, and M. P. Toglia, Suggestibility of children's memory: Psycholegal implications. *Journal of Experimental Psychology: General, 116,* 38–49 (1987).

4. E. F. Loftus, B. Levidow, and S. Duensing, Who remembers best? Individual differences in memory for events that occurred in science museum, *Applied Cognitive Psychology, 6,* 93–107 (1992).

5. J. Morton, R. H. Hammersley, and D. A. Bekerian, Headed records: A model for memory and its failures, *Cognition, 20,* 1–23 (1985).

6. M. McCloskey and M. Zaragoza, Misleading postevent information and memory for events: Arguments and evidence against memory impairment hypotheses, *Journal of Experimental Psychology: General, 114,* 1–16 (1985).

7. C. C. Chandler, How memory for an event is influenced by related events: Interference in modified recognition tests, *Journal of Experimental Psychology: Learning, Memory, and Cognition, 17,* 115–125 (1991).

8. R. F. Belli, Influences of misleading postevent information: Misinformation interference and acceptance, *Journal of Experimental Psychology: General, 118,* 72–85 (1989).

9. E. F. Loftus, Made in memory, in *The Psychology of Learning and Motivation,* Vol. 27, G. Bower, Ed. (Academic Press, Orlando, FL, 1991).

10. D. S. Lindsay, Misleading suggestions can impair eyewitnesses' ability to remember event details, *Journal of Experimental Psychology: Learning, Memory, and Cognition, 16,* 1077–1083 (1990).

11. Loftus and Hoffman, note 3, p. 103.

13

Des Power

Very Long-Term Retention of a First Language Without Rehearsal

SUMMARY

A case study is presented of an American sign language-using deaf woman whose life circumstances were such that she had no opportunities to use her sign language over nearly 40 years, but whose recall of its lexicon and syntax were almost unimpaired when she resumed its use after that period. Implications for the role of memory in first language learning are compared with results for second languages, and the role of rehearsal and interference in remembering over very long periods is considered.

In recent years memory researchers have turned increasingly to the study of memory in 'natural' or 'everyday' contexts to supplement traditional restricted and artificial laboratory studies (Neisser, 1982; Bahrick and Karis, 1982; Harris and Morris, 1984; Johnston and Hasher, 1987). Recent studies have been not only of remembering and forgetting in natural contexts, but have also been of these phenomena over very long periods (up to, for example, 50 years in Bahrick's (1984a) study of recall of Spanish learned in school and university and Bahrick and Hall's (1991) of school and university mathematics).

Bahrick (1984a) has shown that recall of Spanish learned in school and university as a second language shows a discontinuous function; with different degrees of forgetting taking place in the first 3–6 years after learning, and then virtually no loss of material for at least 25 years thereafter. He therefore posits the existence of a 'permastore' in memory, particularly for 'semantic' materials (of which language is a prime example). The extent to which learned material is entered into permastore varies with level of original training, the original grade achieved, and the nature of the response required at later testing, with those trained to higher levels and obtaining higher original grades retaining more. Bahrick was also able to show that amount of retention was unrelated to opportunities for rehearsal and he concluded that 'very significant portions of semantic knowledge remain perfectly accessible for decades without being used at all' (p. 23). He is also of the view that interference from later learning is not particularly important in determining level of forgetting, but that the major factor at work is the level of original learning, particularly for semantic material which typically is learned over long periods so that 'extension of the re-exposure to information over long time periods produces a cumulative effect which eventually gives permanence to responses and renders them invulnerable to most interference effects' (p. 25).

Neisser (1984) objected to the static nature of Bahrick's permastore ('a mental fallout shelter', p. 33) and suggested instead that, given the nature of memory as 'reconstruction' of past learning (Bartlett, 1932), the very long-term recall found by Bahrick is better interpreted in structural terms. 'Information that is tied into an extensive and redundant cognitive structure ... is sharply resistant to forgetting; isolated pieces of information ... are much more vulnerable (Neisser, 1984: 34). Neisser suggests that the concept of permastore is thus not necessary, 'because subjects can generate the right responses from a cognitive structure that they still possess' (p. 34). Bahrick (1984b) defended himself against Neisser's comments, but did not advance an argument that could well reconcile the two positions, namely that what is entered into permastore is just that 'extensive and redundant cognitive structure' of Neisser's that generates the correct responses, even half a lifetime later.

Language is regarded as the nonpareil 'semantic' phenomenon, and is undoubtedly also highly structured at several levels, including the semantic, phonological, syntactic and lexical. Bahrick's (1984a) research was on the retention of a second language learned in school, undoubtedly a semantic phenomenon; however, study of the retention of a first language would also be of great interest as the conditions under which a first language is learned even better fit the criteria for entry of learned material to permastore.

Semantic memory content is typically acquired over extended time periods during which exposure or active rehearsal is limited to relatively short periods spaced at intervals ... The ... results of successive relearning sessions ... [which] may continue over a period of several months or years ... produces a cumulative effect which eventually gives permanence to responses and renders them invulnerable to most interference effects (Bahrick, 1984a: 25).

This description fits very well the process of first language acquisition as described, for example, by Brown (1973, 1977) and the writers in Snow and Ferguson (1977). It is therefore of interest to examine the 'forgetting' of a first language and natural environments in which this can occur are available. The major one is 'isolation' (to a greater or lesser extent) from other speakers of one's language by migration to another language and culture or by solitariness for long periods (for example, like Robinson Crusoe).

Crusoe's experiences were, of course, mostly from Defoe's imagination, so his report of Crusoe speaking English to Friday (and indeed teaching it to him) after 25 years' solitude and then speaking Portuguese, Latin and Spanish to the mariner he rescued from the cannibals after not using these languages for 27 years, must be treated with some caution (even though it does accord with Bahrick's data!). However, there are real accounts of the return to language use of marooned individuals, several of which are reported by Shinagel (1975) in his critical edition of *Robinson Crusoe*. Indeed, Shinagel quotes the reports of the people who rescued Alexander Selkirk (the 'original' of Crusoe; Selkirk was, in fact, only marooned for 4 years and 4 months) that, 'At his first coming on board us, he had so much forgot his language for want of use, that we would scarce understand him, for he seemed to speak his words by halves' (Shinagel, 1975: 252). Other observers, however, who were present, do not mention any differences in Selkirk's speech, though one does comment on the strangeness of his 'Aspect and Gesture' (Shinagel, 1975: 256). While of interest, this does not constitute much evidence.

Perhaps more reliable are the accounts of captives of the American Indians held in Indian cultures for long periods. In the 111 volumes of *The Garland library of narratives of North American Indian captives* (Washburn, 1977) are many such reports. This evidence, however, is equivocal, perhaps because retention of language was rarely a major theme of these reports. In some cases, language seems to have been retained, as in the case of a Spaniard, Artiz, who, after 11 years with the Indians of Florida (1528–39), is reported to have saved himself from being killed by fellow Spaniards by saying in Spanish, 'I am a Christian—do not kill me, nor these poor men who have given me my life' (Drake, 1851: 18). On the other hand, there are reports of English being completely lost in environments where there were no English speakers, particularly (as would be predicted) when the captive was taken as a child.

An account in Australia of William Buckley ('the Wild White Man') who spent 32 years with Victorian Aborigines, indicates that he had entirely lost his English, and even 2 years after his return to speaking English, it was reported that 'his knowledge of his mother tongue [is] very imperfect' (Sayers, 1967:xi).

Interestingly, in view of the data on retention of American sign language to be reported below, there is evidence that there is some loss of one sign language when a signer moves to another country. Battison and Jordan (1976) report that when deaf signers move,

> by all reports they forget their own signs as rapidly as they acquire the sign language of their new country... [and] when one of these expatriates has visitors from his native country [they]... report that they have difficulty readjusting to their first language and that it takes several days of interaction with their guests before they begin to feel normal. They also report that they can understand but not express themselves very well in these situations (p. 62).

The issue of the relationship between the conditions of learning and the 'maintenance conditions' over a period before remembering is required is of great interest to educators. If the major influence on remembering occurs at the learning point rather than during the maintenance interval, then an understanding of the kind of point of learning conditions that maximize remembering will be of great value in planning teaching/learning sequences (Power, 1981; Bahrick and Hall, 1991).

The relationship between point of learning and maintenance conditions is complex as far as language learning is concerned and it is very difficult to find 'real-world' experimental conditions that will allow for these variables to be manipulated. As noted above, language learning takes place over a long series of repeated encounters, and it is virtually impossible to eliminate maintenance rehearsal of one's own language. As Bahrick and Karis (1982) point out,

> if we continue to live in a given environment, we are constantly re-exposed to the sources of much of our common knowledge. For example, we continue to hear, read, speak, and write our language. As a result, there is little likelihood of forgetting the relevant information (p. 431).

A singular opportunity to consider these relationships has occurred with the presence of a subject who did not use her first language for over 20 years, but who, because of a very isolated life, did not have an interfering second language. The subject in question is a user of a strikingly different language, American Sign Language (ASL).

RETENTION OF SIGN LANGUAGE: A CASE STUDY

Sign Language

Evidence has accumulated over the past 20 years or so that the various sign languages of deaf communities are indeed 'natural languages', and that they share most of the linguistic and psychological characteristics of spoken languages, the obvious major difference being the use of the manual/visual rather than the oral/aural modalities (Klima and Bellugi, 1979; Wilbur; Power, 1988).

A major characteristic which sign languages share with spoken languages is the presence of a syntactic structure which enables the generation of sentences. Syntax in the sign language concerned in this study (ASL) uses word order, body movement and 'tension differences' in such movement, and 'face work', consisting of raising eyebrows or squeezing them together, moving and tilting the head, etc., all of which have syntactic/semantic significance; for example, one difference between *Yes—No* and *Wh*-questions is that in the former the eyebrows are raised, but in the latter brought together (Humphries, Padden, and O'Rourke, 1980). ASL is also distinguished by its incorporation of classifier handshapes into nominals, a distinctive use of position in space gestures for the pronominal system, a unique agent suffix and gestural systems for pluralization and tense marking.

A few deaf children learn sign languages in the normal way from deaf parents, but the majority of sign language users learn it from age-peers and older pupils in school, especially in state residential schools (Higgins and Nash, 1987). Most countries have a stable sign-using deaf community which is increasingly being recognized to have most of the characteristics of a non-English speaking cultural minority; for example a shared history, sense of unique identity, possession of a common language, etc. (Power, 1988).

A Case Study

A unique case of linguistic isolation has become available with the discovery of a now 72-year-old signing deaf woman who was completely isolated from other deaf signers for 20 years and had only very few contacts for another 17 years, yet who retained the syntactic structure of her ASL intact over that period and even lost very few lexical items during that same period.

Maggie Lee Sayre was born in Kentucky in 1920. She is profoundly deaf (apparently congenitally, probably hereditarily, although there is no known record of deafness in either of her parents' families). She had one sibling, a sister a year older who was also deaf and who died aged 16. Maggie attended the Kentucky State residential school for the deaf from ages 7 to 19. The school at that time used signed English or pidgin sign English in school, and the pupils used ASL outside the classroom. Signed English uses a mixture of signs from sign language and finger-spelling (where there is a gesture for each letter of the alphabet) to reproduce English syntax on the hands. Pidgin sign English, like all pidgins, uses characteristics of both English and the local sign language (Wilbur, 1979). Maggie did well at school and left in 1940 fluent in ASL, with a large lexicon of signs. She also had good written English, but virtually no intelligible speech.

After leaving school she returned to live with her parents, who were subsistence commercial fishers in the 'Shantyboat Culture' on the Tennessee River and its tributaries. Maggie's parents could not sign; her father was functionally illiterate and her mother nearly so. They were also both reported to be very reticent individuals, and communication among the three was minimal, being carried largely by the nonverbal routine of the 'daily round' and a few non-syntactic 'home signs' (gestures which had achieved standard but non-conventional communicative meaning within the family). Maggie was able to understand very little English via lip-reading.

Because the nature of the Sayres' lives isolated them from frequent contacts with hearing/speaking people, and there were no other signing people around, Maggie had no opportunity for using her ASL and virtually no interference from English on it. In this way of life, Maggie had no contact with ASL in the 21 years 1940–60. From 1960 to 1977 she had a few visits (not more than an afternoon annually) from a deaf signing couple who came to know of her. Her mother died in 1970 and her father in 1977. From about 1977 Maggie had regular contact with the deaf couple who had previously visited her and other deaf and hearing signers at a church she began to attend. She and her father had set up the boat on land near a town in Tennessee in 1971.

Maggie today is alert and well, and living in a nursing home in Tennessee.

In 1982 Maggie came to the attention of some Tennessee folklorists who were studying the Shantyboat Culture (Rankin, 1990). During all her nearly 50 years on the river she had been taking photographs of their unique way of life, and had amassed an extensive photographic record of it. Selected photographs were used in a Smithsonian exhibition of her work in 1986 and at Gallaudet University in 1987. An account of her life appeared in the Summer, 1987 issue of *Gallaudet Today* (Smith, 1987).

PROCEDURE

In July 1987 the writer, accompanied by a registered and experienced ASL interpreter, visited Maggie in Tennessee and conducted several interviews with her and other deaf and hearing signers who knew her well; one of the deaf signers being one of the couple who had begun occasionally visiting her in 1960. The interpreter, together with a deaf lady who had known Maggie at school, made a follow-up visit to elucidate several points in August, 1990.

RESULTS

Evidence from people who knew the school Maggie attended indicated that Maggie was a fluent user of ASL when she left in 1940, with a large and idiomatic lexicon and full command of the elements of ASL syntax described above. The evidence of another fluent deaf user of ASL about her ability in 1960 is that, despite her lack of opportunity to use it, her syntax was intact and there was little, if any, loss of items from her lexicon. This deaf informant (and Maggie herself) thought she had forgotten some signs, but not many. In fact, Maggie's memory for lexical items is remarkable, because upon her visit to Gallaudet in 1987, a hearing ASL interpreter whose parents had attended the Kentucky school remarked that Maggie was still using 'old-fashioned' signs that she had not seen for years; these signs, because of Maggie's isolation, not having undergone the changes over time that constant use had done to them with signers in the deaf community.

As far as her syntax was concerned, my informant was of the view that in 1960 it was intact. She was closely questioned in both visits about the above-mentioned 'facework' and 'holding' of the question sign, head and shoulder movement, etc. These were all reported to be standard, with apparently no elements missing. Maggie's use of tense marking by time words was normal, as was the use of repetition for pluralization. She still incorporated her classifiers into nominals in the standard way and used the space and movement parameters of the pronoun system in a completely standard way as she would have done 20 years earlier.

Although my informant was recalling the status of Maggie's signing of some years before, it is likely that her recall (and that of my other informants for a later period) was accurate, because deaf sign users are very sensitive to the 'correctness' of ASL use and have many opportunities to contrast its correct use with competing systems such as pidgin sign English and signed English. They are therefore very aware of departures from standard use, and my informant would have recognized any such departures in Maggie's use and reported them.

This report of Maggie's signing is confirmed at the point of her re-entry to a signing community both by the above informant and two other deaf informants who have also known her since 1977. Despite only very infrequent use of signs 1960–77 (less than once a year for an afternoon), Maggie's lexicon and syntax were to all intents and purposes what they had been when she left school 37 years previously: a singular example of the retention of a semantic system over a very long period with no loss of structure and very little even of lexical items.

It is of note that there were few opportunities for 'interference effects' to be at work over those years. Maggie is effectively dependent on sign language as she has no useful speech and her reticent parents spoke little to her, and both she and those who know her report that she obtains almost nothing useful from lip-reading. Her parents were functionally illiterate, so they did not write English to her. It was reported that the family received rare letters from relatives, and very occasionally magazines or newspapers. Maggie's written English is good and she read these infrequent materials and wrote very occasional replies. In general, then, the chance of interference from English upon her sign language was very slight.

For the reasons outlined Maggie had very few occasions for overt rehearsal of her signing; she certainly had no opportunities for rehearsing it by using it with other fluent signers. It is therefore of interest whether Maggie much covertly rehearsed her ASL by 'talking to herself' on her hands, daydreaming in signs or using signs in her sleeping dreams. On both occasions when she was interviewed Maggie said she didn't ever talk to herself in sign, and my informants said they had rarely seen her sign to herself and then only isolated words, not discourse. Maggie also said she doesn't 'dream', either in the day or while asleep, and while it is impossible to evaluate this claim, it does not seem likely that such events could have been a major source of rehearsal of her ASL. What 'rehearsal' may have been going on at deeper non-conscious thinking levels, and the form which it might take, remains an intriguing and unanswerable question.

DISCUSSION

The evidence from this case study confirms for a first language Bahrick's (1984a) finding for a second language learned in school that it is retained with virtually no overt rehearsal over very long periods, in this case almost 40 years; confirming his claim that 'very significant portions of semantic memory remain perfectly accessible for decades without being used at all' (1984: 23).

It is of interest that details of what was remembered do not agree at all points with Bahrick's results. He found, for example, that recall for grammar of Spanish was one of only two of his subscores which continually declined over the period examined, and 'shows no clear evidence of stabilizing during the retention interval' (p. 17). On the other hand, recall for vocabulary fell off relatively quickly at first, but then stabilized. The opposite seems to have occurred in this case: there was no apparent loss of syntactic structure (grammar) over a very long period, and what little forgetting did occur was of lexical items which were quickly recovered on return to a signing environment. We have noted that Battison and Jordan (1976) found that living in a different sign language environment interfered with the use of one's native sign language, and similar phenomena have been reported by migrants about their life in a non-native culture. It is tempting to hypothesize that the absence of an 'interfering grammar' in Maggie's case could be responsible for this phenomenon, and that the 'competing' grammatical structure of English or another sign language hastened the loss of the second language syntax in Bahrick's study. Lexical items may not be so readily entered into a structure, and therefore may more likely be forgotten because of the gradual weakening of associationistic bonds; down to a level highly correlated with level of original learning (which is higher in the case of a first language), and which wold account for the slighter loss of vocabulary in this case than with Bahrick's second language learners. Syntactic devices entered into a structure ('rule of grammar') may follow a less associationistic forgetting path, with whole 'chunks' of Spanish syntax lost because of interference from others in the competing English domain.

The present data also support Bahrick's finding that the amount of retained knowledge bears little relationship to rehearsal. Opportunities for overt or covert rehearsal for this subject were virtually non-existent over this very long period, but almost no forgetting occurred. It seems that material learned in the way that a first language is, in 'successive learning sessions... over a period' (Bahrick, 1984a: 25) is virtually permanent, and educators must seek methods for classroom learning that will as closely as possible replicate that process, especially for materials like language and living skills which are crucial to the personal and social development of the learner (see also Bahrick and Hall, 1991).

These results are also in accord with developing evidence in the literature; e.g. Conway, Cohen, and Stanhope (1991), in a study of the retention of a course in cognitive psychology, found that the pattern of forgetting or retention of such material supported the view that 'specific and detailed knowledge may be retained in memory over very long retention periods' and that 'knowledge was retrieved from memory, rather than reconstructed by schemata' (p. 409).

Hence, while Neisser (1984) is correct in stating that modern cognitive psychology prefers a 'memory as reconstruction' hypothesis over what he calls the 'reappearance' hypothesis, so that 're-membering is like problem-solving rather than like reproduction,' and that 'constructive recall is the rule, literal recall is the exception' (p. 33), there is evidence here that not all remembering need be reconstructive. It is difficult to see how the correct recall of syntactic structures of a language could in any sense be reconstructive, it can only be 'literal' in Neisser's sense. One may indeed 'reconstruct' the memory of a prior event in one's 'autobiography', and that reconstruction can be influenced by any number of factors both historical (in the personal sense) and contemporaneous, but one does not reconstruct a syntactic rule in this sense. Either one recalls it (or parts of it) or one does not. One cannot build into the 'recollection' of how to ask a question in Spanish or American Sign Language any plausible elements which either oneself or an observer can accept as 'correct' without the whole structure. Clearly, literal remembering is at work here, and needs to be included in any theory of memory.

ACKNOWLEDGEMENTS

This research was done while I was Visiting Distinguished International Scholar at the Gallaudet Research Institute, Gallaudet University, and I am grateful to the Institute for its support. The author thanks Jean Lindquist who acted as interpreter and advisor in contacts with Maggie Sayre, Harry Bahrick for his encouragement and helpful advice, and Gordon Elias for critical reading of an early version of the manuscript. Special thanks are due to Maggie Sayre, a truly remarkable deaf lady, for her patience in helping with our elucidation of her life.

REFERENCES

Bahrick, H. (1984a). Semantic memory content in permastore: fifty years of memory for Spanish learned in school. *Journal of Experimental Psychology: General,* 113, 1–29.

Bahrick, H. (1984b). Associations and organization in cognitive psychology: a reply to Neisser, *Journal of Experimental Psychology: General,* 113, 36–37.

Bahrick, H. and Hall, L. K. (1991). Lifetime maintenance of high school mathematics content. *Journal of Experimental Psychology: General,* 120, 20–33.

Bahrick, H. and Karis, D. (1982). Long-term ecological memory. In C. R. Puff (ed.), *Handbook of research methods in human memory and cognition* (pp. 427–465). New York: Academic Press.

Bartlett, F. C. (1932). *Remembering.* Cambridge: Cambridge University Press.

Battison, R. M. & Jordan, I. K. (1976). Communication with foreign signers: fact or fancy. *Sing Language Studies,* 15, 53–68.

Brown, R. (1973). *A first language: the early stages.* Cambridge, MA: Harvard University Press.

Brown, R. (1977). Introduction. In C. Snow and C. Ferguson (eds), *Talking to children: Language input and acquisition* (pp. 1–27). Cambridge: Cambridge University Press.

Conway, M. A., Cohen, G. and Stanhope, N. (1991). On the very long-term retention of knowledge acquired through formal education: twelve years of cognitive psychology. *Journal of Experimental Psychology: General,* 120, 395–409.

Drake, S. G. (1951). *Indian captives or life in the wigwam.* Auburn: Derby & Miller.

Harris, J. E. and Morris, P. E. (1984). *Everyday memory, actions and absentmindedness.* London: Academic Press.

Higgins, P. and Nash, J. (1987). *Understanding deafness socially.* Springfield, IL: C. C. Thomas.

Humphries, T., Padden, C. and O'Rourke, T. J. (1980). *A basic course in American sign language.* Silver Spring, MD: T. J. Publishers.

Johnson, M. K. and Hasher, L. (1987). Human learning and memory. In M. R. Rosenzweig and L. W. Porter (eds), *Annual review of psychology,* (vol. 38). pp. 631–668.

Klima, E. and Bellugi, U. (1979). *The signs of language.* Cambridge, MA: Harvard University Press.

Neisser, U. (1982). *Memory observed: Remembering in natural contexts.* San Francisco, CA: W. H. Freeman.

Neisser, U. (1984). Interpreting Harry Bahrick's discovery: what confers immunity against forgetting? *Journal of Experimental Psychology: General,* 113, 32–35.

Power, D. J. (1981). Principles of curriculum and methods development in special education. In W. Swann (ed.), *The practice of special education* (pp. 435–447). London: Blackwell.

Power, D. J. (1988). Vox silentii: Australian sign language and the deaf community. *Vox,* 1, 44–48.

Rankin, T. (1990). The photographs of Maggie Lee Sayre: A personal vision of houseboat life. In J. Hardin (ed.), *Folklife annual 90.* Washington, DC: Library of Congress, American Folklife Center.

Sayers, C. E. (ed.). (1967). *The life and adventures of William Buckley by John Morgan.* Melbourne: Heinemann. (1st edn, Hobart: Archibald MacDougall, 1852.)

Shinagel, M. (1975). *Daniel Defoe, Robinson Crusoe, an authoritative text: Backgrounds and sources, criticism.* New York: Norton.

Smith, D. (1987). Maggie Lee Sayre: Her photographs capture a vanished way of life. *Gallaudet Today,* 17(4), 2–9.

Snow, C. and Ferguson, C. (eds). (1977). *Talking to children: language input and acquisition.* Cambridge: Cambridge University Press.

Washburn, W. E. (ed.). (1977). *The Garland library of narratives of North American Indian captives.* New York: Garland (111 vols.).

Wilbur, R. B. (1979). *American sign language and sign systems.* Baltimore, MD: University Park Press.

14

K. Anders Ericsson, William G. Chase, and Steve Faloon

Acquisition of a Memory Skill

Abstract: *After more than 230 hours of practice in the laboratory, a subject was able to increase his memory span from 7 to 79 digits. His performance on other memory tests with digits equaled that of memory experts with lifelong training. With an appropriate mnemonic system, there is seemingly no limit to memory performance with practice.*

One of the most fundamental and stable properties of the human memory system is the limited capacity of short-term memory. This limit places severe constraints on the human ability to process information and solve problems (1). On the other hand, this limit (about seven unrelated items) stands in apparent contrast to documented feats of memory experts (2). Whether these memory skills are the result of extensive practice or of exceptional ability has often been disputed. The goal of this research is to analyze how a memory skill is acquired.

An undergraduate (S.F.) with average memory abilities and average intelligence for a college student engaged in the memory span task for about 1 hour a day, 3 to 5 days a week, for more than 1½ years. S.F. was read random digits at the rate of one digit per second; he then recalled the sequence. If the sequence was reported correctly, the next sequence was increased by one digit; otherwise it was decreased by one digit. Immediately after half the trials (randomly selected), S.F. provided verbal reports of his thoughts during the trial. At the end of each session, he also recalled as much of the material from the session as he could. On some days, experiments were substituted for the regular sessions.

During the course of 20 months of practice (more than 230 hours of laboratory testing), S.F.'s digit span steadily improved from 7 to almost 80 digits (Figure 1). Furthermore, his ability to remember digits after the session also improved. In the beginning, he could recall virtually nothing after an hour's session; after 20 months of practice, he could recall more than 80 percent of the digits presented to him. On one occasion (after 4 months of practice), we tested S.F.'s memory after the session with a recognition test (because recognition is a much more sensitive measure of retention

Figure 1

Average Digit Span for S.F. as a Function of Practice

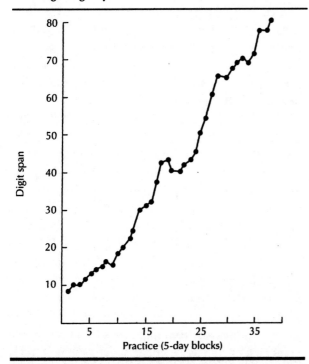

Digit span is defined as the length of the sequence that is correct 50 percent of the time; under the procedure followed, it is equivalent to average sequence length. Each day represents about 1 hour's practice and ranges from 55 trials per day in the beginning to 3 trials per day for the longest sequences. The 38 blocks of practice shown here represent about 190 hours of practice; interspersed among these practice sessions are approximately 40 hours of experimental sessions (not shown).

than recall is); he not only recognized perfectly 3- and 4-digit sequences from the same day, but also recognized sequences from earlier in the week.

With only a few hundred hours of practice, S.F. would be classified as a beginner at most skills. However, in his field of expertise, memory for random digits, he compares favorably with the best-known mnemonists, such as Luria's S. and Hunt and Love's V.P. (2). For example, after about 6 months of practice, we set S.F. the task of recalling a matrix of 50 digits because data on this task are available for both S. and V.P. S.F.'s study times and recall times were at least as good as those of the lifetime memory experts.

The key to understanding this skill comes from analyses of S.F.'s verbal reports and his performance on various experimental tests. We will first describe two essential components of this skill: (i) his mnemonic associations and (ii) his retrieval

structures. Then we will address the question of whether or not S.F. was able to increase his short-term memory capacity.

The most essential part of S.F.'s skill is his mnemonic associations, which he described in great detail in his verbal reports. The principle of a mnemonic is to associate unknown material with something familiar; the advantage is that it relieves the burden on short-term memory because recall can be achieved through a single association with an already-existing code in long-term memory. What S.F. did was to categorize 3- and 4-digit groups as running times for various races (3). For example, 3492 was recoded as "3 minutes and 49 point 2 seconds, near world-record mile time" (4). During the first 4 months, S.F. gradually constructed an elaborate set of mnemonic associations based initially on running times and then supplemented with ages (893 was "89 point 3, very old man") and dates (1944 was "near the end of World War II") for those sequences that could not be categorized as times. Running times (62 percent) and ages (25 percent) account for almost 90 percent of S.F.'s mnemonic associations.

There are several lines of evidence concerning the mnemonic associations. On the basis of S.F.'s verbal reports, we were able to simulate his mnemonic associations, that is, to abstract a set of rules that categorizes a sequence of digits as 3- and 4-digit running times. When we compared the simulation to the verbal reports, between 85 and 95 percent of the time the computer categorized the digit sequences as S.F. did. By means of the simulation, we were also able to determine which sequences of digits would be categorized as running times and which would not. On the basis of this analysis, we presented S.F. with sequences that could not be associated with running time categories. (This was before S.F. started to use ages to supplement his running times, after about 2 months of practice.) When S.F. was faced with these uncodable sequences, his performance dropped almost to his beginning level. In another experimental session we did the opposite: We presented him with sequences that could all be coded in terms of running times. His performance jumped by 22 percent (from an average of 16 to an average of 19.5 digits).

The mechanism whereby S.F. recodes single digits into 3- and 4-digit units is not sufficient to account for his performance. If S.F. originally had a digit span of 7 digits, and he then learned to re-code digits into 4-digit groups, how could he re-member the order of more than seven groups of digits—that is, more than 28 digits? The answer to this question comes from an analysis of his retrieval structures.

Like most people, S.F. initially tried to hold everything in a rehearsal buffer, which stored ma-terial in a phonetic code. When he first used his mnemonic associations (session 5), he demon-strated the first rudimentary use of a retrieval struc-ture. He recoded the first 6 digits as two running times, if possible, and he held the last 4 to 6 digits in his rehearsal buffer. He then tried to recall the two running times in order while rehearsing the last few digits. This strategy worked well, and he gradu-ally perfected it over the course of the first 30 ses-sions until he could recall as many as 18 digits by recoding three groups of 4 digits each as running times and holding the last 6 digits in his rehearsal buffer. At this point, he began to experience real difficulty in keeping the order straight for more than three or four running times (Figure 1, blocks 8 and 9).

The next important advance came when S.F. in-troduced organization into his retrieval structure by segmenting his groups into subgroups: He used two 4-digit groups followed by two 3-digit groups and the rehearsal group. From this point, S.F. improved his performance rapidly by increasing the number of groups within each subgroup, until he began to experience the same difficulty as before. The sec-ond plateau in his performance curve (around block 21 in Figure 1) is associated with difficulty in re-membering the order of more than four groups within a supergroup. Introducing another level of organization by subdividing these supergroups al-lowed S.F.'s performance to improve rapidly so that he now averages almost 80 digits. His current re-trieval organization can be described as a hierarchy with three levels, and his retrieval structure for 80 digits can be illustrated in the following way, with spaces corresponding to levels in the hierarchy:

444 444   333 333   444 333   444 5

Besides the verbal descriptions, there is a great deal of additional evidence that S.F. uses hierarchi-cal retrieval structures. Probably the most straight-forward evidence comes from his speech patterns during recall, which almost invariably follow the same pattern. Digit groups are recalled rapidly at a normal rate of speech (about 3 digits per second) with pauses between groups (about 2 seconds be-tween groups, on average, with longer pauses when he has difficulty remembering). At the end of a su-pergroup, however, there is a falling intonation, generally followed by a longer pause (5).

In several experiments, we verified that groups are retrieved through the hierarchical structure rather than through direct associations between groups. In one experiment, instead of asking for recall after presenting the digits, we presented S.F. with a 3- or 4-digit group and asked him to name the group that preceded it or followed it in the se-quence. He required more than twice as long, on the average, if the preceding or following group crossed a supergroup boundary (10.0 seconds) than if it did not (4.4 seconds). In another experiment, after an hour's session, we presented S.F. with 3- and 4-digit groups from that session and asked him to recall as much as he could about each group. He invariably recalled the mnemonic associations he had generated, and he often recalled a great deal about the location of the group within the hierarchy, but he was virtually never able to recall the pre-ceding or following group.

After all this practice, can we conclude that S.F. increased his short-term memory capacity? There are several reasons to think not. (i) The size of S.F.'s groups were almost always 3 and 4 digits, and he never generated a mnemonic association for more than 5 digits (6). (ii) He almost never allowed his rehearsal group to exceed 6 digits. (iii) He generally used three groups in his supergroups and, after some initial difficulty with five groups, never al-lowed more than four groups in a supergroup. (iv) In one experimental session, S.F. was switched from digits to letters of the alphabet after 3 months of practice and exhibited no transfer: His memory span dropped back to about six consonants.

These data suggest that the reliable working ca-pacity of short-term memory is about three or four units, as Broadbent has recently argued (7), and that it is not possible to increase the capacity of short-term memory with extended practice. Rather, in-creases in memory span are due to the use of mnemonic associations in long-term memory. With an appropriate mnemonic system and retrieval structure, there is seemingly no limit to improvement in memory skill with practice.

REFERENCES AND NOTES

1. G. A. Miller, *Psychol. Rev.* **63,** 81 (1956); A. Newell and H. A. Simon, *Human Problem Solving* (Prentice-Hall, Englewood Cliffs, N.J., 1972).

2. A. R. Luria has documented the case history of one exceptional person, S., who seemed to remember large amounts of trivial information for years by means of visual imagery [*The Mind of a Mnemonist* (Avon, New York, 1968)], and E. Hunt and T. Love have described another exceptional person, V.P., who could remember large amounts of material by means of elaborate linguistic associations in several languages [in A. W. Melton and E. Martin, Eds., *Coding Processes in Human Memory* (Winston, Washington, D.C., 1972), p. 237].

3. S.F. is a good long-distance runner who competes in races throughout the eastern United States. He classifies running times into at least 11 major categories, from half-mile to marathon, with several subcategories within each.

4. The category label by itself was not sufficient to retrieve the exact digits presented. A complete understanding of the precision of mnemonic associations will require an answer to the more general question of how meaningful associations work.

5. Pauses, intonation, and stress patterns are well-known indicators of linguistic structures [M. A. K. Halliday, *Intonation and Grammar in British English* (Mouton, The Hague, 1967); K. Pike, *The Intonation of American English* (Univ. of Michigan Press, Ann Arbor, 1945)]. In one memory span study, we compared the grouping patterns indicated by the prosodic features in recall with the grouping patterns reported by S.F. in his verbal protocols, and agreement was virtually perfect.

6. The mnemonic associations of lightning calculators appear to be limited to 3 or 4 digits [G. E. Müller, *Z. Psychol. Ergänzungsband* 5 (1911)].

7. D. A. Broadbent, in *Studies in Long Term Memory,* A. Kennedy and A. Wilkes, Eds. (Wiley, New York, 1975), p. 3.

8. Supported by contract N00014-78-C-0215 from the Advanced Research Projects Agency and by grant MH-07722 from the National Institute of Mental Health. We thank J. R. Anderson, M. T. H. Chi, W. Jones, M. W. Schustack, and H. A. Simon for their valuable comments.

On the Internet...

Mind/Brain Resources

This site lists resources that researchers in cognitive science or philosophy of mind might find useful, including artificial intelligence and cognitive science links.
http://mind.phil.vt.edu/www/mind.html

Cognitive Neuroscience Lab Et Cetera

This Stanford University site contains links to neuroscience/psychology resources, general science resources, and Internet resources.
http://www-psych.stanford.edu:80/~gabra/GabMisc.html

The Wonders of the Mind

At this site, 12 world-class psychologists, neuroscientists, roboticists, and psychiatrists give you the big picture on how the mind works in the brain.
http://www.hypermind.com/mind/MIND.HTM

Part❖4

Varieties of Thought

Judy S. DeLoache

❖

Alan M. Leslie

❖

Jeffery Scott Mio and Arthur C. Graesser

❖

Mary Kister Kaiser, John Jonides, and Joanne Alexander

❖

Richard E. Mayer, Anne Bovenmyer Lewis, and Mary Hegarty

❖

Jean Bédard and Michelene T. H. Chi

❖

Robert S. Lockhart

Varieties of Thought

There are two themes in this section. The first is that thought is built on symbols and therefore involves layers of information. Layering, in turn, results in indirectness between an original input and its ultimate meaning. The theme of indirectness appears in the articles on the development of young children's ability to symbolize, on autistic individuals' inability to appreciate the existence of other minds, and on the use of metaphor to convey humor.

The second theme centers on the way in which people interpret and solve problems. Clearly, how people look at a problem will have a big effect on whether and how they solve it. This theme is found in the articles on people's attempts to solve puzzles about mathematics and about the physical world, on the nature of expertise, and on why knowledge may or may not be applied in novel situations. While exploring both themes, you will encounter a variety of subject populations, methodologies, and hypotheses about the way people reason and solve problems.

THIS SECTION BEGINS WITH CHILDREN'S ATTEMPTS TO GO BEYOND THE INFORMATION given through the construction of analogies. This topic is introduced by Judy S. DeLoache in "Early Understanding and Use of Symbols: The Model Model." As she points out, early childhood development entails entry into a world that places a premium on symbolization, or how to understand one thing in terms of something else. Children learn about pictures, numbers, writing systems, maps, and the like, all of which involve the use of one thing to represent another.

DeLoache explores symbolization through experiments that assess young children's ability to transfer their knowledge from a scale model to the real thing. For example, the model might be a tiny replica of an ordinary room. While the child is watching, the experimenter places an object somewhere in the model room, such as under a pillow. The child is then asked to find the larger analogue object in the ordinary room. DeLoache consistently finds that 3-year-old children do very well on this task, whereas 2½-year-old children do poorly. DeLoache states that the younger children behave as if they "do not realize . . . that they have any way of knowing—other than by guessing—where it [the object] is."

DeLoache explains these and other results in terms of a theory that includes various independent variables, intervening variables, and resulting behaviors. The independent variables include the salience of the source symbol, the similarity (iconicity) between the symbol and its referent, and instructions given to the child about the symbol and its referent. If, for example, the symbol (e.g., the scale model) is overly salient for children, then their ability to map the symbol to the referent may be hindered. De-

134

Loache focuses on the intervening variables of "dual representation," defined as the ability to conceive of a symbol as both a concrete reality and as referring to something else, and on "representational insight," which is an awareness of representational abilities, amounting to an awareness that symbol and referent are related. DeLoache closes with some cautionary statements about young children's ability to symbolize—for example, in cases of courtroom testimony involving the use of anatomically correct dolls.

ALMOST ALL CHILDREN DEVELOP SYMBOLIC ABILITIES; otherwise, thought and most social interaction would be impossible. But what happens when some symbolic abilities are missing? For example, when other people speak and interact with us, we assume that they have minds and that their minds can do things, such as desire, refer, pretend, and imagine. This is the starting point for the article by Alan M. Leslie, "Pretense, Autism, and the Theory-of-Mind Module." Leslie states that childhood autism is characterized by " a relatively focused and specific impairment in the capacity to reason about mental states." That is, autistic children do not develop a *theory of mind*, sometimes called "mindblindness."

How can we determine that someone lacks a theory of mind? One way involves false beliefs. To illustrate, Leslie describes the Sally-and-Anne procedure that is used with children: Sally puts candy in a cupboard and leaves the room, but Anne comes into the room and moves the candy to a drawer. When Sally comes back for her candy, where will she think it is? Research indicates that 4-year-old children will attribute a false belief to Sally—she will look in the cupboard—but younger children will predict that Sally will think the candy is in the drawer. However, if the location of the desired object (e.g., candy) is not known and must be guessed, then, regardless of what the child guesses, the experimenter can say that Sally thinks it is somewhere else. In this circumstance, the younger children can better predict where Sally will look.

Leslie draws the connection between false belief and childhood autism by looking at shared pretense. If a child treats a toy block as a truck, then in order for the pretense to be shared, another person must also understand that the block symbolizes a truck. Leslie states that even 2-year-olds have this sort of ability, and so he credits them with being

able to represent a "propositional attitude," the idea that someone else can pretend, desire, and believe something. However, children with autism do not possess this attitude; thus, their performance on the Sally-and-Anne task is much poorer than that of other children. Other research reported by Leslie suggests that this mindblindness may be unique to mental states. That is, autistic children often perform well on tasks that involve attribution of causation in the physical-causal realm. However, these children do not seem to take other people's knowledge into account—knowledge that might cause them to say or do something. If this mindblindness hypothesis is on the right track, it might help explain autistic children's deficits in social competence, communication, and imagination.

IT SHOULD NOT BE SURPRISING NOW TO FIND THAT AUTIStic individuals also have difficulty understanding figurative language. Saying something like "her eyes popped out" to such individuals may well lead them to look on the floor for those eyes. Autistic persons are notoriously literal. Metaphors (e.g., "She's a peach"), proverbs (e.g., "People who live in glass houses shouldn't throw stones"), and other forms of figurative language pose a puzzle for them.

In general, figurative language is an indirect way of saying something, in that someone says something but means something else. The something else is what someone has in mind and is really trying to convey, and so the autistic individual's problem with figurative language is understandable. And figurative language requires a symbolic attitude in which a literal meaning (what is actually said) serves to promote a different, figurative meaning (what is actually meant). In the case of metaphor, if someone says, "Sharon is a peach," that person does not mean that Sharon is literally a peach but that she has some qualities that we might attribute to peaches, such as producing a pleasant impression. The standard terminology for describing metaphor is that there is a topic (Sharon), a vehicle (peach) that comments on the topic, and a ground, which is whatever concepts might be sensibly attributed to the topic by the vehicle. The topic and vehicle are said to be in tension because the topic is being placed in an unusual category.

This discussion sets up the next article, "Humor, Language, and Metaphor," by Jeffery Scott

Mio and Arthur C. Graesser. These authors note that metaphors are often used for humorous effect, and since humor can lighten otherwise serious situations, such metaphors can be therapeutic. Moreover, while humor often builds on incongruity, metaphor likewise requires an incongruity between literal and figurative meaning. Mio and Graesser report an experiment that further links humor and metaphor via a test of the disparagement, or superiority, theory of humor. This theory holds that humor arises from disparaging remarks about something with the intent of feeling somehow superior to it. In the experiment, participants were asked to judge which of a pair of metaphors was funnier, where one metaphor was disparaging (e.g., "My surgeon is a butcher among doctors") and the other was uplifting (e.g., "My butcher is a surgeon among meat cutters"). Disparaging metaphors were judged funnier overall, although men overwhelmingly preferred the disparaging metaphors while only about half of the women did, theoretically because men are more aggressive than women.

THE SECOND THEME OF PART 4 INVOLVES THE UNDERstanding of problems and why problems are either solved or not solved as a result. In "Intuitive Reasoning About Abstract and Familiar Physics Problems," Mary Kister Kaiser, John Jonides, and Joanne Alexander examine people's reasoning about curvilinear motion in both familiar and abstract domains. They suggest that people solve problems in familiar domains by drawing on specific experiences in those domains rather than by reasoning via underlying physical laws. Evidence for this was obtained in two experiments. In the first, Kaiser et al. asked subjects to indicate the path that a ball would take when exiting a spiral tube that was elevated at one end (the abstract problem). Subjects were also asked to indicate the path that a stream of water would take if a hose was connected to the tube (the familiar problem). Kaiser et al. found that subjects produced far more correct predictions for the water problem than the ball problem, regardless of the order in which they attempted to solve the problems. Moreover, successfully completing the water problem first did not enhance performance on the ball problem. A second experiment introduced another familiar problem—a bullet exiting a curved rifle barrel—in order to more fully explore the effects of solution transfer

to the abstract problem. Again, subjects gave more accurate predictions for the familiar problems, and there was no transfer from the familiar to the abstract. This supports Kaiser et al.'s conclusion that familiar problems are so realistic that they are solved by drawing on concrete experiences. More reflective reasoning is merely a default stategy.

THE PROBLEMS THAT ARISE FROM FAULTY PROBLEM REPresentation are seen more clearly in Richard E. Mayer, Anne Bovenmyer Lewis, and Mary Hegarty's article "Mathematical Misunderstandings: Qualitative Reasoning About Quantitative Problems." In it, Mayer et al. describe various studies of high school and college students' performance on mathematical story problems. These problems contained verbal statements about the quantitative relationship between two variables. For example: "Discount Heaven sells a box of three long-sleeve shirts for $50. This is $5 less per box than the price at Shirt Palace. How much do 3 boxes of shirts cost at Shirt Palace?"

Mayer et al. assert that mathematical problem solving involves both qualitative and quantitative reasoning. The former refers to the translation of each verbal statement into a mental representation; integration of these representations into a larger, coherent *mental model*; and a plan to break the problem into manageable parts. Quantitative reasoning refers to actual mathematical computations. For the shirt problem above, a common error is to do the reverse of what is required—students subtract $5 from $50, get $45, and then multiply by 3 to get $135. Of course, the problem is properly represented as $50 + $5 = $55, which, when multiplied by 3, gives $165. Apparently, students are led astray by the key word *less* and end up misrepresenting the problem. This suggests that we should concentrate on the processes involved in solving math problems, since they ultimately determine what the computations yield as the product.

Mayer et al. present numerous findings that confirm their thesis. Examination of student solution protocols revealed that inconsistent problems, which contain a statement that arouses the wrong mathematical operator (e.g., "less" in the shirt example), produce many more reversal errors than do consistent problems. Furthermore, measurement of the students' eye fixations indicated that better problem solvers fixated longer on inconsistent than consistent problems (i.e., poorer performers were less sensitive to the linguistics of the problems). Mayer et al. also demonstrate that if less accurate problem solvers are instructed about the types of statements that occur in problems and how to diagram them, then performance can be enhanced.

IF ABSTRACT CURVILINEAR MOTION PROBLEMS ARE DIFFIcult for neophytes, and if students have problems constructing the proper representations for math problems, what of experts? In an article entitled "Expertise," Jean Bédard and Michelene T. H. Chi look at the question of how to distinguish experts from nonexperts. They discuss expertise in terms of several categories. First, experts obviously know a lot more about a domain than nonexperts, and this knowledge is highly structured, cross-linked, and built on the use of underlying principles. Thus, experts can overcome the salience and press of literal, concrete information and categorize events in terms of these principles. Second, experts can better select out and infer the relevant features of a problem. Third, experts are more likely to use forward reasoning strategies by starting with the givens and moving toward the goal, rather than using backward reasoning by starting with the goal. Fourth, experts make better decisions than nonexperts, although real-world problems do not always yield this result. Finally, Bédard and Chi note that expertise is limited to a particular domain—physics experts may not be able to fix a car, for example—and experts can be disadvantaged if they apply their expertise inflexibly.

IF EXPERTISE IS LIMITED TO A PARTICULAR DOMAIN, IS this true of all aspects of thinking? Surely we are capable of using what we know in more than a narrow context. This is not an idle question, as everyday life presents quite different situations—some new—that call for flexibility of thought. Moreover, there is currently a great debate about the value of critical thinking in our educational system. Ideally, students should learn more than facts, as important as these are. They must also learn to analyze, infer from, synthesize, and skeptically consider the facts.

Robert S. Lockhart addresses this issue in "The Role of Conceptual Access in the Transfer of Thinking Skills." Essentially, Lockhart claims that while the generalizability of knowledge depends on having learned some general rules, it "hinges much more critically on factors that control access to those rules." Lockhart starts with this example: Someone throws a rock into a lake, but it rests on the lake surface for several weeks before it sinks to the bottom. This scenario may sound puzzling until we realize that it may be winter and the rock landed on ice. This scenario may arouse what Lockhart calls content- or thematically based memories, such as of other cases of rocks being thrown into lakes. However, the content of the story does not easily allow *abductive remembering*, which involves the arousal of concepts (e.g., winter, ice) that will allow an understanding of the target scenario.

Lockhart then provides cases in which abductive remembering has broken down, owing to an inflexibly applied prior learning or to learning that does not incorporate memory cues that will arouse the appropriate explanatory concepts. Lockhart contends that people do not readily transfer analogies to new realms, practice using a concept does not necessarily mean that the concept will be used in a new problem, and even telling people what constitutes the basis for a concept does not guarantee that the concept will be learned any faster. In each of these cases, Lockhart argues that effective cuing of the appropriate explanatory structures may be lacking. An important notion here is *encoding specificity*, which means that remembering will occur to the extent that the cues that are present during remembering are similar to the cues that were present during original learning. But Lockhart warns that the mere concreteness and presumed familiarity of an input do not guarantee effective problem solving. An input must somehow activate relevant background knowledge.

Lockhart concludes that "the skill of effective remembering and of effective thinking both hinge on the cognitive system being trained in such a way that the data of experience are able rapidly to trigger the cognitive structures appropriate to the task at hand." This long statement basically says that just knowing something is not enough for the knowledge to transfer. A physician may know a lot about disease, for example, but effective use of this knowledge depends on being able to "read" the cues that a patient presents so that the appropriate inferences can be made.

15

Judy S. DeLoache

Early Understanding and Use of Symbols: The Model Model

The hallmark of human cognition is symbolization: There is nothing that so clearly distinguishes us from other creatures as our creative and flexible use of symbols. Cultural creations such as writing systems, number systems, maps, and models—to name a few—have enabled human knowledge and reasoning to transcend time and space.

My working definition of an external, artifactual symbol is that it is any entity that someone intends to stand for something other than itself. Note that this definition is agnostic about the nature of symbols; virtually anything can be a symbol, so long as some person intends that it be responded to not as itself, but in terms of what it represents. Adults are so experienced and skilled with symbols and symbolic reasoning that they simply assume that many of the novel entities they encounter will have symbolic import. They appreciate that such entities should be responded to as representations of something other than themselves—and readily do so. My research reveals that children only gradually adopt this assumption. Despite the centrality of symbolization in human cognition and communication, young children are very conservative when it comes to detecting and reasoning about symbol–referent relations.

SYMBOLIC DEVELOPMENT

Becoming a proficient symbolizer is a universal developmental task; full participation in any culture requires mastery of a variety of culturally relevant symbols and symbol systems, in addition to language and symbolic gestures. Children make substantial progress in this task in the first years of life. In Western societies, older infants and toddlers start to learn about pictures and pictorial conventions. Most preschool children are taught the alphabet and numbers, many begin to read, and some even start to do simple

From Judy S. DeLoache, "Early Understanding and Use of Symbols: The Model Model," *Current Directions in Psychological Science,* vol. 4, no. 4 (August 1995). Copyright © 1995 by The American Psychological Society. Reprinted by permission of Cambridge University Press.

arithmetic. Many young children also encounter a variety of less common symbols, such as maps, models, musical notation, and computer icons.

Symbolic development plays a prominent role in many theories of child development, and there is a substantial body of empirical work focusing on the development of particular symbol systems, especially drawing, reading, and mathematical competence.[1] My research addresses the general issue of how very young children first gain insight into novel symbol–referent relations and how they begin to use symbols as a source of information and a basis for reasoning.

In our research, my colleagues and I present young children with a particular symbolic representation—most often a scale model, picture, or map—that provides information needed to solve a problem. Use of the symbol requires (a) some awareness of the relation between symbol and referent, (b) mapping the corresponding elements from one to the other, and (c) drawing an inference about one based on knowledge of the other. The majority of our research has involved scale models. Because young children rarely, if ever, encounter real models in which the symbol maps onto a specific referent, we can use scale models to examine how children first gain insight into and exploit a novel type of symbol–referent relation.

In our standard task, the model stands for a room (either a full-sized real room or a tentlike, portable room). The model is very realistic, and there is a high degree of physical similarity between the objects—items of furniture—within the model and the room. The model is in the same spatial orientation as the room, but it is located outside the room, so the child can see only one space at a time. The model–room relation is explicitly and elaborately described and demonstrated for the 2- to 3-year-old children. In the task, children watch as a miniature toy is hidden behind or under a miniature item of furniture in the model, and they are told that a larger version of the toy is hidden with the corresponding piece of furniture in the room. ("Watch! I'm hiding Little Snoopy here. I'm going to hide Big Snoopy in the same place in his big room.") If the children appreciate the relation between the two spaces, then their knowledge of the location of the miniature toy in the model can be used to figure out where to search for the larger toy in the room, and vice versa. (It does not matter whether subjects see the hiding event in the model or the room. For convenience, I refer to the situation in which the hiding event occurs in the model.)

In numerous studies, 36-month-old children have typically succeeded in this task (> 75% error-less retrievals), but 30-month-olds have usually performed very poorly (< 20% correct).[2-5] Failure in the task is not due to memory or motivational factors: Virtually all children can retrieve the toy they actually observe being hidden in the model. Nevertheless, the younger children fail to relate their knowledge of the model to the room. These children understand that there is a toy hidden in the room, and they readily search for it. What they do not realize is that they have any way of knowing—other than by guessing—where it is.

A MODEL OF SYMBOL UNDERSTANDING AND USE

Research conducted with this and related tasks has led to the development of a heuristic, conceptual model of young children's understanding and use of symbols (see Fig. 1). (To avoid confusion, henceforth, I use the term Model, with a capital *M*, to refer to the conceptual model.) Although this Model is intended to apply to symbol use more broadly, in this review, I use our work with scale models to illustrate the Model's features. The Model incorporates several factors we have discovered to be important in young children's symbol use (left side of Fig. 1), including characteristics of the symbol itself (salience), the symbol–referent relationship (iconicity), the symbol user (experience), and the social context (instruction). As is apparent from the figure, these factors interact in complex ways to determine performance.

The end point of the Model is the behavior of using a symbol as a source of information (right side of Fig. 1), which always requires mapping between symbol and referent. Numerals must be mapped onto the appropriate quantities; the individual elements on a road map must be mapped onto the corresponding roads and cities in the real world. In the model task, the individual object—items of furniture—within the model must be mapped onto the corresponding objects in the room. The relation between the hidden toy and its hiding place must also be mapped from one space to the other.

Figure 1

A Heuristic Model of Children's Understanding and Use of Symbols.

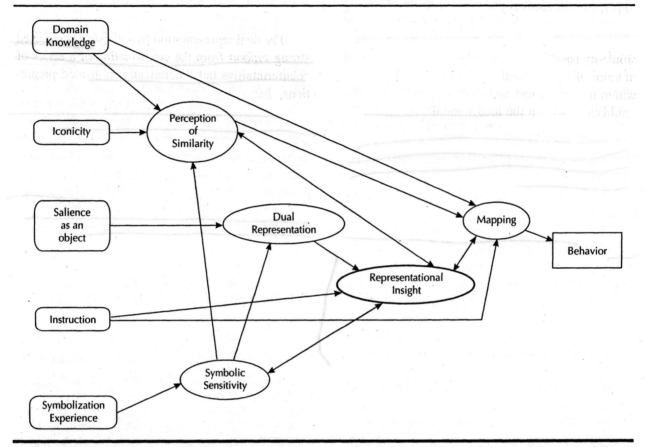

The five rounded rectangles on the left represent factors demonstrated or hypothesized to affect the behavior of interest (symbol use), represented by the rectangle on the far right. The ellipses represent intervening variables assumed to mediate between the manipulated factors and children's behavior. Because we have not yet investigated the role of domain knowledge, it is not discussed in this article.

Representational insight, the basic realization of the existence of a symbol–referent relation, is the pivotal element in the Model. The level of awareness of this relation varies from explicit metacognitive knowledge that a given symbol represents some particular referent, such as an adult might have, to an implicit and inexpressible sense of relatedness, such as a young child might have. My research has repeatedly shown both that representational insight can be surprisingly difficult for young children to achieve and that developmental progress can be very rapid.

It is obvious that the social context of symbol use is important. Much symbolic development involves direct instruction by other, more knowledgeable people. Children are explicitly taught the alphabet and numbers and how to read and do math. In the model task also, direct instructions play an important role: Three-year-olds succeed in the standard task in which the relation between the model and room is explicitly described and demonstrated for them, but they perform very poorly when less complete instructions are given.[6] Children have to be told about the model–room relation to achieve representational insight.

Another variable that plays an important role in young children's symbol use has to do with the symbol–referent relation. Iconicity refers to physical similarity between symbol and referent. Many symbol–referent relations are purely arbitrary and conventional, with no physical resemblance at all— for example, numerals, letters, and musical notation. Some are partially iconic: Maps preserve spatial relations, but have few other iconic features. other symbols are highly iconic: A color photograph, for example, closely resembles its referent. Except for size, the scale model used in my research looks very much like the room it represents.

Iconicity generally 'facilitates symbol use: The more a symbol resembles its referent, the easier it is to perceive the similarity between the two. Perception of similarity facilitates both the achievement of representational insight and mapping. In the model task, similarity has been shown to be very important, both in terms of surface similarity of the individual objects within the two spaces and in terms of the overall resemblance between the model and the room. For example, 3-year-olds are highly successful if the furniture in the two spaces is highly similar, but they perform poorly if there is a low level of similarity. When object similarity is high and, in addition, model and room are similar in overall size, even 2½-year-olds succeed in the model task.[3]

Note that the Model specifies two-way influences between representational insight and perception of similarity. A child who realizes that a symbol and referent are related will presumably search for similarity between the elements within them, thus leading to improved mapping. For example, in the model task, a child who realizes that the model and room are related will actively look for similarities between the individual items within the spaces.

DUAL REPRESENTATION

Another important factor is the salience of the physical properties of the symbol. All symbols of the sort under consideration have both a concrete and an abstract nature. A consequence is that understanding and using them requires what I have termed dual representation—simultaneously representing both the concrete and the abstract nature of a symbol.[2] To the extent that one's attention is drawn to the physical properties of a symbol, it will be more difficult to appreciate its symbolic status. As Langer[7] said, a peach would be a poor symbol because "we are too much interested in peaches themselves."

To succeed in our task, the child must mentally represent the model both as a real, concrete object (or set of objects) and, at the same time, as an abstract symbol for something other than itself. The high salience of the model and young children's keen interest in it prevent them from representing it both ways. They pay attention to the model itself, encoding and remembering the location of the hiding

event in it, but that memory representation remains separate from their mental representation of the room. Hence, they fail to use their knowledge about the model to draw an inference about the room.

The dual representation hypothesis has received strong support from the confirmation of a series of counterintuitive but theoretically motivated predictions. First, I reasoned that because a picture is much less salient and interesting as an object than a model is, substituting a picture for the model should make our task easier (even though two-dimensional stimuli are generally less informative and effective than three-dimensional ones).[2] As predicted, 2½-year-old children succeeded when pictures, but not a model, were used to convey the location of a hidden toy.

Second, we attempted to decrease the physical salience of the model by placing it behind a window, thus preventing the children from touching it or interacting directly with it. We reasoned that denying children access to the model would decrease its salience as an object, hence making it easier for them to achieve dual representation. The predicted improvement in the performance of a group of 2½-year-olds occurred. In a third study in this series, we attempted instead to increase the salience of the model by letting children play with it for several minutes before testing them in the standard task. The idea was that playing with and manipulating the model would make it more salient as an object and hence would make dual representation more difficult to achieve. The predicted poor performance by a group of 3-year-olds occurred.[8]

We recently conducted an even more stringent test of dual representation by attempting to eliminate the need for it.[9] In this study, we endeavored to convince a group of 2½-year-old children that a "shrinking machine" could shrink a troll doll and a room. Our reasoning was that if children believe the machine has shrunk the room (into the scale model of that room), then there is no representational relation between model and room. Instead, there is an identity relation: The model *is* the room. Hence, the task of retrieving the hidden toy is simply a memory problem. Therefore, we predicted that 2½-year-olds, who typically fail the standard model task, would succeed in the nonsymbolic shrinking-room task.

In the orientation, the child was introduced to "Terry the Troll" (a troll doll with vivid fuschia hair) and was shown "Terry's room" (a tent-like, portable room that had been used in many previous model studies). Then the shrinking machine (an oscilloscope with flashing green lights) was introduced, and its remarkable powers were demonstrated. The troll was placed in front of the machine, which was "switched on," and the child and experimenter waited in the adjoining area, listening to computer-generated "sounds the shrinking machine makes while it's working." The child then returned to discover a miniature troll in place of the original one. The child was then shown that the machine could also make the troll "get big again." A similar demonstration showed the power of the machine to shrink and enlarge Terry's room. The sight of the model in place of the room was very dramatic.

The child then watched as the experimenter hid the larger doll somewhere in the portable room. After waiting while the machine shrank the room, the child was asked to find the hidden toy. The miniature troll was, of course, hidden in the model in the place corresponding to where the child had seen the larger troll being hidden in the room. Thus, just as in the model task, the child had to use his or her knowledge of where the toy was hidden in one space to know where to search in the other. However, in this task, the child thought the room and model were the same thing. (Both the experimenters and the parents were convinced that all but one child firmly believed the shrinking-room scenario. Remember, most of these children also believe in the tooth fairy.)

As predicted, performance was significantly better in this nonsymbolic task than in a control task involving the usual symbolic relation between the model and the room. This superior performance occurred even though the shrinking-room scenario was more complicated and the delay between the hiding event and the child's retrieval was much longer than in the standard model task. This study thus provides very strong support for the dual representation hypothesis.

DEVELOPMENTAL PROGRESS

A key element in the Model is the individual's symbolization experience, which includes both general experience with a variety of symbols and specific experience with any particular type of symbol.

Such experiences lead to the development of symbolic sensitivity, a general expectation or readiness to look for and detect the presence of symbolic relations between entities. Experience responding to a given entity as a representation of something other than itself increases an individual's readiness to respond to other entities in an abstract rather than concrete mode.[10] Symbolic experience, and hence symbolic sensitivity, increases naturally with age.

Evidence for the role of symbolic sensitivity comes from a series of standard transfer-of-training studies. Children who are first tested in a relatively easy task (i.e., one in which they detect the symbol–referent relation and perform well) subsequently perform better in a more difficult task (i.e., one their age group normally fails). Thus, $2\frac{1}{2}$ year-olds who did well using a picture to guide their search for a hidden toy subsequently succeeded using a model as a source of information. Children of the same age also showed significant transfer from a relatively easy model task to the standard task. Three-year-old children who first participated in the task with high similarity between model and room were subsequently successful with low similarity between the two spaces, although 3-year-olds typically fail the latter task.[5]

Symbolic sensitivity is the primary mechanism for developmental change in the Model. As a function of experience using symbols, children increasingly expect and look for relations between entities. As children become more sensitive to the possibility of symbolic relations, they become capable of detecting them with less support. Thus, high levels of iconicity are less important for older children than for younger children, less explicit instructions suffice, and so forth. Dual representation is more readily achieved: Anticipating a symbolic relation, children focus less on the concrete characteristics of a symbol and more on its abstract, representational function. (General cognitive development is also obviously important in symbolic development, but it is not formally incorporated into the Model.)

IMPLICATIONS AND APPLICATION

The Model described here has a number of clear practical implications. One cannot take for granted that children will detect a symbolic relation, no matter how obvious it is to older individuals. There are no fully transparent symbols. Only through experience do young children come to appreciate the abstract, representational relation that holds between a symbol and referent, regardless of how physically similar they may be.

Educational materials are often designed with the assumption that three-dimensional materials—"manipulables"—will help children acquire abstract concepts (e.g., various blocks are often used to teach number concepts and arithmetic). It is assumed that the relation between the object symbols and the concepts will be obvious or readily figured out. My research indicates that this assumption cannot be made blithely—and will not always be valid. Hence, the utility of any such educational aids cannot simply be taken for granted.

Similarly, anatomically explicit dolls are commonly used in investigations of suspected child abuse on the assumption that the self–doll relation will be obvious to young children and will help them provide more complete and accurate testimony. Recent research in my laboratory and others questions this assumption. There is increasing evidence that, as predicted by dual representation, very young children do not find it natural or easy to use a doll as a representation of themselves.[11]

In conclusion, children start early to acquire the variety of symbols needed for full participation in their culture. However, the representational nature of any given symbol may not be clear to them. Understanding and using a symbol depends on the interaction of many factors, including characteristics of the symbol and its referent, the child's prior experience with symbols, and the information given to the child about the nature and meaning of the symbol.

ACKNOWLEDGMENTS

The research summarized in this review was supported by Research Grant HD-25271 and Training Grant HD-07205 from the National Institute for Child Health and Human Development. I thank Renée Baillargeon, Gerald Clore, Larry Jones, and Don Marzolf for helpful comments on earlier versions of the manuscript. I also thank Kathy Anderson for her invaluable contributions to this research.

NOTES

1. For theories on the development of symbolization, see, e.g., H. Werner and H. Kaplan, *Symbol Formation* (Wiley, New York, 1967); L. S. Vygotsky, *Mind in Society*, M. Cole, V. John-Steiner, S. Scribner, and E. Souberman, Eds. (Harvard University Press, Cambridge, MA, 1978). For summaries of research on particular symbols, see, e. g., J. Goodnow, *Children Drawing* (Harvard University Press, Cambridge, MA, 1977); U. Goswami and P. E. Bryant, *Phonological Skills and Learning to Read* (Erlbaum, Hove, England, 1990); R. Gelman and C. R. Gallistel, *The Child's Understanding of Number* (Harvard University Press, Cambridge, MA, 1978). For recent reviews of research on the development of representation, see C. Pratt and A. Garton, Eds., *The Development and Use of Representation in Children* (Wiley, Chichester, England, 1993); R. R. Cocking and K. A. Renninger, Eds., *The Development and Meaning of Psychological Distance* (Erlbaum, Hillsdale, NJ, 1993).

2. J. S. DeLoache, Rapid change in the symbolic functioning of very young children, *Science, 238* 1556–1557 (1987); J. S. DeLoache, Symbolic functioning in very young children: Understanding of pictures and models, *Child Development, 62,* 736–752 (1991).

3. J. S. DeLoache, D. V. Kolstad, and K. N. Anderson, Physical similarity and young children's understanding of scale models, *Child Development, 62,* 111–126 (1991).

4. G. A. Dow and H. L. Pick, Young children's use of models and photographs as spatial representations, *Cognitive Development, 7,* 351–363 (1992).

5. D. P. Marzolf and J. S. DeLoache, Transfer in young children's understanding of spatial representations, *Child Development, 65,* 1–15 (1994).

6. J. S. DeLoache, Young children's understanding of the correspondence between a scale model and a larger space, *Cognitive Development, 4,* 121–129 (1989).

7. S. K. Langer, *Philosophy in a New Key* (Harvard University Press, Cambridge, MA, 1942), p. 75.

8. Described in J. S. DeLoache and N. M. Burns, Symbolic development in young children: Understanding models and pictures, in Pratt and Garton, note 1.

9. J. S. DeLoache, K. F. Miller, K. S. Rosengren, and N. Bryant, *Symbolic development in young children: Honey, I shrunk the troll*, paper presented at the meeting of the Psychonomic Society, Washington, DC (November 1994).

10. J. S. DeLoache and D. P. Marzolf, When a picture is not worth a thousand words, *Cognitive Development, 7,* 317–329 (1992).

11. J. S. DeLoache, The use of dolls in interviewing young children, in *Memory and Testimony in the Child Witness*, M. S. Zaragoza, J. R. Graham, G. C. N. Hall, R. Hirschman, and Y. S. Ben-Porath, Eds. (Sage, Thousand Oaks, CA, 1995); J. S. DeLoache and D. P. Marzolf, The use of dolls to interview young children: Issues of symbolic representation, *Journal of Experimental Child Psychology* (in press).

16

Alan M. Leslie

Pretense, Autism, and the Theory-of-Mind Module

Even mundane social life depends on the ability to comprehend other minds and their informational states. We rely heavily on commonsense folk psychology, or "theory of mind," to understand other people's behavior and to predict their reactions. A critical component of this commonsense knowledge is the concept of a *propositional attitude*. We often construe behavior as mediated by an agent's holding or taking an attitude to a proposition *p* (e.g., believing, hoping, or pretending that *p)*. Recent research shows that even preschool children have an impressive and spontaneous grasp of this mental source of action.

The acquisition of the knowledge and skills necessary to understand another person's mind has become a topic of interest to developmental psychologists.[1] One potentially important line of work in this area concerns the nature of cognitive deficits in the neurodevelopmental disorder known as childhood autism. Although early biological damage to the growing brain is likely to have a number of different consequences for cognitive development, there is increasing evidence that, in autism, one of the effects is a relatively focused and specific impairment in the capacity to reason about mental states.

EXPERIMENTAL TESTS OF THE CHILD'S THEORY OF MIND

Folk psychology arises naturally during the preschool years. One of the most striking demonstrations of this development comes from the study of attribution of false beliefs. Imagine the following scene in which Sally is tricked by Anne. Sally puts her candy in a cupboard and goes out to play. Naughty Anne comes in, finds the candy, and moves it to a nearby drawer. Now Sally comes back for her candy. Where does Sally think her candy is? Where will she look for it? Working at the Universities of Salzburg and

Sussex, respectively, Wimmer and Perner[2] used scenarios such as this one to show that 4-year-old children could figure out what Sally wrongly thinks. The children were able to attribute a false belief to Sally and thus to predict her erroneous behavior. Children younger than 4, however, would predict Sally's behavior based on the candy's current position, as if Sally would know this.

In a further study, Perner, Leekam, and Wimmer[3] developed the "Smarties" task, which also tests for understanding false belief. (Smarties are a type of candy known and loved by European children.) The child is shown a Smarties box and asked what it contains. "Smarties" is the invariable reply. The child is then shown that, actually, the box contains only a pencil. The pencil is placed back in the box, and the lid is closed again. The child is reminded that his or her friend is outside waiting to come in. Then the test question is asked: "What will your friend say [/think] is in the box when we first show it to him?" Again, most 4-year-olds correctly predict "Smarties," whereas most 3-year-olds expect the friend to say, "pencil."

The study of false belief has become to dominate much of the effort in this area since these findings. Interest in false belief arose initially out of Premack and Woodruff's[4] article on the question of whether or not chimpanzees have a theory of mind. In a commentary on that article, Dennett[5] suggested that a crucial test of animals' understanding would involve not just belief but false belief. In understanding false belief, animals must understand a belief that is not their own and therefore does not reflect reality as they construe it. Wimmer and Perner took up this idea and developed the above scenarios, testing not chimpanzees but human children instead.

Other, simplified, versions of false belief tasks have been developed. For example, Wellman and Bartsch[6] found that 3-year-olds can pass a version of the Sally-and-Anne task in which the position of the target object is not known but guessed. Whatever the child guesses, the experimenter says that Sally thinks it is some other place. When asked to predict Sally's search behavior, then, the child has to predict on the basis of Sally's different belief. Under these circumstances, most 3-year-olds succeed. Apparently, their efforts to represent Sally's belief are not swamped by current reality, if reality is only guessed at and not known for sure.

SHARED PRETENSE: AN EARLY INDICATOR OF MENTALISM

The preschool child makes relatively slow progress in understanding situations in which people act on false beliefs. Two-year-olds, however, understand at least one kind of situation in which people act in response to imagined circumstances: shared pretense. In shared pretense, one person's behavior communicates an imaginary situation to the other person. I analyzed this ability, which first emerges between 18 and 24 months, by means of a cognitive model that identified the main properties of the internal representations required.[7] These representations turned out to express the key information contained in propositional attitudes, leading me to suggest that these same representational mechanisms probably underlie the child's capacity to acquire and elaborate different theories of mind. In the preschooler's "concept" of pretense, we glimpse the specific innate basis of our capacity spontaneously to acquire a "theory of mind."

Pretending, in the sense I was interested in, is a playful activity and does not have an ulterior motive, such as to deceive. It should also be distinguished from being confused: If I pretend that a banana is a telephone, I know perfectly well what the banana really is. To engage in shared pretense, I have to understand that someone else can have a pretend-type attitude to the imaginary situation of the banana being a telephone. Just such an ability is found in 2-year-olds. Their ability to represent a propositional attitude is an index of their capacity to acquire a theory of mind—including, for example, an ability to employ a concept of belief.

Perhaps the easiest way to see the connection between understanding pretense in others and theory of mind is to consider the following. Suppose you are faced with trying to understand why some particular physical event has happened (e.g., why your automobile's engine keeps cutting out). You will consider only explanations based on actual circumstances, dismissing explanations based on imagined circumstances as irrelevant. When it comes to understanding the behavior of people, however, things are different. In such cases, we often consider imaginary circumstances because we know that people sometimes behave in relation to circumstances that are not real. A metal button can be attracted only by a magnet that is really there, but a deluded Sally can be "attracted" to an empty box by a piece of chocolate that is no longer there. Or perhaps there never was a piece of chocolate— perhaps Sally is just pretending there is something in the box. In either case, Sally is behaving with respect to a situation that is only imaginary.

AUTISM: EVIDENCE FOR MODULARITY?

The single capacity to pretend and to understand pretense in others has important implications. It implies the existence of a domain-specific processing mechanism whose task is to understand behavior in relation to mental states. This mechanism is essentially innate and, in some sense, a specific part of the brain. If all this were true, then we might find an organic brain disorder that detrimentally affects this mechanism while leaving many other capacities relatively intact. There should be individuals whose capacity to pretend and to understand pretense in others is impaired. Individuals with this sort of organic damage should also have problems with intentional communication[8] and specific difficulties in acquiring and elaborating a theory of mind. Finally, such developmental difficulties should give rise to a peculiarly limited social life. Together with my colleagues in London, Simon Baron-Cohen and Uta Frith, I began working on these conjectures when it seemed to us that childhood autism might fit this profile.[9]

What was already known about autism was that pretense and imaginative abilities, intentional communication, and social competence are all impaired. Indeed, these three features are central to the behavioral diagnosis of autism. There were good reasons for thinking that autism has a biological origin, and the pioneering work of Hermelin and O'Connor[10] showed that autism involves cognitive deficits. What we needed to discover was whether autistic children also show any inordinate difficulty with theory-of-mind concepts. We started with false belief.

We presented three groups of children with a task adapted from Wimmer and Perner[2]—essentially the Sally-and-Anne scenario outlined earlier. One of these groups consisted of normal 4-year-olds, the other two of Down syndrome and autistic children. We deliberately arranged that the autistic group had a mental and chronological age consid-erably higher than that of the other groups. In fact, their IQs were in the borderline to normal range (mean = 82), whereas the children with Down syndrome averaged an IQ of 64. We went to these lengths to ensure that any difficulty the autistic children might have with this task would not be due to general intellectual level. This point was important because our hypothesis was that autism involves a specific brain mechanism. The results of this study were clear. Although around 85% of both the normal and Down's groups correctly predicted Sally's false belief, only 20% of the autistic group did so, despite their intellectual and age advantage.

Autistic children may lack understanding of mental states, but do they lack *only* an understanding of mental states? In a follow-up study, we used a picture-sequencing task to compare, across these same three groups, the children's ability to understand mental and physical events. Some sequences depicted physical-causal events, and some sequences depicted events that, it seemed to us, could be appreciated only if one took into account the mental states of the protagonists. The results were again striking. The autistic children showed a specific difficulty. They performed well on the physical-causal events but slumped to chance performance on the mental state stories. The younger normal children were near ceiling on the latter stories, and even the more retarded Down's group outperformed the autistic group. Finally, our analysis of the children's verbal descriptions of the stories showed that the autistic children produced much more physical-causal language but much less mental state language than the other two groups. In sum, the autistic children appeared to be disadvantaged when it came to understanding events that required a "theory of mind." Incidentally, we also included sequences depicting social interactions that we thought could be understood without reference to mental states. On these sequences, the autistic children did as well as the normal children and better than the Down's children.

The findings of these initial studies have subsequently been confirmed and extended in a number of ways.[11] For example, Baron-Cohen showed that even those autistic children who pass a basic false belief task fail a more complex ("second order") version that Down's children often pass. Frith and I demonstrated that high-ability autistic children have difficulty with true belief as well as false belief. Perner, Frith, Leekam, and I showed that most autistic children fail the Smarties task and do not take into account what another person knows while communicating with that person. These basic findings have received support from studies by other workers.[12]

The classical view of autism, originated by Kanner[13] and currently championed by Hobson,[14] is that it is primarily an affective disorder, but the specific pattern of spared and impaired abilities seems hard to explain in terms of a general affective disorder. Instead, Frith and I[15] have argued that autism involves a cognitive impairment specifically affecting metarepresentational capacity. Frith[16] provided the first detailed consideration of the connection between theory-of-mind deficits and the clinical picture of autism. Baron-Cohen[17] showed that not all "theoretical" concepts in autistic children are impaired. Roth and I[18] found that although normal 3-year-old children failed standard false belief tasks, they could attribute propositional attitudes to participants in a conversation. Our autistic subjects, however, failed to perform even at this 3-year-old level.

Further evidence that autistic children are not simply "delayed 3-year-olds" comes from recent work[19] that extended Zaitchik's[20] elegant "false photographs" tasks to show that autistic children perform well (better than normal 4-year-olds) on a task that is structurally similar to a false belief task. This task involves not beliefs but photographs that become false by going out-of-date. This superior performance extends to understanding a false map, leading to the conclusion that autistic children are not impaired *generally* in problem solving that, like "theory of mind," requires executive functioning or counterfactual reasoning. These results support the idea that autism involves a damaged theory-of-mind module.

THE THEORY-OF-MIND MODULE

I have argued that the normal and rapid development of theory-of-mind knowledge depends on a specialized mechanism that allows the brain to attend to invisible mental states.[21] Very early biological damage may prevent the normal expression of this theory-of-mind module in the developing brain, resulting in the core symptoms of autism.[22]

NOTES

1. See, e.g., J. Astington, P. Harris, and D. Olson, Eds., *Developing Theories of Mind* (Cambridge University Press, 1988); G. Butterworth, P. L. Harris, A. M. Leslie, and H. Wellman, *Perspectives on the Child's Theory of Mind* (Oxford University Press, Oxford, 1991).

2. H. Wimmer and J. Perner, Beliefs about beliefs: Representation and constraining function of wrong beliefs in young children's understanding of deception. *Cognition, 13,* 103–128 (1983).

3. J. Perner, S. R. Leekam, and H. Wimmer, Three-year-olds' difficulty with false belief: The case for a conceptual deficit, *British Journal of Developmental Psychology, 5,* 125–137 (1987).

4. D. Premack and G. Woodruff, Does the chimpanzee have a theory of mind? *Behavioral and Brain Sciences, 4,* 515–526 (1978).

5. D. C. Dennett, Beliefs about beliefs, *Behavioral and Brain Sciences, 1,* 568–570 (1978).

6. H. M. Wellman and K. Bartsch, Young children's reasoning about beliefs, *Cognition, 30,* 239–277 (1988).

7. A. M. Leslie, *Pretend play and representation in the second year of life,* paper presented to British Psychological Society Developmental Conference, Oxford (1983, September); A. M. Leslie, Pretense and representation: The origins of "theory of mind," *Psychological Review, 94,* 412–426 (1987).

8. S. Baron-Cohen, Social and pragmatic deficits in autism, *Journal of Autism and Developmental Disorders, 18,* 379–402 (1988); U. Frith, A new look at language and communication in autism, *British Journal of Disorders of Communication, 24,* 123–150 (1989); A. M. Leslie and F. Happé, Autism and ostensive communication: The relevance of metarepresentation, *Development and Psychopathology, 1,* 205–212 (1989).

9. S. Baron-Cohen, A. M. Leslie, and U. Frith, Does the autistic child have a "theory of mind"? *Cognition, 21,* 37–46 (1985); S. Baron-Cohen, A. M. Leslie, and U. Frith, Mechanical behavioural and intentional understanding of picture stories in autistic children, *British Journal of Developmental Psychology, 4,* 113–125 (1986).

10. B. Hermelin and N. O'Connor, *Psychological Experiments With Autistic Children* (Pergamon, London, 1970).

11. S. Baron-Cohen, The autistic child's theory of mind: A case of specific developmental delay, *Journal of Child Psychology and Psychiatry, 30,* 285–297 (1989); A. M. Leslie and U. Frith, Autistic

children's understanding of seeing, knowing and believing, *British Journal of Developmental Psychology, 6,* 315–324 (1988); J. Perner, U. Frith, A. M. Leslie, and S. R. Leekam, Exploration of the autistic child's theory of mind: Knowledge, belief and communication, *Child Development, 60,* 689–700 (1989).

12. See, e.g., R. Eisenmajer and M. Prior, Cognitive linguistic correlates of "theory of mind" ability in autistic children, *British Journal of Developmental Psychology, 9,* 351–364 (1991); J. Russell, N. Mauthner, S. Sharpe, and T. Tidswell, The "windows task" as a measure of strategic deception in preschoolers and autistic subjects, *British Journal of Developmental Psychology, 9,* 331–349 (1991).

13. L. Kanner, Autistic disturbances of affective contact, *Nervous Child, 2,* 217–150 (1943).

14. R. P. Hobson, On acquiring knowledge about people, and the capacity to pretend: A response to Leslie (1987), *Psychological Review, 97,* 114–121 (1990).

15. A. M. Leslie and U. Frith, Prospects for a cognitive neuropsychology of autism: Hobson's choice, *Psychological Review, 97,* 122–131 (1990).

16. U. Frith, *Autism, Explaining the Enigma* (Blackwell, Oxford, 1989).

17. S. Baron-Cohen, The autistic child's theory of mind: How specific is the deficit? *British Journal of Developmental Psychology, 9,* 301–314 (1991).

18. D. Roth and A. M. Leslie, The recognition of attitude conveyed by utterance: A study of preschool and autistic children, *British Journal of Developmental Psychology, 9,* 325–330 (1991).

19. A. M. Leslie and L. Thaiss, Domain specificity in conceptual development: Neuropsychological evidence from autism, *Cognition* (in press); S. Leekam and J. Perner, Does the autistic child have a "metarepresentational" deficit? *Cognition* (in press).

20. D. Zaitchik, When representations conflict with reality: The preschooler's problem with false beliefs and "false" photographs, *Cognition, 35,* 41–68 (1990).

21. A. M. Leslie, The theory of mind impairment in autism: Evidence for a modular mechanism of development? in *The Emergence of Mindreading,* A. Whiten, Ed. (Blackwell, Oxford, 1991). pp. 63–78.

22. U. Frith, J. Morton, and A. M. Leslie, The cognitive basis of a biological disorder: Autism, *Trends in Neurosciences, 14,* 433–438 (1991).

17

Jeffery Scott Mio and Arthur C. Graesser

Humor, Language, and Metaphor

It has long been assumed that humor and metaphor are connected. However, little direct empirical examination of this connection exists. We sought to directly test a popular theory of humor—the disparagement theory—in a metaphor form. Thirty male and 30 female introductory psychology students judged 32 metaphor pairs. One half of the pairs disparaged the topic of the metaphorical sentence, whereas the other half of the pairs uplifted the topic. Consistent with the disparagement theory, the disparaging metaphors were perceived to be more humorous than their uplifting counterparts. Moreover, men showed a much greater propensity to follow this pattern. We then discussed the advantages of simultaneously examining humor and metaphor to gain insight into both areas.

As Greenwald (1977) cautioned, "I'm very concerned about psychologists becoming interested in humor. It is almost as bad as the fact that the Church has become interested in sex. They will begin to take the pleasure out of that" (p. 161). At the risk of taking some of the pleasure out, the purpose of this article is to examine humor. We feel that insights may arise from humor by examining the connection between humor and metaphor.

One of the most imposing obstacles to overcome in investigating humor is its paradoxical nature. Levine (1977) specified some of humor's paradoxes:

1. Laughter has been used to show scorn and derision for things we do not like but sympathy and affection for things we do like.
2. Jokes have conveyed hostility or shared intimacy.
3. Humor exposes hypocrisy or hides unpleasant truths.
4. Laughter without restraint is evidence of madness or of mental health.
5. Laugher is used to allay anxiety or as a relief from anxiety.

With such differing functions of humor, it is no wonder that the systematic investigation of humor has proven to be such a daunting task.

From Jeffery Scott Mio and Arthur C. Graesser, "Humor, Language, and Metaphor," *Metaphor and Symbolic Activity,* vol. 6, no. 2 (1991). Copyright © 1991 by Lawrence Erlbaum Associates, Inc. Reprinted by permission.

HISTORICAL ROOTS AND THEORIES OF HUMOR

Theories of Humor

Humor has been a topic of interest at least since the time of the ancient Greeks. Through this period, three general theories of humor have emerged (Morreall, 1987; Raskin, 1985). *Superiority theories* encompass the more modern versions of disparagement, aggression, and hostility. These theories emphasize the elements of humor that make us feel superior in some manner. A person, an institution, or an idea serves as an object of our disparagement or aggression in order for us to feel superior to that object. *Incongruity theories* encompass incongruity-resolution, surprise, and script-opposition theories. These theories emphasize the disparity between expectations and reality. For example, in jokes, the punch line is at variance with expectations established in the body of the joke. *Relief theories* encompass arousal-relief (or -release), tension-relief (or -release), and physiologically based theories. These theories emphasize our psychological and/or physiological arousal followed by an arousal reduction. Morreall (1987) examined the philosophical roots of these theories. Table 1 is a compilation of Morreall's discussion. As one can see, the superiority tradition has been in existence for a longer period of time than the other two traditions. However, at least since the time of Descartes, theorists have merged and/or integrated more than one of the stances.

Aggression

The superiority theories of humor have enjoyed the longest history of support. In discussing Thomas Hobbes's stance, Morreall (1987) stated, "Laughter is nothing but an expression of our sudden glory when we realize that in some way we are superior to someone else" (p. 19). Thus, superiority theories have an aggressive component attached to them. This aggressive component is among the most studied of humor components (e.g., Bryant, 1977; Feinberg, 1978; Gill, 1982; Graesser, Long, & Mio, 1989; Zillmann & Cantor, 1976). In Freud's (1905/1960) famous work on humor, he emphasized the breakthrough of sexual and/or aggressive drives manifested in a socially acceptable manner. However, even the sex-gratifying joke had an aggressive quality to it. In his later writing on this topic (Freud, 1927/1961), he discussed how humor as a defense mechanism signified the individual's personal triumph over adversity.

Zillmann and his colleagues (e.g., Cantor & Zillmann, 1973; Zillmann, 1983; Zillmann & Bryant, 1974; Zillmann & Cantor, 1972, 1976) have long been interested in the aggressive component of humor. Their findings (not surprisingly) suggest that indiscriminate aggression is not humorous. However, when one or more of the following is present, humor is enhanced:

1. The object of the aggression is not seriously injured.
2. There are social/environmental cues for laughter.
3. The object is a hated rather than a loved object.
4. There is an equal level of aggressive retaliation.
5. The object is a member of a different class than the aggressor and/or the audience.

Graesser et al. (1989) examined what aspects of a joke make it funny to an audience. Among the stimulus questions asked were those relating to the prevailing theories of humor including arousal relief (e.g., Berlyne, 1967; Rothbart, 1977), incongruity resolution (e.g., Suls, 1972, 1977, 1983), disparagement (e.g., La Fave, Haddad, & Maeson,

Table 1
Morreall's Classification of Theorists by Types of Humor Theories Advocated

Superiority	Incongruity	Relief
Plato (428–348 BC)	[Descartes]	[David Hartley]
Aristotle (348–322 BC)	Francis Hutcheson	Herbert Spencer
Cicero (106–43 BC)	(1694–1746)	(1820–1903)
Thomas Hobbes	[David Hartley]	Sigmund Freud
(1588–1679)	Immanuel Kant	(1856–1939)
Rene Descartes	(1724–1804)	George Santayana
(1596–1650)	Arthur Schopenhauer	(1863–1952)
David Hartley	(1788–1860)	
(1705–1757)	William Hazlitt	
[Freud]	(1778–1830)	
	Søren Kierkegaard	
	(1813–1855)	
	[Freud]	

1976; Zillmann & Cantor, 1976), and script juxta-position–opposition (e.g., Raskin, 1985). Of these theories, only disparagement reliably predicted the subjects' funniness ratings of jokes.

The Graesser et al. (1989) findings do not discount the contributions of the other approaches to humor in general, because there are more aspects to humor than joke forms. However, these results do suggest that the aggressive or disparaging component is a necessary part of what makes jokes funny. For example, consider the following joke:

> Two women were comparing notes on the techniques of their respective boyfriends. "He kissed my hand," boasted one. "It's the way that a man with experience kisses." The other replied, "A man with experience should have better aim."

Here an arousal-relief interpretation of the joke would suggest that the body of the joke would rouse us in some manner (particularly because it deals with sex) and our laughter would relieve us from the tension caused by suppressing our arousal. An incongruity-resolution interpretation would suggest that the body of the joke established one set of expectations (e.g., that the first woman and her boyfriend are wise about sexual matters), but the punch line is inconsistent with this expectation. Humorous enjoyment is experienced when this discrepancy is solved. Finally, a script juxtaposition–opposition interpretation would suggest that differing scripts that are opposite to one another come into play (e.g., "experienced lovers" script vs. an "inexperienced lovers" script). Although all these elements might (or must) be present, Graesser et al.'s (1989) findings suggest that it is the notion that the second woman is disparaging the first woman and/or her boyfriend that makes this joke funny.

Sex Differences

If aggression is an important part of humor, then there must be sex differences in the use and appreciation of humor. This is because of the long-acknowledged sex differences in aggressive expression (e.g., Brody, 1985; Maccoby & Jacklin, 1974). Such sex differences in humor expression seem to hold true. Males express more humor than fe-males (e.g., McGhee, 1979; Pollio & Edgerly, 1976), appreciate more aggressive humor (e.g., Cantor, 1976; McGhee, 1979), and elicit more humorous responses from audiences (e.g., Gadfield, 1977; Sheppard, 1977). One reason why males engage in more humorous expression is that the "clever" person is the one controlling the flow of the communication process, especially with an audience present, so males also seem to want to be in control.

Freud (1905/1960) suggested that jokes may persuade an audience to adopt a speaker's position because the humorous remark may be overestimated in substance. For example, in the second 1984 Presidential Debate between Ronald Reagan and Walter Mondale, there was a concern that President Reagan was too old to hold the position for another 4 years. When asked if age should be a factor in considering a candidate, Reagan said, "No, and I don't think Fritz Mondale's youthful inexperience should be held against him." Instead of coming back with a clever response to recapture the audience's favor, Mondale simply laughed along with the audience. Many political commentaries that followed the debate singled out Reagan's humorous remark as the event that cemented his re-election bid.

McGhee (1979) felt that the sex differences observed in humor expression were due to socialization factors. He based this conclusion primarily on the fact that these differences are not manifested until the late preschool years. Parents seem to encourage their male children to "clown" or "perform" more than their female children. Also, people of higher status tend to tell more jokes than people of lower status, and unfortunately in this society, males are given higher status than females. In joke expression, higher status people are allowed to disparage lower status people, whereas lower status people tend to engage more in self-deprecation. This pattern seems to follow the male–female pattern, as men tend to enjoy disparaging humor more than women, whereas women tend to enjoy disparaging humor when women were the ones being disparaged. These differences tend to dissipate the more a woman adopts a feminist stance.

Although acknowledging the aggressive component of humor, Chapman (1976) contended that humor was a socially acceptable and physically harmless way of discharging motivational arousal.

Humor is a way of expressing a feeling and/or social intimacy. If his position is correct, it is not surprising that males would engage in humor more than females, because males are more societally limited, relative to females, in the ways in which they can express intimate feelings (Brody, 1985). This indirect expression of intimacy enables males to maintain a masculine stance while still addressing their intimacy needs.

HUMOR AND METAPHOR

Elements of the connection between humor and metaphor can be seen throughout the literature. For example, Gardner (1980) contended that the ability to understand metaphors precedes the ability to understand humor. After these cognitive complexities to understand metaphors have developed, we gain a fundamental delight in making connections between two seemingly disparate concepts. Two areas seem relevant to connecting humor with metaphor: (a) humor as it arises in therapy and (b) paradoxes in both humor and metaphor.

Therapy and the Humor–Metaphor Connection

One of the more popular models of metaphor understanding is the *domains interaction* model (Sternberg, 1982; Tourangeau & Sternberg, 1981, 1982). This model suggests that metaphors that seem to be more pleasing are those that connect markedly disparate concepts. This model has stimulated many experiments (e.g., Boswell, 1986; Hansen & Halpern, 1987; Kelly & Keil, 1987; Marschark & Hunt, 1985; Trick & Katz, 1986). However, the essence of this model was anticipated long ago by Freud (1905/1960) in his discussion of "good" and "bad" jokes. According to Freud, a bad joke seems to be one where a leap from one circle of ideas to another circle is taken when there is not a link between the two circles at that time. A good joke links two disparate circles of ideas of observing the similarities between them. The more distance between the circles of ideas, the funnier the jokes are. This supports Freud's economy notion of psychic discharge, where little psychic energy is expended to resolve such disparate domains to produce a pleasing outcome.

Metaphors invite the listener to entertain the comparison being made instead of challenging its logic. For example, if a therapist were to interpret a couple's marital problems by saying, "You are like your mother," the wife may respond by saying, "No I am not. She does this, and I do that." However, if the therapist were to say, "*You are mothering your husband,*" the wife may wonder if she really were and try to examine how her behavior was similar to her mother's. Lusterman (1988) equated humor's power with the metaphor's power. Humor, too, is powerful, yet disarming. Because telling a joke in psychotherapy is not expected, it increases attention. Lusterman told the following ethnic joke to a family of the same ethnicity. The parents were in their 50s with a 28-year-old son who was living at home and had never held a steady job. The family thwarted any attempt at the therapist's logical challenges to their situation, leaving the therapist frustrated and bored with them. (The ethnic nature of the joke has been removed from our retelling to encourage a nondisparagement position.)

> Mrs. *X* went to a plush hotel. The manager noticed that the chauffeur had picked up Mrs. *X*'s good-looking son and carried him into the lobby. The manager said, "What a nice-looking son you have. It is too bad he cannot walk." Mrs. *X* replied, "What do you mean he cannot walk? Thanks to God he doesn't have to!"

The family responded with laughter, then became silent and reflective. The mother said she did not see anything wrong because the boy was in the lap of luxury. The son asked what would happen to the boy in the future, for the lack of the use of his legs will cause atrophy. The father said he felt like the chauffeur. Each member of the family returned to the theme of the joke several times. One time, the son turned to his mother and said, "*Don't Mrs. X me!*" The mother referred to Mrs. *X*'s fallacies. The father wondered when the boy wold regain the use of his legs. These all indicated that the joke had made an impact upon the family. Lusterman reported that a few months later, the son secured a full-time job, then shortly thereafter, got his own apartment. A 1-year follow-up on this family revealed that the therapeutic gains had been maintained. Lusterman credited the joke he told as the key event that dislodged the family's inertia.

A second example of the metaphoric use of a joke in therapy comes from Levine (1977). He was dealing with a 40-year-old woman who detested all aspects of her relationship with her husband. When confronted with her choice of remaining married to him, she resisted by speculating that loneliness may be a worse alternative. Levine related a joke about a man whose job was to clean up after all the circus animals and give enemas to constipated elephants. A friend offered to get him another job away from the circus that paid better and was less menial, to which the man replied, "What, and give up show biz?" The patient was at first indignant, then laughed, then was able to discuss in a meaningful way the redeeming qualities about her marriage that kept her in it.

In summary, jokes can often serve as a metaphorical illustration of key issues with which the client and therapist are struggling. If correctly timed and delivered with good humor, they can greatly enhance the therapeutic process.

Paradoxes and the Humor–Metaphor Connection

Earlier, we discussed Levine's (1977) identification of some paradoxes of humor. Metaphor understanding requires a paradox of a different sort. According to some (e.g., Searle, 1969, 1979), metaphors require people to process a literal statement while grasping its figurative meaning. For example, in the nominal metaphor, *"Juliet is the sun,"* the receiver needs to understand the literalness of this statement, recognize its falseness, and calculate the figurative meaning of it. Glucksberg (1987, 1990), on the other hand, suggested that such statements are to be taken literally. The receiver is to consider "Juliet" to be an exemplar of "sun." However, the metaphor can only be correctly understood if the receiver also recognizes the extralinguistic task of calculating the meaning while recognizing that Juliet is not equated with the sun, or that "Juliet" is not an alternative name for the "sun." Thus, both the Searle and the Glucksberg positions require the paradox of tolerating the literal with the figurative. This position is consonant with the positions of those advocating the use of metaphors in

persuasive communication, where metaphors signify the juxtaposition of the rational with the irrational (e.g., Chaiken & Stangor, 1987; Jamieson, 1985; Mio, 1988; Reardon, 1981).

The paradox in humor that most closely ties it to metaphors involves the incongruity of elements. In examining the philosophical roots of humor, Morreall (1987) cited Francis Hutcheson (1674–1746) as directly connecting humor with metaphor:

> Genius in serious literature consists in the ability to trigger ideas of greatness, novelty, and beauty in the reader through the use of apt metaphors and similes. *Comic* genius, he continues, is largely the ability to use somewhat *inappropriate* metaphors and similes to trigger ideas that clash with each other. (p. 26)

Pollio (1983) conceives of humor as a two-stage process: (a) puzzlement at incongruity and (b) resolution of incongruity. As readers of the metaphor literature will recognize, this seems to be akin to the metaphor notions of *tension* and *ground*. Tension is created by the dissimilarity between the topic and vehicle, and the metaphor is solved when the appropriate ground is discovered.

Lang (1988) examined Proust's metaphor usage. Proust juxtaposed dissimilar or irreconcilable terms in his writings. This form of metaphor has been termed a *diaphor* by Wheelwright (1962). Lang interpreted the Proustian metaphor/paradox as injecting humor by drawing attention to the dissimilarity in the text. This technique disconcerts the reader because it avoids "the banal predictability of the commonplace" (Lang, 1988, p. 159).

Therefore, both humor and metaphor contain paradoxes that seem to be central to the understanding of both. However, the paradoxes are of a different sort and demand different cognitive processes of the receiver. In humor, the paradox can be copresent (Hershkowitz, 1977; Leventhal & Safer, 1977), whereas in metaphor, the paradox must be solved. Leventhal and Safer (1977) stated what when jokes are explained, they cease to be funny. However, when metaphors are explained, they increase understanding of the intended meaning.

OUR STUDY

Given the connection between humor and metaphors cited in the literature, we sought to empirically explore this connection. Because the disparagement model of humor has received the most support, we decided to examine the relative humorousness of disparaging and nondisparaging metaphors. We predicted that disparaging metaphors would be perceived as more humorous than their nondisparaging counterparts. Moreover, given the disparity between male and female displays of aggression, we predicted that males would perceive disparaging metaphors as much more humorous than would females.

Method

Subjects.
Sixty students (30 women, 30 men) from Washington State University's Department of Psychology human subject pool served as subjects for this study to fulfill course requirements or to receive extra credit.

Materials.
In a preliminary task, we generated what we took to be 40 high-status and 40 low-status items. High-status items included things such as "surgeon," "general," and "Harvard," whereas low-status items included things such as "butcher," "ape," and "sewer." To affirm our intuitions, we had 24 subject-pool students judge these items as representing high or low status. Our intuitions were confirmed (e.g., "surgeon" was judged to be high status, whereas "butcher" was judged to be low status), as there was nearly perfect concordance with our assessments.

From our list of high- and low-status items, 32 metaphors were constructed having the high-status items in the topic position and the low-status items in the vehicle position. In effect, the high-status items were being disparaged by being compared with the low-status items. We also constructed 32 metaphors interchanging the high- and low-status items, thus uplifting the low-status items by comparing them with the high-status items. For example, mirror metaphors were *"My surgeon is a butcher among doctors"* versus *"My butcher is a surgeon among meat cutters,"* and *"A general is an ape among military officers"* versus *"An ape is a general among jungle animals."* All 64 metaphors we used appear in the Appendix. As can be seen, every attempt to make the metaphors understandable was taken, such as (a) including the

topic's domain, (b) using an appropriate article of speech to introduce the topic, and (c) matching place with place and animate object with animate object.

We paired the mirror metaphors together. Next we constructed four-page booklets from these metaphors, with 8 metaphor pairs per page. The disparaging and uplifting sentences were each presented first in 16 of the metaphor pairs with the orders interspersed in a random fashion. We employed a completely counterbalanced Latin-square design on the four pages to control for order effects.

Procedure.
Subjects were tested in groups of 5 to 10, depending on the days and times for which they signed. We employed a two-alternative forced-choice procedure. Subjects were instructed to place a check mark in front of the metaphorical sentence that struck them as being funnier than the other sentence. They were allowed to work at their own pace.

Results

Disparaging Versus Uplifting Metaphors.
Mean difference scores were calculated for each subject by subtracting that subject's number of uplifting-metaphor endorsements from his or her number of disparaging-metaphor endorsements. If the two types of metaphors were judged to be of equal funniness, we would expect a mean difference score of 0. Overall, the mean difference score was 5.00. This yielded reliable differences between item endorsements, $t(59) = 3.50$, $p < .001$. Disparaging metaphors were perceived to be more humorous than their uplifting metaphorical counterparts.

Sex Differences.
Men obtained a mean difference score of 8.40, whereas women obtained a mean score of 1.60. This difference was statistically significant, $t(58) = 2.47$, $p < .05$. Men appeared to reliably judge disparaging metaphors as being more humorous than did females.

An alternative analysis yielded a clearer picture of the pattern of men's and women's responses. Of the men, 25 preferred the disparaging metaphors over the uplifting metaphors, 4 preferred the uplifting ones over the disparaging ones, and 1 showed no preference. Of the women, 16 preferred the disparaging metaphors over the uplifting ones, 8 preferred the uplifting ones over the disparaging ones, and 6 showed no preference. The overall analysis yielded a significant difference, $X^2(1, N = 53) = 12.54, p < .001$. This indicates an overall difference in the distribution of responses in the two groups. We also conducted separate binomial analyses on the distributions by sex. Men significantly preferred disparaging metaphors ($p = .0001$), whereas women showed much less propensity to prefer disparaging metaphors ($p = .0438$).

Discussion

Results showed a strong preference for disparaging metaphors over uplifting metaphors with respect to humor. Those metaphors that compared a relatively high-status item with a relatively low-status item were found to be more humorous than those metaphors that compared low-status items to high-status ones. This is consistent with past disparagement or superiority theories of humor (e.g., Zillmann & Cantor, 1976).

Also consistent with past findings (e.g., Cantor, 1976; McGhee, 1979), men responded much more to the humor in disparaging metaphors than to the uplifting metaphors. On the other hand, women only displayed marginal preference for such metaphors. This is also in keeping with general sex differences in aggression (e.g., Brody, 1985). Because males are more aggressive than females, it would stand to reason that males would prefer more aggressively derived humor than would females. An interesting question relevant to this matter would be if androgynous individuals (cf. Bem, 1984) would respond similarly or in an attenuated fashion.

Our results demonstrate that the heretofore theorized connection between humor and metaphor seems to have validity. Predictions from one domain (humor) were supported in the other domain (metaphors). These predictions held true for both the general form of the metaphor and for sex differences previously observed. Thus, the systematic investigation of other connections between humor and metaphor seems warranted.

As discussed elsewhere (e.g., Graesser et al., 1989; Morreall, 1987; Raskin, 1985), three general theories of humor have been consistently supported throughout the years: superiority, incongruity, and

relief. Our study was derived from only one of these general theories. We feel that the simultaneous examination of humor and metaphor across all three humor theories will help reveal important aspects of both domains.

First, from the standpoint of studying metaphors to better understand humor, studies such as ours could be useful. Disparagement or aggression does seem to be part of a humor appreciation. In disparaging a high-status individual or institution, we are making ourselves superior to those objects. If we were to examine the incongruity theory of humor, topic and vehicle disparities could be measured, with greater disparities predicted to be more humorous. Finally, relief theories of humor could be further examined by measuring the tension caused by the juxtaposition of the topic and the vehicle terms. Again, the greater the tension, the greater the predicted humorousness.

The value of such studies may not necessarily be the confirmation or disconfirmation of existing theories of humor. Given that these theories have been well established, additional evidence from metaphorical forms of humorous utterances may be uninteresting, other than merely affirming the connection between the two areas. However, metaphorical forms, particularly nominal metaphors similar to ones we used in this study, are easily generated. After establishing the relation between metaphors and specific theories of humor, we could then ask subjects to construct a humorous metaphor, given a particular topic. For example, we could ask someone to construct a humorous metaphor comparing a surgeon to something else (e.g., "*My surgeon is a _____ among doctors*"). In completing this metaphor, we could further examine the cognitive processes through which individuals go in constructing their metaphors. We could also measure variability among elements such as disparagement, incongruity, and tension by asking others to compare the given topics with the subject-generated vehicles on these dimensions.

Reciprocally, examination of humor can add insight into our understanding of metaphors. Gibbs has argued (e.g., Gibbs, 1989; Gibbs & Gerrig, 1989) that what makes metaphors seem "special" are the *products* that result from metaphor understanding. This contrasts with one of the main lines of metaphor research—that of examining the processes involved in comprehending metaphors. In examining humorous metaphors, we can observe laughter, snickers, facial contortions, and other products of humor. In order for this humor to have been apprehended, the metaphors themselves must have been understood.

Gibbs (1989) gave an example of a person (Rob) asking another (Denise) if a third (Gladys) had a good memory. Denise replies, *"Gladys is just like an elephant."* Denise could have replied by saying that Gladys had a very good memory, but this would have most likely prevented Rob from processing Denise's response beyond its determinate meaning. However, if Rob and Denise shared the knowledge that Gladys was quite heavy, Rob would have further appreciated the cleverness of Denise's response. Another person, not knowing Gladys's physical appearance, would most likely treat Denise's response as if it meant that Gladys had a very good memory. Does this person really "understand" Denise's metaphor as fully as Rob does? We think not.

We do not intend to imply that humor and metaphor should be equated. As mentioned earlier, metaphors explained increase understanding, whereas jokes explained cease to be funny. However, the simultaneous investigation of humor and metaphor can lead to interesting products of understanding. We offer this study as an important first step in this direction.

ACKNOWLEDGMENT

We extend our appreciation to Chanda Binder, Debra L. Long, Robert McIntosh, Nora P. Reilly, James I. Salomon, Michael K. Smith, Lynnette Socci, Kay Lynn Stevens, and Eric Wahlund for their contributions to this project.

REFERENCES

Bem, S. L. (1984). Androgyny and gender schema theory: A conceptual and empirical integration. In T. B. Sonderegger (Ed.), *Nebraska Symposium on Motivation* (Vol. 32, pp. 179–226). Lincoln: University of Nebraska Press.

Berlyne, D. E. (1967). Arousal and reinforcement. In D. Levine (Ed.), *Nebraska Symposium on Motivation* (Vol. 15, pp. 1–110). Lincoln: University of Nebraska Press.

Boswell, D. A. (1986). Speakers' intentions: Constraints on metaphor comprehension. *Metaphor and Symbolic Activity, 1,* 153–170.

Brody, L. R. (1985). Gender differences in emotional development: A review of theories and research. *Journal of Personality, 53,* 102–149.

Bryant, J. (1977). Degree of hostility in squelches as a factor in humour appreciation. In A. J. Chapman & H. C. Foot (Eds.), *It's a funny thing, humour* (pp. 321–327). Oxford, England: Pergamon.

Cantor, J. R. (1976). What is funny to whom?: The role of gender. *Journal of Communication, 26,* 164–172.

Cantor, J. R., & Zillmann, D. (1973). Resentment toward victimized protagonists and severity of misfortunes they suffer as factors in humor appreciation. *Journal of Experimental Research in Personality, 6,* 321–329.

Chaiken, S., & Stangor, C. (1987). Attitudes and attitude change. *Annual Review of Psychology, 38,* 575–630.

Chapman, A. G. (1976). Social aspects of humorous laughter. In A. J. Chapman & H. C. Foot (Eds.), *Humor and laughter: Theory, research and applications* (pp. 155–185). New York: Wiley.

Feinberg, L. (1978). *The secret of humor.* Amsterdam: Rodopi.

Freud, S. (1960). Jokes and their relation to the unconscious. In J. Strachey (Ed. and Trans.), *The standard edition of the complete psychological works of Sigmund Freud* (Vol. 8, pp. 9–243). London: Hogarth. (Original work published 1905)

Freud, S. (1961). Humor. In J. Strachey (Ed. and Trans.), *The standard edition of the complete psychological works of Sigmund Freud* (Vol. 21, pp. 159–172). London: Hogarth. (Original work published 1927)

Gadfield, J. J. (1977). Sex differences in humour appreciation: A question of conformity? In A. J. Chapman & H. C. Foot (Eds.), *It's a funny thing, humour* (pp. 433–435). Oxford, England: Pergamon.

Gardner, H. E. (1980). Children's literary development: The realms of metaphors and stories. In P. E. McGhee & A. J. Chapman (Eds.), *Children's humor* (pp. 91–118). Chichester, England: Wiley.

Gibbs, R. W., Jr. (1989). Understanding and literal meaning. *Cognitive Science, 13,* 243–251.

Gibbs, R. W., Jr., & Gerrig, R. J. (1989). How context makes metaphor comprehension seem "special." *Metaphor and Symbolic Activity, 4,* 145–158.

Gill, R. B. (1982). New directions in satire: Some psychological and sociological approaches. *Studies in Contemporary Satire, 9,* 17–28.

Glucksberg, S. (1987, November). *Understanding metaphors: Beyond similarity.* Paper presented at the annual meeting of the Psychonomic Society, Seattle.

Glucksberg, S. (1990). Understanding metaphorical comparisons: Beyond similarity. *Psychological Review, 97,* 3–18.

Graesser, A. C., Long, D. L., & Mio, J. S. (1989). What are the cognitive and conceptual components of humorous text? *Poetics, 18,* 143–163.

Greenwald, H. (1977). Humour in psychotherapy. In A. J. Chapman & H. C. Foot (Eds.), *It's a funny thing, humour* (pp. 161–164). Oxford, England: Pergamon.

Hansen, C. C., & Halpern, D. F. (1987, November). *Using analogies to improve comprehension and recall of scientific passages.* Paper presented at the annual meeting of the Psychonomic Society, Seattle.

Hershkowitz, A. (1977). The essential ambiguity of, and in, humour. In A. J. Chapman & H. C. Foot (Eds.), *It's a funny thing, humour* (pp. 139–142). Oxford, England: Pergamon.

Jamieson, G. H. (1985). *Communication and persuasion.* London: Croom Helm.

Kelly, M. H., & Keil, F. C. (1987). Metaphor comprehension and knowledge of semantic domains. *Metaphor and Symbolic Activity, 2,* 33–51.

La Fave, L., Haddad, J., & Maeson, W. A. (1976). Superiority enhanced self-esteem and perceived incongruity in humor theory. In A. J. Chapman & H. C. Foot (Eds.), *Humor and laughter: Theory, research and applications* (pp. 63–91). New York: Wiley.

Lang, C. D. (1988). *Irony/humor.* Baltimore: Johns Hopkins University Press.

Leventhal, H., & Safer, M. A. (1977). Individual differences, personality, and humour appreciation: Introduction to symposium. In A. J. Chapman & H. C. Foot (Eds.), *It's a funny thing, humour* (pp. 335–349). Oxford, England: Pergamon.

Levine, J. (1977). Humour as a form of therapy: Introduction to symposium. In A. J. Chapman & H. C. Foot (Eds.), *It's a funny thing, humour* (pp. 127–137). Oxford, England: Pergamon.

Lusterman, D. D. (1988, August). Humor as metaphor. In R. A. DiGuiseppe (Chair), *Eclectic uses of metaphor in psychotherapy.* Symposium conducted at the annual meeting of the American Psychological Association, Atlanta.

Maccoby, E. E., & Jacklin, C. N. (1974). *The psychology of sex differences.* Stanford, CA: Stanford University.

Marchark, M., & Hunt, R. R. (1985). On memory for metaphor. *Memory & Cognition, 13,* 413–424.

McGhee, P. E. (1979). *Humor: Its origin and development.* San Francisco: Freeman.

Mio, J. S. (1988, August). *On men of zeal: Metaphors and the Iran–Contra hearings.* Paper presented at the annual meeting of the American Psychological Association, Atlanta.

Morreall, J. (1987). *The philosophy of laugher and humor.* Albany: State University of New York Press.

Pollio, H. R. (1983). Notes toward a field theory of humor. In P. E. McGhee & J. G. Goldstein (Eds.), *Hand-*

book of humor research: Vol. 1. Basic issues (pp. 213–230). New York; Springer-Verlag.

Pollio, H. R. & Edgerly, J. W. (1976). Comedians and comic style. In A. J. Chapman & H. C. Foot (Eds.), *Humor and laughter: Theory, research and applications* (pp. 215–242). London: Wiley.

Raskin, V. (1985). *Semantic mechanisms of humor.* Dordrecht, Netherlands: Reidel.

Reardon, K. K. (1981). *Persuasion: Theory and context.* Beverly Hills, CA: Sage.

Rothbart, M. K. (1977). Psychological approaches to the study of humour. In A. J. Chapman & H. C. Foot (Eds.), *It's a funny thing, humour* (pp. 87–94). Oxford, England: Pergamon.

Searle, J. R. (1969). *Speech acts.* Cambridge, England: Cambridge University Press.

Searle, J. R. (1979). Metaphor. In A. Ortony (Ed.), *Metaphor and thought* (pp. 92–123). Cambridge, England: Cambridge University Press.

Sheppard, A. (1977). Sex role attitudes, sex differences, and comedians' sex. In A. J. Chapman & H. C. Foot (Eds.), *It's a funny thing, humour* (pp. 365–368). Oxford, England: Pergamon.

Sternberg, R. J. (1982). Understanding and appreciating metaphors. *Cognition, 11,* 203–244.

Suls, J. (1972). A two-stage model for the appreciation of jokes and cartoons: An information-processing analysis. In J. H. Goldstein & P. E. McGhee (Eds.), *The psychology of humor* (pp. 81–100). New York: Academic.

Suls, J. (1977). Cognitive and disparagement theories of humour: A theoretical and empirical synthesis. In A. J. Chapman & H. C. Foot (Eds.), *It's a funny thing, humour* (pp. 41–45). Oxford, England: Pergamon.

Suls, J. (1983). Cognitive processes in humor appreciation. In P. E. McGhee & J. H. Goldstein (Eds.), *Handbook of humor research; Vol. 1. Basic issues* (pp. 39–57). New York: Springer-Verlag.

Tourangeau, R., & Sternberg, R. J. (1981). Aptness in metaphor. *Cognitive Psychology, 13,* 27–55.

Tourangeau, R., & Sternberg, R. J. (1982). Understanding and appreciating metaphors. *Cognition, 11,* 203–244.

Trick, L., & Katz, A. N. (1986). The domain interaction approach to metaphor processing: Relating individual differences and metaphor characteristics. *Metaphor and Symbolic Activity, 1,* 185–213.

Wheelwright, P. E. (1962). *Metaphor and reality.* Bloomington: Indiana University Press.

Zillmann, D. (1983). Disparagement humor. In P. E. McGhee & J. H. Goldstein (Eds.), *Handbook of humor research: Vol. 1. Basic issues* (pp. 85–107). New York: Springer-Verlag.

Zillmann, D., & Bryant, J. (1974). Retaliatory equity as a factor in humor appreciation. *Journal of Experimental Social Psychology, 10,* 480–488.

Zillmann, D., & Cantor, J. R. (1972). Directionality of transitory dominance as a communication variable affecting humor appreciation. *Journal of Personality and Social Psychology, 24,* 191–198.

Zillmann, D., & Cantor, J. R. (1976). A dispositional theory of humor and mirth. In A. J. Chapman & H. C. Foot (Eds.), *Humor and laughter: Theory, research and applications* (pp. 93–116). New York: Wiley.

APPENDIX

Disparaging Metaphors

- *"Harvard is a sewer among elite universities."*
- *"A princess is a whore among royalty."*
- *"An ace is a mule among airplane pilots."*
- *"Princeton is the kindergarten of elite universities."*
- *"A stud is an animal among men."*
- *"A Nobel laureate is a janitor among honored people."*
- *"The White House is a shack among leaders' residences."*
- *"Yale is a tavern among elite universities."*
- *"My surgeon is a butcher among doctors."*
- *"A gold medalist is a rodent among sports figures."*
- *"This officer is a bum among leaders."*
- *"Miss America is a beetle among women."*
- *"The Taj Mahal is a dump among palaces."*
- *"Caesar was the worm of emperors."*
- *"This Prime Minister is the cobbler of world leaders."*
- *"This champion is a pimp among winners."*
- *"This university is a preschool among learning institutions."*
- *"This king is a pauper among rulers."*
- *"The President is a cockroach among world leaders."*
- *"The Pentagon is a cave among government buildings."*
- *"The Secretary of State is a beggar among cabinet members."*
- *"This chief is a fool among leaders."*
- *"A general is an ape among military officers."*
- *"This diplomat is a shoe-shine boy among statesmen."*

- *"The Ivy League is a hell among university systems."*
- *"Wall Street is an opium den among business sites."*
- *"Medical school is a brothel among learning institutions."*
- *"The Attorney General is a dog among government workers."*
- *"My doctor is a garbageman among professionals."*
- *"The queen is a bag lady among rulers."*
- *"A lawyer is a thief among professionals."*
- *"A virtuoso is a knave among artists."*

Uplifting Metaphors

- *"This sewer is the Harvard of waste systems."*
- *"A whore is a princess among street people."*
- *"A mule is an ace among work animals."*
- *"This kindergarten is the Princeton of primary schools."*
- *"An animal is a stud among living creatures."*
- *"A janitor is a Nobel laureate among workers."*
- *"This shack is the White House among poor dwellings."*
- *"This tavern is the Yale among drinking establishments."*
- *"My butcher is a surgeon among meat cutters."*
- *"A rodent is the gold medalist among animals."*
- *"This bum is an officer among beggars."*
- *"The beetle is a Miss America among insects."*
- *"This dump is the Taj Mahal of disposal areas."*
- *"The worm is a Caesar of the garden."*
- *"This cobbler is the Prime Minister of shoe repairers."*
- *"This pimp is a champion among street people."*
- *"This preschool is a university among primary schools."*
- *"This pauper is a king among the downtrodden."*
- *"The cockroach is the President of insects."*
- *"This cave is the Pentagon among caverns."*
- *"A beggar is the Secretary of State among street people."*
- *"This fool is a chief among the downtrodden."*
- *"An ape is a general among jungle animals."*
- *"This shoe-shine boy is a diplomat among workers."*
- *"Hell is the Ivy League among unpleasant places."*
- *"This opium den is a Wall Street among shady areas."*

- "*A brothel is a medical school among shady areas.*"
- "*A dog is the Attorney General among animals.*"
- "*My garbageman is a doctor among workers.*"
- "*The bag lady is a queen among street people.*"
- "*A thief is a lawyer among criminals.*"
- "*A knave is a virtuoso among servants.*"

18

*Mary Kister Kaiser, John Jonides,
and Joanne Alexander*

Intuitive Reasoning About Abstract and Familiar Physics Problems

Previous research has demonstrated that many people have misconceptions about basic properties of motion. In two experiments, we examined whether people are more likely to produce dynamically correct predictions about basic motion problems involving situations with which they are familiar, and whether solving such problems enhances performance on a subsequent abstract problem. In Experiment 1, college students were asked to predict the trajectories of objects exiting a curved tube. Subjects were more accurate on the familiar version of the problem, and there was no evidence of transfer to the abstract problem. In Experiment 2, two familiar problems were provided in an attempt to enhance subjects' tendency to extract the general structure of the problems. Once again, they gave more correct responses to the familiar problems but failed to generalize to the abstract problem. Formal physics training was associated with correct predictions for the abstract problem but was unrelated to performance on the familiar problems.

Recent studies have demonstrated that many adults hold erroneous beliefs concerning fundamental laws of motion (McCloskey, 1983; McCloskey, Caramazza, & Green, 1980). For example, when asked to predict the trajectory of a ball exiting a curved tube, many college students respond that the ball will continue to curve, at least for some period of time. McCloskey and his colleagues explain such erroneous predictions as evidence that, when people are asked to reason abstractly about motion, their intuitive models frequently resemble a medieval impetus theory rather than a Newtonian model. The Newtonian model holds that, in the absence of external force, objects maintain a linear path. Alternatively, the impetus theory holds that setting an object in motion imparts to the object an internal energy, or

From Mary Kister Kaiser, John Jonides, and Joanne Alexander, "Intuitive Reasoning About Abstract and Familiar Physics Problems," *Memory and Cognition*, vol. 14, no. 4 (1986), pp. 308–312. Copyright © 1986 by The Psychonomic Society, Inc. Reprinted by permission.

impetus, that maintains the object's motion along its initial trajectory, be it linear or curvilinear.

Suppose people were asked to reason about problems that evoked actual motion events with which they are familiar. Would they make the same impetus-like error? Research in other cognitive domains raises the possibility that they would not: whereas many adults make errors in reasoning about abstract logic problems, performance is much better on problems that are logically equivalent to the abstract problems but that make reference to familiar situations. For example, in Wason's (1966) selection task, subjects were presented with cards showing a letter on one side and a number on the other. They were required to choose which cards needed to be examined to determine the validity of the statement: "If a card has an A on one side, then it has a 4 on the other." When presented four cards showing an "A," a "B," a "4," and a "7," many subjects responded that the "A" and "4" cards must be examined (instead of the logically correct "A" and "7"), an error termed "affirming the consequent." Other logical errors, such as insisting that all cards must be examined, were also observed. This would suggest that adults make systematic errors in logical reasoning, much as McCloskey's work suggests that adults make systematic errors in mechanical reasoning.

However, research has shown that subjects can solve problems that are formally identical to the selection task if they are presented in realistic, thematic contexts (see Evans, 1982). Drawing on the now-defunct British postal rule requiring more postage for sealed than unsealed envelopes, Johnson-Laird, P. Legrenzi, and M. S. Legrenzi (1972) asked subjects to examine letters for violations of the rule, "If the letter is sealed, then it has a 5d stamp on it." This problem is formally identical to Wason's (1966) selection task. Older subjects, familiar with the postal system, performed far better on the envelope task than on Wason's task. Younger subjects who had no previous experience with the postal rule performed no better on the envelope task.

Our Experiment 1 is concerned with the possibility that familiarity may breed success: We examined whether or not people would give more accurate trajectory predictions on a somewhat familiar motion problem than on a more abstract version of the problem. In addition to examining performance on the two

problems, we were interested in whether or not subjects would recognize the similarity between the problems and perform better on the abstract problem if it was presented after the familiar one.

EXPERIMENT 1

Method

Subjects.
Eighty college students (40 males and 40 females) were recruited in the hallway of a classroom building at the University of Michigan. Half of the students (20 males and 20 females) had taken physics courses in either high school or college.

Materials and Procedures.
A clear plastic spiral tube was mounted on a 60 × 80 cm plywood board that lay flat on a level table. The tube was 2.2 cm in diameter and formed a spiral of 540° rotation with an interior diameter of 25 cm (see Figure 1a). One end of the tube was elevated such that it appeared that a ball or liquid inserted in the elevated end would travel through the tube at a moderate speed. Half of the subjects were given the following instructions: "Suppose I take this ball bearing and place it in this (the elevated) end of the tube. It would roll around the tube and come out here (indicate mouth of tube). I'd like you to draw the path that the ball would take when it exited the tube." Once the subject had produced a response, a second problem was presented: "Okay, now imagine that we connect a hose to the elevated end of the tube and send water through it. The water would flow through the tube and come out here (at the mouth of the tube). Could you draw the path that the main part of the stream of water would take when it came out of the tube?" The other half of the subjects were administered the problems in the opposite order.

The ball problem has been used by a number of researchers to investigate people's understanding of curvilinear motion (e.g., McCloskey et al., 1980). Typically, a sizable proportion of subjects' answers include references to nonexistent forces and influences (e.g., curvilinear momentum). The

Figure 1

Schematics of Apparatus Employed in Experiment 1 (a) and Experiment 2 (a and b)

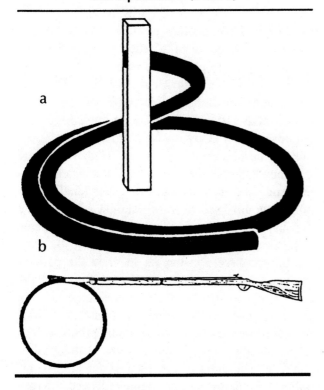

water problem was chosen since water shooting from a curved garden hose is a closely related event that is familiar to most people. Since most subjects have seen that the curvature of the hose does not affect the water's path, we hoped that people would draw upon this experience in solving the problem.

Subjects made their predictions by drawing a path on a 28 × 55 cm piece of paper placed on the board at the mouth of the tube. Subjects were asked to describe verbally the path they drew to clarify any ambiguity. The experimenter recorded the subject's gender, and inquired about his or her coursework in physics. Subjects were thanked and paid for their participation.

Results

A response was coded as correct if the path arced no more than 10° throughout its length and was tangent to the point of exit. Examples of correct and incorrect responses are illustrated in Figure 2. Subjects produced far more correct predictions for the water problem than for the ball problem. Fifty-

three people (31 men and 22 women) drew linear paths for the water problem, compared with 31 subjects (22 men and 9 women) for the ball problem. This effect was highly significant ($x^2(1) = 12.13$, $p < .005$). Log-linear analyses demonstrated a strong gender effect for the ball problem [$x^2(1) = 9.45$, $p < .005$] and a lesser gender effect for the water problem [$x^2(1) = 4.59$, $p < .05$]. Physics training had a marginal effect on performance on the ball problem [$x^2(1) = 2.93$, $p < .10$] but no significant effect on performance on the water problem [$x^2(1) = 1.21$].

To examine whether or not subjects transferred their correct solutions on the water problem to the more abstract ball problem, we tested for a problem-order effect among those subjects who answered the water problem correctly. Were subjects who demonstrated a correct understanding of the water problem more likely to answer the ball problem correctly if it was administered second? Of the 53 subjects who gave a correct response to the water problem, 27 were administered the ball prob-

Figure 2

Examples of Correct and Incorrect Responses on the Water and Ball Problems in Experiment 1

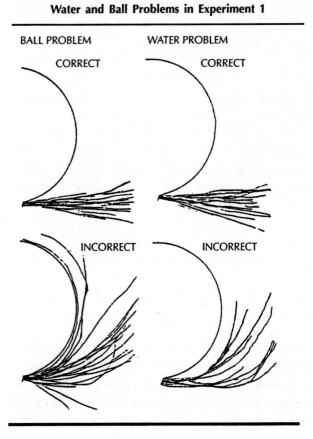

lem first. Ten of these subjects (37%) were correct on the ball problem. The other 26 subjects answered the ball problem after correctly answering the water problem. Fifteen of them (58%) were correct on the ball problem. This difference is not significant ($x^2 = 2.26$, $p > .10$). Thus, correctly solving a familiar problem on curvilinear motion immediately prior to attempting an abstract curvilinear problem did not significantly enhance performance on the latter.

EXPERIMENT 2

The lack of transfer in Experiment 1 is quite striking, especially since the abstract problem was administered immediately after the common-sense problem and even used the same apparatus. Why did subjects fail to reason analogically from the water problem to the ball problem? Is it possible to improve subjects' transfer by offering more than one common-sense exemplar? These were addressed in Experiment 2.

The literature on analogical problem solving suggests that a critical obstacle to solution transfer is the failure to recognize the relevant similarities among problems (D. Gentner & D. R. Gentner, 1983; Holyoak, 1984). Providing multiple exemplars of a solution type often enhances people's ability to recognize abstract similarities (Holyoak, 1984). We investigated whether providing a second common-sense motion problem increased the likelihood of solution transfer to the abstract problem. Furthermore, we asked subjects to justify their predictions, particularly when their solutions for the two types of problems differed.

Method

Subjects.

Eighty-one University of Michigan female students participated in the experiment. Forty-three of them had taken physics courses in either high school or college. Subjects were recruited from a subject pool at the university and were paid for their participation.

Materials and Procedure.

Subjects were administered one abstract and two familiar curvilinear motion problems. The ball problem from Experiment 1 was the abstract problem. One of the familiar problems was the water problem of Experiment 1. The other problem required subjects to predict the path of a bullet when fired from a rifle with a curved barrel. The rifle was oriented such that the curved barrel lay flat on a horizontal surface, similar to the curved-tube apparatus. A pilot study indicated that, although people had never used such a weapon, many insisted that they had seen them used (in cartoons and movies) and professed an intuitive understanding that bullets would have to travel straight regardless of the shape of the barrel. The experimental apparatus is schematized in Figures 1a and 1b.

Subjects were instructed to draw the path of the ball, the water, or the bullet upon exiting the curved tube or barrel. Forty of the subjects were given the two familiar problems (water and rifle) first, followed by the abstract (ball) problem. The other subjects were administered the abstract problem first. The order of presentation for the two familiar problems was counterbalanced across subjects. After they had made all three predictions, 41 of the subjects (every other subject) were asked to explain their predictions and to justify any discrepancies in the paths.

Results

Subjects' responses were coded as in Experiment 1. The patterns of subjects' predictions are shown in Table 1. It should be noted that a fairly conservative classification scheme was used for the familiar problems: Subjects had to produce correct predictions for both familiar problems to be classified as accurate on that problem type. Very few subjects (12) gave incorrect predictions for both familiar problems.

Even with such a classification scheme, subjects were found to give more accurate predictions for the familiar problems than for the abstract problem [$x^2(1) = 4.24$, $p < .05$]. As in Experiment 1, there was no evidence of transfer of correct solutions from the familiar to the abstract problems [$x^2(1) = 1.29$]. Having correctly solved two familiar

Table 1

Table 1

Patterns of Subjects' Responses for Abstract and Common-Sense Curvilinear Motion Problems (Experiment 2)

	Number of Subjects		
Pattern of Responses	Common-Sense Problems First	Abstract Problem First	Total
Accurate Predictions for all Problems	11(6)	17(14)	28(20)
More Accurate Predictions for Common-Sense Problems	10(7)	13(5)	23(12)
More Accurate Prediction for Abstract Problem	8(2)	3(2)	11(4)
Inaccurate Predictions for Common-Sense and Abstract Problems	13(3)	6(4)	19(7)

Note—Numbers in parentheses indicate number of subjects with formal physics training.

curvilinear problems did not enhance subjects' performance on the abstract problem.

How did subjects who gave correct responses for the familiar problems justify their erroneous responses to the ball problem? Examination of these subjects' protocols indicated three basic justifications: First, in the case of the rifle, subjects noted that the barrel had less curvature (360°) than did the ball apparatus (540°). Second, in the case of the water, subjects contended that liquids and solids had different motion properties; water would not acquire curvilinear "momentum" the way a ball would. Finally, subjects cited several irrelevant dynamic properties, notably speed, pressure, and weight. Speed was most often seen as a determining factor. Subjects reported that since the bullet (and sometimes the water) would travel faster than the ball, there would be less tendency for the bullet (and water) to "pick up" curvature from the tube. Two examples of subjects' protocols are given in the Appendix. Both of these subjects gave correct responses to the two common-sense problems but curvilinear responses to the abstract problem.

Most subjects who gave correct responses to all three problems noted the underlying similarity. Newton's first law of motion (or some more vernacular version) was often cited, as was the tendency of objects to move in a "natural" path (i.e., a straight line). The remainder of these subjects either were unable to justify their correct responses or acknowledged that they were just guessing.

Experience-based explanations were given for all problems, although more were given for the familiar problems than for the ball problem. Interestingly, incorrect responses were sometimes justified with inappropriate experiences, such as citing whirlpools as a basis for a curvilinear path for water.

GENERAL DISCUSSION

The data from both experiments indicate that people give more accurate predictions to some curvilinear motion problems than to others. Furthermore, a correct solution on one type of problem is not generalized to another, usually because irrelevant differences are noted in the problems.

One model that is generally consistent with the data holds that subjects apply formal physical principles to both kinds of problems, but that their principles are inaccurate and include such irrelevant factors as the object's velocity and the amount of tube curvature. Certainly, protocols indicate that subjects employ a number of inappropriate physical properties in their justifications. Subjects' allusions to specific experiences may merely reflect an attempt to provide concrete examples of their basic, abstract beliefs. However, if such a model is correct, it is not clear why these misconceptions should impact on subjects' ball predictions more often than on their water or rifle predictions. It would be rather serendipitous that the familiar problems we selected tapped more accurate formal physical principles than did the abstract problem we chose.

An alternative interpretation of the data is that people are able to reason more appropriately about motion problems when they are related to specific, concrete, familiar experiences. The facilitation of reasoning that results from placing an abstract problem in a familiar context has been examined in other cognitive domains, notably in the area of deductive reasoning. Context effects, or "facilitation by realism," have been found to affect performance on syllogistic reasoning (Wilkins, 1928) as well as on a number of variations of the Wason selection task (see Evans, 1982, for a summary). As in our motion problems, however, the facilitation did not generalize to subsequent abstract problems.

Evans (1982) has discussed context effects and the lack of solution transfer from the familiar to the abstract deductive reasoning problem. He argues that the studies that demonstrate the greatest context effects (e.g., Johnson-Laird et al., 1972) may present problems that are too realistic. That is, they do not require subjects to reason at all, but rather allow for a solution based on specific experiences. Such a model would certainly explain the lack of transfer: the relevant similarity in the problems is not recognized since the familiar problem is never processed in formal terms.

We propose a similar model for our subjects' performance. Subjects draw on specific experiences to solve the common-sense problems, and need not employ formal reasoning. The abstract problem, evoking no specific memory, requires subjects to draw upon their formal understanding of physics (which is often erroneous). Thus, we suggest that subjects apply a two-stage approach to solving these problems. First, they search for a specific solution based on relevant experiences. If this search fails, they default to a reasoning process employing formal understanding of mechanics. Such default reasoning models have been proposed in many areas of cognitive psychology (e.g., Siegler, 1981) and artificial intelligence (e.g., Reiter, 1980).

The striking lack of transfer can also be accounted for by such a model. Reasoning by analogy is dependent upon recognizing the relevant similarities of the base problem and the target problem (D. Gentner, 1982). Since the relevant similarities of the common-sense and abstract problems exist only at the level of formal analysis, it is necessary that the common-sense problems be viewed in formal terms for transfer to occur. However, subjects' protocols suggest that most people are able to map the common-sense problem to experience-based solutions on a very concrete level. Since the common-sense problems are only considered on a concrete level, similarity recognition is not possible. The use of two common-sense problems in our Experiment 2 did not improve subjects' solution transfer, although other researchers have found the provision of multiple exemplars to enhance subjects' awareness of formal similarities among problems (Holyoak, 1984).

Finally, our model explains why people demonstrate inconsistency in their reasoning concerning motion problems. Many people who give impetus-type responses to one problem will provide a correct prediction on the next. We suggest that this is because people do not always draw upon their formal representation of physics, but only do so when they are unable to find an acceptable solution based on specific experiences in their memories. The problem of deciding what is or is not a relevant experience is still an issue, but our main point is that people draw on their formal models only after such a solution-by-analogy method fails. In the problems we employed, subjects usually failed to find a relevant experience for the abstract problem and dismissed the common-sense problems as irrelevant based on extraneous factors (e.g., velocity, substance). What we propose, therefore, is that reasoning by analogy is the default strategy most people apply to motion problems (particularly if they lack formal physics training). Only when people are unable to map the target problem to an appropriate base do they draw upon formal representations. It is then that errors reflecting an impetus model of physics emerge from many individuals.

REFERENCES

Evans, J. St. B. T. (1982). *The psychology of deductive reasoning.* London: Routledge & Kegan Paul.

Gentner, D. (1982). Are scientific analogies metaphors? In D. S. Miall (Ed.), *Metaphor: Problems and perspectives* (pp. 106–132). Brighton, Sussex, England: Harvester Press.

Gentner, D., & Gentner, D. R. (1983). Flowing waters or teeming crowds: Mental models of electricity. In D. Gentner & A. Steven (Eds.), *Mental models* (pp. 99–130). Hillsdale, NJ: Erlbaum.

Holyoak, K. J. (1984). Analogical thinking and human intelligence. In R. J. Sternberg (Ed.), *Advances in the psychology of human intelligence* (Vol. 2, pp. 199–230). Hillsdale, NJ: Erlbaum.

Johnson-Laird, P. N., Legrenzi, P., & Legrenzi, M.S. (1972). Reasoning and a sense of reality. *British Journal of Psychology, 63,* 395–400.

McCloskey, M. (1983). Intuitive physics. *Scientific American, 248*(4), 122–130.

McCloskey, M., Caramazza, A., & Green, B. (1980). Curvilinear motion in the absence of external forces: Naive beliefs about the motion of objects. *Science,* **210,** 1139–1141.

Reiter, R. (1980). A logic for default reasoning. *Artificial Intelligence, 13,* 81–132.

Siegler, R. (1981). Developmental sequences within and between concepts. *Monographs of the Society for Research in Child Development,* **46**(2).

Wason, P. C. (1966). Reasoning. In B. M. Foss (Ed.), *New horizons in psychology 1* (pp. 135–151). Harmondsworth, England: Penguin.

Wilkins, M. C. (1928). The effect of changed material on the ability to do formal syllogistic reasoning. *Archives of Psychology* (New York) No. 102.

APPENDIX

Sample Subject Protocols from Experiment 2

Subject 20

Q: Could you explain for each of the situations why you thought the objects took the paths you drew?

A: I guess when I think in terms of bullets, bullets always go straight; when it came out of the gun, I figure it would go straight. And the water, water also seems to go straight out, no matter how much like a garden hose is twisted around, so I imagine the water coming out straight. The ball, I imagine, staying next to the tube, like just following around the tube.

Q. Could you tell me how the speed of the object affects the path it takes?

A. If it were going really fast, it would go straighter than if it were going slow.

Q: Why is that?

A: When you roll a ball very slowly, it tends to go off to the side, where if you throw it faster, it takes a straighter path. I guess maybe it's the gravity behind it. . . . well, it's not even gravity, I guess; it's more like inertia, or the energy it has.

Q: Could you tell me your background in physics?

A: Two years in high school. I got As.

Subject 21

Q: Could you explain why you thought the objects took the paths you drew?

A: I'm going to assume that the ball's going to come out slower here, and because it's been going around and not going real fast, it's going to take the path it had, and curve around. With the gun, the curve was less on the tube, and there's more force, so it's going to be going more straight forward. I don't know the physics behind it, but since it hadn't been going real slow, it's going to take the most direct path, which will be straight. With the water, it's the same reasoning as with the shotgun, it's coming out faster, so it's going to take the direct path, and that's more out straight.

Q: How does the speed of the object affect the path it takes?

A: The faster the object goes, the straighter or more direct path it will take.

Q: Why is that? What about its going faster makes it take a straighter path?

A: Gravity's going to want to hold it in more to the circular path, but when it's going faster, then you get away from the effects of gravity.

Q: What's your physics background?

A: Very limited. Just reading on my own, and what they threw in chemistry. . . . I got an A in chemistry.

This research was supported in part by NIMH Training Grant T32-MH16892 to the first author and in part by a grant from AFOSR to the second author. Portions of this paper were presented at the Annual Meeting of the Midwestern Psychological Association, Chicago, May, 1985.

We would like to thank Michelene Chi, Alice Healy, and Michael McCloskey for their helpful comments.

19

Richard E. Mayer,
Anne Bovenmyer Lewis,
and Mary Hegarty

Mathematical Misunderstandings: Qualitative Reasoning About Quantitative Problems

SUMMARY

In this [selection], we summarize a research program on students' misunderstandings of mathematical story problems. A mathematical misunderstanding occurs when the problem solver constructs a mental model of the problem situation that conflicts with the information in the problem statement. In particular, we examine difficulties that students have in reasoning about problems containing relational statements, such as "Gas at Chevron is 5 cents more per gallon than gas at ARCO." We report a series of studies in which relational statements cause systematic errors in the recall of story problems, in the pattern of solution errors, in the pattern of solution times, in students' eye fixations, and in the effectiveness of remediation training. This research supports the idea that instruction in mathematical problem solving should focus on the development of qualitative reasoning skills—such as how to build a mental model of the problem situation—in addition to quantitative reasoning skills—such as executing computational procedures.

Reprinted from Richard E. Mayer, Anne Bovenmyer Lewis, and Mary Hegarty, "Mathematical Misunderstandings: Qualitative Reasoning About Quantitative Problems," in J. I. D. Campbell, ed., *The Nature and Origins of Mathematical Skills* (Elsevier Science, 1992), pp. 137–153. Copyright © 1992 with kind permission from Elsevier Science - NL, Sara Burgerhartstraat 25, 1055 KV Amsterdam, The Netherlands.

INTRODUCTION

Mathematical Misunderstandings

In mathematical problem solving, a problem solver begins with a verbal statement of a situation describing quantitative relations among different variables, and must end with a solution, which is derived by combining the given quantities in a manner consistent with the described situation. The cognitive processes involved in mathematical problem solving include: *translation*—converting each statement in the problem into an internal mental representation, *integration*—combining the relevant information into a coherent mental representation, *planning*—devising and monitoring a plan that breaks the problem into parts (including metacognitive processes of monitoring one's solution attempts), and *execution*—carrying out the computations or operations for each step in the plan (Mayer, 1985, 1989, 1991; Mayer, Larkin & Kadane, 1984).

Thus, successful mathematical problem solving involves both qualitative and quantitative reasoning. The first three cognitive processes, i.e., translation, integration, and planning, involve qualitative reasoning, which includes constructing a qualitative model of the situation described in the problem (Greeno, 1987, 1989; Kintsch & Greeno, 1985); in contrast, the process of execution involves quantitative reasoning, which includes combining the numerical values in the problem to derive the quantitative solution. *Mathematical misunderstandings* occur in qualitative reasoning when the problem solver's model of the problem situation conflicts with the information in the problem statement.

One of the major accomplishments of qualitative reasoning about quantitative problems is the production of a model of the problem situation (Greeno, 1987, 1989; Kintsch & Greeno, 1985). Kintsch and Greeno (1985) characterized this type of reasoning as a special case of text comprehension in which a propositional textbase is formed and organized into a *problem model*, a mathematical representation of the actions and relations expressed in the problem. In a later version of this problem-comprehension model, a distinction is made between situation models—which are qualitative representations of problem text in everyday terms, such as comprehending that a boat is travelling upstream—and corresponding problem models—which express these qualitative representations in formal mathematical terms such as an equation (Lewis & Nathan, 1991; Nathan, Kintsch & Young, in press). Thus, construction of a problem model involves formally quantifying the informal situation information. In terms of this problem-comprehension model, mathematical misunderstandings occur when the problem solver's problem model does not accurately reflect the situation described in the problem, that is, when the problem solver is unable to construct a correct situation model of the problem, or is unable to make a correct correspondence between this situational understanding and the mathematical formalisms of a problem model.

In this [selection], we explore the nature of high school and college students' mathematical misunderstandings of a particularly difficult type of word problem—*compare problems* (Hudson, 1983; Morales, Shute & Pellegrino, 1985; Riley & Greeno, 1988; Riley, Greeno & Heller, 1983). Compare problems are story problems that include a proposition describing a quantitative relation between two variables, such as, "Gas at Chevron is 5 cents less per gallon than gas at ARCO." In particular, we review the role of problem representation in mathematical problem solving, summarize five approaches that we have used in our research program to study how students understand and misunderstand mathematical problems, and conclude with suggestions for mathematics education.

An Example of Mathematical Misunderstanding

A well-documented example of a mathematical misunderstanding is based on the following problem (Hegarty, Mayer & Green, in press; Lewis and Mayer, 1987; Lewis, 1989):

> At ARCO gas sells for $1.13 per gallon.
> This is 5 cents less per gallon than gas at Chevron.
> How much do 5 gallons of gas cost at Chevron?

This is a two-step compare problem because two computations are required and the second sentence compares the cost of gas at ARCO to the cost of gas at Chevron using the relational term, "less . . .

than." The college and junior college students we tested in our program of research found this to be a difficult problem (Hegarty, Mayer, & Green, in press; Lewis, 1989; Lewis & Mayer, 1987). The most common incorrect answer was $5.40 based on computations such as these:

$$1.13 - .05 = 1.08$$
$$1.08 \times 5 = 5.40$$

We refer to this mistake as a *reversal error* because the problem solver performs the opposite operation of what is actually required—e.g., subtraction instead of addition in the first step. In spite of many years of mathematics education, including practice in solving hundreds of word problems, approximately 15% to 35% of the college students that we tested in various studies produced reversal errors on two-step compare problems like the ARCO problem. De Corte and his colleagues have extended this research, showing that young children display the same pattern of errors on one-step compare problems (De Corte, Vershaffel & Pauwels, 1989).

Why is the ARCO problem so difficult? Computationally, the problem is straightforward and our students rarely made arithmetic errors. Conceptually, however, the problem is demanding. Students who rely on key words to understand the problem will see the word "less" and therefore be inclined to subtract (rather than add) the first two numbers in our example. Briars & Larkin (1984) have shown that a key word approach to understanding word problems can be effective for some word problems commonly found in mathematics textbooks, in spite of the fact that reliance on key words is a superficial heuristic that does not work on problems such the ARCO problem. Thus, reversal errors on problems such as the ARCO problem seem to signal mathematical misunderstandings rather than computational failures on the part of the problem solver.

The distinction between the key word approach to solving word problems and a model-based approach has also been explored in the artificial intelligence research literature. Bobrow (1968) developed a program, called STUDENT, that solves mathematical story problems by identifying key words in the program statement and converting the quantities and key words into mathematical equations from which the problem can be solved. This program was successful in solving many problems that occur in

mathematical textbooks, but had some limitations as a theory of problem solving. In particular, Paige and Simon (1966) found that in converting story problems into equations, some human subjects did not always translate directly from the problem statement, but first constructed an "auxiliary representation" of the problem situation and derived the equations from this. On the other hand, some less able problem solvers did translate directly and these solvers failed to notice that the following problem describes an impossible situation (Paige & Simon, 1966, p. 87):

> A board was sawed into two pieces. One piece was two-thirds as long as the whole board and was exceeded in length by the second piece by 4 feet. How long was the board before it was cut?

If a program like STUDENT solved the ARCO problem, relying on the key words to derive the appropriate operations, it might commit the type of reversal errors that we observed in some of our students. In contrast, students who first build a qualitative model of the situation described in the problem should be better able to determine that gas at ARCO is less than gas at Chevron and therefore select the proper mathematical equation (Kintsch & Greeno, 1985). One way to correctly represent the cost-per-gallon-of-gas is on a number line (Lewis, 1989):

$$|\!\!\leftarrow\!\text{-----------------}|\text{-}|\text{------------------}\!\rightarrow\!|$$
ARCO Chevron

After constructing this qualitative representation, students can recognize that to determine the price of gas at Chevron they must add the difference in price to the cost of gas at ARCO. We hypothesize that this external, spatial representation helps students create a link between their situational understanding of the problem and the proper mathematical representation of the situation.

As suggested by Paige and Simon (1966), the difference between a key-word and a model-construction approach to problem representation exemplifies a possible difference between successful and unsuccessful problem-solvers. The ARCO example suggests that errors occur when students focus on *product*—getting a numerical answer—rather than *process*—building a qualitative representation of the problem that makes sense and enables the creation of an appropriate solution plan. Put another way, the ARCO example suggests that errors occur when students view word problems primarily as an invitation to engage in *quantitative reasoning*—carrying out computations based on numbers in the problem—rather than *qualitative reasoning*—understanding the situation described in the words of the problem and then devising an appropriate plan.

The theme of this [selection] is that problem understanding should be viewed as a basic mathematics skill, that is, students need to acquire skill in qualitative reasoning about quantitative problems. The kind of instructional program we propose differs radically from current practice in which mathematics instruction emphasizes quantitative computation as the primary goal in mathematical problem solving.

Understanding a problem has long been recognized as one of the premier skills required for successful mathematical problem solving (Cummins, Kintsch, Reusser & Weimer, 1988; Greeno, 1987; Kintsch & Greeno, 1985; Mayer, 1985, 1991; Mayer, Larkin & Kadane, 1984; Polya, 1965; Wertheimer, 1959). *Problem understanding* occurs when a problem solver converts the words of the problem into an internal mental representation of the problem situation. In the case of word problems involving numerical quantities, the problem solver must construct a qualitative model of the situation described in the problem. Nathan, Kintsch & Young (in press) refer to this process as the construction of a situation model, and we argue that a crucial skill for mathematical problem solving is the ability to construct a qualitative, situation model of the problem information and relate this model to mathematical formalisms. In the following sections we describe five approaches we have taken in trying to understand the nature of mathematical misunderstandings—recall, solution errors, solution times, eye fixations, and remediation.

RECALL: DIFFICULTIES IN REMEMBERING COMPARE PROBLEMS

Our study of mathematical misunderstandings began with an analysis of approximately 1100 word problems collected from mathematics textbooks commonly used in California's junior high schools (Mayer, 1981). We sorted the problems into "families" that each shared the same general situation, such as motion problems which involved the formula distance = rate × time. In all, we identified approximately 24 families including motion, current, age, coin, work, part, dry mixture, wet mixture, percent, ratio, unit cost, markup/discount/profit, interest, direct variation, inverse variation, digit, rectangle, circle, triangle, series, consecutive integer, arithmetic, physics, and probability. This extends the list of 18 problem categories proposed by Hinsley, Hayes and Simon (1977).

Within each family, there were several different formats, which we called "templates," yielding a total of approximately 100 templates. For example, there were 13 different templates for motion problems including overtake (one vehicle overtakes another), closure (two vehicles converge on the same point from different directions), speed change (one vehicle changes speed during a trip), and round trip (one vehicle makes a round trip). In this [selection], we use the term "type" to refer to a problem template.

The structure of any template can be expressed as a unique list of propositions with each proposition consisting of an assignment proposition, a relational proposition, or a question proposition. An assignment gives a single numerical value for some variable, such as "the cost of candy is $1.70 per pound" or "one vegetable oil contains 6% saturated fats." A relation gives a single numerical relation between two variables, such as "the length is $2\frac{1}{2}$ times the width" or "the rate in still water is 12 mph more than the rate of the current." A question asks for a numerical value of some variable, such as "how much time will it take to empty the tanks" or "how many miles will the first car have gone before it is passed." In addition, problems could contain relevant or irrelevant facts.

The psychological reality of such problem categories has been demonstrated by Hinsley, Hayes and Simon (1977). In a series of verbal protocol studies, they found that students recognized each of the standard types of problems, often within reading the first few words of the problem. Students were also able to sort problems into categories based on problem type, suggesting that students possessed schemas for basic problem types.

Our research focused on students' recall of story problems. In order to examine students' comprehension of problems, we asked college students to study a series of eight algebra story problems that were presented individually in printed form and then, as a recall test, we asked the students to write down the problems they had just read (Mayer, 1982). For example, one of the problems was the following current problem:

> A river steamer travels 36 miles downstream in the same time that it travels 24 miles upstream. The steamer's engine drives in still water at a rate 12 miles per hour more than the rate of the current. Find the rate of the current.

This problem consists of two assignments, two relations, and a question, which can be specified as:

> miles downstream = 36
> miles upstream = 24
> time upstream = time downstream
> rate of steamer in still water = rate of current + 12
> rate of current = UNKNOWN

A common error in recalling the current problem was to change a relation proposition into an assignment proposition:

> A river boat goes 36 miles down the river and 24 miles up the river. If its engines push the boat 12 mph in still water, find the current speed.

In this example, the problem is also converted from a version that rarely appeared in math books (twice per 1100 problems) to a more common version (nine times per 1100 problems). Uncommon problem types (or templates) occurred once or twice per 1100 problems in textbooks whereas common problem types occurred from nine to 40 times per 1100 problems.

Overall, the results indicated a *proposition-type effect:* propositions about relations were approximately three times more likely to be misrecalled than propositions about assignments (29% and 9% errors, respectively), and there were 20 instances of students recalling a relation as an assignment versus only one instance of the reverse. These results suggest that students have difficulty in mentally representing propositions that express a numerical relation between two variables—that is,

relational propositions may require more cognitive processing than assignments.

Our results also indicated a *schema-familiarity effect:* problem types commonly found in mathematics textbooks were more easily recalled than uncommon problem types (e.g., the correlation between probability of recall and the relative frequency with which a problem type occurred in textbooks was $r = .942$), and there were 17 instances of students converting a less common problem type into a more common one versus no cases of the reverse. Cummins, Kintsch, Reusser and Weimer (1988) also found that students tended to miscomprehend difficult word problems by converting them into simpler problems. These results support the view (Hinsley, Hayes & Simon, 1977) that problem categorization plays an important role in the representation of story problems.

SOLUTION ERRORS: DIFFICULTIES IN SOLVING COMPARE PROBLEMS

The next approach to our study of mathematical misunderstanding was an examination of the solution protocols of students who solved a series of story problems (Lewis & Mayer, 1987). We asked college students to show their work as they solved a series of 24 story problems, including problems that contained relational propositions. Some of the relational propositions were called *consistent* because the relational term primed the appropriate arithmetic operation (e.g., contained "less" when the appropriate operation was to subtract or contained "more" when the appropriate operation was to add); others were *inconsistent* because the relational term primed an inappropriate arithmetic operation (e.g., contained "less" when the appropriate operation was to add or contained "more" when the appropriate operation was to subtract).

For example, a consistent problem was:

> At ARCO gas sells for $1.13 per gallon.
> Gas at Chevron is 5 cents less per gallon than gas at ARCO.
> How much do 5 gallons of gas cost at Chevron?

In contrast, an inconsistent problem was:

> AT ARCO gas sells for $1.13 per gallon.

This is 5 cents less per gallon than gas at
Chevron.

How much do 5 gallons of gas cost at Chevron?

Each problem contains an assignment (ARCO =
1.13 per gallon), a relation (ARCO − .05 = Chevron, or ARCO + .05 = Chevron), an assignment
(number of gallons = 5), and a question (total cost
= UNKNOWN).

The results indicate an *error-consistency effect:*
inconsistent problems, which contain a relational
statement that primes an incorrect operation, lead
to far more reversal errors (i.e., adding when subtraction is required or subtracting when adding is
required) than consistent problems, which contain
a relational statement that primes an appropriate operation. For example, over the course of several
studies, college students made reversal errors on
less than 2% of the consistent problems but on 15%
to 35% of the inconsistent problems. This result
suggests that students have difficulty in constructing and using a representation corresponding to the
situation portrayed in relational statements.

SOLUTION TIMES: DIFFICULTIES IN PLANNING SOLUTIONS FOR COMPARE PROBLEMS

The third approach in our research program was to
pinpoint the locus of the error consistency effect
using eye-fixation methodologies (Hegarty, Mayer
& Green, in press). We asked college students to
view a series of problems presented on a computer
monitor and to state a solution plan for each. For
example, a solution plan for the inconsistent version of the ARCO problem is, "Add a dollar eighteen to five cents, then multiply by five." Thus,
unlike previous studies, students did not engage in
computing a numerical answer (execution); instead,
they engaged solely in the qualitative aspects of
mathematical problem solving (translation, integration, and planning). To better evaluate students'
qualitative reasoning processes, we recorded their
eye fixations as they read each problem until they
produced a solution plan.

Reflecting the *error-consistency effect* found by
Lewis and Mayer (1987) and by Lewis (1989), students made more errors in devising plans for inconsistent compare problems than for consistent
compare problems. This result suggests that the
consistent effect occurs during the qualitative
phases of problem solving rather than during the
quantitative computations in the execution phase.

A new aspect of this study is a more detailed
picture of the problem-solvers' processing times.
When we look only at highly accurate students, for
example, we find a *time-consistency effect* in which
more time is allocated to inconsistent compare
problems (e.g., 27 seconds) than consistent compare problems (e.g., 23 seconds). Interestingly, the
effect is not present during the initial reading of
the problem (translation phase) but is seen in the
period between initial reading and producing a solution plan (integration and planning phases). Thus,
the time consistency effect seems to be localized in
the integration and planning phases rather than the
translation and execution phases of problem solving.

The time-consistency effect was not found
for less accurate students. Overall, students who
produced many errors did not spend more time
processing inconsistent problems than consistent
problems. De Corte, Vershaffel, and Pauwels (1989)
obtained a similar pattern of time effects with
younger children. This suggests that less-accurate
students may not be sensitive to the linguistic
structure of problems. This lack of recognition that
inconsistent problems require more careful
processing can account for the higher error rate
on inconsistent problems.

EYE FIXATIONS: DIFFICULTIES IN PROCESSING WORDS AND NUMBERS IN COMPARE PROBLEMS

The eye-fixation data provide some preliminary
new information concerning how highly accurate
students process word problems. As an initial step,
we developed an eye-fixation protocol for each student on the ARCO problem. The protocol listed
each line that the student fixated, in order; each
line on the protocol contained all of the words
and/or numbers fixated before the student's eyes
moved to another line.

If students read our word problems as they
would read familiar narrative prose we could expect
their eye movements to progress systematically

from line to line, with few *rereadings*—that is moving one's eyes from the current line to a line that had previously been fixated (Just & Carpenter, 1987). In contrast, our students reread a portion (or all) of a previously read line an average of 13.2 times, suggesting that they experienced difficulty in understanding the problem. An analysis of these rereadings revealed three interesting patterns—a fixation-funnel effect, a fixation-selection effect, and a fixation-consistency effect.

First, we found a *fixation-funnel effect* in which students tended to fixate fewer words and/or numbers when their eyes moved back to a line they have previously read. Whereas students fixed almost all of the words and numbers on each line during the initial reading, they most commonly fixated only one or two items on subsequent rereadings. For example, approximately 39% of the rereadings involved looking at one word or number and 26% of the rereadings involved looking at two words or numbers.

Second, we found a *fixation-selection effect* in which students tended to fixate on words and numbers during the initial reading of the problem but to focus disproportionately on numbers during subsequent rereadings. For example, students reread the numbers in the ARCO problem approximately three times while rereading other information approximately once. These patterns are consistent with the idea that successful students begin by trying to build a qualitative model of the problem situation—using mainly the words in the problem statement—and then later fill in the model with specific numbers.

Third, we found a *fixation-consistency effect* in which students reread the numbers in inconsistent and consistent problems about the same number of times but reread the words more often in inconsistent than consistent problems. For example, in the second line of the ARCO problem, students given the inconsistent version reread "Chevron" an average of 1.4 times compared to .5 for students given the consistent version and reread "less" 2.6 times compared to 1.5 for the consistent version; however, students given the inconsistent version reread "5 cents" an average of 2.9 times compared to 3.5 times for students given the consistent version. This finding suggests that the additional processing time required to correctly process inconsistent problems can be accounted for by students building a situation model of the problem—based on the words rather than the numbers in the problem.

REMEDIATION: ELIMINATING ERRORS VIA REPRESENTATION TRAINING

The foregoing solution-time and eye-fixation results suggest that more-accurate students build a qualitative model of the situation described in the problem before planning their solution. Thus, the final approach we used in our research program was to provide less-accurate students with direct instruction in how to construct qualitative situation models for compare problems (Lewis, 1989). The instruction, called *representation training*, consisted of two sessions. In the first session, the instructor presented the definitions and examples of the three types of statements in word problems (i.e., assignments, relations, and questions), the instructor noted that problems with relations were called compare problems and that relational statements were generally more difficult to understand than assignments, and students learned to label statements in example problems with A for assignment or R for relation or Q for question. In the second session, the instructor demonstrated how to use a diagram to represent the information in two-step compare problems, and provided feedback as students diagrammed several practice problems. [See box for a typical diagram procedure worksheet.] Students did not actually solve any word problems during the training.

Does teaching students how to recognize and represent relational statements affect their problem solving performance? To answer this question, Lewis gave counterbalanced pretests and post-tests to students who received the training (trained group) and those who did not (control group). The tests included eight two-step compare problems, such as described in the previous sections, and four three-step compare problems, such as "Alfredo is 25 years old. He is 7 years younger than Pedro who is 3 years older than Dennis. How old will Dennis be in 8 years?" Although two-step problems (i.e., requiring two computations) were presented in the training, no three-step problems (i.e., requiring three computations) were presented so three-step problems may be viewed as transfer problems. The

Diagramming Procedure for a Sample Problem

Sample Problem

Megan has saved $420 for vacation. She has saved ⅕ as much as James has saved. James has been saving for his vacation for 6 months. How much has he saved each month?

Diagramming Steps

1. Draw a number line and place the variable and the value from the assignment statement in the middle of the line.

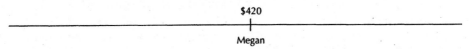

2. Tentatively place the unknown variable (James's savings) on one side of the middle.

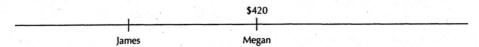

3. Compare your representation with the information in the relation statement, checking to see if your representation agrees with the meaning of the relation statement. If it does, then you can continue. If not, then try again with the other side.

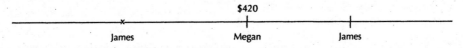

4. Translate your representation into an arithmetic operation. If the unknown variable is to the right of the center, then the operation is an increase, such as addition or multiplication. If the unknown variable is to the left of the center, then the operation is a decrease, such as subtraction or division.

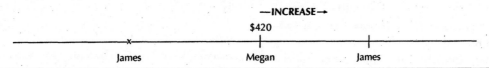

problems given during training were different from those given on the pretest or on the post-test.

On the pretest both groups made many errors on compare problems, especially on inconsistent problems—replicating the *error-consistency effect* found by Lewis and Mayer (1987). For example, in one study, the probability of making a reversal error was approximately .02 for consistent and .30 for inconsistent problems. However, almost all of the errors were eliminated on the post-test for the trained group whereas most of the errors remained for the control group. For example, on two-step problems, the error rate fell from 15% on the pretest to 1% on the post-test for the trained group and from 16% to 9% for the control group. Training also had a strong effect on students' performance on the transfer problems: On three-step problems, the error rate fell from 23% on the pretest to 7% on the post-test for the trained group and from 20% to 19% for the control group.

These results can be described as a *representation-training* effect: training in how to recognize and represent relational statements improves students' problem-solving performance. These results are consistent with the idea that a major impediment to successful problem solving is the student's failure to understand the problem. Importantly, instruction aimed at improving students' qualitative reasoning about word problems also improved their quantitative answers.

CONCLUSION

In this [selection] we presented evidence that understanding what a word problem says is a major source of difficulty for mathematical problem solvers. We also provided encouraging evidence that problem-representation skills can be taught successfully to students who possess adequate computational skills. Each of the major effects that we found (such as proposition-type, error-consistency, time-consistency, fixation-consistency, and representation-training effects) can be viewed as different measures of the same cognitive processes. Our program of research on mathematical problem solving suggests both theoretical and practical implications.

Theoretical Implications

Our work is consistent with an emerging theme in the cognitive science literature concerning the place of qualitative and quantitative reasoning in mathematical problem solving (Hall, Kibler, Wenger & Truxaw, 1989). Our findings complement research on how students solve physics problems in which expert problem solvers reason qualitatively about a problem before and while they begin making quantitative computations (Larkin, 1983; Larkin, McDermott, Simon & Simon, 1980; White & Frederiksen, 1987). Similarly, our results suggest that successful students actively attempt to construct a qualitative model of the problem situation before and while they engage in quantitative computations; in contrast, errors are more likely to occur when students engage in quantitative reasoning before they have constructed a qualitative representation of the problem.

Practical Implications

Our work is also consistent with the educational pleas for emphasis on process rather than product (Bloom & Broder, 1950) and for emphasis on understanding rather than responding (Brownell, 1935). In particular, our work is consistent with the idea that students often need instruction and practice in representing and planning of word problems. Greeno (1987, p. 70) has noted that "students need to recognize quantities and relations among quantities" and suggests that "explicit representations of the quantities and their relations" could be helpful in instruction. Lewis' (1989) use of number lines provides one method of improving students' skills in representing the situation in word problems and deriving a corresponding plan. Willis & Fuson (1988) provide another example of how practice in constructing visual representations of word prob-

lems can improve mathematical problem-solving performance.

In summary, our research points to the crucial role of qualitative reasoning about quantitative problems. Understanding the situation presented in the words of the problem is a fundamental skill required for solving word problems. Mathematical misunderstandings—in which students fail to construct appropriate qualitative models of the problem situation—are likely to contribute to incorrect answers in students who possess computational skill, and therefore, learning to "think situationally" (Nathan & Young, 1990) should be a central focus of mathematics instruction.

REFERENCES

Bloom, B. S. & Broder, L. J. (1950). *Problem-solving processes of college students: An exploratory investigation.* Chicago: University of Chicago Press.

Bobrow, D. G. (1968). Natural language input for a computer problem-solving system. In M. Minsky (Ed.), *Semantic information processing.* Cambridge, MA: MIT Press.

Briars, D. J. & Larkin, J. H. (1984). An integrated model of skill in solving elementary word problems. *Cognition and Instruction, 1,* 245–296.

Brownell, W. A. (1935). Psychological considerations in the learning and teaching of arithmetic. In *The teaching of arithmetic: Tenth yearbook of the National Council of Teachers of Mathematics.* New York: Columbia University Press.

Cummins, D., Kintsch, W., Reusser, K. & Weimer, R. (1988). The role of understanding in solving word problems. *Cognitive Psychology, 20,* 439–462.

De Corte, E., Vershaffel, L. & Pauwels, A. (1989). *Third-graders' comprehension of compare problems: Empirical validation of Lewis and Mayer's consistency hypothesis.* Unpublished manuscript, University of Leuven.

Greeno, J. G. (1987). Instructional representations based on research about understanding. A. H. Schoenfeld (Ed.), *Cognitive science and mathematics education.* (pp. 61–88). Hillsdale, NJ: Erlbaum.

Greeno, J. G. (1989). Situation models, mental models, and generative knowledge. In D. Klahr and K. Kotovsky (Eds.), *Complex information processing: The impact of Herbert A. Simon.* Hillsdale, NJ: Erlbaum.

Hall, R., Kibler, D., Wenger, E., & Truxaw, C. (1989). Exploring the episodic structure of algebra story problem solving. *Cognition and Instruction, 6,* 223–283.

Hegarty, M., Mayer, R. E. & Green, C. E. (in press). Comprehension of arithmetic word problems: Evidence from students' eye fixations. *Journal of Educational Psychology, 84.*

Hinsley, D., Hayes, J. R., & Simon, H. A. (1977). From words to equations. In P. Carpenter and M. Just (Eds.), *Cognitive processes in comprehension* (pp. 89–106). Hillsdale, NJ: Erlbaum.

Hudson, T. (1983). Correspondences and numerical differences between disjoint sets. *Child Development, 54,* 85–90.

Just, M. A. & Carpenter, P. A. (1987). *The psychology of reading and language comprehension.* Newton, MA: Allyn and Bacon.

Kintsch, W. (1988). The use of knowledge on discourse processing: A construction-integration model. *Psychological Review, 95,* 163–182.

Kintsch, W. & Greeno, J. G. (1985). Understanding and solving word arithmetic problems. *Psychological Review, 92,* 109–129.

Larkin, J. H. (1983). The role of problem representation in physics. In D. Gentner & A. L. Stevens (Eds.), *Mental models* (pp. 75–98). Hillsdale, NJ: Erlbaum.

Larkin, J. H., McDermott, J., Simon, D. P. & Simon, H. A. (1980). Expert and novice performance in solving physics problems. *Science, 208,* 1335–1342.

Lewis, A. B. (1989). Training students to represent arithmetic word problems. *Journal of Educational Psychology, 81,* 521–531.

Lewis, A. B. & Mayer, R. E. (1987). Students' miscomprehension of relational statements in arithmetic word problems. *Journal of Educational Psychology, 79,* 363–371.

Lewis, A. B. & Nathan, M. J. (1991). A framework for improving students' comprehension of word arithmetic and word algebra problems. In L. Birnbaum (Ed.), *Proceedings of the International Conference on the Learning Sciences* (pp. 305–314). Charlottesville, VA: Association for the Advancement of Computing in Education.

Mayer, R. E. (1981). Frequency norms and structural analysis of algebra story problems. *Instructional Science, 10,* 135–175.

Mayer, R. E. (1982). Memory for algebra story problems. *Journal of Educational Psychology, 74,* 199–216.

Mayer, R. E. (1985). Mathematical ability. In R. J. Sternberg (ed.), *Human abilities: An information processing approach* (pp. 127–150). San Francisco: W. H. Freeman.

Mayer, R. E. (1989). Introduction to special section on cognition and instruction in mathematics. *Journal of Educational Psychology, 81,* 452–556.

Mayer, R. E. (1991). *Thinking, problem solving, cognition (Second edition).* New York: Freeman.

Mayer, R. E., Larkin, J. H. & Kadane, J. (1984). A cognitive analysis of mathematical problem solving ability. In R. J. Sternberg (ed.), *Advances in the psychology of human intelligence, Volume 2* (pp. 231–273). Hillsdale, NJ: Erlbaum.

Morales, R. V., Shute, V. J. & Pellegrino, J. W. (1985). Developmental differences in understanding and solving simple word problems. *Cognition and Instruction, 2,* 41–57.

Nathan, M. J., Kintsch, W. & Young, E. (in press). A theory of algebra word problem comprehension and its implications for the design of learning environments. *Cognition and Instruction.*

Nathan, M. J. & Young, E. (1990). Thinking situationally: Results with an unintelligent tutor for word algebra problems. In A. McDougell & C. Dowling (Eds.), *Computers and education* (pp. 187–216). New York: North-Holland.

Paige, J. M. & Simon, H. A. (1966). Cognitive processes in solving algebra word problems. In B. Kleinmuntz (Ed.), *Problem solving: Research, method, and theory.* (pp. 51–119). New York: Wiley.

Polya, G. (1965). *Mathematical discovery: On understanding, learning, and teaching problem solving.* New York: Wiley.

Riley, M. S. & Greeno, J. G. (1988). Developmental analysis of understanding language about quantities and of solving problems. *Cognition and Instruction, 5,* 49–101.

Riley, M. S., Greeno, J. G., & Heller, J. I. (1983). Development of children's problem-solving ability. In H. P. Ginsberg (Ed.), *The development of mathematical thinking* (pp. 153–196). New York: Academic Press.

Wertheimer, M. (1959). *Productive thinking.* New York: Harper & Row.

White, B. Y. & Frederiksen, J. R. (1987). Qualitative models and intelligent learning environments. In R. W. Lawler & M. Yazdani (Eds.), *Artificial intelligence and education, Volume One* (pp. 281–306). Norwood, NJ: ABLEX.

Willis, G. B. & Fuson, K. C. (1988). Teaching children to use schematic drawings to solve addition and subtraction word problems. *Journal of Educational Psychology, 80,* 192–201.

20

Jean Bédard and Michelene T. H. Chi

Expertise

In the past two decades, there has been a significant amount of research on the nature of expertise. Researchers have examined expertise with respect to a variety of tasks, such as problem solving of either puzzles (e.g., Tower of Hanoi puzzle), games (e.g., chess, go), or classroom problems; decision making; troubleshooting mechanical systems; or diagnosing illnesses. The studies have shown that a large, organized body of domain knowledge is a prerequisite to expertise. This knowledge influences the perceptual processes and strategies of problem solving. Thus, it is important to understand how experts' knowledge is organized. We begin with a presentation of the differences in knowledge between experts and novices. The impact of the differences on problem solving and transfer is then discussed. Finally, the limitations of expertise are examined.

KNOWLEDGE

Knowledge can be discussed in terms of its quantity or its structure. There is no question that experts possess a greater quantity of domain-relevant knowledge than do novices, by definition. The amount of knowledge that experts possess can be measured in a variety of ways. However, it is not merely the fact that experts have more knowledge that is important; more crucially, they have their knowledge organized in particular ways, ways that make that knowledge more accessible, functional, and efficient.

The Amount of Knowledge

A classic study of expert-novice differences in the amount of knowledge was carried out by Chase and Simon.[1] Using a recall method, they found that chess experts can recall a greater number of pieces from a chess position than novices. This recall superiority can be explained by the greater number of chess patterns (such as a castle-king position) that experts recognize, and each pattern tends to contain more pieces than a novice's patterns. For example, it is estimated that a chess master has roughly 50,000 patterns in memory, a good player has 1,000, and a poor player has very few. These results have been replicated for schematic drawings of electronic circuit boards, computer programs, internal accounting controls, and medical problem solving, just to name a few.

The Structure of Knowledge

A large amount of domain knowledge is not the only factor responsible for the demonstration of expert-level performance; the organization of this knowledge is also important, although the amount and the organization tend to be correlated.

One way to capture the organization is to see what information experts and novices use to make categorization decisions. A classic demonstration used a card-sorting technique for assessing how experts and novices classify problems.[2] Each card contained the text and diagram for a physics problem. The novices tended to sort problems on the basis of literal, surface features, such as the type of objects involved (e.g., an inclined plane). The experts tended to sort the problems on the basis of the principles used to solve the problems (e.g., conservation of energy). Similar results have been found for categorizing problems in mathematics, computer programming, and genetics and for categorizing real-world objects such as cameras, rice bowls, electronic circuit diagrams, or pictures of dinosaurs.

In addition, experts' knowledge is extensively cross-referenced, with a rich network of connections among concepts. Novices have fewer and weaker links among concepts. In a study of diagnostic reasoning of experts and novices, Feltovich, Johnson, Moller, and Swanson[3] found that novices' knowledge of diseases is anchored in the most prototypical features of the diseases and lacks information on connections to other diseases or on shared feature of classes of diseases. Experts' knowledge of diseases is extensively cross-referenced, with rich networks of connections among diseases with similar symptoms.[4]

In sum, experts have a greater tendency to base the organization of their knowledge on meaning, whereas novices base their organization on the surface features of the information presented. Also, experts have more and stronger links among concepts, suggesting that there is a greater degree of connectedness and cross-referencing, and the pattern of connections and cross-referencing can result in a better structure.

PROBLEM SOLVING

The greater amount and better organization of experts' knowledge, as compared to that of novices, results in the two groups demonstrating different problem-solving behaviors. Differences have been captured in problem representations, problem-solving strategies, and the quality of the decisions.

Problem Representation

A representation of a problem consists of the person's interpretation or understanding of the problem. Such an interpretation must be based on the person's domain-related knowledge and organization of this knowledge. One way to begin representing a problem is to classify it as a particular type, because people presumably have solution procedures attached to each "type" of problem. To classify a problem, one needs to pick out the relevant features or must infer additional aspects about the problem given the explicitly stated features. Both of these feature-identification processes are more efficient and superior among experts, because of their richer knowledge base.

For instance, consider the familiar physics problem: A block is suspended from a spring, which is attached to the ceiling. Given the initial displacement of the block (how far the spring is stretched), calculate the amplitude and period of the resulting oscillation. In solving this problem, experts translate the literal cues from the problem statement, such as "block," "spring," and "suspended," into derived features, such as "mass(m)," "spring-constant (k)," and "gravity (g)." This translation may then activate a category of problems, such as "mass-spring oscillation problems."[2] Thus, experts represent problems on the basis of the derived features. For novices, the process of constructing a representation also involves the activation of a category, except that novices' problem categories are based largely on literal features, such as "the spring."[2]

Differences between experts' and novices' representations are even more apparent in ill-defined problems. An ill-defined problem is a problem whose structure lacks definition in some respect (initial state, set of permissible operators, or goal state[5]). In solving an ill-defined problem, such as one in political science, experts spend a considerable amount of time developing a problem representation by adding many domain-specific and general constraints to the problem—as if they are modifying the problem from an ill-defined to a well-defined one. Novices, however, attempt to solve the problem directly without defining it.[6] Thus, experts and novices essentially construct different representations for the same problem. The constructed representation determines the success of the problem solving.

Problem-Solving Strategies

In searching for a solution, a problem solver may use strategies such as means-ends analysis, subgoaling (generating and solving a subgoal as a step toward solving the goal), generate-and-test, or analogical reasoning. Experts and novices tend to use the same general problem-solving strategies. In a medical diagnosis task, for example, novices and experts both used a generate-and-test strategy in which hypotheses are generated in response to items of patient data and then are tested for confirmation or disconfirmation. Experts, however, tended to generate the *correct* hypothesis more often than novices.

One prominent strategy in which differences between experts and novices have been found is means-ends analysis. Means-ends analysis is simply the strategy of problem solving in which the goal is to reduce the difference between the end state and the current state. One can work either backward or forward using this strategy. With a backward-driven strategy, the problem solver works backward from the goal to the problem givens. With a forward-driven strategy, the problem solver works from the problem givens and uses applicable operators, without regard to the goal. There have been numerous studies examining expert and novice problem solving in domains such as physics, medicine, political science, and accounting. The results of these studies indicate that experts' use a

forward-driven strategy and novices use a backward-driven strategy.

In mechanics problems, for example, Simon and Simon[7] found that an expert works from the variables given in a problem, successively generating equations that can be solved from the given information. A novice starts with the goal—finding the value for the unknown of the problem—and then generates an equation containing the unknown of the problem. If the equation contains a variable that is not among the givens, the novice selects another equation to solve for that variable, and so on.

Working forward is riskier than working backward in problem solving because operations are executed without first checking to see if they lead toward the goal. It seems more intelligent to organize the problem solving around the goal. Why, then, do experts work forward? It seems that working forward is more efficient if the problem solver knows enough about the domain to recognize the problem type. Once the type is selected, the expert builds a problem representation and executes the solution procedure associated with that problem type. This explanation implies that the choice of a problem-solving strategy is knowledge driven. When problem solvers possess sufficient knowledge about the domain, they use a forward-driven strategy. Otherwise, they use a backward-driven strategy. Thus, experts do work backward when confronted with an unfamiliar problem that cannot be categorized as an instance of a known problem type. Experts in thermodynamics, for example, work backward when confronted with unfamiliar problems.

In summary, experts use recognition processes that are based on a large repertoire of structured knowledge to build a problem representation. The nature of that representation determines to a large extent the strategy used during problem solving. When the problem matches an existing prestored problem type, problem-solving procedures are triggered, and these procedures make the problem-solving process appear forward working. When recognition does not suffice, experts resort to general problem-solving strategies and, as is the case for novices, use a backward-solving approach. Thus, although it may be correct to characterize differences in the way experts and novices use forward versus backward reasoning, these differences are driven by the availability of the problem type, and not the availability of the strategies per se. Therefore, the point is not that experts are better able to use more sophisticated strategies, or use their strategies more competently, but rather that a strategy applied to a well-organized knowledge base produces a more competent performance. This interpretation can be seen more clearly using the generate-and-test strategy, as exemplified in medical diagnoses. In this case, the more accurate hypothesis generated by the expert physician, given a set of symptoms, does not arise because the expert is better at using the generate-and-test strategy.

Decision Quality

In game and classroom problems, experts' superior knowledge structure and strategies allow them to perform the tasks more quickly and to produce more accurate solutions than novices. Researchers have examined the relationship between knowledge and decision quality in real-world problems, too, and these results seem to parallel those for classroom problems. In marketing, for example, effective salespeople have been found to have category structures containing more descriptors of both customers' traits and sales strategies and to exhibit more sophisticated sales scripts than ineffective salespeople.[8]

In some real-world problems, however, results of the studies carried out indicate that expert judgment is seldom better than that of novices and is easily improved on when replaced with simple mathematical models. In public accounting, for example, there were no significant relationships between expertise and decision quality.[9] Why do experts in some real-world problems perform so poorly? Why is there a discrepancy between real-world problems and other types of problems? Researchers have just recently started studying these questions. The following four factors may explain these differences: the degree of structure of the problem, the approach (cognitive science or behavioral decision theory) used to study the problem solving, the lack of a "right answer" or of a correct solution procedure, and mismatch between the expertise of the subjects and the task. For example, expert physicians were found to be slightly better than novices and worse than a simple regression model in selecting candidates for internships and

residencies.[10] This poor performance by physicians may be explained by the fact that selecting interns is not a task at which physicians are experts. Personnel selection requires a great deal of knowledge about how past experience, intelligence, knowledge, skills, abilities, and motivation lead to outcomes such as high performance.

TRANSFER OF EXPERTISE

One of the characteristics of expertise is that it is task specific. There appears to be little transfer from high-level proficiency in one domain to proficiency in other domains. This result has been found across a large range of problems. For instance, although go and gomoku are played on the same board and with the same pieces, go experts' recall of gomoku displays is poor and vice versa. Voss, Greene, Post, and Penner[6] compared the problem-solving behavior of expert political scientists, expert chemists, and novice political scientists in solving real-world problems related to Soviet agriculture. They found that the chemists' protocols, on the whole, were much like those of novices, sparse and dealing with low-level, specific problems that were subproblems for the experts. Patel, Evans, and Groen[11] compared the performance of subjects from three medical subspecialties, cardiology, surgery, and psychiatry, in solving a problem in the domain of cardiology. Cardiologists' diagnoses were more accurate than those of surgeons and psychiatrists. The lack of transfer between problems confirms the role of an appropriate knowledge base, both declarative and procedural, in accounting for expertise.

The reviewed literature indicates that, in general, there is no transfer of proficiency between domains. Within a specific domain, however, there is transfer from one task to another. If learning is the construction of conditional rules, then within a domain, transfer of learning from one task to another is determined by the number of rules the two tasks share. The extent to which a person, having learned a text editor, transfers positively to a second text editor depends on the number of rules the two editors share.[12] Thus, the lack of transfer in the studies of political science and medicine may be due to very few rules being shared by the experts' domains.

PITFALLS OF EXPERTISE

In some situations, novices not only can perform as well as experts, but actually surpass experts. One can handicap experts in at least three ways: by putting them in a situation in which they cannot make use of their greater knowledge base, by selecting a task in which interpreting the problem at a deeper level may interfere with problem solving, and by selecting a task for which a standard response may be inappropriate. An example of the first case is to present expert chess players with randomized chess positions (i.e., the pieces on the board have been placed randomly). In such conditions, the experts' recall of the chess positions is slightly worse than novice players'.[1] The second case can be illustrated by a recognition task. Baseball experts, more often than novices, falsely recognize synonym sentences about baseball as being the original sentence that was presented.[13] One interpretation is that experts store the semantics of the sentences, thus confusing their surface distinctions, whereas novices remember verbatim sentences. Similarly, novice computer programmers surpass experts in answering concrete questions about how a program functions because the experts' representations no longer include the details of how the program functions.[14] The third case can be illustrated by a transfer of knowledge from one situation to another. Marchant, Robinson, Anderson, and Schadewald[15] presented a court decision about the deductibility of a business expense to expert and novice accountants and required them to make a decision about the deductibility of a business expense in a similar case. Significantly more novices than experts transferred the knowledge from the court decision to the new case. Apparently, tax experts had a highly proceduralized general strategy of deducting all business expenses, which led to inflexibility.

SUMMARY

A fundamental goal of science is to find invariants. The studies described here support five invariants of expertise. First, experts, by definition, know more about their domain than do novices. Second, experts not only know more, but their knowledge is better organized. Third, on the basis of their greater knowledge and better organization, experts perform better than novices in domain-related tasks. Fourth, experts' skill is domain specific: There is very little transfer to unrelated domains. Finally, there are also many situations in which experts do not excel.

ACKNOWLEDGMENTS

Preparation of this article was supported in part by an OERI Institutional Grant for the National Center on Student Learning. The opinions expressed do not necessarily reflect the position of the sponsoring agency, and no official endorsement should be inferred.

NOTES

1. W. Chase and H. A. Simon, Perception in chess, *Cognitive Psychology, 4,* 55–81 (1973).

2. M. T. H. Chi, P. Feltovich, and R. Glaser, Categorization and representation of physics problems by experts and novices, *Cognitive Science, 5,* 121–152 (1981).

3. P. J. Feltovich, P. E. Johnson, J. H. Moller, and D. B. Swanson, LCS: The role and development of medical knowledge in diagnostic expertise, in *Readings in Medical Artificial Intelligence,* W. J. Clancey and E. H. Shortliffe, Eds. (Addison-Wesley, Reading, MA, 1984).

4. G. Bordage and R. Zacks, The structure of medical knowledge in the memories of medical students and general practitioners: Categories and prototypes, *Medical Education, 18,* 406–416 (1984).

5. H. A. Simon, The structure of ill-structured problems, *Artificial Intelligence, 4,* 181–201 (1973).

6. J. F. Voss, T. R. Greene, T. Post, and B. C. Penner, Problem-solving skill in the social sciences, in *The Psychology of Learning and Motivation* (Academic Press, New York, 1983).

7. D. P. Simon and H. A. Simon, Individual differences in solving physics problems, in *Children's Thinking: What Develops?* R. Siegler, Ed. (Erlbaum, Hillsdale, NJ, 1978).

8. H. Sujan, M. Sujan, and J. R. Bettman, Knowledge structure differences between more effective and less effective salespeople, *Journal of Marketing Research, 25,* 81–86 (February 1988).

9. J. Bédard, Expertise in auditing: Myth or reality? *Accounting, Organization and Society, 14,* 113–131 (1989).

10. E. J. Johnson, Expertise and decision under uncertainty: Performance and process, in *The Nature of Expertise,* M. T. H. Chi, R. Glaser, and M. J. Farr, Eds. (Erlbaum, Hillsdale, NJ, 1988).

11. V. L. Patel, D. A. Evans, and G. J. Groen, Biomedical knowledge and clinical reasoning, in *Cognitive Science in Medicine: Biomedical Modeling,* D. Evans and V. Patel, Eds. (MIT Press, Cambridge, MA, 1989).

12. M. K. Singley and J. R. Anderson, The transfer of text-editing skill, *International Journal of Man-Machine Studies, 22,* 403–423 (1985).

13. H. R. Arkes and M. R. Freedman, A demonstration of the costs and benefits of expertise in recognition memory, *Memory and Cognition, 12,* 84–89 (1984).

14. B. Adelson, When novices surpass experts: The difficulty of the task may increase with expertise, *Journal of Experimental Psychology: Learning, Memory, and Cognition, 10,* 483–495 (1984).

15. G. Marchant, J. Robinson, U. Anderson, and M. Schadewald, Analogical transfer and expertise in legal reasoning, *Organizational Behavior and Human Decision Processes, 48,* 272–290 (1991)

RECOMMENDED READING

Chi, M. T. H., Glaser, R., and Farr, M. J. (Eds.). (1988). *The Nature of Expertise* (Erlbaum, Hillsdale, NJ).

21

Robert S. Lockhart

The Role of Conceptual Access in the Transfer of Thinking Skills

As with most important matters in philosophy, education, or psychology, the question of whether critical thinking can be taught as a generalizable skill is one that affords no simple answer. In unraveling the complex network of issues involved, it is instructive to consider this same question applied to a simpler case, that of memory, because remembering is an aspect of cognition that raises many of the same questions but, unlike critical thinking, remembering provides some clear answers.

REMEMBERING AS A TRANSFERABLE SKILL

In what sense is remembering a transferable skill and in what sense is it content bound? If we ask whether practice at remembering improves memory generally, the only possible answer is that it "all depends," a sure sign that the question is badly phrased. It was once thought that the memorizing involved in learning Latin would improve memory ability in general in much the same way that exercising a muscle increases its strength. This muscle metaphor is quite misleading: learning Latin is likely to improve memory for little else besides Latin. There are many other examples suggesting that skilled remembering is highly content bound, one of the best documented of these being the highly skilled memory for digit strings. Chase and Ericsson (1981, 1982) trained one subject (S. F.) to a point where he could repeat up to 80 digits immediately after presentation. It took some 250 days of practice to achieve this impressive level. The technique was not complicated. Over the course of his practice session, S. F. learned to exploit his extensive knowledge of track times, grouping the digits into sets of three or four digits each, and then coding them as running times for various races. For example, 3492 might be coded 3:49.2, close to the world

From Robert S. Lockhart, "The Role of Conceptual Access in the Transfer of Thinking Skills," in Stephen P. Norris, ed., *The Generalizability of Critical Thinking: Multiple Perspectives on an Educational Ideal* (Teachers College Press, 1992), pp. 54–65. Copyright © 1992 by Teachers College, Columbia University. Reprinted by permission. All rights reserved.

record time for running the mile. Needless to say this prodigious feat of memory is highly content specific; it works only for digit strings. When S. F.'s memory for letter strings was tested, it was found to be no better than it had been before.

Should these examples be taken to mean that memory cannot be taught as a generalizable skill? Obviously not. It has been known since earlier times (see Yates, 1966) that remembering can indeed be taught as a generalizable skill. Consider mnemonic techniques such as the method of loci that were once taught in highly respectable courses in rhetoric, and which are still to be found in books on how to improve your memory. It is interesting that these techniques are now less frequently taught despite the ample experimental evidence that they do work. They work because they embody and exploit certain general principles of memory processes, the most basic of which was stated succinctly by William James: "The art of remembering is the art of thinking . . . our conscious effort should not be so much to *impress* or *retain* (knowledge) as to *connect* it with something already there" (James, 1983, p. 87).

James's statement might be thought of as a principle for generating particular mnemonic techniques—a meta-mnemonic strategy—in that virtually all mnemonic techniques work by using the properties of the rememberer's existing knowledge to structure and pattern the material that is to be remembered. In the method of loci, for example, the items to be remembered are associated with locations in some familiar space and the structure of this known space then becomes the basis of a subsequent retrieval plan; one simply "visits" each location and retrieves its associated item. It is a mnemonic technique well-suited to situations in which order is important, such as the points of a speech.

So the answer to the question of whether practicing memory improves memory in general is both yes and no. Although techniques such as the method of loci have wide application, other forms of skilled remembering are quite content bound, because the knowledge that structures the novel material requiring memorization is content specific and highly specialized. A laboriously acquired digit span of eighty would leave you with a letter span no better than before. On the other hand, knowing the general principle contained in the above quotation from William James and applying it in the form

of general mnemonic strategies can improve memory over a wide range of content. The important differences among these various mnemonic techniques is the specificity of the knowledge being used to structure the material to be remembered. But in all applications, the skill of effective remembering hinges on the cognitive system being trained in such a way that the data of experience are able rapidly to trigger knowledge structures that in turn have the capacity to organize incoming information in ways that facilitate remembering.

The general lesson to be learned from the memory example is this: the fact that a high level of cognitive performance in a given content area fails to generalize does not warrant the conclusion that the process cannot be taught as a generalizable skill. Conversely, if a cognitive process can, in fact, be taught as a generalizable skill, it does not follow that any one particular form of practice will produce that generalization.

Are there more specific lessons to be drawn? Can we make a direct analogy between remembering and critical thinking? We might argue that, as with mnemonic strategies, the teachable skills underlying critical thinking vary in their generality. Certain basic rules such as those of propositional logic have wide generality; whereas other skills necessary for critical thinking are more content bound and are designed for more specialized purposes, analogous to mnemonic techniques used in memorizing digit strings. For example, evaluating evidence supporting the claim that Napoleon lost 22,000 men crossing the Berizina River in his retreat from Moscow in 1812, clearly calls on different skills from those needed to evaluate the claim that oatbran lowers blood cholesterol levels. But, so the argument continues, despite these obvious differences, the critically thinking historian and scientist both share a great deal. They both possess a common disposition of reflective scepticism (McPeck, 1981) and, obviously, they both exploit the same basic rules of syllogistic or propositional reasoning. Moreover, given the general conclusion in the preceding paragraph, the fact that no amount of practice at evaluating historical claims such as those about Napoleon's army will lead to an improvement in the ability to evaluate nutritional claims such as those for the health benefits of oatbran is irrelevant to the basic issue at hand. And so it might be concluded that in teaching critical thinking, one should first teach those basic aspects of critical thinking with wide generality and, once they have been mastered and a disposition of reflective scepticism has been acquired, then add additional content-specific skills as needed.

This analysis is seductively straightforward but seriously incomplete. It ignores at least one important problem, and it is this problem that I will explore in the remainder of this paper. I will label it the problem of abductive access or abductive memory. In outline, my argument will be that generalizability depends not only on the generality of the rules for rational thought, but hinges much more critically on factors that control access to those rules. That is, whereas certain schema for critical thinking may have wide application, they may in fact be content bound in their application by virtue of the fact that access to these schema is content bound. It is this access relation between content and schema that I will label abductive remembering.

ABDUCTIVE REMEMBERING

I have taken the term "abductive" from C. S. Peirce in order to capture the idea that this particular form of memory is a transition from data to theory, from the "givens" or thematic content of a problematic situation to those abstract cognitive structures (such as concepts, inference schema, scripts, and so forth) needed to structure the data in such a way as to resolve the problem. My intent is simply to distinguish abductive remembering from the more usual content- or thematically based remembering, although, of course, in any particular problem-solving situation a specific act of remembering might be both.

Perhaps the simplest example of abductive remembering occurs when simple riddles are solved. For example, most people find puzzling the statement "John threw the rock out into the lake. It landed on the surface and rested there for several weeks before sinking to the bottom five meters below" until they receive a hint such as "ice" or "winter" or think of it themselves. The initial failure to make sense of statements such as these is a failure of abductive remembering—the puzzling sentence fails to access the concept that is essential to its comprehension. On the other hand, being reminded of other stories of throwing rocks into lakes would

be an example of content- or thematically based remembering. Many problems (serious ones as well as the trivial examples given here) constitute riddles precisely because the data, for reasons to be discussed below, function as effective content-based cues, but fail to cue abductively (that is, to cue the retrieval of relevant concepts or schema) if there is a change of content. Similarly, many apparent errors in problems involving critical thinking can be traced to the way in which content and context, rather than the problem's formal underlying structure, control and bias abductive memory.

The class of phenomena known as mental set or mental blocks (Adams, 1976) constitutes a good example of the manipulation of abductive memory. A very dramatic example is that of Levine (1971). Subjects were shown a sequence of cards, each containing two side-by-side circles, one large and one small, with the large circle sometimes to the left of the small one, sometimes to the right. They were required to learn a simple discrimination rule (for example, large) applied to these pairs of circles. Under normal conditions, subjects learned such a rule in an average of about three trials. If, however, this same problem is preceded by a set of other problems for which the rules to be learned consist of position sequences, and size is irrelevant (for example, left, right, left, right . . .), then an average of 62 trials was required; indeed 28 of 60 subjects had not solved the simple discrimination problem after 115 trials.

This breakdown in thinking skill is a consequence of the contextual biasing of abductive memory: a previously strong data-to-concept association is undermined or "overwritten" by the repeated association of that same class of data to an inappropriate concept or hypothesis space. Conversely, a strong abductive association between data and an inadequate concept can block retrieval of a weaker association required to solve the problem. Scientific discovery is full of such examples but the best known is probably Kepler's replacement of the circle with the ellipse. Kepler's insight was also Peirce's favorite example of abduction. In experimental psychology, the best example of a problem made difficult by a strong a priori abductive association is probably Wason's notorious "2 4 6" problem (Wason & Johnson-Laird, 1968). In this problem, subjects are instructed that their task is to discover a number-series rule by generating data and asking whether or not such data conform to the rule. They are given an initial instance of the rule, the series 2 4 6. This initial instance is, of course, strongly associated with the rule "ascending even numbers" which, in fact, is not the rule the experimenter has in mind. It is not uncommon for intelligent subjects to take over thirty minutes to discover the rule "any set of ascending numbers," or, indeed, not to discover it at all and give up the task.

Abductive Memory and Tulving's Encoding Specificity Principle

Many of the observed failures to obtain generalization or transfer from the solving of one problem to the solving of novel, isomorphic problems can be thought of as a failure of abductive memory, and understood in terms of what we know about memory access. Perhaps the best example of failure to obtain transfer is the work on analogical transfer. Gick and Holyoak (1983) studied analogical transfer using Duncker's classic radiation problem: how can a patient with an inoperable tumor receive radiation strong enough to destroy the tumor but not harm surrounding tissue? This problem requires for its normal solution the application of a "convergence schema" in which a series of low-powered rays are simultaneously focused on the tumor from many directions. Efforts to increase solution rates to this problem by prior presentation and solving of an analogous problem—one with quite different content but also requiring application of the convergence schema—have consistently failed. One of the reasons for this failure is not difficult to see, but it illustrates an important principle. Solving the radiation problem requires that its specific content (the "givens") abductively access the convergence schema. There is no reason to suppose that prior training that establishes some other content as an effective cue to that schema should enhance the cue-effectiveness of a quite different content. Indeed, the data that Tulving (1983) has amassed in support of his encoding specificity principle should lead us not to expect such transfer. To assume otherwise is to make the common mistake of supposing that memory is a matter of stamping in the response (in this case the schema) without regard to the fact that all remembering is dependent on the building in of effective retrieval cues.

One subsidiary result from Gick and Holyoak's work helps illustrate this point. Whereas most of their experiments were concerned with the effects on problem solving of solving prior analogous problems, one (Experiment 2) was an attempt to teach subjects the convergence schema explicitly, with the help of a diagram and without any accompanying story. They found that this attempt to teach the schema directly had very little beneficial effect. A parallel result was obtained some forty years earlier by Clark Hull in his famous study of concept learning. Hull (1920) used Chinese ideographs as stimuli, with a conceptual class being defined by the presence of an invariant component figure hidden within the ideograph. In Experiment E, Hull presented subjects with the defining common element without any context at all. That is, they were essentially given the answer. Granted that under normal conditions the identification of the defining component within the context of the entire ideograph is a major aspect of the task's difficulty, it might be expected that such a "give-away" condition would yield a substantial improvement in the rate of learning. Hull found that it produced no improvement at all. Again, the conclusion is that exposure to a solution-giving concept will be ineffective if that exposure does not incorporate elements that will function in the context of the novel problem as effective retrieval cues to access that concept.

More recent experimental work has repeatedly shown that giving subjects "practice" by having them use a concept or schema in one context does little to increase the likelihood that they will use that concept or schema when it is needed to solve a subsequently presented problem, unless the conditions are such that the initial context lays down concept-related retrieval cues that will be activated by the subsequent problem. Of course one condition that achieves this cuing is similarity of surface or thematic content but this result is no more interesting than it is surprising, since our concern is with transfer of conceptual access across changes in surface content.

Let me illustrate this point by describing the results from a simple demonstration experiment. The task is one inspired by Werner and Kaplan (1963) in which subjects are required to discover the meaning of a nonsense word, given its use in a set of English sentences. Subjects are told that it is a word in a foreign language and that they are to work out its English translation. For example, the pseudo-foreign word might be "julvert" and the sentences might be:

Most people have many julverts;
If a julvert runs into too many difficulties it may cease to exist;
A julvert may form gradually over a long period of time, or may form very quickly;
We may use some of our julverts more than others;
A person cannot have a julvert completely on their own;
Close julverts can be rare and difficult to come by.

Before attempting to solve a number of these problems, subjects are given a set of single sentences. Each of the English words that will be the solutions for the subsequent translation problems occurs in one of these sentences. Various techniques are used to ensure that subjects attend to these critical words. For example, the word might be underlined and subjects asked to judge the appropriateness of the word's meaning for that sentence. In one condition, this practice sentence reappears as one of the set of five sentences in the translation task, except that the English word is replaced with the pseudo-foreign word. In a second condition, there is no such repetition of the prior sentence. Compared to a control measure (in which there is no prior presentation of the solution at all), subjects in the sentence repetition condition show substantial facilitation measured in terms of either speed or accuracy. Subjects who were exposed to the solution, but within the context of a sentence not repeated in the test set, show no facilitation whatsoever, despite the strenuous efforts to highlight the word in the initial phase, and despite the fact that under these conditions subjects can free-recall most of the solution words if asked to do so. That is, the solutions are readily available under one set of retrieval conditions, but not under the conditions of the translation task.

The lesson to be drawn from this and similar results is that whereas problem solving (and effective thinking generally) depends on effective abductive remembering (content-cuing of conceptual structure), normal memory processes operate on a content-to-content basis. That is, under normal conditions transfer is governed by similarity of thematic content, not by similarity of the conceptual structure. The problem of generalizability is not therefore solved by simply "stamping in" the con-

ceptual structure, but rather by increasing the abductive cue-effectiveness of different forms of content.

Content Specificity in a Propositional Reasoning Task

This same kind of analysis can be seen more clearly by examining empirical studies of the role of thematic content in simple reasoning problems. The literature contains many examples of reasoning problems that are formally equivalent (isomorphic) but which vary in their difficulty depending on their content. Probably the best known example of such a problem, and certainly the one experimentally most studied, is Wason's (1966) four-card selection task. In its original form it consisted of showing subjects four cards each with a letter on one side and a single digit on the other. Subjects in the experiment are informed about the cards, but are shown only one side of each card. What they might see is "A," "D," "4," and "7" on cards one through four respectively. Subjects are given a rule: "If a card has a vowel on one side, then it has an even number on the other side." They are then instructed, "Your task is to say which of the four cards you need to turn over in order to find out whether the rule is true or false." The answers most frequently given are "only A" and "A and 4," both of which are wrong; all but a small minority of subjects fail to appreciate the falsifying potential of the "7" card.

For a short period of time, it was thought that this apparent failure of rationality could be attributed to the abstract nature of the materials used in the task since several subsequent experiments showed a considerable improvement in subjects' performance when digits and letters were replaced with content that was more realistic and concrete. The most dramatic of these early demonstrations was that of Johnson-Laird, Legrenzi, and Legrenzi (1972) who instructed subjects to imagine that they were postal workers whose job it was to sort letters and to determine whether the following rule had been violated: "If a letter is sealed, then it has a 5d [d = penny] stamp on it." Subjects were shown four envelopes: the fronts of two envelopes, with a 5d and 4d stamp respectively, and the backs of two envelopes, sealed and unsealed respectively. This version is, of course, isomorphic with the original version, but unlike that version which yielded 15 percent correct answers, the percentage of correct responses for the realistic version was 81.

Subsequent findings have made it apparent that such a difference cannot be attributed in any simple way to the contrast between abstract and realistic materials. The literature contains many examples of failed replications; realistic content seems to help for some types of content and not in others, for some subject populations and not in others. For example, the envelope version of the problem, so effective with British subjects in 1972, produced no facilitation for American subjects used by Griggs and Cox (1982), the latter subjects having had no experience with this former regulation of the British post office. Such a conclusion is further supported by a result reported by Golding (1981) that the facilitation is not obtained with younger British subjects who have had no experience with the since discontinued regulation, and by the result of Cheng and Holyoak (1985) who found that facilitation is obtained with subjects from Hong Kong where the rule is familiar.

These kinds of results (and there are many others; see Evans, 1982 for a review) seem to argue strongly for a highly content-dependent view of logical reasoning, and this is exactly the conclusion drawn by a number of psychologists (for example, Griggs & Cox, 1982; Manktelow & Evans, 1979). These writers claimed that rather than use general rules of inference, subjects draw upon domain-specific experience. It now seems clear, however, that such a conclusion is overly pessimistic. In supporting this claim I will draw on the work of Cheng and Holyoak (1985) who, as noted above, also used the envelope problem as one of their tasks. Cheng and Holyoak's experiments show that it is not the specific experience (for example, with rules governing the stamp value required with sealed and unsealed letters) that is critical, but rather whether or not the content of the task activates more general schema that embody appropriate rules of inference. They term such schema *pragmatic reasoning schema,* and what they show experimentally is that correct reasoning ceases to be narrowly content bound, provided the novel content accesses the appropriate schema. Let me offer two examples, one from Cheng and Holyoak (1985) and one from a quite different source.

Cheng and Holyoak argue that the pragmatic reasoning schema relevant to the envelope problem is one that they term a "permission schema," in which performing a particular action requires that a certain precondition be satisfied. They formalize the schema in terms of a simple production system. If one examines the particular realistic problems (ones that are isomorphic to the four-card selection task) that have yielded high levels of correct performance, they do seem to fit a permission schema. For example, the rule "if he is drinking beer then he is over eighteen years of age" or the rule "if a purchase exceeds thirty dollars, then the receipt must have the signature of the manager on the back," both yield high levels of performance. Cheng and Holyoak show that American subjects who normally perform poorly on the envelope task will perform much better if they are given a rationale for the task that serves as an effective cue to activate the permission schema. Thus it is not the familiarity of the literal content that is critical but rather whether or not the particulars of the problem access an appropriate schema.

The second example concerns the activation of causal schema, and another well-worn problem, the taxicab problem first introduced by Kahneman and Tversky (1972). The standard version of the problem is as follows:

A cab was involved in a hit-and-run accident at night. Two cab companies, the Green and the Blue, operate in the city. You are given the following data:

1. Eighty-five percent of the cabs in the city are Green and 15 percent are Blue.
2. A witness identified the cab as Blue. The court tested the reliability of the witness under the same circumstances that existed on the night of the accident and concluded that the witness correctly identified each one of the two colors 80 percent of the time and failed 20 percent of the time.

What is the probability that the cab involved in the accident was Blue rather than Green?

Application of Bayes's theorem gives the answer as 0.41; the model response is 0.80. The usual interpretation of this result is that subjects ignore the differential base-rates (a priori probabilities) of the two cabs and equate the answer with the reliability of the witness. However, a slight modification of the problem yields a sharp change in subjects' responses, even though the two versions are formally equivalent. The modified version involves replacing the incidental base rate of cabs with a causal base rate of accidents: "Although the two companies are roughly equal in size, 85 percent of cab accidents in the city involve Green cabs and 15 percent involve Blue cabs." With this form of the problem base rate is no longer ignored.

A further example involving causal schema is the frequent ambiguity between causal and diagnostic schema and the dominance of the former over the latter. The confusion is captured in joking statements such as, "the likelihood of death is greater among those who have made a recent visit to their doctor than those who have not," which is a joke precisely because it evokes a causal schema which after a moment's reflection is replaced with the more appropriate diagnostic schema. Tversky and Kahneman (1982) provide a detailed analysis of this ambiguity.

The point of these examples is that reasoning is governed neither by general abstract rules on the one hand, nor by the particularities of experience on the other, but by conceptual structures or schema of intermediate levels of generality. Subjects were able to reason correctly about the envelope problem, not by being made familiar with that particular situation, but by ensuring that abductive memory accesses an appropriate reasoning schema.

Expertise

There have been many recent studies contrasting the problem-solving strategies of experts and novices. Abductive memory provides a way of thinking about certain aspects of these results. One general finding is that experts have specialized reasoning schemas, especially in well-structured domains such as physics. But expertise in physics does not consist merely in "possessing" such schemas, since real physics problems do not come with a label indicating which schema to use. Expertise also includes the ability to discern from the surface features of a problem the schema appropriate to its solution. Thus in a study comparing experts and novices in the area of physics, Chi, Feltovich, and Glaser (1981) had subjects sort problems into classes on the basis of "similarity." Novices tended to form categories on the basis of relatively surface features of the problems, whereas experts sorted the

problems with respect to those underlying physical laws relevant to the problem's solution. Thus a novice might group problems on the grounds that they all dealt with blocks on an inclined plane; the expert was more likely to form groups based on criteria such as that they all involve the principle of conservation of energy. Physics experts have well-trained abductive memories, at least for the domain of physics.

THE GENERALITY OF MNEMONIC STRATEGIES AND OF THINKING SKILLS

The above analysis makes clear one of the reasons why the teaching of generalizable memory skills is so much more straightforward than the corresponding teaching of thinking skills. Once a mnemonic technique has been taught and mastered, there is little confusion as to which technique to use and when to apply it. The situation with reasoning is quite different: practice with an abstract rule, no matter how general its application, does not guarantee that it will be accessed in the context of the content of a particular problem. Practice at reasoning modus tollens (reasoning that if *p* implies *q*, then *not q* implies *not p*), for example, does not in itself guarantee success in the Wason four-card selection task.

There is, however, a common principle. The skill of effective remembering and of effective thinking both hinge on the cognitive system being trained in such a way that the data of experience are able rapidly to trigger the cognitive structures appropriate to the task at hand. In the case of memory, extensive practice enabled Chase's and Ericsson's subject S. F. to achieve a digit span of eighty digits because the digits triggered knowledge that served to restructure a "randomly" ordered sequence into something more meaningful. Once this process is understood, the feat is not more mysterious than most people's ability to remember a sequence of eighty letters—provided the letters are ordered so as to form English words that in turn form a sentence. To the person who reads only Swahili, however, such a letter string may well appear as random as strings of digits appeared to S. F. before he developed his "digit vocabulary." More importantly, this same understanding makes the question of transfer quite transparent. Although both ordinary reading and S. F.'s memory for digits are clearly teachable skills, and although they both embody a common set of laws of memory, there is no need to hold a workshop to establish that there will be no direct transfer from one domain to the other.

Corresponding arguments can be applied to thinking skills. Although there may be a set of common principles underlying sound reasoning, training is not just a matter of "knowing" these principles. Rather the skill to be taught is that of correctly "reading" a specific content as an instance embodying that principle. From this point of view, training thinking skills is not dissimilar from teaching diagnostic skills to a trainee physician. The skill involved is being able to "read" specific content as clues to an underlying process that is not directly observable but which holds the key to making correct inferences. In both cases the problem of transfer is that the same underlying principle may manifest itself in a bewildering array of symptoms. Skill will generalize only with adequate exposure to this range of symptoms; no amount of practice with the principles themselves will do the job. As Margolis (1987) has argued, there is much to be gained from adopting the view that thinking is a form of pattern recognition.

ACKNOWLEDGMENT

Preparation of this manuscript was supported by an operating grant from The Natural Sciences and Engineering Research Council of Canada.

REFERENCES

Adams, J. L. (1976). *Conceptual blockbusting.* New York: Norton.

Chase, W. G., & Ericsson, K. A. (1981). Skilled memory. In J. R. Anderson (Ed.), *Cognitive skills and their acquisition* (pp. 141–189). Hillsdale, NJ: Erlbaum.

Chase, W. G., & Ericsson, K. A. (1982). Skill and working memory. In G. H. Bower (Ed.), *The psychology of learning and motivation* (Vol. 16, pp. 1–58). New York: Academic Press.

Cheng, P. W., & Holyoak, K. J. (1985). Pragmatic reasoning schemas. *Cognitive Psychology, 17,* 391–416.

Chi, M. T. H., Feltovitch, P. J., & Glaser, R. (1981). Categorization and representation of physics problems by experts and novices. *Cognitive Science, 5,* 121–152.

Evans, J. St. B. T. (1982). *The psychology of deductive reasoning.* London: Routledge and Kegan Paul.

Gick, M. L., & Holyoak, K. J. (1983). Schema induction and analogical transfer. *Cognitive Psychology, 15,* 1–38.

Golding, E. (1981). The effect of past experience on problem solving. Paper presented at the Annual Conference of the British Psychological Society, Surrey University.

Griggs, R. A., & Cox, J. R. (1982). The elusive thematic-materials effect in Wason's selection task. *British Journal of Psychology, 73,* 407–420.

Hull, C. L. (1920). Quantitative aspects of the evolution of concepts. *Psychological Monographs, 28,* (Entire Issue).

James, W. (1983). *Talks to teachers on psychology and to students on some of life's ideals.* Cambridge, MA: Harvard University Press.

Johnson-Laird, P. N., Legrenzi, P., & Legrenzi, S. M. (1972). Reasoning and a sense of reality. *British Journal of Psychology, 63,* 395–400.

Kahneman, D., & Tversky, A. (1972). Subjective probability: A judgment of representativeness. *Cognitive Psychology, 3,* 430–454.

Levine, M. (1971). Hypothesis theory and nonlearning despite ideal S-R reinforcement contingencies. *Psychological Review, 78,* 130–140.

Manktelow, K. I., & Evans, J. St. B. T. (1979). Facilitation of reasoning by realism: Effect or non-effect. *British Journal of Psychology, 70,* 477–488.

Margolis, H. (1987). *Patterns, thinking, and cognition.* Chicago: The University of Chicago Press.

McPeck, J. (1981). *Critical thinking and education.* New York: St. Martin's Press.

Tulving, E. (1983). *Elements of episodic memory.* Oxford: Oxford University Press.

Tversky, A., & Kahneman, D. (1982). Causal schemas in judgment under uncertainty. In D. Kahneman, P. Slovic, & A. Tversky (Eds.), *Judgment under uncertainty: Heuristics and biases* (pp. 117–128). New York: Cambridge University Press.

Wason, P. C. (1966). Reasoning. In B. Foss (Ed.), *New horizons in psychology* (pp. 135–151). Harmondsworth, Middlesex: Penguin.

Wason, P. C., & Johnson-Laird, P. N. (Eds.) (1968). *Thinking and reasoning.* Harmondsworth, Middlesex: Penguin.

Werner, H., & Kaplan, B. (1963). *Symbol formation.* New York: Wiley.

Yates, F. A. (1966). *The art of memory.* London: Routledge & Kegan Paul.

http://www.dushkin.com

On the Internet...

Berkeley Psychophysiology Laboratory Home Page

The Berkeley Psychophysiology Laboratory is a research laboratory located in the Department of Psychology at the University of California, Berkeley. The research facility studies human emotion by examining the subjective experience of emotion, emotional behavior, and physiological reactivity to emotional stimuli.
http://socrates.berkeley.edu/~lorenmc/bpl.html

Facial Analysis Page

The Perceptual Science Laboratory at the University of California, Santa Cruz, has put together this facial analysis page, which provides information and resources on researchers such as Paul Ekman.
http://mambo.ucsc.edu/psl/fanl.html

Part❖5

The Emotional Mind

William Raft Kunst-Wilson and R. B. Zajonc

❖

Richard J. McNally

❖

Daniel M. Wegner and David J. Schneider

❖

Daniel B. Wright

The Emotional Mind

Until relatively recently, and for reasons that can only be speculated about, cognitive psychologists have not investigated emotion. In the late 1950s and 1960s cognitivists were mainly concerned about establishing new views about memory, language, and thought. Emotion was not a high-priority topic. There has also always been the view, not always explicit or well articulated, that emotion is a very messy area and might not repay any analytic effort. Moreover, experts in other areas of psychology—clinical, personality, social, and developmental—had been studying emotion for a long time. From the cognitivists' perspective, then, emotion was therefore somehow already covered. Or emotion was viewed in a territorial way—emotion is "their" area of study. Another, more theoretical factor is that emotion often seems to run a different course than cognition. When we consider the mind-body issue, one of the first things that comes to mind is the apparent separateness of emotion. All common human experience is that emotions have a life of their own and that it is hard to think our way either into or out of emotions. Emotions seem to be all those things that cognition is not—automatic and involuntary, relentless, compelling, and hot. In contrast, cognition is stereotypically effortful and voluntary, episodic, mundane, and cold. Indeed, one of the longer-running controversies in psychology concerns the priority of emotion over cognition.

In some respects, the early cognitive psychological treatment of emotion was similar to the way the early radical behaviorists treated mental imagery; that is, as a taboo topic. Since about 1980 all this has changed. A wide variety of emotions and feelings, including mood, depression, pain, repression, stress, anxiety and fear, memory for traumatic and significant events, and obsessive thinking, have been studied. The articles in this section consider research on the apparent automatic nature of emotion; its biasing effect on attention, memory, and thought; and whether or not its effects require unique theoretical mechanisms.

This section begins with the classic study reported by William Raft Kunst-Wilson and R. B. Zajonc in "Affective Discrimination of Stimuli That Cannot Be Recognized." The results of the authors' experiment suggest that if a stimulus makes even minimal contact with long-term memory, it may take on some emotional significance, even if it does not arouse more explicit, presumably conscious recognition processes.

In their study, Kunst-Wilson and Zajonc presented irregular octagons five times, each for one millisecond (enough time to effect chance recognition), with the added instruction to subjects that they would not be able to see what was presented. Subjects were then asked which of a pair of octagons (old and new) they preferred, and then which they judged to be old. The results indicated that recognition was at chance but that old (originally shown) stimuli were preferred 60 percent of the time. It was concluded that "individuals can apparently develop preference for objects in the absence of conscious recognition." Familiarity, even if unavailable to normal memorial routes to recollection, seems to promote a warm, cozy feeling.

Such results raise questions not only about the automaticity of emotion but about the separability of emotional and cognitive systems. This same question has surfaced in research on subliminal processing, a controversial area. Other literatures in psychology have touched upon the same question— "incidental learning," "learning without awareness," "subception," and some attention studies come to mind here. Recently, this general topic has been dubbed "implicit memory," in which experience affects performance on a task that does not seem to require conscious processing. That is, people remember something but without any awareness that they are remembering it. For example, when provided with only a few letters for a word (e.g., _l_p_a_t), amnesic patients may fill in the blanks with letters that yield the word "elephant," although they cannot recall this word from a list of just-presented words, and they cannot say why they filled in the blanks that way. In this case, the word "elephant" has *primed* memory in a way that eludes conscious access. Thus, the issues of the effect of minimally processed stimuli and of nonstrategic, automatic remembering simply will not go away.

THE RESULTS REPORTED BY KUNST-WILSON AND ZAjonc suggest that there may be a built-in, ever-present bias for processing some stimuli in an affective way. But what if normal biases are overextended and go beyond ordinary concerns about oneself and the world? Richard J. McNally looks into this in "Cognitive Bias in Panic Disorder." According to McNally, panic disorder has a base rate of about 2 percent in the population and is characterized by anxiety attacks that involve dizziness, rapid heart rate, and feelings of impending doom. Attempts to pinpoint a biological basis for the disorder have been largely unsuccessful. However, one psychological theme that has emerged is that those who are afflicted with panic disorder are overly concerned with bodily states of arousal. This suggests, in turn, that "for panic sufferers, cognitive representations of arousal seem closely linked in memory with those of threat" and that memory structures involving fear may bias the processing of various inputs.

McNally documents the prediction that panic sufferers do in fact show various kinds of cognitive biases. For example, panic patients with agoraphobia were more likely than normal individuals to interpret ambiguous statements (e.g., "You feel discomfort in your chest area. Why?") as threatening. Similarly, panic patients showed attentional bias to fear-related words (e.g., "breathless") in that they had longer response delays than nonsufferers in naming the color in which the words were printed. These patients also showed memory biases for anxiety-related words but not for more positive emotional words. McNally points out that while other psychopathological groups (e.g., generalized anxiety disorder and posttraumatic stress disorder) also show cognitive biases, these biases show a different pattern than those for panic sufferers. However, although panic seems automatic, it is hard to separate automatic from strategic processing and equally hard to say whether the cognitive biases involved are causes or consequences of anxiety.

IF DIFFERENT PSYCHOPATHOLOGICAL GROUPS ARE COGNItively biased in processing stimuli, might these biases occur in normal individuals and be explainable by general mechanisms? What is happening when a panic sufferer obsesses about negative thoughts? One possibility is suggested by Daniel M. Wegner and David J. Schneider in "Mental Control: The War of the Ghosts in the Machine." Here the topic is unwanted thoughts and what people do about them. What do we do in order to not think about an upcoming need for surgery, a frustrating interpersonal situation, a dying relative, or a recurring negative memory from childhood? Wegner and Schneider argue that we control such thoughts in order to demonstrate self-control, to keep the thoughts secret, and to keep mental peace. The mechanism of control is one of *primary suppression*, by which attention is purposely kept away from the negative thought, and *auxiliary concentration*, by which a different thought is focused on. Experimental work on this topic involved having subjects verbalize their thoughts for five minutes, then do it again with the instruction "Try not to think of a white bear" (and ring a bell if they did), and do it one more time while specifically thinking about a white bear. In general, bell ringing tended to decrease in the second period, but compared to control groups, the experimental group showed more bell ringing in the last five-minute period. In other words, once the subjects who had tried to suppress the thought were free to think about the white bear, the thought "rebounded" and subjects seemed more preoccupied with it. Follow-up studies on this rebound effect suggested that *unfocused distraction* strategies, in which subjects thought about all sorts of things in order to suppress, tended to guarantee a rebound because a multiplicity of mental cues had become associated with the unwanted thought. *Focused distraction*, in which a single thought was used to suppress, was a more successful strategy. The "war of the ghosts" could be reduced to a skirmish if a single suppressor thought was used. This article may further understanding of the panic sufferer's dilemma: It may be that obsessive negative thoughts become associated with a wide range of stimuli, internal and external, in which case the scope of the disorder expands.

THE QUESTION OF THE SPECIAL VERSUS THE GENERAL theoretical status of emotional states also arises in conjunction with the last article in this section, "Recall of the Hillsborough Disaster Over Time: Systematic Biases of 'Flashbulb' Memories," by Daniel B. Wright. Flashbulb memories are memories that people have for highly emotional and significant events, such as the death of a loved one or a national disaster. Many Americans claim to have flashbulb memories for the assassination of President John F. Kennedy in 1963. This was the source of the original 1977 study on flashbulb memories by Roger Brown and James Kulick. These investigators argued that some highly emotional and consequential events may trigger a special brain mechanism that they called *Now Print*. This mechanism freezes the event, which results in a vivid and strong memory for it. Thus, people who have flashbulb memories can presumably access them in an encapsulated and literal form, as if the memory is retained forever in this form and is not subject to any sort of distortion. This special mechanism hypothesis is inconsistent with the reconstruction hypothesis, which holds that the recall of essentially all (episodic) long-term memories involves a reconstructive process. That is, memories are not simply lifted whole and without elaboration from some tape-recorder-like mechanism. They are pieced together with the help of inferences that change the original event.

More recent research on flashbulb memories finds that these memories can be quite inaccurate: people forget aspects of the original memory or even have totally false recollections. Wright's study specifically looked at whether or not flashbulb memories show the same kind of systematic biases as ordinary memory. Thus, it was a challenge to the special mechanism hypothesis.

Wright studied the memory sequalae of the Hillsborough disaster, as it was called, in which 95 people were crushed to death at a soccer game in Liverpool, England, in 1989. Wright used a cross-sectional, time-series method in which three different groups of university students filled out a survey two days, one month, or five months after the disaster. The students rated their emotional reactions to this event, their enthusiasm for soccer, and the importance of the event for them and for society. They also indicated the circumstances they were in when they heard about the event and what it reminded them of.

The results indicated that while ratings of emotional reaction and soccer enthusiasm remained constant across the three periods, the ratings rose for personal and societal importance. Moreover, with time, the ratings for personal importance moved upward toward those for emotion, meaning that the correlation between these ratings increased across the sessions. Wright also found that as time passed, memory did in fact recede, a greater percentage of the subjects said that they were watching television when the disaster occurred, and they more often recalled being with their families. Moreover, passage of time also promoted more generic memories of disasters than of specific soccer events. Wright concluded that the occurrence of the various systematic biases was more consistent with the view that ordinary reconstructive processes were at work rather than a special memory mechanism. According to Wright, a workable explanation of flashbulb memories must acknowledge their schematic character and social function.

22

William Raft Kunst-Wilson
and R. B. Zajonc

Affective Discrimination of Stimuli That Cannot Be Recognized

Abstract: *Animal and human subjects readily develop strong preferences for objects that have become familiar through repeated exposures. Experimental evidence is presented that these preferences can develop even when the exposures are so degraded that recognition is precluded.*

A substantial body of evidence demonstrates that the mere repeated exposure of a stimulus object increases its attractiveness (*1*). Both human (*2*) and animal subjects (*3*) exhibit the exposure effect with a variety of stimuli, exposure methods, and outcome measures of stimulus attractiveness.

In addition to its effects on preferences, exposure experience also allows the individual to learn a great deal about the stimulus object, so that the ability to recognize, discriminate, and categorize the object generally improves. Traditionally, theorists have assumed that this cognitive mastery resulting from experience with the stimulus mediated the growth of positive affect [for example, Harrison's response competition theory (*4*) and Berlyne's theory of optimal arousal (*5*)]. Thus, as the individual comes to "know" the stimulus better, his affective reaction to it is likely to become increasingly positive. For example, much of the literature on esthetic reactions to music suggests that experience leading to the recognition of familiar patterns and the ability to anticipate development is pleasurable and makes the composition attractive (*6*).

Recent research, however, suggests that overt affective responses may be unrelated to prior cognitive outcomes which result from stimulus exposure. For example, Moreland and Zajonc (*7*) have shown by a correlational analysis that repeated exposure increases preference for stimuli even when recognition is held constant, and Wilson (*8*) has demonstrated by experimental methods that auditory stimuli gain in attractiveness by virtue of

From William Raft Kunst-Wilson and R. B. Zajonc, "Affective Discrimination of Stimuli That Cannot Be Recognized," *Science,* vol. 207 (February 1, 1980), pp. 557–558. Copyright © 1980 by The American Association for the Advancement of Science. Reprinted by permission.

repeated exposure, even when their registration and subsequent recognition had been considerably impaired in the course of a dichotic listening task.

In the present experiment, a more stringent test was used to determine whether the exposure effect could be obtained when recognition was drastically reduced. Through preliminary studies, the conditions of stimulus exposure were systematically impoverished until recognition performance was brought down just to a chance level. A new group of subjects was then exposed to stimuli under these impoverished conditions, and judgments of attractiveness and measures of recognition memory for these stimuli and for stimuli not previously exposed were obtained. The results revealed clear preferences for exposed stimuli, even though subjects in a recognition memory test could not discriminate them from novel stimuli.

The experiment consisted of an exposure phase and of a test series. The stimuli were 20 irregular octagons constructed by a random process. Octagons of this type were used previously in exposure research, and subjects found no difficulty in making clear cognitive and affective discriminations among them (9). The 20 stimuli were divided into two sets of ten, sets A and B. In the exposure phase, half of the subjects saw set A and half set B. All subjects saw sets A and B in the test series. During the exposure phase, subjects fixated the center of a 23 by 17 cm rear projection screen mounted at the end of a viewing tunnel 91 cm long. Five exposures of each stimulus from the set of ten stimuli were shown in a random sequence. The octagons were solid black on white background; because of their high contrast, chance recognition could be obtained only after exposures were reduced to a 1-msec duration and illumination was lowered by a neutral density (ND8X) and a red gelatin filter. The instructions to subjects at the beginning of the exposure phase were that the experiment consisted of two parts and that during the first part slides would be shown on the screen at durations so brief that one could not really see what was being presented. Nevertheless, the subject was instructed to pay close attention to the flashes, even if nothing could be distinguished, and to acknowledge verbally the occurrence of each flash.

The second part of the experiment required subjects to make paired comparisons between slides from set A and set B. Now the slides were pre-

Figure 1

Proportion of Correct Recognition and Affective Discriminations for First Judgments in Each Category

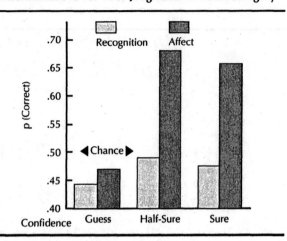

sented under adequate viewing conditions (exposure time was extended to 1 second). For each of the ten pairs, all containing one octagon previously exposed and one new, the subjects had to indicate (i) the one they liked better and (ii) the one they thought had been shown previously. For both judgments, confidence ratings were obtained on a three-point scale: "sure" (3 points), "half-sure" (2 points), and "guess" (1 point). Two groups of 12 subjects were studied, one making affective judgments of the ten stimulus pairs first and recognition judgments of the same pairs afterward, and another for whom the order of these judgments was reversed.

Recognition performance was very close to chance (48 percent accuracy). Affect responses, however, did reliably discriminate between old and new stimuli: old stimuli were liked better than new ones 60 percent of the time ($x^2 = 8.44$, $P < .01$). Overall, 16 of the 24 subjects preferred old to new stimuli, but only 5 of the 24 recognized old stimuli as such at better than the chance level. Of the 24 subjects, 17 discriminated better between old and new stimuli in their affective judgments than in their recognition responses, while only 4 showed superiority of recognition memory over affective judgments.

Subjects' confidence ratings show an interesting pattern (Figure 1). When they reported they were just guessing, recognition accuracy and affective discrimination were both at chance levels (47 and 48 percent, respectively). Recognition accuracy did not improve when subjects were either "half-sure" or "sure" of their recognition judgments (49 and 45 percent). In contrast, at these levels of confidence, affective discrimination was considerably more accurate (63 and 60 percent).

These effects are slightly more pronounced when the affective and recognition judgments were obtained first, and were therefore unbiased by prior responses to the test stimuli. Accuracy for affective judgments made prior to recognition judgments tended to be higher than the overall levels, while accuracy for recognition-first judgments tended to remain about the same.

Confidence in affective preferences was substantially higher than in recognition judgments. Mean confidence in affective discrimination was 2.29, while confidence in recognition judgments was 1.60 [$t(23) = 6.66$, $P < .01$] [10]. The tendency for affective preferences to be rendered more rapidly than recognition judgments (2.76 and 2.97 seconds, respectively) was not significant.

Individuals can apparently develop preferences for objects in the absence of conscious recognition and with access to information so scanty that they cannot ascertain whether anything at all was shown. The results thus suggest that there may exist a capacity for making affective discriminations without extensive participation of the cognitive system [11]. In fact, evidence of this sort, together with data on the influence of affective judgments on recall and recognition [12, 13], has been taken to indicate that partially independent systems may encode and process affect and content [12, 14].

The fact that with minimal stimulus information, some forms of discrimination can be performed while others are not possible is not new. Studies of perceptual vigilance and defense have yielded findings obtained with modern methods and under conditions that satisfy the most stringent experimental criteria—findings that can no longer be seriously ignored [15]. The large number of clear subliminal effects reported warrant the belief that various forms of affect-linked reactions are possible with only minimal access to the content. Shevrin [16], for example, found physiological and behavioral effects with 1-msec exposures. The recent work of Blum and Barbour [17], using hypnosis, confirms that affective reactions of various forms can take place with the content almost entirely suppressed.

Evidence for processing that occurs without an apparent access to the physical properties of verbal stimuli has been repeatedly reported. For example, subjects can identify a word sooner than they are able to identify its letters [18], and they can identify the semantic category of a word without being able to identify the word itself [19]. Of course, what stimulus cues or internal processes allow the subject to make affective discriminations on the basis of what must surely be minimal processing of stimulus information cannot be established on the basis of what is now known. Perhaps from the point of view of survival value, however, it should not be entirely surprising that these affective discriminations can be made with so little stimulus information [20]. Since affective reactions to a stimulus may readily change without any changes in the stimulus (as a result of repeated exposure, for example), these reactions must be based not only on the properties of the stimulus itself, but on information related to some internal states of the individual. Further empirical work may reveal the different bases of affective and cognitive judgments, should they indeed be partially separate and independent.

REFERENCES AND NOTES

1. R. B. Zajonc, *J. Pers. Soc. Psychol. Monogr. Suppl.* **9,** 1 (1968).

2. A. A. Harrison, in *Advances in Experimental Social Psychology*, L. Berkowitz, Ed. (Academic Press, New York, 1977), vol. 9, pp. 218–252.

3. W. F. Hill, *Psychol. Bull.* **85,** 1177 (1978); R. B. Zajonc, in *Man and Beast: Comparative Social Behavior*, J. F. Eisenberg and W. S. Dillon, Eds. (Smithsonian Institution Press, Washington D.C., 1971), pp. 48–73.

4. A. A. Harrison, *J. Pers. Soc. Psychol.* **9,** 363 (1968).

5. D. E. Berlyne, *Percep. Psychophys.* **8,** 279 (1970); *Aesthetics and Psychobiology* (Appleton, New York, 1971).

6. H. K. Mull, *J. Psychol.* **43,** 155 (1957).

7. R. L. Moreland and R. B. Zajonc, *J. Pers. Soc. Psychol.* **35,** 191 (1977).

8. W. R. Wilson, *ibid.* **37,** 811 (1979).

9. P. H. Hamid, *Br. J. Psychol.* **64,** 569 (1973).

10. Unlike recognition, preferences cannot be construed as right or wrong. In an attempt to correct for this source of bias, subjects in another experiment were

led to believe that their affect judgments would be compared with those of art critics, and "subjective impressions of familiarity" were requested in the place of recognition judgments. Even under these conditions, subjects' confidence in their affect judgments remained significantly higher.

11. Explanations involving response bias, such as that individuals use less stringent criterion for liking than for recognition judgments, cannot be readily invoked because a forced-choice procedure eliminated response biases of this kind.

12. N. H. Anderson and S. Hubert, *J. Verb. Learn. Verb Behav.* **2,** 379 (1963).

13. G. H. Bower and M. B. Karlin, *J. Exp. Psychol.* **103,** 751 (1974); K. E. Patterson and A. D. Baddeley, *J. Exp. Psychol. Hum. Learn. Mem.* **3,** 406 (1977).

14. M. I. Posner and C. R. R. Snyder, in *Attention and Performance,* V. P. M. A. Rabbitt and S. Dornic, Eds. (Academic Press, New York, 1975), pp. 87–103; R. B. Zajonc, paper presented at the First Ontario Symposium of Personality and Social Psychology, London, Ontario, 27 August 1978.

15. M. H. Erdelyi, *Psychol. Rev.,* **81,** 1 (1974).

16. H. Shevrin and D. E. Fritzler, *Science* **161,** 295 (1968).

17. G. S. Blum and J. S. Barbour, *J. Exp. Psychol. Gen.* **108,** 182 (1979).

18. J. C. Johnston and J. L. McClelland, *Science* **184,** 1192 (1974).

19. A. J. Marcel and K. E. Patterson in *Attention and Performance,* J. Requin, Ed. (Erlbaum, Hillsdale, N.J., 1978), vol. 7, pp. 209–226.

20. There is no implication that one of these processes is more accessible to awareness. Either the affective or the cognitive process can become consciously available, depending on a variety of factors.

21. Supported in part by a fellowship from the John Simon Guggenheim Foundation and by HEW grant 5RO2-NU00572.

23

Richard J. McNally

Cognitive Bias in Panic Disorder

Panic disorder is characterized by unexpected anxiety attacks involving symptoms such as dizziness, breathlessness, rapid heart beat, and fears of impending death, insanity, or loss of self-control. Panic attacks are harmless, and rarely last more than a few minutes. Yet many people who experience them become apprehensive about their recurrence and avoid situations that do not permit easy escape should panic strike (e.g., crowded shopping malls, airplanes). If avoidance becomes widespread, panic disorder with agoraphobia is diagnosed.[1] Agoraphobia is characterized by fearful avoidance of public places where panic might occur. Most people who develop panic disorder exhibit at least some agoraphobic avoidance.

Panic disorder is a common condition that afflicts about 2% of the population. It occurs more often in women than in men, typically develops in early adulthood, and has a fluctuating, chronic course if not treated with cognitive-behavior therapy, medication, or both.[1]

The sudden, seemingly "spontaneous" eruption of arousal that characterizes panic has prompted considerable research into its biological basis. Yet aspects of the syndrome defy a purely biological analysis. Not everyone who experiences surges of arousal experiences terror, and not everyone who experiences an attack becomes apprehensive about further attacks and develops panic disorder. Accordingly, psychological factors may figure in the etiology of the syndrome. For example, people who consider arousal symptoms potentially harmful are probably those most at risk for developing the disorder should they experience such symptoms. Indeed, concerns about arousal are so prominent in people with panic disorder that many theorists conceptualize the syndrome as primarily a "fear of fear."[1]

STUDIES ON COGNITIVE BIAS IN PANIC DISORDER

These observations suggest that the psychopathology of panic lies partly in the semantic representation of arousal. For panic sufferers, cognitive representations of arousal seem closely linked in memory with those of threat.

From Richard J. McNally, "Cognitive Bias in Panic Disorder," *Current Directions in Psychological Science,* vol. 3, no. 4 (August 1994). Copyright © 1994 by The American Psychological Society. Reprinted by permission of Cambridge University Press.

Their chronic hypervigilance for bodily symptoms, moreover, implies that these "fear structures" are primed and readily accessible to bias information processing in ways likely to exacerbate pathological anxiety. Accordingly, researchers have investigated whether panic patients are characterized by interpretive, attentional, and memory biases for threat. Although informal clinical observations have long suggested that cognitive processes are disturbed in panic disorder, researchers have only recently applied objective paradigms potentially capable of discriminating between those processes that are dysfunctional and those that are not.

Interpretive Bias for Threat

In everyday life, people encounter many situations whose meaning is not obvious. Tightness in the chest may signify heart trouble, or merely sore muscles. A noise in the middle of the night may signify an intruder, or merely windows rattling in the wind. Any tendency to interpret such ambiguous stimuli as threatening ought to increase the likelihood of one's becoming anxious. Although a bias for disambiguating stimuli as threatening ought to be associated with anxiety in general, it ought to be especially evident in people suffering from panic disorder.

In a study on interpretive bias,[2] panic patients with agoraphobia, recovered panic patients, and normal control subjects provided the first explanation that came to mind after reading ambiguous scenarios involving either an external stimulus (e.g., "You wake with a start in the middle of the night, thinking you heard a noise, but all is quiet. What do you think woke you up?") or an internal stimulus (e.g., "You feel discomfort in your chest area. Why?"). For each scenario, subjects then ranked three experimenter-provided explanations (one threatening) in terms of their likelihood of coming to mind in a similar situation. In contrast to recovered panickers and normal control subjects, panic patients with agoraphobia more often provided threatening interpretations for both external and internal scenarios, and they more often ranked the threatening experimenter-provided explanation as the one most likely to come to mind. In a subsequent investigation,[3] panic patients without agoraphobia exhibited an interpretive bias only for ambiguous scenarios concerning internal cues.

Taken together, these studies suggest that interpretive bias may spread beyond ambiguous bodily sensations to other stimuli when pure panic disorder evolves into agoraphobia.

Attentional Bias for Threat

If cognitive representations of arousal, fear, and threat are primed and readily accessible in panic disorder, patients ought to attend selectively to such information in the modified Stroop color-naming paradigm. In this paradigm, subjects are shown words of varying emotional significance and are asked to name the colors in which the words are printed while ignoring the meanings of the words. A delay in color naming occurs when the meaning of the word captures the subject's attention despite the subject's effort to attend to the color of the word. In one study, consistent with the hypothesis that panic patients have an attentional bias for threat, they exhibited delayed color naming for words related to fear (e.g., panic), bodily sensations (e.g., breathless), and catastrophe (e.g., insane).[4] In a subsequent experiment,[5] panic patients exhibited greater interference for catastrophe words than for positive words of equal but opposite valence (e.g., carefree).

Memory Bias for Threat

Panic patients are troubled by distressing thoughts that come to mind seemingly automatically, and especially under conditions of arousal. Accordingly, they ought to exhibit a memory bias for recalling anxiety-relevant material in a free-recall paradigm, and physiological activation ought to enhance this bias if cognitive representations of arousal and threat are closely linked for panic patients.

In a study concerning memory bias for threat,[6] panic patients and normal control subjects rated the self-descriptiveness of adjectives either related (e.g., *nervous)* or unrelated (e.g., *polite)* to anxiety before either exercising (high arousal) or relaxing (low arousal). Immediately thereafter, subjects attempted to recall the previously rated material. Panic patients recalled more anxiety than nonanxiety words, whereas control subjects exhibited the opposite pattern. Arousal tended to enhance the recall bias for threat in the panic disorder group. Additional analyses revealed that the memory bias for threat in that group was not attributable to either a response bias or a general self-descriptive recall bias. In a subsequent experiment,[7] panic patients exhibited memory biases for threatening material but not for material of positive emotional valence.

COGNITIVE BIASES IN OTHER ANXIETY DISORDERS

Attempts to elucidate cognitive biases associated with pathological anxiety have not been confined to research on panic disorder. Indeed, most work has concerned generalized anxiety disorder (GAD).[8] Researchers have uncovered similarities and differences across the anxiety disorders. One important similarity concerns the Stroop paradigm. Threat-related interference effects occur not only in panic disorder and GAD, but also in simple phobia, obsessive compulsive disorder (OCD), social phobia, and post-traumatic stress disorder (PTSD). The modal finding has been that patients exhibit interference only for threatening material directly pertinent to their central concerns. For example, Vietnam combat veterans with PTSD exhibit marked interference for words related to trauma (e.g., *body-bags*), but not for material disturbing for OCD patients (e.g., *feces*).[9]

An apparent difference among the anxiety disorders concerns memory bias for threat. Panic patients display enhanced recall for threatening material, and PTSD patients exhibit poor recall for everything except material related to trauma.[10] In contrast, GAD patients exhibit no recall bias for threat.[11] There is some evidence, however, that biases for threat in GAD (and PTSD) are detectable on indirect tests of implicit memory, which do not require conscious recollection of having seen threatening material earlier in the experiment.[10,11] Discrepant findings across studies indicate that firm conclusions about the nature and extent of memory bias in anxiety would be premature.

AUTOMATIC AND STRATEGIC COGNITIVE BIASES

Psychopathologists studying anxiety have increasingly endeavored to distinguish automatic from strategic (i.e., voluntary, conscious, controlled) cognitive biases, and to devise tasks that capture automatic processes uncontaminated by strategic influence. The motivation for targeting automaticity arises from the phenomenology of pathological anxiety: Panic attacks, generalized anxiety, and phobias appear involuntary, thereby implying that the underlying mechanisms are automatic, not strategic. Moreover, the distinction between automatic and strategic biases may have therapeutic significance; automatic biases are unlikely to be easily altered by verbal psychotherapy.

Two issues complicate investigation of automatic cognitive biases in the anxiety disorders. First, it is unclear in what sense these biases are "automatic." Traditional views hold that automatic processes are rapid, involuntary, resource-independent, and capable of occurring outside awareness, but these attributes of automaticity do not always covary. Phenomenology suggests that being rapid and being involuntary are most relevant to the anxiety disorders, rather than being resource-independent or capable of occurring outside of awareness.

A second issue concerns the ability of existing paradigms to parse the relative contributions of automatic and strategic processes to task performance. Many tasks designed to tap automatic (or strategic) processes are subject to contamination from strategic (or automatic) influences. To circumvent the need for process-pure tasks, Jacoby[12] has devised a framework to estimate the relative contributions of automatic and strategic influences in a variety of paradigms. His process-dissociation framework has yet to be applied to the study of cognitive bias in the anxiety disorders.

ARE BIASES CAUSES OR CONSEQUENCES OF PATHOLOGICAL ANXIETY?

Most research relevant to cognition and panic concerns people who already have panic disorder. Accordingly, it is impossible to determine whether biases favoring the processing of threatening information are causes or consequences of panic attacks.

To determine whether cognitive biases contribute to the etiology of panic disorder, investigators need to establish that these biases antedate the occurrence of panic. Longitudinal study of high-risk populations provides a method for answering this question. One promising high-risk group is psychiatrically healthy people with high anxiety sensitivity. Anxiety sensitivity refers to the degree of fear that anxiety symptoms are harmful.[13] People with high anxiety sensitivity are especially prone to panic under conditions of arousal. In one recent experiment,[14] healthy subjects who had never experienced a panic attack, but who scored as high as panic disorder patients on the Anxiety Sensitivity Index (ASI), were far more likely than low-anxiety-sensitive subjects to panic after inhaling carbon dioxide, a gas that produces intense, but harmless, arousal symptoms. Additional analyses revealed that carbon dioxide–induced panic could not be explained by preinhalation levels of state or trait anxiety.

It remains to be seen whether people identified as at risk for panic disorder by the ASI respond similarly to panic patients on non-self-report measures of pathological information processing. Moreover, it remains to be seen whether these people subsequently develop panic disorder—and, more important, whether the development of the syndrome might be prevented through early intervention efforts.

ACKNOWLEDGMENTS

Support for the author's research was provided by National Institute of Mental Health Grant MH 43809.

NOTES

1. D. H. Barlow, *Anxiety and Its Disorders: The Nature and Treatment of Anxiety and Panic* (Guilford Press, New York, 1988).

2. R. J. McNally and E. B. Foa, Cognition and agoraphobia: Bias in the interpretation of threat, *Cognitive Therapy and Research, 11,* 567–581 (1987).

3. D. M. Clark, A cognitive model of panic attacks, in *Panic: Psychological Perspectives*, S. Rachman and J. D. Maser, Eds. (Erlbaum, Hillsdale, NJ, 1988).

4. R. J. McNally, B. C. Riemann, and E. Kim, Selective processing of threat cues in panic disorder, *Behaviour Research and Therapy, 28,* 407–412 (1990).

5. R. J. McNally, B. C. Riemann, C. E. Louro, B. M. Lukach, and E. Kim, Selective processing of emotional information in panic disorder, *Behaviour Research and Therapy, 30,* 143–149 (1992).

6. R. J. McNally, E. B. Foa, and C. D. Donnell, Memory bias for anxiety information in patients with panic disorder, *Cognition and Emotion, 3,* 27–44 (1989).

7. M. Cloitre and M. R. Liebowitz, Memory bias in panic disorder: An investigation of the cognitive avoidance hypothesis, *Cognitive Therapy and Research, 15,* 371–386 (1991).

8. A. Mathews, Why worry? The cognitive function of anxiety, *Behaviour Research and Therapy, 28,* 455–468 (1990).

9. R. J. McNally, S. P. Kaspi, B. C. Riemann, and S. B. Zeitlin, Selective processing of threat cues in postttraumatic stress disorder, *Journal of Abnormal Psychology, 99,* 398–402 (1990).

10. S. B. Zeitlin and R. J. McNally, Implicit and explicit memory bias for threat in post-traumatic stress disorder, *Behaviour Research and Therapy, 29,* 451–457 (1991).

11. A. Mathews, K. Mogg, J. May, and M. Eysenck, Implicit and explicit memory bias in anxiety, *Journal of Abnormal Psychology, 98,* 236–240 (1989).

12. L. L. Jacoby, A process dissociation framework: Separating automatic from intentional uses of memory, *Journal of Memory and Language, 30,* 513–541 (1991).

13. S. Reiss, R. A. Peterson, D. M. Gursky, and R. J. McNally, Anxiety sensitivity, anxiety frequency and the prediction of fearfulness, *Behaviour Research and Therapy, 24,* 1–8 (1986).

14. M. J. Telch and P. J. Harrington, *The role of anxiety sensitivity and expectedness of arousal in mediating affective response to 35% carbondioxide*, paper presented at the annual meeting of the Association for Advancement of Behavior Therapy, Boston (November 1992).

RECOMMENDED READING

McNally, R. J. (1990). Psychological approaches to panic disorder: A review. *Psychological Bulletin, 108,* 403–419.

McNally, R. J. (1994). *Panic Disorder: A Critical Analysis* (Guilford Press, New York).

Rachman, S., and Maser, J. D., Eds. (1988). *Panic: Psychological Perspectives* (Erlbaum, Hillsdale, NJ).

24

Daniel M. Wegner and David J. Schneider

Mental Control: The War of the Ghosts in the Machine

Sometimes it feels as though we can control our minds. We catch ourselves looking out the window when we should be paying attention to someone talking, for example, and we purposefully return our attention to the conversation. Or we reset our minds away from the bothersome thought of an upcoming dental appointment to focus on anything we can find that make us less nervous. Control attempts such as these can meet with success, leaving us feeling the masters of our consciousness. Yet at other times we drift back to gaze out the window or to think again of the dentist's chair, and we are left to wonder whether mental control is real—and, if it is, how we might exercise it effectively.

THE NATURE OF MENTAL CONTROL

One way to approach this problem is to assume that mental control is a real phenomenon, ask people to exercise it, and see what happens. Some noteworthy regularities in the effects of mental control become evident on following this line of inquiry. This chapter is about experiments we have conducted in which people are asked to control their minds while they are describing the course of their thoughts. We begin by describing the course of our own thoughts.

A "Tumbling-Ground for Whimsies"

Mental control is connected to two of the most important controversial concepts in psychology—consciousness and the will. Even William James, a champion of the study of things mental, warned that consciousness has the potential to make psychology no more than a "tumbling-ground for whimsies" (1890, Vol. 1, p. 163). Psychology since James has echoed his concern. Although the idea of altogether abolishing consciousness from psy-

From Daniel M. Wegner and David J. Schneider, "Mental Control: The War of the Ghosts in the Machine," in James S. Uleman and John A. Bargh, eds., *Unintended Thought* (Guilford Press, 1989). Copyright © 1989 by Guilford Press, a division of Guilford Publications, Inc. Reprinted by permission.

chology only held sway at the peak of behaviorism, even after a cognitive revolution there remains a preference for the study of mind through its processes rather than its conscious content. The will, in turn, is relegated to the status of illusion by many—among them Gilbert Ryle, who called it the "ghost in the machine" (1949, p. 15). The question, then, of whether the will can operate upon consciousness is doubly troubling.

James held that we exert our wills by "effort of attention" (1890, Vol. 2, p. 562). He voiced the useful intuition that we do one thing as opposed to another by steering our consciousness. *How* we do this, however, is unclear. We appear to attend to one thing as opposed to another by—well, by just doing so. James's account only indicates that the willful movement of consciousness from one object to another feels like work, and that this movement can be contrasted with those cases in which our attention is drawn, seemingly without our effort, by forces beyond our will. Mental control is, in this light, one of the irreducible elements of conscious experience. This irreducibility is one of the puzzling aspects of mental control that has left those inclined to deal with this issue talking of ghosts and whimsies.

It is possible to study the operation of mental control in a useful way, however, without any further insight into this puzzle. One need only assume that there is a cognitive process responsible for activating and deactivating attentional mechanisms according to priorities that are reflected in conscious thoughts. A scientific understanding of this process does not require that we be able to see into it as we do it, any more than a science of movement requires that we have insight into the enervation of our muscles as we walk like a chicken. It is time to set aside the dissection of the conscious experience of willing, and study instead the observable circumstances and consequences of this experience.

There is one other feature of mental control that has given it a reputation as a phantom of the ganglia. Mental efforts sometimes fail, and we do not know enough about mental control to understand why this happens. Sometimes the right idea will not come, despite furrowed brows, squinted eyes, and all the deliberate concentration one can muster. This may not at first seem strange, because efforts of all sorts frequently fail. But we find it surprising because whereas the effort to make a thought ap-

pear on command sometimes does not work, seemingly similar physical efforts rarely fail in the physically healthy. It is odd to say that "I couldn't get it out of my mind" or "I couldn't concentrate on the idea," but it seems most peculiar to say that "I couldn't make my finger move."

Even mental control that is initially successful can subsequently falter. Unlike physical effort, which, once initiated typically suffers few indigenous interferences (i.e., other than from physical restraint), our thoughts seem remarkably capricious. On good days our thoughts are as precise as a hawk gathering small rodents, but more often our thoughts seem like fluttery butterflies that not only fail to stay put for long but are subject to the winds of competing thought. Try as we may, we cannot concentrate on reading a novel or solving an equation when there are interesting distractions nearby. Or we may struggle to make particular thoughts go away in the midst of a sleepless night, only to have them return all too soon. And it is something of a universal tragedy that when we attempt to reject thoughts of hot fudge sundaes from our minds while dieting, we must usually watch as they then march through our imaginations again and again.

The Aims of Mental Control

There are two general goals to which we aspire in controlling our minds: having something in mind, and not having it in mind. Psychology gives us many terms for each. Having something in mind is "thinking," "attending," "retrieving," "perceiving," "encoding," and so on; not having something in mind is "forgetting," "denying," "repressing," "avoiding," "filtering," and so forth. The activities in which we engage when we consciously attempt to achieve one of these states are most generally called "concentration" and "suppression," respectively. Although there are other potential goals for mental control—one, perhaps, for each mental operation people can perform—it is clear that these are most fundamental. If we could not concentrate or suppress, it seems there would be little else we could do to our minds.

Normally, when we are thinking of one thing, we are not thinking of something else. Cognitive psychologists have often held that this dual function of the process of attending suggests the operation of two subprocesses, one that brings items to attention and one that filters out everything else (e.g., Broadbent, 1958). The central idea here is that *both* processes must be operating at all times in order to keep one thing in our conscious attention. If we assume that mental control processes are simply willful versions of such automatic processes, then we can suggest that concentration and suppression are typically associated. In concentrating on X, we suppress not-X; by the same token, in suppressing X, we concentrate on not-X.

By this logic, the two processes are always simultaneous. The reason we have different names for them and experience them as distinct is that we try to do one at a time (and the other follows). So, for instance, we may try to concentrate on writing a book chapter (and suppress thoughts of other things, such as going swimming). Alternatively, we may try to suppress a thought, say, of smoking a cigarette (and concentrate on other things, such as eating). In either case, we are primarily aware of intending only one of the processes, but we nevertheless must use the other process as well in order to fulfill our intention. This is true because both processes are versions of the "effort of attention" described by James, and we cannot move attention toward something without at the same time moving it away from something else.

The simultaneity of concentration and suppression suggests that there are two distinguishable forms of each process. First, there are primary and auxiliary forms of concentration; primary concentration is attending to something because we want to do so, whereas auxiliary concentration is attending to something because we wish to suppress attention to something else. In a similar vein, there are primary and auxiliary forms of suppression. Primary suppression is keeping attention away from something because we want to do so, whereas auxiliary suppression is keeping attention away as a means of concentrating on something else. Primary concentration is thus accompanied by an auxiliary suppression (as when one avoids thinking about the noise down the hall in order to study). And primary suppression brings with it an auxiliary concentration (as when one tries not to think of a broken romance by focusing on a television program.)

Our studies of mental control have centered on the case of primary suppression with auxiliary concentration. This is the form of mental control that people appear most anxious to have, in large part because lapses of suppression announce themselves intrusively. We know quite clearly when an unwanted thought returns to consciousness. In a sense, our plan to suppress marks the thought as something of which we must be wary, and its return is thus heralded by an immediate reorientation to the suppression problem. By contrast, when we merely try to concentrate, it is quite possible to lose sight of the plan and mentally drift away, for minutes or perhaps even days. The only sign that we have failed to concentrate occurs if we happen in our mental meandering to stumble across the concentration target. And even then, the concentration target and our earlier failure do not seem to burst into our minds with nearly the force of a returning unwanted thought.

The reason for examining suppression rather than concentration, in short, is not too far removed from the sheer love of sport. When people concentrate, the purpose of mental control is to maintain a line of thought. In a sense, one part of the mind is cheering on another. But when people suppress, the purpose of mental control is to challenge a line of thought. One part of the mind is set to defeat another. Skirmishes can break out on many mental fields of battle, and the most placid, unsuspecting states of mind can be ambushed from the blue by unwanted thoughts. Thought suppression is thus an occasion for mental conflict, a true war of the ghosts in the machine.

THE CASE OF THOUGHT SUPPRESSION

The fact that we sometimes suppress thoughts because they are painful is no surprise either to introspective laypeople or to readers of Freud. Sometimes mental pain seems as unbearable as its physical counterpart, and one does not have to be a committed hedonist to recognize that painful stimuli are typically avoided. Freud, of course, built much of his theory around such episodes. Although our work has not been much oriented toward Freudian ideas, he offered many masterful insights not only about the unconscious but the conscious part of mental life. We begin by considering his approach, and then turn to the basic problems of why people suppress, how they do it, what effect their efforts have, and how they might do it most competently.

Freud and Forgetting

Unfortunately, Freud was often most vague at the point where he should have been most precise, and it is hard to extract a consistent theory about the mental life from his work. This is especially true in the case of his accounts of suppression and repression. For example, it is commonly assumed that Freud made a sharp distinction between conscious "suppression" and unconscious "repression." In fact, he continuously and throughout his career used the terms interchangeably; furthermore, he never stated explicitly that repression referred only to pushing conscious material into the unconscious (cf. Erdelyi & Goldberg, 1979).

Freud preferred a broad definition of repression: "[T]he essence of repression lies simply in the function of rejecting and keeping something out of consciousness" (1915/1957, p. 105). It is certainly true that many (indeed, most) of the examples he used invoke a stronger and more popular sense of the term, involving the unconscious, but it is also true that he was generally perfectly explicit that removing cathexis (roughly, attention, in this context) from an idea was a sufficient condition for repression, defined as above. As far as we know, the closest he ever came to distinguishing between suppression and repression came in a long footnote in Chapter 7 of *The Interpretation of Dreams:* "For instance, I have omitted to state whether I attribute different meanings to the words 'suppressed' and 'repressed.' It should have been clear, however, that the latter lays more stress than the former upon the fact of attachment to the unconscious" (Freud, 1900/ 1953, Vol. 5, p. 606).

Psychoanalysts have now focused for many years on the notion of unconscious repression to the exclusion of simple suppression. Although Freud himself can surely be faulted for promoting this particular line of orthodoxy in psychoanalytic theorizing, his primary concern was in how we keep former ideas from recurring. This activity could involve suppression alone, and certainly need not depend on either unconscious motivation or memory erasure, the central features of classical repression. Each of these features of the concept of

repression has served in its own way as a theoretical albatross.

The dogma of unconscious motivation, for example, requires that research on repression must typically arrive at the scene after the fact. We cannot know beforehand exactly what unconscious motive might be energized, nor when that motive might act, nor which particular conscious thought it might choose as a repression target; these things are all deeply unconscious. So, according to psychoanalysis, we must typically wait until after a repression has happened and then bring in the research crew to sift the ashes. For this reason, repression has seldom been approached as a cognitive process, and the research in this area has typically settled instead on the far weaker tactic of isolating individuals who tend to repress, and examining their other personality characteristics. This circuitous avenue of inquiry has met with some success (see, e.g., Davis, 1987), but of course cannot clarify the repression process itself.

Classical repression theory does make the strong prediction that memory can be erased, however, so much research has focused on this claim. It is in this domain that the Freudian notion of repression has received its most stunning disconfirmations. Holmes (1974) reviewed a long list of studies of repression and found no clear evidence for the occurrence of forgetting motivated by ego threat. Erdelyi (1985) sympathetically reviewed a series of his own and others' studies of hypermnesia (the retrieval of more information from memory than was retrievable at an earlier point), and concluded that no fully convincing demonstration had yet been made. Although there are many clinical cases of amnesia (e.g., Breznitz, 1983; Rapaport, 1959), and a variety of indications that physical illness or injury can render memory inaccessible (e.g., Yarnell & Lynch, 1973), there is little indication that the widespread and frequent memory losses Freud envisioned are at all so common in daily life. Studies of hypnotic amnesia (see Kihlstrom, 1983) and directed forgetting (e.g., Geiselman, Bjork, & Fishman, 1983) show instead that certain memory processes under voluntary control (e.g., the avoidance of rehearsal at encoding) may on occasion contribute to the occurrence of motivated forgetting.

What all this means is that the topic of thought suppression per se is relatively neglected and misunderstood. Consciously keeping a thought from consciousness is the task of suppression, and we know comparatively little about how such an activity proceeds. Do people control their minds, not by forgetting, but by failing to access thoughts that are nonetheless accessible in memory? Such "selective inattention" could perform many of the tasks that psychoanalysts have counted on unconscious repression to accomplish. Indeed, several theorists have argued that inattention is all we need to avoid painful affect (e.g., Klinger, 1982). One need not forget a thought forever, and also forget the forgetting, merely to remove the thought from one's focus of attention. All that is required is thinking of something else, and continuing to do so.

Why Do We Suppress?

There are many possible answers to the question of why a thought might be unwanted. Freud suggested several answers, but offered no unified picture of why people suppress. His most general theme was that those instinctually driven ideas that fail the censor's and/or superego's tests of acceptability will be suppressed. In Freud's earlier writing, he stressed the unacceptability of ideas as a direct motive for repression, whereas in his later work he was more inclined to stress the anxiety aroused by the ideas as the motive force behind repression. In any event, he never suggested (as did many of his followers) that suppression exists only for "dirty" thoughts. Indeed, in his work on dreams and his subsequent theoretical work, he often referred to pain in the broadest possible sense as a motive for repression.

A broad desire to avoid unpleasantness does not account fully, however, for a number of instances in which people tend to engage in suppression. It is possible to refine this global motive into at least three distinct categories (Wegner, 1988, 1989). One general class of such instances involves efforts at *self-control*. When people diet, try to quit smoking, attempt to get more exercise, try to stop using drugs, want to avoid alcohol, resolve to watch less television, or even attempt to break off a destructive or unhappy relationship, they usually find that they desire to suppress thoughts of the unwanted activity as well. Any straightforward definition of "pleasantness" would not class thoughts of food, alcohol, drugs, and the like as unpleasant, especially to the

person who is feeling deprived; for this reason, it seems useful to suggest that instances of self-control can make thoughts *unwanted*, even though they may not be strictly unpleasant.

A dedicated psychoanalyst might note that the agonies of self-control are consistent in some respects with the struggles Freud envisioned between id and superego. We would concur with this, but expand this characterization to speak of self-control as a clash between habitual, automatic processes spawned by a history of appetitive contact with an entity, and enlightened, controlled processes attempting to redirect behavior. Mental control, in this analysis, is the first step toward any sort of self-control. One must avoid thinking of the addictive object in order to stop the instigation of the addictive behavior. The only way to bypass the exercise of mental control in these circumstances is to act precipitously to prevent oneself from ever performing the unwanted behavior—padlocking the refrigerator in the case of food, perhaps, or avoiding alcohol by moving to Saudi Arabia.

A second source of suppression occurs in the need for *secrecy*. There is nothing that can instigate suppression faster than the threat that something normally private might be made public. The prototypical situation occurs when one encounters a person from whom a secret must be kept. With the person present, it is deeply tempting to blurt out the secret whenever it comes to mind—or at least one worries that this will happen. Thus, one makes a special point of suppressing the secret thought whenever the relevant person is around. The range of relevant people differs for different secrets, of course, and at the extreme one may find oneself suppressing a thought whenever anyone at all is present or even imagined.

This cause of suppression is strongly social in origin, forged in large part by the schism that inevitably develops between our private thoughts and our public lives. Self-deception is, in this sense, the child of social deception. We admire someone from a distance, for example, and because we fear our sentiments will not be reciprocated, we keep quiet about our feelings. We must hold this back each time we are in the person's presence, and we become a dithering caricature of ourselves as we work so hard to be normal. Alternatively, there may be some occurrence in our childhood that we have never troubled to tell anyone about. It may not even be particularly traumatic (in the Freudian sense), but the secrecy alone is enough to make us try not to think of it when we encounter potential audiences (Pennebaker, 1988). Other instances occur when we harbor discriminatory opinions of someone and work extra hard at suppressing our usual disparaging thoughts to keep from appearing prejudiced when the person is around to notice (see Fiske, Chapter 8, this volume). The source of our secrets, in sum, can be concern about any social, moral, or personal blunder, but the most socially unacceptable secrets tend to spawn the greatest suppression.

The third wellspring of suppression can best be called a motive to find *mental peace*. Quite simply, we sometimes observe that we are thinking something too often for our liking. A dream is repeated several nights in a row: we notice we keep toying with a lock of our hair; the unnamed pain in our chest reappears each time we feel stressed; or the same worry about our family's safety comes up over and over. The mere repetition of a thought may be sufficient to suggest to us the need for mental control, and we try not to think of it. Such thoughts are not necessarily abhorrent because of any special unpleasantness, although they can be; rather, we hope to suppress them because we have decided we are thinking them too often. The decision that a thought occurs "too often" will often be based, of course, in some unwanted emotional reaction that the thought engenders. This motive thus can encompass a wide range of what Freud imagined as the beginnings of suppression or repression—all those thoughts that are too disturbing to think because they produce negative affect. For many such thoughts, even one occurrence is too many, and in search of mental peace we put them aside as soon as we can.

These sources of suppression—self-control, secrecy, and mental peace—are not mutually exclusive. Many cases of keeping secrets, for example, can be cast as instances of self-control as well, and the pursuit of mental peace may be the conscious desire that arises during mental control attempts originally set in motion by self-control or secrecy. Partitioning the sources of mental control in this way is not meant to provide an exhaustive system of independent motivational categories. Indeed, these three sources of the urge to suppress could well be seen as subservient to some more general

motive, such as esteem maintenance, control, or the like. This partition is useful as a way of highlighting the principal everyday circumstances in which mental control is engaged: when we are dissatisfied with ourselves, when we hide things from others, and when we are not at peace in our minds.

How Do We Suppress?

The strategies people use to suppress unwanted thoughts can be described as either direct or indirect. A direct strategy, as noted earlier, is primary suppression through auxiliary concentration—actively trying to think of something else. The indirect strategies are many; they include such devices as using alcohol, engaging in strenuous physical activity, or performing some palliative action that makes the unwanted thought less intrusive (e.g., coming back home to check whether the stove was really left on). When suppression is auxiliary to the attempt at primary concentration, we may also call the suppression attempt indirect. Many forms of psychotherapy can also be classed as indirect forms of suppression, in that attempts at problem-solving, emotional expression, cognitive restructuring, and the like are commonly addressed toward the elimination of unwanted thoughts. Only "thought stopping" (Wolpe & Lazarus, 1966) verges on a direct therapeutic approach. With this technique, the client is taught to call out "stop" whenever an unwanted thought occurs in a therapeutic session, and is encouraged to continue this procedure covertly outside the session.

When people are asked to describe their own strategies for coping with everyday obsessions and worries, the most frequently mentioned tactic is the perfectly direct one—simple self-distraction (Rachman & de Silva, 1978). Respondents say they try to think about something else. People who report worrying too much appear to point to this tactic as well. They blame their worry on a personal inability to distract themselves, claiming that for them, worry subsides only in the presence of attention-demanding environmental events (Borkovec, Robinson, Pruzinsky, & DePree, 1983). The accuracy of self-reports of the relative usage of different tactics is debatable, however, because certain tactics may simply be more evident to the self-reporter than others, independent of their actual usage. Suffice it to say that in everyday life, the suppression of thoughts by direct mental control happens enough that people notice it.

In the laboratory, this tactic is easily observed as well. Subjects in our initial study of thought suppression were asked to spend a 5-minute period verbalizing the stream of their thoughts for tape recording (Wegner, Schneider, Carter, & White, 1987, Experiment 1). They were prompted to think aloud, verbalizing every thought, feeling, or image that came to mind, and were assured that the recordings would be completely confidential. The subjects were then asked to continue their reporting, but some were now to follow an additional instruction: "In the next 5 minutes, please verbalize your thoughts as you did before, with one exception. This time, try not to think of a white bear. Every time you say 'white bear' or have 'white bear' come to mind, though, please ring the bell on the table before you."

Subjects given this instruction typically began by describing their plan to suppress: "Okay, then, I'll think about the light switch instead," or "I guess I'll talk about my sister's operation." As a rule, this auxiliary concentration succeeded for some time, as the subject talked on about the chosen replacement for "white bear." But overall, the self-distraction tactic was not very successful: Subjects rang the bell a mean of 6.1 times in 5 minutes and mentioned a white bear a mean of 1.6 times in the period as well. The degree of thinking about a white bear did decrease over the experimental session, however, such that by the final minute of the period most subjects no longer reported more than one occurrence (mention or bell ring).

We made another observation in this study about how people suppress, and though it did not seem important at the time, it has turned out to be a crucial one. Most of the time, people carried out their suppression by concentrating in turn on each of a wide variety of different items; this seemed to be a kind of *unfocused self-distraction,* a wandering of thought to one item after another, seemingly in search of something that might be truly interesting. The flip side of this approach, then, was a tactic of *focused self-distraction,* always turning to one thing as a distracter whenever the unwanted thought intruded. This second sort of distraction is the only thing that psychologists encourage people to do in research on how distraction can dull pain, emotion,

and the like (see McCaul & Malott, 1984), so no one has ever really considered the unfocused variety before—despite its apparently greater popularity. As it turned out, the subsequent effects of thought suppression are highly dependent on the difference between the focused and unfocused strategies.

With What Effect Do We Suppress?

The white-bear study was arranged to examine also what happens to thinking when the need for suppression is over. The subjects who were asked to suppress in the experiment were asked in a final time period to continue their stream-of-consciousness reports, this time with the instruction to think of a white bear. These subjects showed a level of thinking about a white bear (15.7 bells and 14.4 mentions) significantly greater than that shown by subjects in a comparison group who were asked from the start (immediately after the practice period) to think about a white bear (11.8 bells and 11.5 mentions). In short, the mere act of avoiding a thought for 5 minutes made subjects oddly inclined to signal a relative outpouring of the thought when thinking about it was allowed. We found not only that the absolute level of thinking of a white bear was greater in this group, but also that there was an accelerating tendency to think of a white bear over time. That is, whereas thinking about a white bear in all the other conditions of the experiment declined over the 5-minute session, in those subjects expressing after suppression, the level of thinking continued to increase.

This pattern suggests a "rebound" effect—an increase in preoccupation with a thought that was formerly suppressed. Much of our work on thought suppression has been prompted by the many parallels between this effect and a wide array of familiar phenomena in psychology. Certainly, Freud (1914/1958) was among the first to point out that an attempt to deny or repress a thought might lead to a subsequent obsession (conscious or unconscious) with that thought. But other observers have remarked on many kindred effects: The suppression of grief following a loss appears to hamper coping and amplify the later grieving that is exhibited (Lindemann, 1944); the suppression of thoughts about a surgery prior to its occurrence foreshadows great anxiety and distress afterwards (Janis, 1958); the suppression of thoughts about eating may be one of the features of dieting that leads to later relapse and binge eating (Polivy & Herman, 1985); the suppression of thoughts about early traumatic occurrences can portend later physical illness and psychological distress (Pennebaker, 1985: Silver, Boon, & Stones, 1983); the failure to express emotions can lead to subsequent emotional problems (Rachman, 1980). In short, the rebound effect in the white-bear study reminded us of many things, and we wondered whether it might provide a laboratory setting within which these phenomena might be explored.

The first step in such exploration must be the development of a theoretical understanding of the phenomenon. Why is it that suppression yields a later rebound of preoccupation? At this point, the distinction we observed between focused and unfocused self-distraction again becomes relevant. If someone spends the entire suppression period in unfocused self-distraction, it is likely that the person will think about many things, both in the laboratory setting and outside it. Each of these things will be concentrated on for a short time, usually as a replacement for a white-bear thought. All these topics will then become linked to a white bear in the person's mind by virtue of their single common quality—they are *not white bears*. Many different distractors, in short, become associated with the unwanted thought. It makes sense, then, that when these former distractors are encountered once more (say, in the later period when expression is invited), they serve as reminders of the earlier unwanted thought. The rebound may stem, then, from the special way in which people enlist their ongoing thoughts to help distract them from the thought they are trying to suppress.

We have tested this idea in several ways. In our first follow-up on the white-bear study (Wegner, Schneider, Carter, & White, 1987, Experiment 2), we tested this explanation by replicating the original experiment with one exception: Some of the subjects in the group who were asked to suppress white-bear thoughts were given a brief instruction to engage in *focused* self-distraction. They were told after the suppression instruction, "Also, if you do happen to think of a white bear, please try to think of a red Volkswagen instead." This group,

when later given the chance to express thoughts of a white bear, did so at a significantly reduced level. Unlike the subjects in this study who were allowed to go their own way (and who typically used the unfocused, "think-about-anything" method), these individuals experienced a noteworthy drop in the rebound of the unwanted thought.

One lesson to be gleaned from this study is that wild-eyed ranging about for distractors is not a good method for thought suppression. True, this may be all that seems possible in the face of a particularly daunting unwanted thought. But it is more likely that one will defeat the rebound effect by choosing one special distractor and turning to it whenever the unwanted thought comes to mind. This tactic presumably prevents all the other things one might think about—whether they arise in memory or are instigated by observation of one's surroundings—from becoming cues to the unwanted thought. The focused distractor becomes the primary cue to that thought, and because it is not especially salient during the later expression period, there is no strong cuing of the unwanted thought to yield a rebound of preoccupation.

We find that in talking to people about this experiment, several have reported using their own versions of focused self-distraction. Often, the single distracter that is chosen in these cases is a religious one—thoughts of God, engaging in prayer, and so on. Others report doing arithmetic in their heads. In any case, we would predict that the single focused distractor might become a fairly strong reminder of the unwanted thought if suppression went on long enough, and thus could itself become unwanted (unless it were somehow absolved of its distressing tone by virtue of pairing with other, more positive experiences). We did not test these kinds of conjectures in the red-Volkswagen study, but they do suggest an interesting line of inquiry.

A different set of derivations from the observation of unfocused self-distraction was tested, however, in subsequent research (Wegner, Schneider, McMahon, & Knutson, 1989). This research examined the hypothesis that thought suppression in a particular context tends to "spoil" that context for the person; it makes that context an unusually strong reminder of the unwanted thought. This notion follows from the idea that when people engage in unfocused self-distraction, they pick many of the different distracters they will use from their current surroundings. These surroundings, later on, can become reminders of the unwanted thought and so may serve to cue the rebound of preoccupation when expression is allowed.

This research called for some subjects to complete the usual sequence of thought suppression followed by expression (or the comparison sequence of expression followed by suppression) in one context—a laboratory room in which a set of slides on a single theme was being shown. Subjects saw either a slide show of classroom scenes, or one of household appliances. Other subjects participated with different slide shows appearing during the initial and later periods of the experiment. We expected that subjects in this latter group who suppressed in the context of one slide show and then expressed in the context of another would show little of the rebound effect, and this is what happened. The degree to which the participants expressed the thought following suppression in a different context was reliably less than the amount of expression following suppression in a constant context. Therefore, the rebound effect was most pronounced when people distracted themselves by thinking about their surroundings, and then thought of the surroundings again when they were allowed to consider the formerly suppressed thought.

The implications of these findings are quite practical. The results suggest, for example, that residential treatment facilities for addictions, alcoholism, overeating, and the like may have a common benefit. Getting away from home during treatment may help, all by itself. Because people suppress thoughts of their forbidden behaviors in the strange surroundings of the facility, they may come to associate many of the features of the facility with their particular self-control problem. When they leave, however, these reminders are left behind, the rebound of preoccupation is disrupted, and there would seem to be a much greater likelihood of long-term success for the treatment. When we are bothered by unwanted thoughts at home or at work, though, it is tempting to suppress them right there. This strategy is likely to fail, for when we try to divest ourselves of a thought in a place, we seem in a sense to leave it there—only to find it again when we return.

Our work on suppression to date indicates, in sum, that people do not do it very well. The question that begins this section ("With what effect do we suppress?") must be met at this time with a disappointing reply: Apparently, we suppress with only temporary and incomplete success. Although our research subjects have been able to reduce their thinking about an innocuous item, a white bear, to relatively low levels in a short time, they nonetheless are not able simply to shut off the thought at will. And once the thought is suppressed, an invitation to return to it appears to have the ironic effect of prompting renewed preoccupation that proceeds at a level beyond what might have occurred had suppression never been started. This effect, too, can be overcome under certain circumstances, but it seems that people's natural proclivities (to use unfocused self-distraction and to stay in the same surroundings) work against them to make the task of long-term suppression most difficult. The effects of thought suppression, it seems, are not usually what we want them to be.

How Might We Suppress More Effectively?

Inevitably, the discussion of thought suppression comes around to home remedies: What should people do when they have unwanted thought? This is one of the great problems of our field, one of the main reasons why clinical psychology and psychotherapy were invented. It should be obvious that our research program is not yet mature enough even to have spawned clinical research, let alone to have yielded solid suggestions for psychotherapy or self-help. With this caveat out of the bag, we feel a bit better about offering our preliminary and untested nostrums.

Our simplest advice would be to avoid suppression, to stop stopping. The work we have conducted and the research by others we have reviewed seems to identify suppression as a strategy that can produce consequences every bit as discomfiting as the unwanted thoughts toward which it is directed. At the extreme, it may be that thought suppression can be the cause rather than the cure of unwanted thoughts, serving over time and in the right circumstances to produce "synthetic obsessions" that can be as painful as those derived from traumas (Wegner, 1988, 1989). Often people use thought suppression to deal with unwanted thoughts when a better strategy would be to work on the unwanted realities that those thoughts represent. We are not recommending that all suppression is nonsense, for there are some junctures at which it seems the only proper solution. When on the brink of a tall building one gets the urge to throw oneself off, it is surely best to suppress the thought. But we do believe that thought suppression is often a mental Band-Aid, a stopgap solution that can create its own problems.

If one must suppress, there are better and worse ways to do it. The research to this point suggests that suppression is likely to be more successful in the long run if we use a limited range of distracters—things we can focus on repeatedly, rather than sorting recklessly through every other thought that might be available. And in this enterprise, it may be best, too, if to do our suppression today, we get away from home or away from the environs we will have to inhabit later. There is the real possibility that the suppressed thoughts will be cued by the very context in which we suppressed them, climaxing our struggle to suppress with a very disappointing conclusion.

That's it. We hesitate to offer more advice at this point, because we believe there are enough unanswered questions that to offer advice now would be premature. We cannot be certain, after all, that white-bear-type studies capture the same processes that occur when people in everyday life attempt to suppress thoughts. The white-bear experiment adds the artificial requirement that people must report their thoughts aloud, for example, and it deals with thoughts that are not nearly as emotional as the ones people usually attempt to suppress.

Work on these things is currently underway. In one study (Chandler & Wegner, 1987), evidence of a rebound effect was found even when people were not asked to ring bells or report white-bear thoughts. It was arranged instead for them to talk freely "off the top of their heads" about any or all of five different topics written on a page before them. They did this during the usual white-bear experiment design: One group was asked first not to think of a white bear, then to think of it; another group did thinking first and then not thinking. The topics had been scaled ahead of time for their relevance to "white bear" ("iceberg" being very relevant, for example, and "gym shorts" being much less relevant). What we found was that subjects assigned to think of a white bear after suppression,

as compared to those assigned to think about it from the outset, talked more about white-bear-relevant thoughts and less about thoughts irrelevant to white bears. So, even without the artificial thought-reporting requirement, an effect very much like the rebound effect was observed.

And in another recent set of experiments, the question of how people suppress more involving and emotional thoughts has been under scrutiny. Wenzlaff, Wegner, and Roper (1988) looked at how depressed and nondepressed people handle unwanted thoughts. Mildly depressed college students (as determined by the short form of the Beck Depression Inventory; Beck & Beck, 1972) and their nondepressed counterparts were asked to read a page-long story and imagine themselves in the starring role of either a very positive incident (e.g., finding a missing child) or a very negative one (e.g., being in a serious car accident). They were then asked to write their ongoing thoughts on three blank pages, and were paced through the pages to allow 3 minutes for each. In a column down the right side of each page, they were to make a check mark each time the thought of the story they had read came to mind.

Some subjects were put up to the task of suppression; they were asked not to think of the story, if they could. Others were not given any special instruction, and were merely told to describe whatever was on their minds. When we counted the marks subjects made, and also their written mentions of the target thought, we found that depressed subjects had a particularly difficult time suppressing negative thoughts. Nondepressed subjects were generally able to suppress both positive and negative thoughts, and depressed subjects did a fine job of suppressing positive thoughts. But when the depressed people tried to suppress a negative thought, they succeeded at first, only to experience a later resurgence of negative thinking. By the third page of writing, their reporting of the negative thought was back up to the same level as that of depressed subjects who had not even tried to suppress.

Further analyses of this study, and further experiments, have explored how this unusual resurgence takes place. What seems to happen is that depressed people distract themselves from negative thoughts by using *other negative thoughts*. These then serve as strong reminders of the thought that was first unwanted, and so return the depressed persons to the initial problem in short order. Non-depressed people, in turn, use positive distracters to get away from negative thoughts, and so leave the whole arena of negative thinking behind. This suggests again that the nature of the self-distraction strategy people use can be very important in determining how successful their thought suppression will be. So, if there is one last piece of advice we can sneak in, it is to look on the bright side. Positive self-distraction may be a generally useful technique whenever we have negative unwanted thoughts—even if we are not depressed at the time, but particularly if we are.

CONCLUSIONS

We should tie up at least one loose end before we draw the chapter to a close. We should explain the allusion to F. C. Bartlett that occurs in the odd mix of metaphors in the chapter subtitle. His story of the "War of the Ghosts" (1932) was used in his classic research on how people transform information in their minds. Although the story itself is not strictly relevant to our concerns, his general approach to psychology is right on target. One of the ideas that Bartlett championed was the role of motivation and affect in cognition, and that is a basic issue in this chapter.

Mental control must be counted as a central form of motivated cognition. Although motivation may affect our thoughts of many things, coloring our views of others and ourselves (see, e.g., Sorrentino & Higgins, 1986), its influence on thought is seldom held in such sharp relief as when we are motivated to control our thoughts directly. Mental control requires conscious motivation, and its success and failure can often appear in our conscious thoughts as well. So, although certain purists in both the cognitive and motivational camps of psychology would prefer not to use both explanatory networks at the same time in any domain of study, in the case of mental control this is simply impossible. Mental control is just too clear a case of motivated thought for either the motivation or the thinking to be ignored.

Our studies of thought suppression reveal that people engage in sensible activities when they are asked to suppress a thought in the laboratory. They try to think of other things, and over time they often

can succeed. But thought suppression has ironic and troubling effects as well, in that the suppressed thought can return, sometimes to be more absorbing than it was at the start. It is therefore evident that motivated thinking may not have the clear-cut success we sometimes find with motivated physical activities. When we want to brush our teeth or hop on one foot, we can usually do so; when we want to control our minds, we may find that nothing works as it should. A war of the ghosts in the machine, it seems, may leave us with defeated spirits.

ACKNOWLEDGMENTS

We thank Toni Wegner, James Pennebaker, and the editors for helpful comments on an earlier draft.

REFERENCES

Bartlett, F. C. (1932). *Remembering.* Cambridge, England: Cambridge University Press.

Beck, A., & Beck, R. (1972). Screening depressed patients in family practice: A rapid technique, *Postgraduate Medicine, 52,* 81–85.

Borkovec, T. D., Robinson, E., Pruzinsky, T., & DePree, J. A. (1983). Preliminary exploration of worry: Some characteristics and processes. *Behaviour Research and Therapy, 21,* 9–16.

Breznitz, S. (Ed.). (1983). *The denial of stress.* New York: International Universities Press.

Broadbent, D. (1958). *Perception and communication.* Oxford: Pergamon Press.

Chandler, G., & Wegner, D. M. (1987). *The effect of thought suppression on preoccupation with associated thoughts.* Unpublished manuscript, Trinity University.

Davis, P. J. (1987). Repression and the inaccessibility of affective memories. *Journal of Personality and Social Psychology, 53,* 585–593.

Erdelyi, M. H. (1985). *Psychoanalysis: Freud's cognitive psychology.* San Francisco: W. H. Freeman.

Erdelyi, M. H., & Goldberg, B. (1979). Let's not sweep repression under the rug: Toward a cognitive psychology of repression. In J. F. Kihlstrom & F. J. Evans (Eds.), *Functional disorders of memory* (pp. 355–402). Hillsdale, NJ: Erlbaum.

Freud, S. (1953). The interpretation of dreams. In J. Strachey (Ed.), *The standard edition of the complete psychological works of Sigmund Freud* (Vol. 4, pp. 1–338; Vol. 5, pp. 339–627). London: Hogarth Press. (Original work published 1900)

Freud, S. (1957). Repression. In J. Strachey (Ed.), *The standard edition of the complete psychological works of Sigmund Freud* (Vol. 14, pp. 146–158). London: Hogarth Press. (Original work published 1915)

Freud, S. (1958). Remembering, repeating, and working-through. In J. Strachey (Ed.), *The standard edition of the complete psychological works of Sigmund Freud* (Vol. 12, pp. 145–150). London: Hogarth Press. (Original work published 1914)

Geiselman, R. E., Bjork, R. A., & Fishman, D. L. (1983). Disrupted retrieval in directed forgetting: A link with posthypnotic amnesia. *Journal of Experimental Psychology: General, 112,* 58–72.

Holmes, D. S. (1974). Investigation of repression: Differential recall of material experimentally or naturally associated with ego threat. *Psychological Bulletin, 81,* 632–653.

James, W. (1890). *The principles of psychology* (2 vols.). New York: Holt.

Janis, I. (1958). *Psychological stress.* New York: Wiley.

Kihlstrom, J. F. (1983). Instructed forgetting: Hypnotic and nonhypnotic. *Journal of Experimental Psychology: General, 112,* 73–79.

Klinger, E. (1982). On the self-management of mood, affect, and attention. In P. Karoly & F. H. Kanfer (Eds.), *Self-management and behavior change* (pp. 129–164). New York: Pergamon Press.

Lindemann, E. (1944). Symptomatology and management of acute grief. *American Journal of Psychiatry, 101,* 141–148.

McCaul, K. D., & Malott, J. M. (1984). Distraction and coping with pain. *Psychological Bulletin, 95,* 516–533.

Pennebaker, J. W. (1985). Inhibition and cognition: Toward an understanding of trauma and disease. *Canadian Psychology, 26,* 82–95.

Pennebaker, J. W. (1988). Confiding traumatic experiences and health. In S. Fisher & J. Reason (Eds.), *Handbook of life stress, cognition, and health* (pp. 669–682). Chichester, England: Wiley.

Polivy, J., & Herman, C. P. (1985). Dieting and binging: A causal analysis. *American Psychologist, 40,* 193–201.

Rachman, S. (1980). Emotional processing. *Behaviour Research and Therapy, 18,* 51–60.

Rachman, S., & de Silva, P. (1978). Abnormal and normal obsessions. *Behaviour Research and Therapy, 16,* 233–248.

Rapaport, D. (1959). *Emotions and memory.* New York: International Universities Press.

Ryle, G. (1949). *The concept of mind.* London: Hutchinson.

Silver, R. L., Boon, C., & Stones, M. H. (1983). Searching for meaning in misfortune: Making sense of incest, *Journal of Social Issues, 39,* 81–102.

Sorrentino, R. M., & Higgins, E. T. (Eds.). (1986). *Handbook of motivation and cognition: Foundations of social behavior.* New York: Guilford Press.

Wegner, D. M. (1988). Stress and mental control. In S. Fisher & J. Reason (Eds.), *Handbook of life stress, cognition, and health* (pp. 683–697). Chichester, England: Wiley.

Wegner, D. M. (1989). *White bears and other unwanted thoughts.* New York: Viking Press.

Wegner, D. M., Schneider, D. J., Carter, S., III, & White, L. (1987). Paradoxical consequences of thought suppression. *Journal of Personality and Social Psychology, 53,* 1–9.

Wegner, D. M., Schneider, D. J., McMahon, S., & Knutson, B. (1989). *Taking worry out of context: The enhancement of thought suppression effectiveness in new surroundings.* Manuscript submitted for publication.

Wenzlaff, R., Wegner, D. M., & Roper, D. (1988). Depression and mental control: The resurgence of unwanted negative thoughts. *Journal of Personality and Social Psychology, 55,* 882–892.

Wolpe, J., & Lazarus, A. A. (1966). *Behavior therapy techniques.* New York: Pergamon.

Yarnell, P. R., & Lynch, S. (1973). The "ding": Amnesic states in football trauma. *Neurology, 23,* 196–197.

25

Daniel B. Wright

Recall of the Hillsborough Disaster Over Time

SUMMARY

The class of memories, described within the literature as flashbulb memories, are susceptible to the same type of systematic biases as everyday memories. These systematic biases, which are consistent with schematic or reconstructive memory theories, were observed in subjects' recalls of the Hillsborough football disaster. Subjects (n = 247) recalled their circumstances when they first heard about the event, gave ratings of various characteristics of the event and wrote down other events of which Hillsborough reminded them. Each of these measures exhibited systematic biases. It is argued that the most consistent explanation for the phenomena requires ordinary reconstructive memory processes and not a special mechanism as postulated within the original definition of flashbulb memories.

Since Brown and Kulik (1977) introduced the term flashbulb memories, to refer to the recollections of surprising and consequential events which have a 'live quality that is almost perceptual' (p. 74), many studies have examined various characteristics of people's recollections of such events. Brown and Kulik (1977) made a bold conjecture, attributing the vividness and apparent veridicality of these memories to a special mechanism, 'Now Print' (Livingston, 1967), and thus neither attributable to ordinary memory mechanisms nor susceptible to ordinary mechanisms' fallacies. They admit that relying on this particular neural mechanism was for convenience, and their proposed special mechanism is independent of it.

This hypothesis does have great intuitive appeal. Brown and Kulik's main empirical backing was 79 of their 80 subjects having a flashbulb for what they were doing when they heard about John Kennedy's assassination. Other events share for individuals this phenomenological sensation of recall: other assassinations, car accidents, etc. Everyone can think of their own examples where the memory is not only vivid, but has that special, almost perceptual quality where seemingly irrelevant minutiae are easily recalled. It is this aspect, not their vividness *per se,* which Brown and Kulik felt necessitated a special mechanism.

Consider, for example, a subject of ours who vividly, and accurately, recalled eating chili con carne and jacket potatoes when she heard about the Hillsborough football tragedy. She had no relatives involved in the tragedy, she was not watching the match on television, she was not even very interested in football, but the vivid flashbulb-like memory exists. The simplest explanation of why, months later, she could recall what she was wearing, what videos she was watching that day, who she was with etc., is via a special mechanism that imprints one's surroundings.

There are, however, problems with Brown and Kulik's specific proposal, not least of which is often flashbulb memories are wrong. Examples of errant recollections include Neisser's (1982) recall of the attack on Pearl Harbor, Larsen's recall of Olof Palme's assassination (Larsen, 1992) and a variety of subjects' accounts of the Challenger disaster (Harsch and Neisser, 1989). Although Brown and Kulik (1977: 75) were quite specific that flashbulb memories would not be complete representations: 'a flashbulb memory is only somewhat indiscriminate and is very far from complete. In these respects, it is unlike a photograph', vividly recalled errant details are counter to their proposal.

Other problems include the necessity and sufficiency of the required event characteristics: surprise and consequentiality. There exist both vivid memories for events which do not have these characteristics and events which have these characteristics for which there is no perceptual memory. Although the events researched tend to have these characteristics, this may only reflect the limited sampling of events (both by researcher and for Rubin and Kozin's study (1984) by subjects), thus these characteristics coincide only with increased probability of having a particularly vivid memory.

With the lessened power of the special mechanism hypothesis, Occam's razor, the idea that excess assumptions and hypotheses which do not aid the explanatory power should be withdrawn, comes into play. If ordinary memory mechanisms could explain the phenomena, then Brown and Kulik's proposed mechanism could be withdrawn. The problem is that traditional cognitive theorizing has difficulties explaining detailed long-term memory of the sort Brown and Kulik are describing. The ideal explanation needs to address both reconstructive processes and memory's functional role for us as social creatures (cf. Neisser, 1982; Robinson, 1981; Wright and Gaskell, 1992). The memory's perceived permanency can then be attributed to its social function or value, while the inaccuracies may still arise through the reconstructive processes affecting all memories.

To be a valid alternative to the special mechanism hypothesis it is not enough just to show that the memories which can be classified as 'flashbulbs' can be errant (see Pillemer, 1990 and Schmidt and Bohannon, 1988), but that the errors reflect systematic biases inherent in reconstructive processes. This paper will explore this aspect of alternative hypotheses for this class of memories.

Before describing the experiment, two critical points need to be stressed. The first point is about the theoretical possibility of questioning the existence of a special mechanism associated with this class of memories. The second point describes the methodological options one may take in researching this area. Empirically it is difficult to falsify, or even examine, Brown and Kulik's hypothesis. The problem is saying when a flashbulb memory occurs if one is using criteria other than subjects' recalling their personal circumstances when they heard about the event. Not having a way to observe the 'Now Print' mechanism, or any other special mechanism, means that proposing flashbulb-like events which counter in some way the hypothesis are vulnerable to critics (quite rightfully) questioning whether the event is of flashbulb calibre. Brown and Kulik's use of John Kennedy's assassination as an exemplar was an obvious choice, not just because it was a tragic, shocking, important event for almost everyone in the United States, but also because, at least from their sample of two, they had *a prior* knowledge that people were going to have flashbulbs for it.

The second point comes from Rubin and Kozin's (1984) finding that many different types of events have memories which are vivid (Brown and Kulik (1977) agree with this, describing various personal flashbulbs in their introduction). With Rubin and Kozin's empirically backed statement made, researchers can take one of two methodological directions. The first is to sample everyday or ordinary memories (cf. Brewer, 1988; Larsen,

1992; Thompson, 1982; Wagenaar, 1986). This enables researchers to identify event-types which are more likely to become vivid without the possible bias of the researcher sampling the events. The second option is to choose a single event which is likely to be of the type that will result in a 'flashbulb', and look in detail at the patterns of the recall of it. This approach, which is utilized here, has the additional advantage of allowing comparisons between subjects because the event itself is the same for all subjects. Other examples of this strategy include Christianson's (1989) study of Olof Palme's assassination, McCloskey, Wible and Cohen's (1988) study of the Challenger disaster and Pillemer's (1984) study of the attempt on Reagan's life.

About 5 minutes into the 1989 Football Association Cup semi-final between Liverpool and Nottingham Forest at Hillsborough stadium an event of 'flashbulb' calibre occurred. Due to an influx of people through the back of the Liverpool terraces, 95 people at the front were crushed to death.

The purpose of this experiment is first to see if this event is one for which people have vivid flashbulb-like memories (i.e. so that recollections fit into the class of memories discussed in the flashbulb memory literature) and then to observe if various recalled characteristics of people's emotions and recollections of this single event systematically changed over time.

METHODS

Subjects and Design

A cross-sectional time-series design was used in which 247 students at three sessions (2 days ($n = 60$), 1 month ($n = 76$) and 5 months ($n = 111$) after the event) were asked to fill in a short survey. Subjects were recruited from the university cafeteria during lunch hours on Monday. A cross-sectional design, where different subjects were used for each session, was used instead of a repeated-measures design for fear that subjects might either remember previous sessions or in some other way have their memories artificially altered. Although some studies (cf. Harsch and Neisser, 1989) have not found this to be a difficulty, the fear remains.

Materials

Subjects were told this research pertained to how people remember news events. When prompted further, they were told it dealt specifically with the Hillsborough disaster. Subjects estimated their emotional reaction, football enthusiasm, how important they felt the event was for both them personally and for society,[1] their circumstances when they heard about it and of what it reminded them. The rating questions used a seven-point scale, 1 being low, 7 being high.

RESULTS

The first question is whether this event satisfies the flashbulb memory criteria: did people have memories of their personal circumstances when they heard about the Hillsborough disaster. Although this event did not have the global importance associated with the Kennedy assassination, it was felt the shock of this disaster and the accompanying graphic television pictures would make it a likely candidate for flashbulb memories. Brown and Kulik's (1977) criterion to define a memory as a flashbulb was simply saying subjects could recall their circumstances when they heard about the event and were able to recall at least one of the following canonical categories: 'place', 'ongoing event', 'informant', 'affect in others', 'own affect', or 'aftermath'. We used a slightly more stringent criterion: to be a 'flashbulb' memory subjects had to recall either where they were, who they were with, or what they were doing when they heard about the Hillsborough disaster. All 76 subjects tested at 1 month passed according to this criterion and over 90 per cent of the subjects at the 5-month testing also passed.

With confirmation that most of our sample had 'flashbulb' recollections for this event, the remainder of the analysis will examine the stability of these memories. The first comparison looks at how subjects' ratings of their emotional reaction to the event, their football enthusiasm, and ratings of personal and societal importance of the event varied between the three sessions. The second section looks for any significant shift in what subjects said they were doing when they heard about the event.

The final section compares what subjects tended to be reminded of across the three sessions.

Before progressing, a brief word about what it takes to constitute a flashbulb memory is in order. While our subjects' memories were 'flashbulb' memories according to the criterion set out, they may not be of the same class as Brown and Kulik were addressing. There is a large difference between the striking example of flashbulbs described in introductions to articles compared to the more lenient criteria set out in the results sections. John Kennedy's assassination was a more emotional and important event for most people than the Hillsborough disaster (as is true of many other events that have been used in this area). Although most of our subjects' recollections passed the necessary criteria, it may be that the Hillsborough disaster did not have the required 'biological significance' which Brown and Kulik grant Kennedy's assassination. In the end, however, it must be realized that by the criteria set forth by Brown and Kulik, for most of our subjects, recollections of the Hillsborough disaster do constitute flashbulb memories.

Comparing Memory Characteristics Over Time

Comparisons were made across the three sessions for subjects' ratings of the event's personal and societal importance, and their emotional reaction and football enthusiasm. While, for emotional reaction and football enthusiasm, ratings did not change across the three sessions ($F < 1$), both personal importance ($F(2,241) = 3.59$, $p = .03$) and societal importance ($t(132) = 2.63$, $p = .01$) rose as time elapsed. Figure 1 illustrates the increase of estimated personal importance compared to estimated emotional reaction. The interaction is also significant ($F(2,241) = 5.42$; $p = .01$).

Often the relationships between variables are hidden by comparing means. By looking at how correlations change over time we can see how the relationships between these characteristics varied. With the exception of football enthusiasm, all the characteristics were moderately positively correlated ($.31 \le r \le .70$) within every session. The surprising result was that, as time passed, the correlation between ratings of personal importance

Figure 1

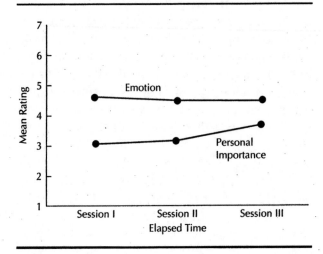

The Mean Personal Importance Ratings Compared to the Mean Ratings of Emotion Impact

and emotional reaction increased from .48 ($n = 58$) to .70 ($n = 110$), which represents a significant change ($z = 2.13$; $p = .03$; using Fisher's method as described by Howell (1987: 240–241). Relationships between the other variables did not significantly change over the three time periods. That the emotion ratings remained basically constant at about 4.5, while the personal importance ratings steadily increased from 3.05 to 3.68 (see Figure 1), *suggests* that as time elapses the personal importance ratings were influenced by the more stable emotional reaction ratings, though the direction of influence cannot be ascertained from these data.

Because the third session occurred in the following academic year, it is possible differences may have resulted because of some difference in the target populations. Third session subjects were asked whether they had been at the university the previous year. All the factors discussed in this paper were tested and there were no statistically significant differences between the third session subjects who were at the university the previous year and those who were not.

It was also necessary to test if the difference between the groups tested at the different sessions was due to varying amounts of interest in football, because it was thought this variable, although not changing its central tendency ($F < 1$), might vary with the sporting season and thereby cause other differences. This was not found; the statistically significant differences in the correlations across sessions remained even when football enthusiasm was partialled out.

How Recalled Circumstances Changed

When comparing subjects' answers for what they were doing, who they were with, and where they were when they heard about the Hillsborough disaster, we are simply looking for overall differences since verification is impossible. Three significant differences were found. The first of these, which was highly predicted, was that for each question more subjects in the third session could not recall anything, compared to the first two sessions, but as stated earlier, this was a remarkably low percentage. Comparing subjects in the final session, they more often forgot what they were doing (17 per cent) than who they were with (14 per cent) or where they were (11 per cent) but these differences are non-significant (Cochran's $Q(2, n = 111) = 5.69; p = .058$).

The second result was that, as time passed, people were more likely to say they were watching television when they found out about the event ($\chi^2(2, n = 223) = 8.32; p = .02$) than doing something else (57.6 per cent of subjects in the third session compared with 36.7 and 39.4 per cent in the first and second sessions). This coincides with Neisser's 'TV priority' (Neisser and Harsh, 1992; Harsh and Neisser, 1989) data for the space shuttle disaster.[2] The visual images displayed for the British public are such that one would predict these images would remain salient the longest.

For analysing the other recalled circumstances, except for the 'who they were with' question, there were too many answers categorized as 'other'. For the 'who' question, the three main answers (family, friends (including boy/girl friends) and alone) were compared (see Table 1). Subjects recalled being alone about the same over the three sessions ($\chi^2(2, n = 231) = .36; p = .83$). As time elapsed, people recalled more often being with their families ($\chi^2(2, n = 231) = 7.68; p = .02$), and less often recalled being with friends ($\chi^2(2, n = 231) = 5.29; p = .07$). The only one of these which is statistically significant at the $a = .05$ level is the increased recall of being with one's family when hearing about the event.

The Events People Were Reminded Of

According to Schank's theory of dynamic memory (1982, 1986), the organization of memory can be examined by exploring what episodes remind people of others. Combining this with the hierarchical organization of event memory into various levels of abstraction as postulated by many researchers (cf. Barsalou, 1988; Conway and Bekerian, 1987; Neisser, 1986a) we would expect, as time elapsed, that people would be reminded of more abstract categories of events when asked what they were reminded of by Hillsborough.

Two hundred of the 247 subjects listed an event of which they were reminded. These events are shown in Table 2. The percentage not being reminded of any event was not statistically different across the three sessions ($\chi^2(2, n = 247) = 1.02, p = .6$). This group differed from the remainder by

Table 1 ━━

Who People Recalled Being With When They Heard About the Hillsborough Disaster

Who they were with	Session I	Session II	Session III	Total
		Session when tested		
Family/relatives	17 (28.8%)	21 (27.6%)	44 (45.8%)	82 (35.5%)
Friends	18 (30.5%)	31 (40.8%)	26 (27.1%)	75 (32.5%)
Alone	18 (30.5%)	21 (27.6%)	25 (26.0%)	64 (27.7%)
Boy/girl friend	5 (8.5%)	3 (3.9%)	2 (1.0%)	10 (8.5%)
Other	1 (1.7%)	0 (—)	0 (—)	1 (0.4%)

Table 2

	Of What Events Hillsborough Reminded People			
	Session when tested			
Event	I	II	III	Total
Heisel stadium	23 (46.9%)	38 (59.4%)	45 (51.7%)	106 (54.0%)
Bradford stadium	9 (18.4%)	8 (12.5%)	7 (8.0%)	24 (12.0%)
Ibrox stadium	1 (2.0%)	0 (—)	1 (1.1%)	2 (1.0%)
Combination of the above	11 (22.4%)	10 (15.7%)	12 (13.8%)	33 (16.5%)
Football in general	2 (4.1%)	5 (7.8%)	9 (10.3%)	14 (7.0%)
Disasters in general	2 (4.1%)	5 (7.8%)	12 (13.8%)	19 (9.5%)
Other	1 (2.0%)	0 (—)	1 (1.1%)	2 (1.0%)

having lower ratings for football enthusiasm, personal importance, and emotional reaction as well as having a higher percentage of people not recalling their encoding circumstances. Unfortunately, these differences confound each other, so no conclusions can be reached about this group.

Of the remaining subjects, most were reminded of either the Heisel stadium disaster, in which a group of Liverpool fans fought with and killed many Italian supporters during a match in Belgium, and/or the Bradford stadium disaster where a fire resulted in the deaths of many football supporters. One subject mentioned another specific football incident—the Ibrox fire in Glasgow.

As described above, there is reason to believe that over time people could be reminded of more general events. Comparing subjects who mentioned specific football events with those who did not, did in fact significantly decrease over time ($\chi^2(2, n = 198)$ 6.92; $p = .03$). This means there was a tendency for more people to be reminded of either more general football items or general disasters after 5 months than immediately after the disaster.

A variety of comparisons were made to see if the dynamic nature of memory could be revealed by people's remindings. The test in which we were most interested compared Heisel remindings with Bradford remindings. It was suggested that the remindings of Heisel (hoolinganism) and Bradford (the fire spread due to an ageing stadium) might vary over time as some initial press reports describe the more unruly nature of the crowd, but it later became clear that crowd management and poor communication were more at fault. The result was

in the predicted direction but was non-significant ($\chi^2(2, n = 132) = 2.65$; $p = .265$).

To summarize this section, the only trend found in subjects' remindings was that people were reminded less of specific football disasters than of more general incidents as time passed. This could be explained by saying the experience, after the elapsed time, had become part of a more general schema.

DISCUSSION

This study is part of a growing literature demonstrating that a special mechanism of the type postulated by Brown and Kulik (1977) is not supported for the class of memories which it is purported to explain. This study adds to the field by presenting data that are best explained by relying on reconstructive memory processes. This is not to say that all the recalls were reconstructed, only that many which would be described as 'flashbulbs' were systematically biased. The shocking aspect of these memories still remains: people recall their personal circumstances of when they heard about many public events long after they occur, and for this a better theory still needs to be developed. The point is that we appear to gain nothing by attributing these processes to special mechanisms. As stated earlier, it is impossible to reject that for some person somewhere a special neural memory mechanism permanently imprints details for certain events; it is just that as data accumulates, it does not appear this explanation is the best approach.

The first key result which supports a reconstructivist explanation was that personal importance and emotional impact became more integrated over time. This dynamic relationship is even more important when coupled with Conway's (1989: 34) finding that as time passes 'ratings of personal importance became reliable predictors of vividness'. Clearly, the emotion–importance–vividness triad is crucial to the dynamic structure of these memories and should be a focus of future research.

The second result, that after 5 months people were more likely to recall hearing about this tragedy with their families, parallels Neisser's baseball/football transformation (Neisser, 1982, 1986b; Thompson and Cowan, 1986) and supports Neisser's theory that the memories are altered so as to cohere with their symbolic status. Perhaps the adage that tragedies bring families closer together only reflects faulty reconstructive memory.

The fact that people recalled hearing about the event on television more often in the third session can be interpreted at two levels of reconstruction. Either people reconstruct their memory of the informing source within a fairly veridical recall of their initial encoding circumstances or they alter their notion of how they originally heard about the event, identifying a more salient episode. Both of these explanations are consistent with the event having salient visual images (as had the Challenger disaster). It is important to realize that the direction of the shift depends on this characteristic of the event. Because visual images of the Hillsborough disaster were both striking and repeatedly shown on television, the shift went in the 'towards television' direction.

The final result, that after 5 months, people were more likely to be reminded of more general incidents, reflects the Hillsborough memory becoming integrated within the nested structure of autobiographical memory (cf. Neisser, 1986a), becoming subordinate to more general event knowledge structures. As this was the only significant difference in remindings, further research needs to be done to verify this finding.

Together, the results show that recall of the Hillsborough disaster varies over time in terms of both subjective characteristics and recalled circumstances, thus favouring a reconstructionist explanation as opposed to Brown and Kulik's special mechanism hypothesis. Acceptance of the schematic nature of these memories, coupled with the growing awareness that the social function of memory is vital (cf. Robinson and Swanson, 1990; Wright and Gaskell 1992), will provide the only workable explanation of flashbulb memories.

ACKNOWLEDGEMENTS

This paper was presented at the International Conference on Memory, University of Lancaster, July 1991. It was prepared as part of the author's doctoral dissertation and as such was supported by a LSE studentship and an ORS scholarship. Helpful comments on earlier drafts from Martin Conway, Julie Dockrell, George Gaskell, Rachel George, Ulric Neisser and an anonymous reviewer are gratefully acknowledged. Requests for reprints should be sent to Daniel Wright, Department of Social Psychology, London School of Economics, London, WC2A 2AE, U.K.

NOTES

1. The third session subjects were not asked about importance for society.

2. This test was done excluding those who could not recall what they were doing. Because more people in the final session could not recall what they were doing, the result is non-significant when including those subjects ($\chi^2(2,247) = 3.03$; $p = .22$). There is the possibility that the significant result was due to more people forgetting they heard about the event on the television and not recalling anything than people with other encoding circumstances, but this does not seem likely.

REFERENCES

Barsalou, L. W. (1988). The content and organization of autobiographical memories. In U. Neisser and E. Winograd (eds), *Remembering reconsidered: ecological and traditional approaches to the study of memory* (pp. 193–243). New York: Cambridge University Press.

Brewer, W. F. (1988). Memory for randomly sampled autobiographical events. In U. Neisser and E. Winograd (eds), *Remembering reconsidered: ecological and traditional approaches to the study of memory* (pp. 21–90). New York: Cambridge University Press.

Brown, R. and Kulik, J. (1977). Flashbulb memories. *Cognition,* **5,** 73–99.

Christianson, S.-Å. (1989). Flashbulb memories: special, but not so special. *Memory and Cognition,* **17,** 435–443.

Conway, M. A. (1989). Vivid memories of novel, important and mundane events (unpublished manuscript).

Conway, M. A. and Bekerian, D. A. (1987). Organization in autobiographical memory. *Memory and Cognition,* **15,** 119–132.

Harsch, N. and Neisser, U. (1989). Substantial and irreversible errors in flashbulb memories of the Challenger explosion. Poster presented at the meeting of the Psychonomic Society, Atlanta, GA.

Howell, D. C. (1987). *Statistical methods for psychology* (2nd edn). Boston, MA: Duxbury Press.

Larsen, S. F. (1992). Potential flashbulbs: memories of ordinary news as the baseline. In E. Winograd and U. Neisser (eds), *Affect and accuracy in recall: Studies of 'flashbulb memories'*. New York: Cambridge University Press.

Livingston, R. B. (1967). Brain circuitry relating to complex behavior. In G. C. Quarton, T. Melnechuck, and F. O. Schmitt, (eds), *The neurosciences: a study program* (pp. 499–514). New York: Rockefeller University Press.

McCloskey, M., Wible, C. and Cohen, N. (1988). Is there a special flashbulb-memory mechanism? *Journal of Experimental Psychology: General,* **117,** 171–181.

Neisser, U. (1982). Snapshots or benchmarks? In U. Neisser, (ed.), *Memory observed: remembering in natural contexts* (pp. 43–48). San Francisco, CA: Freeman.

Neisser, U. (1986a). Nested structure of autobiographical memory. In D. C. Rubin, (ed.), *Autobiographical memory* (pp. 71–81). Cambridge: Cambridge University Press.

Neisser, U. (1986b). Remembering Pearl Harbor: reply to Thompson and Cowan. *Cognition,* 23, 285–286.

Neisser, U. and Harsch, N. (1992). Phantom flashbulbs: false recollections of hearing the news about *Chal-*

lenger. In E. Winograd and U. Neisser (eds), *Affect and accuracy in recall: studies of 'flashbulb memories'*. New York: Cambridge University Press.

Pillemer, D. B. (1984). Flashbulb memories of the assassination attempt on President Reagan. *Cognition,* 16, 63–80.

Pillemer, D. B. (1990). Clarifying the flashbulb memory concept: comment on Mccloskey, Wible, and Cohen (1988). *Journal of Experimental Psychology: General,* **119,** 92–96.

Robinson, J. A. (1981). Personal narratives reconsidered. *Journal of American Folklore,* **94,** 58–85.

Robinson, J. A. and Swanson, K. L. (1990). Autobiographical memory: the next phase. *Applied Cognitive Psychology,* **4,** 321–335.

Rubin, D. C. and Kozin, M. (1984). Vivid memories. *Cognition,* **16,** 81–95.

Schank, R. C. (1982). *Dynamic memory: a theory of learning in computers and people*. Cambridge: Cambridge University Press.

Schank, R. C. (1986). *Explanation patterns: understanding mechanically and creatively*. London: Lawrence Erlbaum.

Schmidt, S. R. and Bohannon, J. N. (1988). In defense of the flashbulb-memory hypothesis: a comment on McCloskey, Wible, and Cohen (1988). *Journal of Experimental Psychology General,* **117,** 332–335.

Thompson, C. P. (1982). Memory for unique personal events: the roommate study. *Memory and Cognition,* **10,** 324–332.

Thompson, C. P. and Cowan, T. (1988). Flashbulb memories: a nicer interpretation of a Neisser recollection. *Cognition,* **22,** 199–200.

Wagenaar, W. A. (1986). My memory: a study of autobiographical memory over six years. *Cognitive Psychology,* **18,** 225–252.

Wright, D. and Gaskell, G. (1992). The construction and function of vivid memories. In M. A. Conway, D. C. Rubin, H. Spinnler and W. A. Wagenaar (eds), *Theoretical perspectives on autobiographical memory* (pp. 275–293). The Netherlands: Kluwer.

 *On the Internet...*

Cognitive Science Society
This is the home page for the Cognitive Science Society.
http://www.umich.edu/~cogsci/

Neuropsychology Central
This site contains a comprehensive directory listing devoted exclusively to the subject of Human Neuropsychology.
http://www.premier.net/~cogito/neuropsy.html

Part❖6
Applications

Judith H. Langlois and Lori A. Roggman

❖

Matthew D. Smith and Craig J. Chamberlin

❖

T. J. Perfect and C. Askew

❖

Michael S. Wogalter and Kenneth R. Laughery

❖

Dean Delis, John Fleer, and Nancy H. Kerr

❖

Stephen J. Ceci and Elizabeth F. Loftus

❖

Ronald P. Fisher and R. Edward Geiselman

Applications

Psychologists have always had an interest in practical applications. That has certainly been the case in the United States and Great Britain, where a pragmatic spirit has permeated the psychological enterprise from its very beginnings in the late nineteenth century. Even during the heydey of behaviorism, the so-called great white rat era, psychologists had an intense interest in practical matters, such as how to raise children, how to deal with emotional problems, and how to lead a happy and productive life. John B. Watson and B. F. Skinner, the founders of behaviorism, wrote copiously about the uses of behavioral principles in everyday life. This interest may seem ironic to some because behaviorism is generally viewed as distant from human concerns, preoccupied as it was (and is) with finding a set of laboratory-inspired principles to explain behavior.

The cognitive psychology that was initiated by Wilhelm Wundt in the late nineteenth century was theoretical and oriented toward basic research and, thus, avowedly impractical. This pattern was repeated by the early cognitivists of the 1950s and 1960s, who focused on shaking off behavioristic concepts and exploring the psychological consequences of the new ideas of information theory, the computer metaphor, and Noam Chomsky's linguistics theories.

By the mid-1970s a freer attitude prevailed, and some cognitivists set about studying the relevance of psychology to law, mathematics, music, psychotherapy, and medicine, as well as to everyday life—memory slips, planning, procrastination, and so on. In the 1980s, although the majority of cognitive psychologists were engaged in basic research in academic settings, there was a headlong rush to explore the practical world. New journals and books on applied topics proliferated. Research was begun on topics that straddle the boundary between pure research and application (e.g., expertise). Cognitivists took the position that everyday life is a rich, valid source of ideas as well as a testing ground for more laboratory-grounded theoretical notions. By the 1990s the boundary between basic and applied research had become quite fuzzy. Indeed, many of the articles in this volume can be seen as applied, even if they do not appear in this section.

One of the dilemmas of basic research is that in order to gain more control over the phenomena being studied—and this in the service of allowing better inferences about cause and effect—inputs and outputs are often simplified. Unfortunately, methodological simplification may lessen the ability to generalize the results to more complex real-life situations (although the right kind of simplification may create a cornucopia of generalization). A more political problem is that many segments of society are resistant to policy changes based on laboratory findings. However, we will see that the methodological dilemma and its political ramifications may be overstated. The articles in this section, although based on research performed in the laboratory, have a clear bearing on the practical issues they address.

In "Attractive Faces Are Only Average," Judith H. Langlois and Lori A. Roggman take a cue from experimental work on prototypes and apply it to the question of facial beauty. Is facial beauty culture bound, or are more universal principles involved? Evolution theory implies that people should prefer average faces because they presumably represent less harmful genes. Research has consistently shown that people represent some events in terms of prototypes and that people experience prototypes, or average events, as familiar even though they have never actually perceived a prototype. Langlois and Roggman reasoned, therefore, that attractive faces could well be prototypical faces. In their experiment they generated computer (digitized) composite faces that incorporated from 2 to as many as 32 individual faces. Ratings of the faces' attractiveness did indeed indicate that the composites (the prototypes) were more attractive than the individual faces and that the more individual faces there were in the composite, the more attractive it was rated.

THE NEXT ARTICLE IN THIS SECTION CONSIDERS SPORTS, which inevitably require attention and response to multiple sources of information. Yet humans have limited resources. Anyone who has learned to drive a car can attest to the initial frustration involved in having to watch the road, avoid various objects, and operate controls with hands and feet, all while trying to understand what an instructor is saying. The late theorist Paul Fitts argued that skills such as this appear to go through three phases: a cognitive or fact phase, in which the goals of a motor sequence are learned; an associative or procedural phase, in which responses are mapped to particular cues in an ultimately automatized way; and a final phase, in which the various elements of the task are guided in an efficient way by the environment. Reaching the final phase defines expertise, which confers a freeing-up of working memory resources and a consequent ability to selectively attend to task-relevant cues and ignore task-irrelevant cues.

This point is nicely illustrated in Matthew D. Smith and Craig J. Chamberlin's article "Effect of Adding Cognitively Demanding Tasks on Soccer Skill Performance." Smith and Chamberlin used a dual-task methodology to assess the effect of secondary tasks on the running speed (the primary task) of soccer players with different levels of expertise. The players first ran through a short slalom course while dribbling a soccer ball (with their feet). They then ran the course while dribbling and simultaneously attempting to identify geometric shapes on a screen at the end of the course. The results indicated that the novice, intermediate, and expert players all ran at about the same speed when no secondary task was required but that each addition of a secondary task (dribbling, then identifying shapes) reduced running speed. The more expert the player, however, the less her speed was reduced by these tasks. The authors argue that, as in this case, even experts' performance can suffer if the secondary tasks "functionally interfere," that is, if they use up the same resources or require the same movements as the primary tasks (such as running and dribbling in soccer).

IN THE SOCCER STUDY, THE PARTICIPANTS' ATTENTION WAS divided and performance was measured on the primary task. What happens when participants are given a primary task but some other, incidental aspect of their attention is of interest? This question was explored by T. J. Perfect and C. Askew in their study "Print Adverts: Not Remembered but Memorable." They sought to demonstrate that a key advertising goal—creation of a positive attitude about a product—can be achieved through an *implicit memory* paradigm. Briefly, implicit memory refers to remembering that occurs without any awareness of the particular episode that gave rise to it. It is not simply that people may not remember where and when they learned something but that they do not know why they are remembering it. For example, people may fill in the blanks on a word test but not know why they filled them in the way they did. Yet it is clear that the filling-in was not at all random. In contrast, on an *explicit memory* test, such as most free-recall and recognition memory tests, people are fully aware of the particulars of their remembering.

Perfect and Askew hypothesized that incidental exposure to advertisements could, through an implicit memory process, produce positive attitudes toward the ads, despite an inability to explicitly recall them. In their experiment, two groups of college students looked at magazines on the pretext that they would be judging layouts. The deliberate exposure group was specifically instructed to look at five different pages in each of several magazines and to decide what the most striking feature was for each ad that appeared there. They had three seconds per page to do this. The incidental exposure group was instructed to find the pages for each of five articles in a magazine and to scan an article for title and main feature headings. For this group, the ads in question appeared opposite the first page of each article, where they might be noticed but only briefly processed. Both groups were then given two tests. First, they received a set of 50 ads, half of which they had been exposed to during the first phase and half that were new. The participants rated the ads on a seven-point scale in terms of their appeal, memorability, distinctiveness, and eye-catching quality. Second, they went through the ads once again and indicated those that they had seen previously.

The results were clear-cut: The deliberate group recognized 60 percent of the ads, whereas the incidental group recognized only 11 percent. However, the target (old) ads were in general rated more positively than the new ads, and the incidental group rated them just as positively as the deliberate group. Moreover, whether participants recognized the old ads or not made no difference, as the unrecognized ads were still rated more positively than the new ads. The authors speculate that the ads that were implicitly remembered may have been rated positively because the participants found it easier to process these ads but, not knowing why, inflated their value. Practically speaking, these results suggest that advertisers might want to assess ad effectiveness with implicit as well as explicit tests and, if changes in the implicit memory of consumers are desired, to use different kinds of ad techniques.

More theoretically, Perfect and Askew's study on implicit memory indicates that subliminal perception effects can be real. But it is not a matter of people having a special, supersensitive, subconscious stimulus-detecting mechanism. Rather, it is a pattern of relationships between briefly processed stimuli, people's claims about the stimuli (i.e., they cannot recognize them), and the empirically observed effect of the stimuli on behavior. Moreover, this line of reasoning requires that, in order to validly claim that subliminal perception has occurred, some minimal level of stimulation must be present.

People cannot be said to remember stimuli that they could not detect in the first place, as some claim occurs in the case of so-called hidden messages in self-help audio tapes.

THE NEXT TOPIC IS IN THE GENERAL AREA OF *HUMAN factors*, which is specifically concerned with improving the efficiency and safety of human performance. For example, some human factors psychologists help design airplane cockpits, automobiles, and doors; others design computer programs that facilitate the human expert's processing of complex systems, such as weather forecasting and disease diagnosis. "Warning! Sign and Label Effectiveness," by Michael S. Wogalter and Kenneth R. Laughery, looks at the factors that affect people's compliance with warning labels. This is an important aspect of everyday life because compliance with labels on tools, drug containers, and other products can protect people against injury, sickness, and potentially life-threatening circumstances.

Wogalter and Laughery discuss compliance in terms of an information-processing model consisting of several stages—the warning information, attention, comprehension, attitudes and beliefs, motivation, and compliance behavior. These stages are organized serially but with feedback loops between the middle four stages. Attention is obviously critical and involves physical aspects (e.g., size) of a warning, but also important is the medium (verbal, visual) that is used. A major question for the comprehension stage is whether or not the intended audience will understand the warning, with implications for the comprehension level at which warnings should be pitched. Pretesting is often done to ensure that consumers understand a warning. Beliefs and attitudes about products, shaped perhaps by prior experience with a similar product, may determine whether or not people will read a warning. People seem to be more concerned about severity of injury than its likelihood, which may be appropriate in some cases but disastrous in others. The motivation stage is mainly a matter of the cost in time and effort of compliance. Labels that are explicit about the negative effects of noncompliance can be effective in overcoming perceived costs. Moreover, seeing other people comply can be contagious.

Wogalter and Laughery note that pictures can play an important role in producing compliance with warning labels. They have effects on every stage—attention, comprehension, attitudes and beliefs, and motivation. One picture may well be worth a thousand words because the information it codes can be put in a compact, coherent, highly memorable imagistic format.

THE IDEA THAT PICTURES AID MEMORY AND UNDERSTANDing is pursued by Dean Delis, John Fleer, and Nancy H. Kerr in "Memory for Music." The background for their study comes from research showing that language inputs will not be comprehended or remembered well unless appropriate schemas are activated. Delis et al. reasoned, therefore, that music might be remembered better if people were asked to construct mental images for some musical passages and that concrete titles (as opposed to abstract titles) would facilitate this process. This is indeed what they found, as the concrete titles condition led to higher vividness ratings and better recognition. Thus, similar principles may apply to memory for both language and music.

FOR ADVERTISING, MUSIC, WARNING LABELS, AND OTHER aspects of everyday life, there is a keen interest in promoting memories that are *veridical*, that is, accurate versions of the original inputs. But what about cases in which people remember things that they claim are veridical but are not and that may also have significant negative effects on the lives not just of the person involved but of other people as well?

In " 'Memory Work': A Royal Road to False Memories?" Stephen J. Ceci and Elizabeth F. Loftus look into the issues surrounding the recovery of so-called repressed memories by means of *memory work* techniques in psychotherapy. They begin by presenting the case of a woman who underwent therapy that included hypnosis, group therapy, anger-venting, and dream analysis. The patient also read books on therapy for childhood abuse, sexual and otherwise. She then began "remembering" being sexually abused as a child by humans and animals and various other horrendous events, and she wound up accusing family members of these crimes. Eventually, she quit therapy, realized that her recovered memories were false, sued her therapist, entered a new form of therapy, and tried to reconcile with her family. Unfortunately, this kind

of scenario has been played out numerous times in recent years.

Ceci and Loftus make numerous points about memory work techniques. First, although an individual may have repressed memories, it is rarely clear how they might manifest themselves in abnormal behaviors if, in fact, they do. Some genuinely abused individuals may be symptom-free. Second, the repressed-memory hypothesis has been overgeneralized and overused, particularly when one realizes that there are other reasons why childhood events may be hard to recall, including normal forgetting and conscious suppression. These mechanisms are better understood than repressed-memory effects, yet therapists rarely consider them. Moreover, the repressed-memory hypothesis does not explain why children who undergo socially sanctioned forms of trauma (e.g., tonsillectomies) generally do not repress these experiences. At the same time, therapists may not be skeptical enough about their own techniques or about the effects they yield— they may not consider that their clients may be constructing false memories. A great deal is known about false memories—they can be vivid, emotional, and easily suggested to nonskeptical clients. They may also be fragmentary and diffuse, properties that therapists often attribute to repressed memories as well. In general, Ceci and Loftus caution therapists who work with clients who begin to have flashbacks about supposed abuse: the abuse may be real or it may not. In Ceci and Loftus's terms, "It would seem wise for therapists, in the course of supporting their clients during the difficult disclosure process, also to attempt to disconfirm memories as they arise."

Ceci and Loftus also consider several often-asked questions about the entire issue of memory repression, making several key points: the therapeutic effectiveness of recovering repressed memories is debatable; therapists should be reasonably skeptical about their clients' memories, especially since they can have disastrous social effects; recovery of a memory does not guarantee that it was repressed; and the problems aroused by memory work techniques are not unique to just a few "bad apple" clinicians.

THE EMPHASIS IN CECI AND LOFTUS'S ARTICLE IS ON the dangers of using techniques that may arouse false memories and their potentially disastrous effects. The last paper in this section is designed to answer the converse question—What can be done to help people to remember things and to remember them in a veridical fashion?

In "Enhancing Eyewitness Memory With the Cognitive Interview," Ronald P. Fisher and R. Edward Geiselman present a technique for helping people to remember crime-related events. Eyewitness testimony for such events is notoriously poor, yet the legal system and juries seem to place great faith in such testimony. Cognizant of this dilemma, Fisher and Geiselman used some basic principles of memory to construct a technique that they believed would improve eyewitness testimony. Specifically, they relied upon the encoding specificity principle (the more similar the recall cues are to the cues in the original learning situation, the better

the recall), the use of multiple recall cues, multiple perspectives for recall, forward and backward recall, and the training of subjects in the use of specific mnemonic techniques. They showed subjects a simulated crime and had law enforcement personnel test their recall two days later using one of three techniques: a standard police interview, an interview with hypnosis, and their specially constructed *cognitive interview*. The results indicated superior recall with the hypnosis interview and the cognitive interview. Moreover, the latter was the technique of choice, since it was less time consuming, required less training, and reduced the effect of potentially misleading questions, which was a factor in the hypnosis situation. The cognitive interview technique is now being used by some police departments and other social agencies.

26

Judith H. Langlois and Lori A. Roggman

Attractive Faces Are
Only Average

Abstract: *Scientists and philosophers have searched for centuries for a parsimonious answer to the question of what constitutes beauty. We approached this problem from both an evolutionary and information-processing rationale and predicted that faces representing the average value of the population would be consistently judged as attractive. To evaluate this hypothesis, we digitized samples of male and female faces, mathematically averaged them, and had adults judge the attractiveness of both the individual faces and the computer-generated composite images. Both male (three samples) and female (three samples) composite faces were judged as more attractive than almost all the individual faces comprising the composites. A strong linear trend also revealed that the composite faces became more attractive as more faces were entered. These data showing that attractive faces are only average are consistent with evolutionary pressures that favor characteristics close to the mean of the population and with cognitive processes that favor prototypical category members.*

What makes a face beautiful? The answer to this question has eluded scientists[1] and philosophers even though interest in the question has continued for centuries. Research in social and developmental psychology, even without a conceptual definition of beauty or a specification of its stimulus dimensions, has nevertheless produced some of the most robust and widely replicated findings in the social and behavioral sciences: Both children and adults respond more positively to attractive rather than unattractive individuals (see reviews by Berscheid & Walster, 1974; Langlois, 1986; Sorell & Nowak, 1981).

Until recently, most researchers interested in attractiveness effects have avoided investigating the stimulus dimensions of beauty, both because of the intractable nature of the problem and because of several well-entrenched assumptions about standards of beauty and preferences for attractiveness. For example, it has been assumed, at least since the publication of Darwin's *Descent of Man* (1871), that standards of beauty are culturally specific and

From Judith H. Langlois and Lori A. Roggman, "Attractive Faces Are Only Average," *Psychological Science*, vol. 1, no. 2 (March 1990), pp. 115–121. Copyright © 1990 by The American Psychological Society. Reprinted by permission of Cambridge University Press.

that attempts to determine universal or underlying dimensions of beauty are futile. It has also been widely held that standards of attractiveness are only gradually learned by children through exposure to the media and culture in which they live.

Both these assumptions, however, have been challenged by new data. First, a number of recent cross-cultural investigations have demonstrated surprisingly high (e.g., .66–.93) inter-rater reliabilities in judgments of attractiveness (e.g., Bernstein, Lin, & McClellan, 1982; Cunningham, 1986; Johnson, Dannenbring, Anderson, & Villa, 1983; Maret, 1983; Maret & Harling, 1985; Richardson, Goodman, Hastorf, & Dornbusch, 1961; Thakerar & Iwawaki, 1979; Weisfeld, Weisfeld, & Callaghan, 1984). The cross-cultural data suggest that ethnically diverse faces possess both distinct and similar structural features; these features seem to be perceived as attractive regardless of the racial and cultural background of the perceiver.

Second, a number of recent studies of infants have demonstrated that when infants 3 to 6 months of age are shown pictures of adult-judged attractive and unattractive faces, they prefer attractive ones (Langlois, Roggman, Casey, Ritter, Rieser-Danner, & Jenkins, 1987; Langlois, Roggman, & Rieser-Danner, in press; Samuels & Ewy, 1985; Shapiro, Eppler, Haith, & Reis, 1987). Thus, even before any substantial exposure to cultural standards of beauty, young infants display behaviors that seem to be rudimentary versions of the judgments and preferences for attractive faces so prevalent in older children and adults.

Taken together, the cross-cultural and infant data suggest that there may be universal stimulus dimensions of faces that infants, older children, and adults cross-culturally view as attractive. The ability to detect these stimulus dimensions may be innate or acquired much earlier than previously believed. Such findings thus compel a more intensified search for answers to the old question of what defines a beautiful face.

THE LENGTH OF NOSES

Most recent attempts to define beauty have taken a feature-measurement approach (Cunningham, 1986; Hildebrandt & Fitzgerald, 1979; Lucker, 1981). While some progress has been made in identifying facial measurements that predict attractiveness ratings, the findings have been contradictory both within and between studies (Cunningham, 1986; Farkas, Munro, & Kolar, 1987). Even if consistent results were to be obtained, the feature-measurement approach would not provide a parsimonious answer to the question of what makes a face attractive. Thousands of measurements of the face are possible (Farkas, 1981), although research so far has employed only a few of the many possible facial measurements. Furthermore, even if we could accurately and reliably predict attractiveness judgments from feature measurements, we would still not know why the combination of certain measurements are perceived as attractive by infants, children, and adults.

Parsimony, Biology, and Cognition

A more parsimonious solution to defining beauty and explaining why certain facial configurations are perceived as attractive is suggested by two distinct fields of inquiry, evolutionary biology and cognitive psychology. Darwin's theory of natural selection (1859), or at least modern day versions of it,[2] suggests that average values of many population features should be preferred to extreme values. In the most ubiquitous form of natural selection, normalizing or stabilizing selection, evolutionary pressures operate against the extremes of the population, relative to those close to the mean (Barash, 1982; Dobzhansky, 1970). Thus, individuals with characteristics (especially some morphological features) that are close to the mean for the population should be less likely to carry harmful genetic mutations and, therefore, should be more preferred by conspecifics (Bumpas, 1899; Schmalhausen, 1949; Symons, 1979). The robust preference shown for attractive individuals has been puzzling in light of this evolutionary fact, given that more attractive individuals are at the extreme rather than in the middle of the distribution of attractiveness ratings.

Results from a second domain of investigation, cognitive and developmental psychology, also converge on the suggestion that the average value of faces should be preferred. It is well known that even young infants are capable of forming concepts and of abstracting prototypes from individual exemplars of a category (Cohen & Younger, 1983;

Quinn & Eimas, 1986). A prototype can be defined as the central representation of a category, as possessing the average or mean value of the attributes of that category and as representing the averaged members of the class (Reed, 1972; Rosch, 1978; Rosch, Mervis, Gray, Johnson, & Boyes-Braem, 1976; Rosch, Simpson, & Miller, 1976). After seeing several exemplars from a category, both infants and adults respond to an averaged representation of those exemplars as if it were familiar; that is, they show evidence of forming mental prototypes, and they rely on such abstracted prototypes to recognize new instances of the category (Quinn & Eimas, 1986: Rosch, 1978; Strauss, 1979).

For example, using schematic faces, Strauss demonstrated that even young infants recognized facial prototypes made from the averaged values of previously viewed facial features rather than from the most frequently viewed features. Infants responded to a prototype or averaged face as highly familiar even though they had never seen it before. Others have also shown that infants will average features from various kinds of visual stimuli to form prototypes (Bomba & Siqueland, 1983; Younger, 1985; Younger & Gotlieb, 1988).

Thus, evidence exists demonstrating that the average value of members of a class of objects is often prototypical, that infants are capable of forming prototypes by averaging features, and that infants assign prototypes special status by recognizing prototypical category members even when they have not seen them before. To the extent that a face is a good example or prototype and is thus easily recognized as a face, infants may show more interest in it than a less prototypical face. These facts imply an explanation for studies showing that infants prefer attractive faces: Perhaps an attractive face is attractive simply because it is prototypical.

If attractive faces are attractive because they represent a prototype or an average of a face, then a prototype created by averaging several faces would be expected to be attractive. Such an attractive "average" face would be consistent with both evolutionary and cognitive theory and would help explain why young infants and adults from diverse cultures prefer attractive faces. Considerable progress may be made in both defining facial beauty and in understanding the broad preferences for a beautiful face if it can be shown that faces representing the average value of the population are judged as attractive.

COMPUTER FACES

To evaluate whether the "average" face is more attractive than the individual faces used to create them, we digitized individual faces, averaged them, and had adults rate the physical attractiveness both of the individual faces and the averaged composite images. We predicted that these average faces would be attractive, that this effect would generalize across different sets of both composite faces and raters, and that composite faces would be more attractive than the mean level of attractiveness of the individual faces used to create them.

To test these hypotheses, we photographed male and female undergraduate students from a standard distance in a full-front view of the face and neck. Background and lighting were identical across subjects. Subjects were asked to pose with a "pleasant but neutral, closed mouth expression." Clothing was draped with a solid light-colored cloth to eliminate all variation in appearance. Subjects wearing glasses or earrings were asked to remove them. Males with facial hair were not included in the population of faces.

The population of facial photographs included a pool of 336 males (including 26 Hispanics and 21 Asians) and a pool of 214 females (including 24 Hispanics and 18 Asians). From each pool, a sample of 96 faces was randomly selected without replacement and randomly divided into three sets of 32 faces from which three composites were created. No face was included in more than one composite set.

Each face was digitized by scanning the photograph with a video lens interfaced with a computer. Using a zoom lens and "joystick" markers, faces were adjusted for size and position by matching the location of the eye pupils and the middle of the lip line across all faces. A 512×512 matrix of numeric gray values then represented each facial image. By arithmetically averaging those matrices, a series of achromatic composite facial images was created. For each set, composites were created at five levels of averaging: two faces, four faces, eight faces, sixteen faces, and thirty-two faces.

These composites were then contrast enhanced to clarify the image. Initially, each image was "smoothed," meaning that each pixel in the matrix was adjusted to the average value of the pixels immediately surrounding it so that any double edges creat[ed] by averaging were minimized. "Extra" edges occasionally remained in the composites with eight or fewer faces and were removed from the image. Subsequently, the gray value difference between each pixel and its surrounding area was doubled so that the resulting smoothed edges were sharpened. Contrast was also enhanced by increasing the range of gray values, similarly to the way the contrast adjustment on a standard television affects the image. The individual faces were smoothed and contrast enhanced in the same manner as the composites to create photographically similar images. The composite and individual faces were then photographed by a matrix camera with direct input from the computer screen.

Each set of individual faces and its corresponding composites were rated for physical attractiveness by a minimum of 65 (range = 65–80) males and females enrolled in undergraduate psychology classes. Three hundred raters participated; some raters evaluated more than one set of faces. The slides of the individual and composite faces from each set were projected in random order and were shown for 10 seconds each. Raters scored each facial image on a 1 to 5 scale ranging from 1 = very unattractive to 5 = very attractive. The raters were told that the photographs were taken from a television screen, to ignore any reduction of photographic quality caused by the TV image, and to judge only the physical attractiveness of faces.

Reliability of the attractiveness ratings was assessed separately for each set of images using coefficient alpha and ranged from .90 to .98. Separate estimates of reliability for male and female raters ranged from .90 for one group of 23 male raters to .98 for one group of 46 female raters. Only three raters from the total of 300 were eliminated from the data set because of low inter-rater correlations with the rest of the raters.

Composite Faces

For each facial image, all ratings were averaged to produce a mean attractiveness score. Table 1 shows the means and standard deviations for each set of individual faces and for each level of the composites. The mean attractiveness scores of the 32- and 16-face male and female composite faces are one standard deviation or more above the mean for the individual male and female faces. Differences in attractiveness scores among levels of the composites were evaluated using analysis of variance (ANOVA) with sex and level of composite as factors. A significant effect for the number of faces entered into the composite was obtained, $F(4, 25) = 3.16$, $p = .03$, but there were no significant effects for sex or for the interaction between sex and composite level. The main effect for composite level was followed up by a test of linearity, which revealed a strong linear effect of increasing attractiveness as more faces were entered into the composite, $F(1, 25) = 10.43$, $p = .004$.

Individual vs. Composite Faces

The individual faces were compared to the composites in three ways for each sex. First, individual faces were compared to the composites using an analysis of variance with a single factor with six levels: the individual face level and each of the five levels of composites (2, 4, 8, 16, 32). This overall test was followed by planned comparisons between the composites at each level of averaging and the individual faces that were averaged into the composite: 32 faces from each of the three sets ($n = 96$) were compared to the three 32-face composites; 16 faces from each of the three sets ($n = 48$) were compared to the three 16-face composites, and so on. Two sample t tests with separate variance estimates were used for these planned comparisons because of differences in the variance and sample size between the individual faces and the composites. Finally, within rater, paired t tests were used to compare raters' judgments of the 32-face composites with their ratings of all the individual faces.

Male Faces

The attractiveness scores of the 96 individual male faces ranged from 1.8 to 3.8 with a mean of 2.51 ($SD = .52$) The ANOVA comparing images of individual male faces with 2-, 4-, 8-, 16-, and 32-face images revealed a significant effect of the number

Table 1

Attractiveness Ratings for Individual and Composite Faces

	n	Mean	SD
Male Faces			
Individual Faces			
Set 1	32	2.60	.53
Set 2	32	2.51	.54
Set 3	32	2.42	.48
Sets 1–3	96	2.51	.52
Composite Faces			
2-face level	3	2.34	.12
4-face level	3	2.45	.61
8-face level	3	2.75	.57
16-face level	3	3.31	.17
32-face level	3	3.27	.08
Female Faces			
Individual Faces			
Set 1	32	2.38	.67
Set 2	32	2.48	.63
Set 3	32	2.42	.66
Sets 1–3	96	2.43	.64
Composite Faces			
2-face level	3	2.87	.49
4-face level	3	2.84	.77
8-face level	3	3.03	.34
16-face level	3	3.06	.18
32-face level	3	3.25	.07

of faces, $F(5, 93) = 2.90$, $p = .017$. The planned comparisons showed that the 32- and 16-face composites were rated as significantly more attractive than their corresponding individual male faces ($t = 10.60$, $p = .001$; $t = 7.24$, $p = .001$, for the 32- and 16-face composites, respectively). The composites made of eight or fewer faces, however, did not differ significantly from their individual faces.

The within-rater analyses revealed that of the 96 individual male faces, only three were judged as significantly more attractive than their corresponding composite, about what would be expected by chance. By comparison, 80 of the individual male faces were rated as significantly less attractive than the composite.

Female Faces

The attractiveness scores of the 96 individual female faces ranged from 1.20 to 4.05, with a mean of 2.43 ($SD = .64$), similar to the mean of the males. The results for the analyses of the female faces were similar to the results for the male faces. There was a significant overall effect of the number of faces in each image revealed by the ANOVA, $F(5, 93) = 2.38$, $p = .043$. The planned comparisons

showed that the 32- and 16-face composites were rated as significantly more attractive than their corresponding individual female faces, but that the other composites did not differ significantly from their individual faces ($t = 10.46$, $p = .001$; $t = 4.83$, $p = .005$, for the 32- and 16-face composites, respectively).

Again, the raters' attractiveness judgments for each individual female face were compared to their ratings of the 32-face composites. Of the 96 individual female faces, only 4 were rated as significantly more attractive than the composites, whereas 75 were judged as significantly less attractive.

DISCUSSION

Galton's Meat-Eaters

In the 1800s, a number of articles and commentaries were published on composite portraits created by Galton and Stoddard in which they superimposed photographic exposures of faces (Galton, 1878; 1883; Stoddard, 1886; 1887). The apparent purpose of these composite portraits was to create graphic representations of types of faces. Galton enjoyed creating composites of criminals, meat-eaters, vegetarians, and tuberculosis patients. Stoddard created composites of the 1883, 1884, and 1886 senior classes of Smith College and of members of the National Academy of Sciences. Although both Galton and Stoddard noted that the composites were "better looking" than their individual components because "the special villainous irregularities in the latter have disappeared" (Galton, 1878, p. 135), their observations were not pursued systematically until now. The data provided here offer empirical evidence that composite faces, at least those of a group of predominantly Caucasian males and females, are indeed attractive and are rated as more attractive than are the individual faces comprising the composite.

Mathematical Averages

The computerized technique of mathematically averaging faces provides several advantages over the photographic method of Galton and Stoddard. First, the images are precisely averaged rather than superimposed by hand based on only roughly equivalent units of time exposure. Second, our technique allowed us to standardize lighting and contrast and to perform precise image enhancement procedures on all of the faces equivalently. Finally, the random selection procedure ensured that faces were included in the composite in an unbiased fashion. Thus, some of the composites were begun with an unattractive face, some with an attractive face; some composites had more unattractive than attractive faces, others had the reverse. The mean attractiveness ratings of the 16- and 32-face composites indicated that the attractiveness of the individual faces in these composites was not an important determinant of the attractiveness of the composite. As Stoddard (1887) discovered, neither was the order in which the faces were entered and averaged.[3]

Despite the technical advantages of a computerized technique over the timed multiple-exposure photography of the last century, we do not presume to have simulated the human mind. Our digitized images, even at 262,144 pixels per image, do not approach the quality of an image of a face viewed live, and our technique only approximates the averaging process that is assumed to occur when humans form mental prototypes. Nevertheless, by using image-processing techniques and by collecting objective and reliable ratings of attractiveness, we have empirically demonstrated that average faces are perceived as attractive. We replicated this finding in two populations, male and female young adults, and in three separate samples from each population using several analytic approaches. Our results demonstrating this robust effect confirm the subjective impressions of those who, in the last century, have viewed composite faces and commented on their striking attractiveness. At the same time, our results will surprise contemporary researchers who have not considered an attractive face to be average.

The attractiveness scores of the composites indicated that faces attain both average values and high attractiveness ratings when 8 to 16 faces are combined into a composite image. Likewise, the variability of the attractiveness ratings of the 16- and 32-face composites was lower than that for most of the other composites and those of all of the individual faces. These statistical findings are mirrored by observation: Inspection of the compos-

ites reveals that the 16- and 32-face composites look very similar to each other, both within and between same-sex composite sets. That this similarity should hold between composite sets is especially interesting given that no individual face appeared in more than one set. Thus, the averaging procedure, in addition to producing attractive faces, also seems to produce a typical face. Other research is consistent with this finding: Faces rated as more attractive are also rated as more typical and less unusual; in turn, faces rated as attractive and typical are rated as more similar to each other than to other faces (Light, Hollander, & Kayra-Stuart, 1981).

The typicalness and "averageness" of attractive faces helps to explain why they are preferred. Faces may be preferred by infants and adults alike if they are perceived as prototypes of a face; that is, as more *facelike*. Unattractive faces, because of their minor distortions (e.g., malocclusions, etc.), may be perceived as less facelike or as less typical of human faces. In the study presented here, although we have not shown that attractive faces are perceived as prototypes, we have demonstrated that prototype faces are perceived as attractive. Conceptually, averaging the gray values of digitized images of faces creates a prototype by definition (Reed, 1972; Rosch, Simpson, & Miller, 1976; Wittgenstein, 1953). Methodologically, averaging matrices of pixels to create prototypes from exemplars is the inverse of procedures used in previous research to create category exemplars from prototypes, such as random distortions of prototype dot patterns (Bomba & Siqueland, 1983; Posner & Keele, 1968). This method of creating a prototype by averaging facial images is also similar to creating a schematic prototype by averaging facial features (Strauss, 1979).

Infants may prefer attractive or prototypical faces because prototypes are easier to classify as a face. Faces are such an important class of visual stimuli for humans, and the perception of faceness in infancy is a critical part of the development of social responsiveness. If humans have evolved to respond to facial configurations for the purpose of extracting relevant social information (e.g., McArthur & Baron, 1983), both infants and adults may respond most strongly to the most facelike or prototypic stimuli in the environment. Because of the importance of the information conveyed by faces for social interaction, humans should therefore have built-in or early developing preferences for them.

Beauty Detectors

The ability of both infants and adults to abstract a prototype by averaging features will not come as a surprise to some biologically oriented theorists. Symons (1979), for example, has proposed an innate mechanism that detects the population mean of anatomical features. In the case of faces, this proposed "beauty-detecting" mechanism averages observed faces; selection pressures are assumed to favor built-in preferences for these average faces over preferences for faces more distant from the mean. Perhaps because of the difficulty of shifting perspectives from ratings of attractiveness to the dimension of faces themselves, however, the field of study concerned with facial attractiveness and its effects on social relations and social behavior has failed to pursue Symons' proposal until now.

Although the nomenclature of the evolutionary and cognitive perspectives is quite different, these perspectives offer more similarity than difference in the predictions made for prototypic or averaged faces and the tendency of infants and adults from diverse cultures to notice and prefer them. The data provided here do not, however, allow us to choose between evolutionary theory, which suggests that preferences for attractive faces are innate, and cognitive theory, which suggests that preferences for attractive faces are acquired early in life through exposure to category exemplars.[4] Indeed, it may be that the mechanism by which such preferences would become built-in is an inevitable outcome of the categorical abstraction of social stimuli. In any case, both the evolutionary and cognitive developmental perspectives bring coherence to the cross-cultural and infant data when the metric of average faceness rather than attractiveness ratings is designated for study.

In their seminal review of physical attractiveness effects, Berscheid and Walster (1974) concluded that there was no answer to the question of what constitutes beauty. Nor could Berscheid and Walster discern a foreseeable answer to this question. The data provided here suggest that attractive faces are those that represent the central tendency or the averaged members of the category of faces.

Such a definition of attractiveness is parsimonious and fits with both evolutionary and cognitive theory. Certain limitations, however, should be noted in these data. Our composites were created by averaging the faces of young, university students from the southwest. Although it is quite unlikely that the faces of these undergraduates differ in any meaningful way from those in other geographical areas of the United States, generality should be ensured by making composites of faces from different geographical locations. Composites of faces from other cultures should also be evaluated. Although a composite of 32 Asian faces will surely look different than that of a Caucasian composite face, we would predict that such an Asian composite face would, nevertheless, be judged as very attractive by both Asian and non-Asian raters.

We also acknowledge that a sample of movie stars might be rated as more attractive than our composites. It may be the case that although averageness is a necessary and critical element of attractiveness, other elements may also be important in influencing judgments of attractiveness. However, whether the digitized versions of faces of movie stars are more attractive in some absolute sense or are merely rated as more attractive because of their exposure and familiarity to raters (e.g., Harrison, 1969; Zajonc, 1968) is unclear and will need to be resolved by future research. Finally, we make no claim that our analysis applies to aesthetics in general; although average faces may be quite attractive, average (i.e., composited) art is not at all likely to be attractive and, in fact, hardly seems to be a useful construct.

We end by noting that the topic of physical attractiveness and its effects on social behaviors and relationships has been described as "undemocratic" (Aronson, 1969). Social scientists may be less disturbed by studying the effects of attractiveness knowing that attractive faces, in fact, are only average.

ACKNOWLEDGMENTS

This work was supported by grants from the National Science Foundation (BNS-8513843) and the National Institute of Child Health and Human Development (HD-21332) to Judith H. Langlois.

We thank Lisa Musselman and the Advanced Graphics Laboratory at the University of Texas for assistance in creating the composite images. This paper profited from discussions with and comments from many people, especially Arnold Buss, David Buss, Leslie Cohen, Donald Foss, Joseph Horn, Kevin Miller, Deborah Tharinger, Del Thiessen, and the reviewers of *Psychological Science*.

NOTES

1. The first psychologist to experimentally study beauty was probably Fechner in 1876 (Osborne, 1953).

2. Darwin himself did not believe there were either common cross-cultural preferences for beauty or common underlying dimensions of beauty.

3. We did not systematically test variations of order. However that the attractiveness of the composites is unrelated to the attractiveness of the faces entered at the beginning of the averaging process is obvious from the nearly identical attractiveness ratings and appearance of the 32-face composites within each gender, compared to the wide range of attractiveness of the first four faces entered into each composite set and from the four-face composites.

4. The ability to categorize is the innate component from this perspective (Cohen, 1988). Unfortunately, the innate versus early acquired distinction cannot be investigated in infants at birth because of the immature status of the visual system (Banks & Salapatek, 1983).

REFERENCES

Aronson, E. (1969). Some antecedents of interpersonal attraction. In W. J. Arnold & D. Levine (Eds.), *Nebraska symposium on motivation* (pp. 143–177). Lincoln: University of Nebraska Press.

Banks, M. S., & Salapatek, P. (1983). Infant visual perception. In P. H. Mussen, M. M. Haith, & J. J. Campos (Eds.), *Handbook of child psychology: Vol. 2, Infancy and developmental psychobiology* (pp. 435–571). New York: Wiley.

Barash, D. P. (1982). *Sociobiology and behavior.* New York: Elsevier North Holland.

Bernstein, I. H., Lin, T., & McClellan, P. (1982). Cross- vs. within-racial judgments of attractiveness. *Perception & Psychophysics, 32,* 495–503.

Berscheid, E., & Walster, E. (1974). Physical attractiveness. In L. Berkowitz (Ed.), *Advances in experimental social psychology* (pp. 157–215). New York: Academic Press.

Bomba, P. C., & Siqueland, E. R. (1983). The nature and structure of infant form categories, *Journal of Experimental Child Psychology, 35,* 294–328.

Bumpas, H. C. (1899). The elimination of the unfit as illustrated by the introduced sparrow. *Biology lectures in marine biology at Woods Hole, Massachusetts, 11,* 209–226.

Cohen, L. B. (1988). An information-processing approach to infant cognitive development. In L. Weiskrantz (Ed.), *Thought without language* (pp. 211–228). New York: Oxford.

Cohen, L. B., & Younger, B. A. (1983). Perceptual categorization in the infant. In E. K. Scholnik (Ed.), *New trends in conceptual representation: Challenges in Piaget's theory?* (pp. 197–220). Hillsdale, NJ: Erlbaum.

Cunningham, M. R. (1986). Measuring the physical in physical attractiveness: Quasiexperiments on the sociobiology of female facial beauty. *Journal of Social and Personality Psychology, 50,* 925–935.

Darwin, C. (1859). *On the origin of species by means of natural selection, or the preservation of favoured races in the struggle for life.* London: Watts & Co.

Darwin, C. (1871). *The descent of man and selection in relation to sex.* London: John Murray.

Dobzhansky, T. (1970). *Genetics of the evolutionary process.* New York: Columbia University Press.

Farkas, L. G. (1981). *Anthropometry of the head and face in medicine.* New York: Elsevier North Holland.

Farkas, L. G., Munro, I. R., & Kolar, J. C. (1987). Linear proportions in above- and below-average women's faces. In L. G. Farkas & I. R. Munro (Eds.), *Anthropometric facial proportions in medicine* (pp. 119–129). Springfield, IL: Charles C. Thomas.

Galton, F. (1878). Composite portraits. *Journal of the Anthropological Institute of Great Britain & Ireland, 8,* 132–142.

Galton, F. (1883). *Inquiries into human faculty and its development.* New York: Macmillan.

Harrison, A. A. (1969). Exposure and popularity. *Journal of Personality, 37,* 359–367.

Hildebrandt, K. A., & Fitzgerald, H. E. (1979). Facial feature determinants of perceived infant attractiveness. *Infant Behavior and Development, 2,* 229–329.

Johnson, R. W., Dannenbring, G. L., Anderson, N.R., & Villa, R. E. (1983). How different cultural and geographic groups perceive the attractiveness of active and inactive feminists. *The Journal of Social Psychology, 119,* 111–117.

Langlois, J. H. (1986). From the eye of the beholder to behavioral reality: The development of social behaviors and social relations as a function of physical attractiveness. In C. P. Herman, M. P. Zanna, & E. T. Higgins (Eds.), *Physical appearance, stigma, and social behavior: The Ontario symposium* (pp. 23–51). Hillsdale, NJ: Erlbaum.

Langlois, J. H., Roggman, L. A., Casey, R. J., Ritter, J.M., Rieser-Danner, L. A., & Jenkins, V. Y. (1987). Infant preferences for attractive faces: Rudiments of a stereotype? *Developmental Psychology, 23,* 363–369.

Langlois, J. H., Roggman, L. A., & Rieser-Danner, L.A. (in press). Infants' differential social responses to attractive and unattractive faces. *Developmental Psychology.*

Light, L. L., Hollander, S., & Kayra-Stuart, F. (1981). Why attractive people are harder to remember, *Personality and Social Psychology Bulletin, 7,* 269–276.

Lucker, G. W. (1981). Esthetics and a quantitative analysis of facial appearance. In G. W. Lucker, K.A. Ribbens, & J. A. McNamara (Eds.), *Psychological aspects of facial form.* Ann Arbor, MI: The Center for Growth and Development, University of Michigan.

Maret, S. M. (1983). Attractiveness ratings of photographs of Blacks by Cruzans and Americans. *The Journal of Psychology, 115,* 113–116.

Maret, S. M., & Harling, G. A. (1985). Cross cultural perceptions of physical attractiveness: Ratings of photos of whites by Cruzans and Americans. *Perceptual Motor Skills, 60,* 163–166.

McArthur, L. A., & Baron, R. M. (1983). Toward an ecological theory of social perception, *Psychological Review, 90,* 215–238.

Osborne, H. (1953), *Theory of beauty: An introduction to aesthetics.* New York: Philosophical Library.

Posner, M. I., & Keele, S. W. (1968). On the genesis of abstract ideas. *Journal of Experimental Psychology, 77,* 353–363.

Quinn, P. C., & Eimas, P. D. (1986). On categorization in early infancy. *Merrill-Palmer Quarterly, 32,* 331–363.

Reed, S. K. (1972). Pattern recognition and categorization. *Cognitive Psychology, 3,* 382–407.

Richardson, S. A., Goodman, N., Hastorf, A. H., & Dornbusch, S. M. (1961). Cultural uniformity in reaction to physical disabilities. *American Sociological Review, 26,* 241–247.

Rosch, E. (1978). Principles of categorization. In E.Rosch & B. B. Lloyd (Eds.), *Cognition and categorization* (pp. 27–47). Hillsdale, NJ: Erlbaum.

Rosch, E., Mervis, C. B., Gray, W. D., Jo... & Boyes-Braem, P. (1976). Basic objects categories. *Cognitive Psychology, 8,* 382–43...

Rosch, E., Simpson, C., & Miller, R. S. (1976). S... tural bases of typicality effects. *Journal of Experimental Psychology: Human Perception and Performance, 2,* 491–502.

Samuels, C. A., & Ewy, R. (1985). Aesthetic perception of faces during infancy, *British Journal of Developmental Psychology, 3,* 221–228.

Schmalhausen, I. I. (1949). *Factors of evolution: The theory of stabilizing selection.* Philadelphia: Blakiston.

Shapiro, B. A., Eppler, M., Haith, M. M., & Reis, H. (1987, April). *An event analysis of facial attractiveness and expressiveness.* Paper presented at the meeting of the Society for Research in Child Development. Baltimore, MD.

Sorell, G. T., & Nowak, C. A. (1981). The role of physical attractiveness as a contributor to individual development. In R. M. Lerner & N. A. Busch-Rossnagel (Eds.), *Individuals as producers of their development: A life-span perspective* (pp. 389–446). New York: Academic Press.

Stoddard, J. T. (1886). Composite portraiture. *Science, 8*(182), 89–91.

Stoddard, J. T. (1887). Composite photography. *Century, 33,* 750–757.

Strauss, M. S. (1979). Abstraction of prototypical information by adults and 10-month-old infants. *Journal of Experimental Psychology: Human Learning and Memory, 5,* 618–632.

Symons, D. (1979). *The evolution of human sexuality.* New York: Oxford University Press.

Thakerar, J. N., & Iwawaki, S. (1979). Cross-cultural comparisons in interpersonal attraction of females toward males. *Journal of Social Psychology, 108,* 121–122.

Weisfeld, G. E., Weisfeld, C. C., & Callaghan, J. W. (1984). Peer and self perceptions in Hopi and Afro-American third- and sixth-graders. *Ethos, 12,* 64–83.

Wittgenstein, L. (1953). *Philosophical investigations.* New York: Macmillan.

Younger, B. A. (1985). The segregation of items into categories by ten-month-old infants. *Child Development, 56,* 1574–1583.

Younger, B., & Gotlieb, S. (1988). Development of categorization skills: Changes in the nature or structure of infant form categories? *Developmental Psychology, 24,* 611–619.

Zajonc, R. B. (1968). Attitudinal effects of mere exposure, *Journal of Personality and Social Psychology Monograph Supplements, 9,* 1–27.

Matthew D. Smith
and Craig J. Chamberlin

Effect of Adding Cognitively Demanding Tasks on Soccer Skill Performance

Summary.—*The effect of adding cognitively demanding elements to the performance of a real-world motor task in which functional interference among the elements in performance existed was investigated across level of expertise. The primary task involved running as quickly as possible through a 15.25-m slalom course. Two secondary tasks were used, dribbling of a soccer ball and identification of geometric shapes projected on a screen located at the end of the slalom course. 4 novice, 5 intermediate, and 5 expert female soccer players served as subjects and performed three trials each of three experimental conditions: running through the slalom course, running through the slalom course while dribbling a soccer ball, and running through the slalom course while dribbling a soccer ball and identifying geometric shapes. Analysis of variance using a 3 (experimental condition) × 3 (level of expertise) design gave significant main effects and a significant interaction. The latter indicated that, although the addition of cognitively demanding elements caused a decrement in performance, the amount of decrement decreased as level of expertise increased. It was concluded that structural interference between elements of performance decreased the positive effect of automation of one element on dual task performance.*

Most sport skills entail concurrent processing of information from a variety of sources and the performance of more than one skill at a time. This particularly true of invasion games such as basketball, soccer, ice hockey, and rugby. Normally, an athlete performing in these games is required to locomote about the environment while manipulating an object and processing information for the purpose of strategic decision-making. Given the cognitive demands of only one of the performance requirements, it can be considered a feat of substantial proportion when we observe a skilled athlete processing multiple inputs of information and performing multiple tasks with minimal performance decrement on any one of the tasks.

Considerable research effort has been expended investigating the mechanisms that underlie an individual's capacity to perform multiple tasks simultaneously. The majority of studies have made use of the dual-task paradigm, wherein a subject is required to respond to more than one stimulus with more than one response, have employed laboratory tasks, and have developed minimal levels of expertise (e.g., Kantowitz & Knight, 1976; Wrisberg & Shea, 1978). A notable exception to this study is another by Leavitt (1979). In this experiment, the author investigated the capabilities of ice hockey players to perform simultaneous multiple tasks across different levels of skill. The primary task that the subjects performed was skating as rapidly as possible through a slalom course of pylons set on the ice, a typical drill incorporated into real-world ice-hockey practice sessions. Two secondary tasks were used—identifying geometric shapes projected onto a screen set at the end of the ice arena and stickhandling a puck. Subjects were measured for the time taken to complete the slalom course under conditions of the primary task alone or in combination with one or both of the secondary tasks.

The results of this study indicated that progressively adding the secondary tasks to the primary task had little effect on the performance of experienced ice hockey players but adversely affected the performance of novice players. This finding appeared to support a model which hypothesizes a decrease in attentional demands as learning progresses, such as that proposed by Fitts and Posner (1967), leading to an automation of elements of the total performance.

The potential for functional interference between the primary and secondary tasks in Leavitt's (1979) study is quite small. The two motor tasks employed (skating and stickhandling) are performed with different limbs. However, in a number of sport skills, functional interference is a problem that must be faced by the performer. For example, the analog of Leavitt's (1979) ice hockey task in soccer would be running while manipulating the ball and observing patterns of action as the basis for further decision-making. In this situation, running and ball manipulation must be accomplished by the same limb. The problem investigated here, then, was whether a similar pattern of results to

Leavitt's (1979) study would be found when functional interference between the primary and secondary tasks was introduced. A reasonable prediction would be that a different pattern of results would be observed, since the act of manipulating a ball with the foot while running could be considered a qualitatively different action to running alone. Therefore, automation of the running action would not affect dribbling a soccer ball to the same extent as automation of the skating action would affect stickhandling a puck.

METHOD

Subjects

Fourteen female soccer players served as subjects and were grouped according to soccer playing experience (novice, $n = 4$, age in years, $M = 13.3$, $SD = 1.0$, playing experience = 15 40-min. physical education class lessons; intermediate, $n = 5$, age in years, $M = 11.8$, $SD = 1.1$, M playing experience = 7 seasons; expert, $n = 5$, age in years, $M = 19.0$, $SD = 1.0$, M playing experience = 24.8 seasons; note that 2 seasons are played per year). All subjects volunteered to participate and informed consent was obtained prior to testing.

Apparatus and Task

The primary task required of subjects was to run as rapidly as possible through a slalom course that consisted of six standard traffic cones set 3.05 m apart on a gymnasium floor. The first secondary task was to dribble a soccer ball and the second secondary task was to identify geometric shapes projected onto a screen at the end of the slalom course.

The arrangement of cones resulted in a total distance from start to finish of 15.25 m. A Kodak Ektagraphic slide projector was set 3.96 m from the last cone in the slalom course on a table that was 68.6 cm in height. A 1.22 m² projection screen was placed 3.96 m from the slide projector. Six slides were loaded into the slide projector. Each slide had two vertical columns of black and white geometric shapes with six or seven randomly ordered shapes in each column. The shapes used were triangles, squares, rectangles, diamonds, and circles, and were either filled or unfilled. When projected on the screen the over-all dimension of the slide was 91.44 cm × 60.96 cm. All timing was done with a Sportline Econosport stopwatch.

Procedure

Each subject ran through the slalom course three times for each of three experimental conditions. The first condition consisted of running through the course as quickly as possible (Condition R). The second condition consisted of running through the course as quickly as possible while dribbling a soccer ball (Condition RD). The third condition consisted of running through the course as quickly as possible while dribbling a soccer ball and identifying geometric shapes (Condition RDS). Each group of subjects were tested during a single testing session. After an adequate warm-up, one subject would perform the three trials of one condition consecutively, followed by each other subject performing their trials of the same condition. This procedure was repeated for the other two conditions. Since trials were kept to a minimum to prevent a learning effect, and fatigue was not a factor, it was deemed unnecessary to counterbalance for an order effect within groups.

Before each trial, the subjects were given a "ready, go" command. Prior to the trials on the condition RDS, the subjects were shown one of the geometric shape slides on the screen. They were instructed to shout out the names of the shapes and to preface the naming with "black" if the shape was filled. The subjects performed the naming function in a top to bottom fashion, beginning with the left column and then proceeding to the right column. As the "ready, go" command was given, the experimenter changed the slide projected on the screen. If an error in the running and dribbling performance occurred, that trial was repeated by the subject.

RESULTS

The dependent variables measured were movement time (MT, time from go command until completion of the slalom course) and, for the Condition RDS, number of shapes identified. For MT, the median

Table 1

Means and Standard Deviations for Movement Time Data by Level of Expertise and Experimental Condition

Level of Expertise		Condition		
		Run	Dribble	Run, Dribble, Shape
Novice	M	3.81	9.00	13.06
	SD	0.24	1.44	2.77
Intermediate	M	3.69	7.94	9.16
	SD	0.17	1.26	0.93
Expert	M	3.27	5.93	7.59
	SD	0.21	0.27	0.62

score of the three trials under each condition was considered representative of a subject's performance. Means and standard deviations for the median data were calculated for each group under each condition (see Table 1). Similarly, the means of the median scores for the number of shapes identified during the RDS condition were also calculated for each group.

Movement Times

Analysis was accomplished using a 3 × 3 (condition × level of experience) analysis of variance with Newman-Keuls follow-up tests for significant effects. Level of significance was established at $p = .05$. Significant main effects for condition ($F_{2,33} = 114.12, p < .01$) and level of experience ($F_{2,33} = 25.49, p < .01$) and a significant interaction of condition by level of experience ($F_{4,33} = 6.54, p < .01$) were found.

Inspection of Figure 1 would indicate that the significant interaction was due to the addition of cognitively demanding elements having the least effect on the expert group and the greatest effect on the novice group. The follow-up Newman-Keuls analyses indicated that there was no difference among the groups during the Run condition. However, all groups were significantly different from each other on the Run-dribble condition, while the novice group was significantly slower than the other two groups at completing the Run-dribble-shapes condition. Within each group, adding cognitively demanding tasks resulted in a significant slowing of performance for all possible comparisons except between the second and third conditions for the intermediate group.

Shape Identification

Analysis of the shape identification data was accomplished using a one-way analysis of variance. There were no significant differences among the three groups in terms of the number of shapes correctly identified while performing under the Run-dribble-shape condition.

DISCUSSION

In this study, the effect of progressively adding cognitively demanding elements to the performance of the primary task of running through a slalom course was examined across three levels of expertise. The intent was to provide a replication of Leavitt's (1979) study, but using a task which introduced some functional interference among the elements of task performance. The addition of cognitively demanding elements had a detrimental effect on the performance of the primary task across all levels of expertise, but the magnitude of this detrimental effect decreased as level of expertise increased.

The results are roughly congruent with those of Leavitt (1979), but there are some interesting differences. Significant is the finding that being required to perform additional elements, such as manipulating a soccer ball and identifying geometric patterns, did decrease performance within the most expert group. In Leavitt's (1979) study, the expert group was able to maintain their performance across all experimental conditions. Two possible reasons can be hypothesized to explain this apparent discrepancy.

First, the level of expertise of the expert group in this study may have been less than that in Leavitt's (1979) study. In our study, female college soccer players from an NCAA Division II program served as subjects for the expert group. In Leavitt's study, collegiate male ice hockey players from major sport universities (roughly congruent to NCAA Division I institutions) in Canada served as subjects for the expert group. An argument can be made for Leavitt's subjects representing a more elite level of performance than the present subjects.

Second, given the functional interference in performance, the dual task of running and dribbling a soccer ball is qualitatively different from the dual task of skating and stickhandling. In ice hockey,

Figure 1

Time to Complete the Slalom Course by Experimental Condition Across Level of Expertise

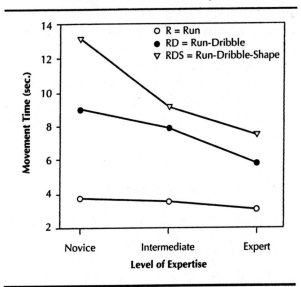

each element of performance is relatively independent of the other. Therefore, automation of a singular element, such as skating, would increase attentional capacity available for the performance of other elements, such as stickhandling and decision-making. Minimal disruption of the skating skill should occur when additional performance elements are required. In soccer, running must be modified when manipulation of the ball is required because there is functional interference between the tasks. Automation of the running action would not have a similar effect in soccer as automation of skating in ice hockey since the act of running while dribbling a soccer ball could be considered a singular skill. The need, then, is to automate the action of running while manipulating the ball as a whole skill.

The previous conclusion, that the effectiveness of automatizing an element of performance is dependent on the independence the element maintains, is very similar to the conclusion that has been drawn from work done on whole-part learning. In that research, increasing the relative independence of a part results in greater effectiveness of using a part learning procedure (e.g., Newell, Carlton, Fisher, & Rutter, 1989; for a more detailed discussion of whole-part learning, see Chamberlin & Lee, in press).

The results of this study and the attentional research completed to date suggest that teachers should not ask novices to perform simultaneous tasks either from the same or different perceptual classes. Also, teachers should first provide some automation in the base element of a task before adding additional elements, although the need is to identify what constitutes the base element. However, these conclusions are tempered by the need for additional research which makes use of real-world tasks. In particular, studies which involve the confound of functional dependence versus independence of the elements of performance should be undertaken.

REFERENCES

Chamberlin, C. J., & Lee, T. D. (in press) Arranging practice conditions and designing instruction. In R. N. Singer, M. Murphey, & L. K. Tennant (Eds.), *Handbook on research in sport psychology.* New York: Macmillan.

Fitts, P. M., & Posner, M. I. (1967) *Human performance.* Belmont, CA: Brooks/Cole.

Kantowitz, B. H., & Knight, J. L. (1976) Testing tapping timesharing: II. Auditory secondary task. *Acta Psychologica,* 40, 343–362.

Leavitt, J. (1979) Cognitive demands of skating and stick handling in ice hockey. *Canadian Journal of Applied Sport Sciences,* 4, 46–55.

Newell, K. M., Carlton, M. J., Fisher, A. T., & Rutter, B. G. (1989) Whole-part training strategies for learning the response dynamics of microprocessor driven simulators. *Acta Psychologica,* 71, 197–210.

Wrisberg, C. A., & Shea, C. H. (1978) Shifts in attention demands and motor program utilitization during motor learning. *Journal of Motor Behavior,* 10, 149–158.

28

T. J. Perfect and C. Askew

Print Adverts: Not Remembered but Memorable

SUMMARY

Attempts to measure advertising effectiveness have relied on explicit memory measures based on recall or recognition. However, recent cognitive research has shown that not only is it possible to measure unconscious effects of prior experience through implicit tests of memory, but that such performance is independent of explicit recollection. The present study sought to determine whether it is possible to demonstrate the same pattern of findings using print advertising in an ecologically valid situation. Eight subjects saw 25 full-page colour magazine adverts in either a deliberate or incidental study condition and subsequently rated (on four salient dimensions) a set of 50 adverts, which included the target adverts. Following the ratings subjects were asked to indicate which of the adverts they recognized as having been in the original set. While the deliberate study group recognized around 60 per cent of the adverts, the incidental study group recognized only 11 per cent. However, both groups showed the same positive bias in attitudes towards the adverts they had been exposed to compared to the ones they had not seen before. Thus, in line with the cognitive literature, it is possible to show shifts in attitudes that are independent of conscious recollection. This data questions advertisers' reliance on explicit memory tests as measures of advertising effectiveness.

There can be little doubt as to the ubiquitous nature of advertising in our society. Every year advertisers spend huge amounts of money in advertising campaigns. For example, in 1989 Unilever spent £81 million, Proctor and Gamble spent £71 million, and Kellogg's spent £48 million on advertising in the UK alone (Flandin, Martin, and Simkin, 1992). Clearly companies seek evidence that this money is well spent and, as a result, measures of advertising effectiveness have considerable economic importance. The research in this area has been largely based on the assumption that purchases are made on the basis of informed choice. For example Lavidge and Steiner (1961) claimed that 'advertising should move people from awareness ... to knowledge ... to liking ... to preference ... to conviction ... to purchase' (cited in Lucas and Britt, 1963: p. 7). Thus the logic used is that in order to make an informed judgement an individual must have the information available, and information can only be available if it is remembered. Hence advertisers have tried to make their adverts as amusing and distinctive as possible, and have tested the efficacy of their adverts using memory measures (see, for example, Friestad and Thorson, 1993; Kellaris, Cox, and Cox, 1993; Keller, 1993; Lucas and Britt, 1963; Schmitt, Tavassoli, and Millard, 1993). However, the evidence that adverts are well remembered is extremely patchy. For example Zielske (1959) showed that after 13 weekly exposures to an advert, 63 per cent of subjects could recall it; After only 6 weeks exposure this figure fell to 20 per cent. After only one exposure, recall fell to 3 per cent after 3 weeks. Further disturbing findings for advertisers come from a study by Bekerian and Baddeley (1980), which evaluated a saturation campaign to inform the public of a forthcoming change in wavelengths for BBC radio stations. Over the course of the campaign, subjects heard the information around 1000 times, yet when asked to locate the new wavelengths on a radio dial, over 70 per cent of responses were 'don't knows', and recall ranged from 12 to 22 per cent.

There seem to be two conclusions to be drawn from research of this kind. Either adverts have no effect, or they have an effect but it is not measured well by the kind of memory tests used so far. It is certainly the case that consumer psychologists have been reluctant to abandon the notion of using memory tests to test the efficacy of adverts (Mitchell, 1993). A further possible role for memory in advertising emerges from consideration of recent work in cognitive psychology, which has drawn a crucial distinction between explicit memory tests, such as free recall and recognition, and implicit memory tests, such as anagram solution, word stem completion, and preference judgements.

Tests such as free recall and recognition are called explicit because a prominent feature of these tests is that they make explicit reference to, and require conscious recollection of, a specific prior episode. In contrast, a test is called implicit when the prior episode is neither required nor made reference to at time of the test, but performance is altered by the previous episode.

Interest in implicit memory largely stemmed from findings in the 1970s that suggested that amnesic patients who perform at extremely poor or even floor levels on tests of explicit memory can perform at normal levels on tests of implicit memory. Warrington and Weiskrantz (1974) reported performance at normal levels in amnesic subjects on word stem completion, despite their inability consciously to remember the words. Similar patterns of results have been reported using a variety of indirect tests with amnesic patients (Shimamura, 1986) and performance on explicit and implicit memory tests have been shown to dissociate in normal individuals (Tulving, Schacter, and Stark, 1982). It is known that while depth of processing, divided attention, intentionality, and generation all affect explicit memory, these factors have either the opposite effect or no effect on implicit memory. Conversely, changes in modality, type font, and physical features of the stimulus all affect implicit memory but have no effect on explicit memory (Roediger, Weldon, and Challis, 1989).

Jacoby (Jacoby, Kelley, and Dwyan, 1989a; Jacoby and Kelley, 1992) has suggested that the dissociation between explicit and implicit memory processes can be understood in terms of the contrast between automatic and consciously controlled information processing. He claims that the representation of a past experience automatically influenced the fluency of processing and so interpretation of later events. These automatic effects are attributed to sources and result in a subjective experience. Because of errors in this attribution process measures of subjective experience are therefore valuable as indirect tests of memory. Several studies have shown that subjects can misattribute fluent processing that is the result of prior experience to sources other than the past. A single prior presentation is sufficient to lengthen the apparent duration of a word, can lead to the misattribution that a statement is true, or that an argument seems to flow, or can lead to a non-famous name being regarded as famous (see Jacoby and Kelley (1992) for a review).

Kunst-Wilson and Zajonc (1980) reported a similar finding using visual stimuli, but within a subliminal perception paradigm rather than an implicit memory paradigm. Initially they presented irregular polygons subliminally on a computer screen; this subsequently led to chance performance in a subsequent recognition test. Despite the inability to recognize 'old' items, subjects displayed an affective preference for the shapes presented previously. Thus the authors concluded that affective reactions to stimuli can be acquired by virtue of exposure to the items even in the absence of conscious awareness.

A review of the literature on mere exposure effects was conducted by Bornstein (1989), who summarized the findings of over 130 studies covering the 20-year period from the discovery of the mere exposure effect. Interested readers are directed to that article for a comprehensive coverage of the issues, but there are several aspects of the findings that are relevant to the present work. In particular, although the effect is robust, it is stronger for more complex stimuli than simple stimuli; it is found with many kinds of affective ratings; it is stronger with shorter presentation times (< 5 s); and it is independent of whether or not the stimulus is recognized at test.

Thus recent cognitive and cognitive neuropsychological research may offer an alternative means of assessing advertising effectiveness. The literature of the past 15 years has demonstrated that two distinct kinds of memory test are susceptible to different kinds of manipulation. Furthermore while cognitive theorists have argued that attributions about items reflect the action of implicit memory, advertisers—who seek to change attitudes—have relied upon explicit measures of advertising effectiveness (see, for example, recent reviews of the memory—advertising literature by Baker, 1993; Keller, 1993; Nedungadi, Mitchell, and Berger, 1993). This gap between the two disciplines seemed ripe for investigation: this point was made recently in review of the consumer psychology literature by Sanyal (1992: p. 802):

> Implicit memory is a reasonably robust framework for many applications in consumer behavior. If the idea of consumer memory is restricted to existing recall/recognition tests then consumer researchers may be ignoring a potentially influential dimension of consumer evaluation and decision making. The notion of consumer memory may thus need to be expanded to include the concept of implicit memory.

The present study aimed to test implicit memory for advertising material by designing an indirect test of memory for magazine adverts. The experiment involved subjects being exposed to full-page colour adverts in either an incidental or deliberate study condition, both conducted under the guise of a market research study. Implicit memory was revealed by a difference in ratings over four scales between seen (target) and unseen (non-target) adverts and was followed by a standard yes/no recognition test. Recognition was favoured over recall or cued recall for two major reasons. First, and most importantly, it utilizes the same cue at test as the implicit measures. Thus any discrimination at test between implicit and explicit measures cannot be attributed to the test cue, because they are the same (i.e. the advert itself). Second, it is the most sensitive measure of what is available to explicit memory. If recall had been used, explicit memory may have been underestimated. If biases in behaviour had been observed for unrecalled information, it would have been difficult to argue that this is due to implicit memory, as the items may have been recalled if a different cue was given, or recognized if re-presented. Thus recognition was used to provide the most inclusive measure of what is available to consciousness at test. In line with Jacoby's work on memory attributions and the findings of Kunst-Wilson and Zajonc (1980) it was expected that target adverts would receive more positive ratings than non-target adverts. It was also expected that this difference in ratings would be driven by implicit memory, and thus would be independent of recognition level, and independent of encoding conditions.

METHOD

Subjects

Baseline Group.

Sixty subjects were used to generate baseline ratings for the adverts; 29 were male and 31 were female, with an age range of 17–35 years and a mean age of 20 years.

Experimental Group.

Eighty subjects (25 male, 55 female) took part in the experiment, with 20 subjects assigned to each of four groups. The age range was 19–58 years with a mean age of 30 years. None of the experimental group had been used to generate the baseline data.

Materials

Ten British national colour magazines were used in the experiment. All were issues released at least two months prior to experimenting. The target adverts were 50 full-page colour adverts within those magazines. No attempt was made to measure exposure to the adverts prior to the test. At test subjects were presented with full-page (A4) colour photocopies of the adverts. An alphabeticised list of the adverts used is given in Appendix 1.

Procedure

Baseline.

Subjects were tested in a group setting. Each subject was asked to rate ten of the target adverts on a seven-point Likert-type scale for the scales 'eye-catching', 'appealing', 'memorable', and 'distinctive'. The scale ranged from 1 = very much more than average, through 4 = average, to 7 = very much less than average. Each advert was rated by twelve subjects in total.

Experimental Group.

All subjects were tested individually in a quiet room. The presentation procedure differed for the incidental and deliberate exposure groups, and will be described separately:

Incidental exposure. Subjects were told that the study aimed to examine factors that make the layout of the magazines appealing and readable. The magazines were then placed in front of them (half received set A, half set B). Subjects were told they were to take each magazine and to turn first to the contents page. Having done so they were given the titles of five articles to which they were to turn. Target adverts appeared facing the leading page of each of these articles. Subjects were asked to find the first page of each article, to scan the article from beginning to end and not to read anything except the title and main feature headings. Subjects completed several questions which related to the articles themselves for each magazine and recorded their own responses. The order of magazine presentation and therefore target adverts, were rotated. After they had seen all the articles the subjects were given 5 min to write their opinions on factors that made magazine layouts appealing.

Deliberate exposure. Subjects in the deliberate exposure group were directly exposed to the same 'target' adverts used for the incidental exposure (again, half saw set A, half set B). Each subject was presented with the magazine set and informed that they would be given five page numbers for each magazine and that each page would be a full page advert (order of presentation was again rotated). The task for each subject was to decide which was the most instantly striking feature of the adverts. A sample list of features was offered by the experimenter; the product, product name, logo, copy, a picture in general, or nothing in particular. The experimenter recorded the responses. Subjects were allowed only 3 s before being asked to turn to the next page. After they had seen all the adverts, subjects were given 5 min to write their opinions on how they believed print adverts could be improved.

Test conditions. The test procedure was the same for both experimental groups. Subjects were presented with 50 colour photocopies of the print adverts (mixed sets A and B), half of which the subjects had been exposed to. Subjects were required to rate each of the adverts on each of the four seven-point Likert scales (eye-catching, appealing, memorable, distinctive) on the basis of their 'first impressions'. The order of presentation of the adverts was reversed for alternate subjects in each group.

On completion of the ratings, subjects were required to turn through the adverts once again and to indicate which of the adverts they recognized as having been present in the magazines they had seen previously.

RESULTS

The first analysis concerned the level of explicit memory for the adverts, as measured by the number of adverts that the subjects claimed to recognize. To control for the possibility that the two groups may differ in willingness to respond, the recognition score used was hits—false positives on the recognition test. A one-way ANOVA on recognition scores showed that the deliberate study group remembered more than the incidental group ($F(1,78) = 152.2; p < .0001$). The mean numbers of adverts recognized by the two groups were 15.1 (SD = 5.48) and 2.8 (SD = 3.07) out of 25 for the deliberate and incidental groups, respectively. Clearly this replicates the standard advantage for deliberate study one would expect with explicit memory, and would be cause for concern to advertisers seeking to reach their target audience with print adverts; within less than 1 hour only 11.2 per cent of adverts studied incidentally are recognized.

The next analyses examined the implicit measures of advertising effectiveness, namely the rating data. Two-way mixed ANOVAs (deliberate versus incidental × targets versus non-targets) were conducted for each of the four rating scales. The mean ratings for each group for targets and non-targets is given in Table 1.

On each of the four scales, targets were rated more positively than non-targets (eye-catching: $F(1,77) = 46.60$, $p < .0001$; appealing: $F(1,77) = 38.19$, $p < .0001$; memorable: $F(1,77) = 28.80$, $p < .0001$; and distinctive: $F(1,77) = 27.34$, $p < .0001$.[1] However, in contrast to the explicit memory

measure, in no case was there a main effect of group ($F < 1$ in all cases), and the only significant interaction was for the rating of memorability ($F(1,77) = 4.34$, $p < .05$). All the others were non-significant (eyecatching: $F(1,77) = 1.04$, NS; appealing: $F(1,77) = 1.52$, NS; distinctive ($F(1,77) = 2.47$, NS).

The lack of interactions between study condition (and hence explicit memory, given the reported differences in recognition) and whether or not the advert had been a target or distractor is particularly compelling evidence that the shift in attitudes is due to implicit memory, and not explicit memory. If there had been effects of both implicit and explicit memory then one would have predicted that there would have been a greater attitude shift in the deliberate condition. This was not the case for the majority of the scales.

Nevertheless, it was decided to conduct a further analysis to investigate whether explicit memory had a role in the attitude shift. The second analysis compared the ratings towards target adverts that the subjects recognized with ratings to unrecognized targets. However, a direct comparison is not feasible because the likelihood of recognition may well be confounded with the inherent memorability, appeal, etc. of the adverts. Thus, for each subject we looked at the appropriate baseline estimates (from the baseline group) for the adverts that had and had not been recognized by each individual, and subtracted these values from the ratings the subjects had given. Thus, for each subject, on each of the four rating scales, two scores were generated—the mean difference score for the adverts that

Table 1

The Mean (and SD) of Ratings for Adverts, on the Four Dimensions of Eye-Catching, Appeal, Memorable, and Distinctive

| | Study condition | | | |
| | Deliberate | | Incidental | |
	T	D	T	D
Eye-catching	3.47	4.06	3.66	4.10
	(.58)	(.73)	(.70)	(.67)
Appeal	3.85	4.43	3.99	4.37
	(.68)	(.71)	(.72)	(.67)
Memorable	4.02	4.64	4.21	4.48
	(.69)	(.71)	(.67)	(.66)
Distinctive	3.97	4.56	4.19	4.49
	(.68)	(.71)	(.71)	(.67)

T, target adverts; D, distractor adverts.
Lower ratings indicate more favourable attitudes.

Table 2

The Mean (and SD) Difference Between Ratings for Adverts and the Baseline Ratings for Adverts
That Were Either Recognized (R) or Non-Recognized (NR)

| | Study condition | | | |
| | Deliberate | | Incidental | |
	R	NR	R	NR
Eye-catching	.32[a]	.18	.13	.20[a]
	(.58)	(.88)	(.84)	(.54)
Appeal	.40[a]	.27[a]	.35[a]	.42[a]
	(.74)	(.75)	(.88)	(.54)
Memorable	.38[a]	.20	.31[a]	.28[a]
	(.69)	(.81)	(.75)	(.51)
Distinctive	.25[a]	.17	.08	.11
	(.73)	(.96)	(.70)	(.52)

R, Recognized adverts; NR, Non-recognized adverts.
[a] These mean differences scores were significantly above zero, where positive values indicate more positive attitudes than baseline.

were recognized, and a similar mean difference score for those that were not. These mean difference scores were entered into a two-way ANOVA (group × recognition status) for each of the four scales. There were no main effects of group, nor recognition status, nor were there any interactions ($F < 1$ in every case). Without wishing to make too much of the null hypothesis, it is clear that this analysis is consistent with the conclusion reached previously: that whether or not the target was recognized, or whether or not it was studied deliberately, made no difference to the shift in attitudes. As Table 2 shows, this is not because there was no effect of prior exposure; the mean differences were all positive, and were significantly above chance for 10/16 scales.[2]

DISCUSSION

The results of the present study are both clear and coherent and, we believe, of some importance for advertising research. Implicit memory for advertising material was clearly manifested in this experiment, with the findings in line with the hypotheses proposed. Although recognition showed a marked decrement from the deliberate to the incidental condition, this manipulation of encoding condition had no effect upon the degree to which the target adverts were rated more positively than non-targets. Thus, even when explicit recognition was close to zero in the incidental condition, implicit memory

effects were apparent, and of the same magnitude as the deeper encoding conditions. Furthermore, when the target adverts that were and were not recognized were analysed separately, there were no differences in attitudes towards those adverts. These findings are in line with those found by Kunst-Wilson and Zajonc (1980), in that it was shown that subjective preference for a stimulus can be acquired by virtue of a single prior exposure, except that in their study subliminal presentation was used to prevent conscious awareness of the stimuli, whereas here the lack of conscious recollection was due to forgetting. This leads to the delicious paradox that while exposure to an advert fails to lead to that advert being remembered, it nevertheless leads to the advert being rated as more memorable (and appealing, distinctive, and eye-catching) than would have been expected.

There are several theoretical accounts of the distinction between the explicit and implicit memory that can be applied to the findings. For example, it has been claimed that they represent separate memory systems (Schacter, 1987), they are the result of different kinds of processing (Roediger and Blaxton, 1987), or that implicit memory is the result of temporary activation of pre-existing representations (Graf and Mandler, 1984). While the present data do not allow one to distinguish between these accounts, the behavioural measure used (making affective judgements) leads us to prefer to discuss the results in terms of Jacoby's attributional theory of memory. According to this account, when presented with an item (e.g. an advert) that has been processed recently (whether deliberately or incidentally), the perceptual system processes this information more fluently. The subjects then need to make an attribution about this added fluency. This can be either an attribution that the event has been dealt with before (i.e. it is a 'memory'), or the attribution can be made to an external source, namely the properties of the adverts themselves. However, given that subjects cannot consciously remember the context of the event (i.e. seeing the advert), they have to generate an alternative reason why the advert is perceived more fluently. Thus, in this account, the advert is rated as more appealing, distinctive, memorable, and eye-catching because the subjects find it easier to process but don't remember why.

One issue that is of theoretical and applied interest follows this account. Jacoby has reported that in some cases when made aware of the reason for the increased fluency, subjects are not susceptible to the memory illusions, and so don't make misattributions, e.g. if aware of the previous presentation, subjects do not make false fame judgements (Jacoby, Woloshyn, and Kelley, 1989b). However, this is not always the case; making subjects aware of the prior occurrence of words does not change judgements of subjective loudness of background noise (Jacoby, Allan, Collins, and Lanwill, 1988). In the present study subjects made more positive judgements whether or not the adverts were recognized. However, the recognition judgements were made after the ratings. Perhaps if subjects were warned in advance a different pattern would have emerged. Clearly this warrants further investigation.

These findings clearly have implications for the measurement of advertising effectiveness. They strongly suggest that explicitly remembering an advert is unnecessary, and perhaps even irrelevant, to the change in attitudes that result from a single exposure to print advertising. Thus advertisers who seek to evaluate the effectiveness of their adverts by recourse to explicit memory tests are likely to underestimate the degree to which their adverts are able to alter attitudes. In the incidental condition of the present study recognition was at 11.2 per cent after less than 1 hour. If we had chosen to use recall no doubt the figure would have been close to zero. Thus the impression garnered from conventional analyses would be that adverts studied inci-

dentally have no effect. None the less, we were able to demonstrate robust changes in attitudes, in a positive direction, on four salient dimensions.

However, it is important not to stretch the data too far. What we have so far illustrated is that attitudes towards adverts can be manipulated in the absence of conscious memory. The next necessary stage of research would be to demonstrate that this change in attitudes transfers to the product. It is also important that we investigate whether the shifts in attitudes occur for all adverts, or just a subset of them. If the latter is the case then we need to determine what factors lead some adverts successfully to change attitudes in the absence of conscious recollection, and others not.

A number of differences between implicit and explicit memory are also pertinent to the advertising field. Whether implicit and explicit memory represent different systems or processes, it remains true that, behaviourally, they are independent, and are driven by different factors. Therefore, if the present claim that implicit memory is a critical determinant of consumer behaviour is valid, this prompts the question of what kind of advertising strategy would best promote implicit memory. This clearly is beyond the scope of the present paper, but given that implicit memory can last much longer than explicit memory (Tulving, Schacter, and Stark, 1982), is sensitive to modality (Jacoby and Dallas, 1981), and surface features (Roediger and Blaxton, 1987), and is insensitive to factors that manipulate explicit memory such as level of processing (Jacoby and Dallas, 1981), intentionality (Basden, Basden, and Gargano, 1993), lag between presentations (Parkin, Reid, and Russo, 1990), and divided attention (Parkin, Reid, and Russo, 1990), clearly the kinds of advertising campaign one would use to promote implicit memory would be very different from those one would use to get people explicitly to remember a brand.

In summary, this small-scale study has achieved its aim. The demonstration that advertising effectiveness can be shown in the absence of explicit recollection has been achieved, and this asks difficult questions about the use of explicit tests as measures of advertising effectiveness. This opens up a wealth of opportunity for applying the accumulated knowledge regarding implicit memory to the applied issues of advertising design and measurement of advertising campaigns. Indeed, by ignoring the wealth of implicit memory research advertising researchers have seemingly limited their ability to demonstrate the true impact of advertising.

APPENDIX 1: ALPHABETICIZED LIST OF ALL THE ADVERTISED PRODUCTS USED

Acuvue Contact Lenses	Lucozade
Aramis	Magnet Trade
Babyliss Bodytoner	Martell
Ballygowan Irish	Maryland Cookies
Spring Water	Milk Marketing Board
Batchelors Slim-a-Soup	National Geographic
Baxi Bermuda	Olympus Sports
Bells Scotch Whisky	Olympus Ecru Cameras
Boddingtons	Pascoes Dog Food
British Gas	Parker Knoll
Calvin Klein—Eternity	Phillips CDi
Champion USA	Prestige Pans
Courvoisier	Prince Sports
Cristal d'Arques	Raymond Weil Watches
Dartington Crystal	Reactolite Rapide
Dishwash Electric	Remy Martin
Duplo	Scheaffer
Gucci	Scholl
Guerlain	Subaru
Hoover	Tag heuer
Hugo Boss	TCP
Isuzu	Tipp-Ex
Johnny Walker	Tisserand Aromatherapy
Johnsons Baby Lotion	Toshiba
Lavazza Filer Coffee	Vax

NOTES

1. The data for one subject in the deliberate encoding condition were lost, and hence the analyses are based on 79 subjects only. However, the results are so robust that it was felt that this would not have altered the findings.

2. Because the responses to the targets were split into hits and misses, this meant that the mean ratings in these analyses were based on fewer responses. Thus the data were noisier and hence not all achieved significance.

REFERENCES

Baker, W. (1993). The relevance accessibility model of advertising effectiveness. In A. A. Mitchell (Ed), *Advertising exposure, memory and choice*. Hillsdale, NJ: Lawrence Erlbaum Associates.

Basden, B. H., Basden, D. R., and Gargano, G. J. (1993). Directed forgetting in implicit and explicit memory tests: A comparison of methods. *Journal of Experimental Psychology: Learning, Memory and Cognition*, **19**, 603–616.

Bekerian, D. A. and Baddeley, A. D. (1980). Saturation advertising and the repetition effect. *Journal of Verbal Learning and Verbal Behavior*, **19**, 17–25.

Bornstein, R. F. (1989). Exposure and affect: Overview and meta-analysis of research, 1968–1987. *Psychological Bulletin*, **106**, 265–289.

Flandin, M. P., Martin, E., and Simkin, L. P. (1992). Advertising effectiveness research: A survey of agencies, clients and conflicts. *International Journal of Advertising*, **11**, 203–214.

Friestad, M. and Thorson, E. (1993). Remembering ads: The effects of encoding strategies, retrieval cues and emotional response. *Journal of Consumer Psychology*, **2**, 1–23.

Graf, P. and Mandler, G. (1984). Activation makes a word more accessible, but not more retrieval. *Journal of Verbal Learning and Verbal Behavior*, **23**, 553–568.

Jacoby, L. L. and Dallas, M. (1981). On the relation between autobiographical memory and perceptual learning. *Journal of Experimental Psychology: General*, **3**, 306–340.

Jacoby, L. L. and Kelley, C. (1992). Unconscious influences of memory. In A. D. Milner and M. D. Rugg (Eds), *The neuropsychology of consciousness*. London: Academic Press.

Jacoby, L. L., Allan, L. G., Collins, J. C., and Lanwill, L. K. (1988). Memory influences subjective experience: Noise judgements. *Journal of Experimental Psychology: Learning, Memory and Cognition*, **14**, 240–247.

Jacoby, L. L., Kelley, C., and Dwyan, J. (1989a). Memory attributions. In H. L. Roediger and F. I. M. Craik (Eds), *Varieties of memory and consciousness: Essays in honour of Endel Tulving*: Hillsdale, NJ: Lawrence Erlbaum Associates.

Jacoby, L. L., Woloshyn, V., and Kelley, C. M. (1989b). Becoming famous without being recognised: Unconscious influences of memory produced by dividing attention. *Journal of Experimental Psychology: General*, **118**, 115–125.

Kellaris, J. J., Cox, A. D., and Cox, D. (1993). The effect of background music on ad processing: A contingency explanation. *Journal of Marketing*, **57**, 114–125.

Keller, K. L. (1993). Memory retrieval factors and advertising effectiveness. In A. A. Mitchell (Ed), *Advertising exposure, memory and choice*. Hillsdale, NJ: Lawrence Erlbaum Associates.

Kunst-Wilson, W. R. and Zajonc, R. B. (1980). Affective discrimination of stimuli that cannot be recognised. *Science, 207*, 557–558.

Lavidge, R. J. and Steiner, G. A. (1961). A model for predictive measurements of advertising effectiveness. *Journal of Marketing, 25*, 59–62.

Lucas, D. B. and Britt, S. N. (1963). *Measuring advertising effectiveness*. New York: Garland Publishing.

Mitchell, A. A. (1963). *Advertising exposure, memory and choice*. Hillsdale, NJ: Lawrence Erlbaum Associates.

Nedungadi, P., Mitchell, A., and Berger, I. E. (1993). A framework for understanding the effects of advertising exposure on choice. In A. A. Mitchell (Ed), *Advertising exposure, memory and choice*. Hillsdale, NJ: Lawrence Erlbaum Associates.

Parkin, A. J., Reid, T. K., and Russo, R. (1990). On the differential nature of implicit and explicit memory. *Memory and Cognition, 18*, 507–514.

Roediger, H. L. and Blaxton, T. (1987). Effects of varying modality, surface features, and retention interval on priming in word fragment completion. *Memory and Cognition, 15*, 379–388.

Roediger, H. L., Weldon, M. S., and Challis, B. H. (1989). Explaining dissociations between implicit and explicit measures of retention: A processing account. In H. L. Roediger and F. I. M. Craik (Eds), *Varieties of memory and consciousness: Essays in honour of Endel Tulving*. Hillsdale, NJ: Lawrence Erlbaum Associates.

Sanyal, A. (1992). Priming and implicit memory: a review and a synthesis relevant for consumer behavior. *Advances in Consumer Research, 19*, 795–805.

Schacter, D. (1987). Implicit memory: history and current status. *Journal of Experimental Psychology: Learning, Memory and Cognition, 13*, 501–518.

Schmitt, B. H., Tavassoli, N. T., and Millard, R. T. (1993). Memory for print ads: understanding relations among brand name, copy and picture. *Journal of Consumer Psychology, 2*, 55–81.

Shimamura, A. (1986). Priming effects in amnesia. Evidence for a dissociable memory function. *Quarterly Journal of Experimental Psychology, 38A*, 619–644.

Tulving, E., Schacter, D. L., and Stark, H. A. (1982). Priming effects in word-fragment completion are independent of recognition memory. *Journal of Experimental Psychology: Learning, Memory and Cognition, 8*, 336–342.

Warrington, E. and Weiskrantz, L. (1974). The effect of prior learning on subsequent retention in amnesic patients. *Neuropsychologia, 12*, 419–428.

Zielske, H. A. (1959). Messages: Their timing and composition. *Journal of Marketing, 23*, 239–243.

29

Michael S. Wogalter and
Kenneth R. Laughery

Warning! Sign and Label Effectiveness

The purpose of warnings is twofold. The first goal is to inform people so they appreciate potential hazards. The second goal is to change behavior, that is, to redirect people away from performing unsafe acts that they might otherwise perform. With today's technology, warnings have become increasingly necessary. Products, equipment, tools, and the environment have become more complex; how they work, their composition, and their inherent hazards are frequently not obvious.

Until the past decade, relatively little empirical research on warnings had been reported—probably because warning research is difficult to do. Some of the difficulties are these:

- Direct behavioral observation of warning effects is time- and labor-intensive because the critical events are infrequent and sporadic.
- Allowing hazardous situations to occur in order to study them poses serious ethical concerns.
- Laboratory studies that permit good experimental control may not be generalizable to other settings. Creating believable risk situations (that are actually safe) in the laboratory is challenging.

In part as a result of these difficulties, research on warnings has proceeded on several methodological fronts employing a variety of techniques. Research has been conducted in the laboratory and in the field and has measured subjective judgments, comprehension, memory, behavioral intentions, and compliance.

STAGES OF INFORMATION PROCESSING

Research on warnings can be organized using an information processing framework. In this article, we adopt an information processing model consisting of a sequence of stages: attention, comprehension, attitudes and beliefs, motivation, and behavior. The basic model is shown in Figure 1. Although this model has limited utility in describing complex mental processes, it is useful in organizing warning research.

In the liner sequence, for a warning to be successful, it must capture attention and be understood. It should agree with existing attitudes and beliefs or be adequately persuasive to evoke a change toward agreement. Finally, the message must motivate the user to comply. Each stage can produce a bottleneck, potentially preventing information from being processed at subsequent stages. For example, a warning that is not comprehended will have little or no influence on beliefs and attitudes, motivation, and behavior.

Much of the research reported to date has focused on attention and comprehension, with a modest amount of effort directed at motivational considerations and relatively little at the role of beliefs and attitudes. Most work on warnings appears in the human factors-ergonomics literature, and much of this research has an applications orientation with the goal of designing more effective warnings.

Warnings are usually transmitted visually (e.g., with signs and labels) or auditorily (e.g., with sounds and speech). Sometimes hazard information is conveyed by other modalities, such as olfaction (e.g., odor added to natural-gas lines to aid leak detection) or touch (e.g., vibrating aircraft control sticks to warn of an impending stall). But these are unusual cases. In this article, we focus on visual warnings. Reviews of auditory warnings can be found elsewhere.[1]

ATTENTION

Most environments are cluttered and noisy, so in order to attract attention, warnings must be conspicuous or salient relative to their context.[2] Principles from basic research on selective attention indicate that factors such as novelty, size, illumination, contrast, and location (both spatial and temporal) affect salience. Additional factors that may help capture attention include a signal word (e.g., "DANGER," "CAUTION"), a signal icon (e.g., triangle enclosing an exclamation point), color (e.g., red is associated with stop and danger in many cul-

Figure 1

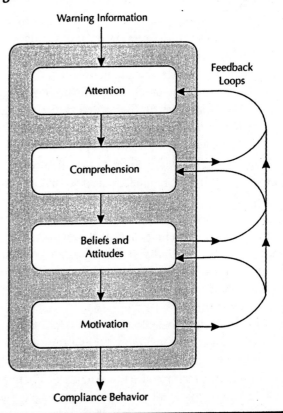

A human information processing model showing a sequence of stages leading to behavior complying with a warning. The model includes feedback to earlier stages.

tures), or a picture (referred to in the warnings literature as a *pictorial*) illustrating the hazard or consequences.[3] For example, one study measuring the time it took people to find warnings on alcoholic beverage labels showed that a warning that was colored red and included a signal icon (triangle enclosing an exclamation point) and pictorial (circle and slash over a car and cocktail glass) was noticed significantly faster (2.07 s) than a warning without these features (2.80 s).[4]

Often, there is limited space on labels for warnings. One alternative is to squeeze in information regardless of the resulting print size. Another alternative is to leave out information and refer to more complete information in another accessible location (e.g., a printed instruction sheet or manual that accompanies the product). Research indicates that a well-located, brief, persuasive safety directive can be effective in getting users to look at more detailed warnings in an accompanying instruction manual.[5]

This approach, however, includes some cost in terms of convenience and time—a serious problem that we address in the section on motivation.

Persons with limited sensory capabilities are of particular concern in designing warnings. If individuals with vision or hearing impairments (e.g., the elderly) are part of the target audience, their capabilities and limitations should be considered (e.g., a larger display might be appropriate). Multimodal presentation (including sound) has shown benefits; it provides redundant cues so that a person occupied by a task employing one modality can receive the information conveyed through another. For example, a field experiment conducted at a shopping mall showed that more people avoided a "wet floor" area when the warning was conveyed through both print and voice (76%) than print (42%) or voice (64%) alone.[6]

An important issue related to attention is habituation: Over time and repeated exposure, a warning will attract less attention despite having many of the salience features already discussed. There are several ways to retard habituation, however. One way is to alter the characteristics of an existing warning from time to time so that it looks different. Another way is provided by recent technology: Warnings can be controlled dynamically by electronics. Sophisticated presentations personalize (e.g., use the targeted individual's name) and vary presentation patterns to delay habituation.[7] Another method of countering habituation is to use interactive warnings, in which the targeted individual has overt physical contact with the warning and is thereby interrupted in performing a familiar task.[8] The interruption serves to call attention to the task and the warning. One study using an incidental task (in which the true purpose of the study is not revealed initially) showed that participants using electrical extension cords with a warning attached to a plastic outlet cover more often connected them to equipment properly (48%, or 29 out of 60) than did participants with a warning lacking interactivity (6.7%, or 2 out of 30).

A related issue is the recent call by industry groups for a standard warning format. The potential benefit is twofold: People will more easily recognize that a section of a sign or label is a warning when they see it, and a standard format decreases development costs. The disadvantage is that standardization promotes similar appearances and conflicts with countermeasures to retard habituation.

COMPREHENSION

The next stage in the model is comprehension. Product and warning designers often assume incorrectly that everyone at risk understands the hazard as well as the designers themselves do.[9] In fact, the target audience (which frequently ranges widely in mental abilities and experience) may not know the information the designers consider, "common sense." Moreover, safety communications should not be written at the average comprehension level of the target audience. Rather, warnings should be understandable to the least-skilled people who can practically be reached. Illiteracy and non-English readers and speakers, of course, pose special problems.

What are reasonable assumptions about comprehension, and what principles can be applied? Generally, individuals with low language ability (children, the poorly educated, non-English readers or speakers, etc.) will not understand warning messages that are written at high reading levels, use technical terms, or describe complex concepts. Thus, one obvious principle of warnings design is to use simple language, to keep the reading level as low as possible, and to minimize technical terminology. The appropriate content depends, however, on the target audience. For example, it may be appropriate for a pharmaceutical company marketing birth control pills to provide different warnings to prescribing physicians than to end users.[10]

Two factors that have been researched extensively are explicitness and the use of pictorials. Explicit messages tell specifics about the hazards, give definitive instructions on what should or should not be done, and explain the consequences for not complying.[11] "Use adequate ventilation" or "May be hazardous to health" are vague messages; comprehension can be improved by using instead specific messages like "Use in a room with forced air or with at least two open windows" or "Can cause lung cancer, which almost always leads to death."

Pictorials can often be used to depict the hazard, the potential consequences, or what to do or not do to avoid the hazard. In addition to capturing attention, well-designed pictorials can communicate large amounts of information in a glance and reach persons who cannot read verbal print messages.[12] However, it is also true that poorly designed pictorials may communicate nothing—or worse, may communicate the wrong message. For example, the verbal warnings for ACUTANE® (Roche Dermatologics, Nutley, New Jersey), a drug that is used to treat severe acne and that also causes severe birth defects, are accompanied by a side-view, outline shape of a pregnant woman within a circle-slash surround. The intended message is that women should not take the drug if pregnant, and women who are not pregnant should take stalwart precautions against getting pregnant if they take the drug. However, some women have incorrectly interpreted the pictorial to mean that the chemical will help them to avoid getting pregnant—a potentially disastrous confusion. In general, pictorials have been used in warnings with varied levels of success.

BELIEFS AND ATTITUDES

In research on warnings, the factors related to beliefs and attitudes have been less frequently examined than the factors related to attention and comprehension. Influential factors at the beliefs-and-attitudes stage include familiarity and perceived hazard. However, before we describe these two influences, we should note that beliefs and attitudes can affect earlier stages of information processing as well. For example, an individual who believes a product or a piece of equipment is safe is less likely to look for a warning than is someone who has doubts about safety. As this example illustrates, in the model shown in Figure 1, the flow of information through the stages is not linear. Probably all of the processing stages influence earlier stages, as shown in the feedback loops on the right side of the figure.

Product familiarity reduces the level of hazard perceived and the likelihood of reading warnings. This familiarity effect derives from beliefs formed from prior exposures and the accumulation of knowledge about the object or task.[13] Conversely, low familiarity leads to more looking, reading, and complying. Even though increased familiarity reduces a warning's effectiveness, familiarity does not necessarily produce unsafe behavior as it generally means the person knows how to deal with the hazards. Nevertheless, beliefs can sometimes be erroneous; people can be overconfident in believing that they know enough to use a product safely. When people are likely to be familiar with a product, it may be necessary to increase the label's salience so they will notice the warning and maybe change their beliefs appropriately.

Hazard perception is closely related to familiarly. The less people perceive a product or task to be hazardous, the less likely they are to notice, look for, or read a warning. But even if they read the warning, they still may not comply with its directives if it does not convince them of the hazard. Research suggests that people's notions of product hazard are almost entirely based on how severely they believe they could be hurt, not necessarily how probable the injuries are.[14]

MOTIVATION

If a warning is noticed, is understood, and fits with a person's beliefs and attitudes, then the remaining element essential to safe behavior is that the warning must motivate (activate) the person to comply with its directives. A critical determinant of motivation is the cost of compliance. Cost can be any expenditure of effort, time, and money. If a person perceives the costs of complying to be greater than the benefits of complying, he or she is less likely to comply than if the benefits appear to outweigh the costs. The required expenditure of even a minimal amount of extra time or effort can reduce compliance dramatically. For example, in a laboratory study in which participants mixed and measured various chemicals, a warning requiring the use of protective equipment (mask and gloves) was complied with significantly less often (17%) when this equipment was 25 feet (8 m) away from the worktable as opposed to being at hand (73%)[15]

Although the cost associated with compliance is a potential hindrance to a warning's effectiveness, the effects of this cost can be counteracted by increasing the perceived cost associated with noncompliance. One motivator is an explicit statement describing the potential negative outcomes that can result if the warning is ignored. Explicit statements provide an appreciation of the potential severity of injury, and this understanding is a major determinant of precautionary intent and actions.[13,14]

Social influence is another motivational factor affecting compliance.[15] One set of experiments showed that if people see another person comply with a warning, they are more likely to comply (e.g., 15 of 18 people, or 83%, donned mask and gloves when a confederate donned them) than if they see another person not comply (3 of 19 people, or 16%, wore the mask and gloves when the confederate failed to put them on). This factor also illustrates the importance of not only warning design, but also personal and environmental factors.

SUMMARY AND IMPLICATIONS

Several implications can be drawn from this broad overview of some of the important issues in the design and implementation of warnings: Warnings should be designed so that they will be noticed and examined, they should be understandable by as large a portion of their intended audience as possible, the message should have persuasive elements to ensure correct beliefs and attitudes, and warnings should motivate people to comply. Attention and comprehension have been considered extensively in research; attitudes and beliefs and motivation are less well researched, and deserve more attention because of their influence on warnings' effectiveness.

We have focused on the factors that improve or maximize warnings' effectiveness. It should be noted, however, that some reports in the literature question the effectiveness of warnings.[16] As can be seen in the data cited in this article, warnings do not always lead to high rates of compliance. Thus, one should not rely on them as the only basis for injury control. Foremost, one should try to design out the hazard, such as by using a safer chemical in a cleaning solution instead of a more dangerous one. However, sometimes hazards cannot be completely designed out, so another strategy is to try to guard against them, such as by having a cover around the sharp blades of a food processor. The point is that because warnings are not 100% reliable, they should not be considered a substitute for good design or safeguards. Warnings are necessary when other hazard-control methods are not possible or practical, or may serve as adjuncts.

How does one know whether a particular warning will be effective? An assessment of effectiveness can, to some extent, be obtained by testing the warning. Testing may involve exposing the warning to a representative sample of the target population and assessing noticeability, readability, comprehension, behavioral intentions, and behavioral compliance. Such efforts pose significant methodological challenges, but the potential value of the results in reducing injury warrants including testing as an integral part of the warning design process.

ACKNOWLEDGMENTS

The authors would like to thank Stephen L. Young for his comments on an earlier version of this article.

NOTES

1. J. Edworthy, S. Loxley, and I. Dennis, Improving auditory warning design: Relationship between warning sound parameters and perceived urgency, *Human Factors, 33,* 205–231 (1991); R. D. Sorkin, Design of auditory and tactile displays, in *Handbook of Human Factors,* G. Salvendy, Ed. (Wiley-Interscience, New York, 1987); M. S. Wogalter and S. L. Young, Behavioural compliance to voice and print warnings, *Ergonomics, 34,* 79–89 (1991).

2. M. S. Sanders and E. J. McCormick, *Human Factors in Engineering and Design,* 7th ed. (McGraw-Hill, New York, 1993); M. S. Wogalter, S. S. Godfrey, G. A. Fontenelle, D. R. Desaulniers, P. R. Rothstein, and K. R. Laughery, Effectiveness of warnings, *Human Factors, 29,* 599–612 (1987); S. L. Young and M. S. Wogalter, Effects of conspicuous print and pictorial icons on comprehension and memory of instruction manual warnings. *Human Factors, 32,* 637–649 (1990).

3. A. Chapanis, Hazards associated with three signal words and four colours on warning signs, *Ergonomics, 37,* 265–275 (1994); L. S. Jaynes and D. B. Boles, The effects of symbols on warning compliance, in *Proceedings of the Human Factors Society 34th Annual Meeting* (Human Factors Society, Santa Monica, CA, 1990); M. S. Wogalter, S. W. Jarrard, and S. N. Simpson, Influence of signal words on perceived level of product hazard, *Human Factors, 36,* 547–556 (1994).

4. K. R. Laughery, S. L. Young, K. P. Vaubel, and J. W. Brelsford, The noticeability of warnings on alcoholic beverage containers, *Journal of Public Policy & Marketing, 12,* 38–56 (1993).

5. M. S. Wogalter, T. Barlow, and S. Murphy, Compliance to owner's manual warnings: Influence of

familiarity and the task-relevant placement of a supplemental directive, *Ergonomics, 38,* 1081–1091 (1995).

6. Wogalter and Young, note 1.

7. B. M. Racicot and M. S. Wogalter, Effects of a video warning sign and social modeling on behavioral compliance, *Accident Analysis and Prevention, 27,* 57–64 (1995); M. S. Wogalter, B. M. Racicot, M. J. Kalsher, and S. N. Simpson, The role of perceived relevance in behavioral compliance in personalized warning signs, *International Journal of Industrial Ergonomics, 14,* 233–242 (1994).

8. R. R. Duffy, M. J. Kalsher, and M. S. Wogalter, Interactive warning: An experimental examination of effectiveness, *International Journal of Industrial Ergonomics, 15,* 159–166 (1995); J. P. Frantz and T. P. Rhoades, A task analytic approach to the temporal placement of product warnings, *Human Factors, 35,* 719–730 (1993); B. P. Hunn and T. A. Dingus, Interactivity, information and compliance cost in a consumer product warning scenario, *Accident Analysis and Prevention, 24,* 497–505 (1992); M. R. Lehto and J. Papastavrou, Models of the warning process: Important implications towards effectiveness, *Safety Science, 16,* 573–598 (1993).

9. K. R. Laughery, Everybody knows: Or do they? *Ergonomics in Design, 1,* 8–13 (1993).

10. K. R. Laughery and J. W. Brelsford, Receiver characteristics in safety communications, in *Proceedings of the Human Factors Society 35th Annual Meeting* (Human Factors Society, Santa Monica, CA, 1991).

11. K. R. Laughery, K. P. Vaubel, S.L. Young, J. W. Brelsford, and A. L. Rowe, Explicitness of consequence information in warnings, *Safety Science, 16,* 597–613 (1993).

12. T. Boersema and H. J. G. Zwaga, Selecting comprehensible warning symbols for swimming pool slides, in *Proceedings of the Human Factors Society 33rd Annual Meeting* (Human Factors Society, Santa Monica, CA, 1989); B. L. Collins, Evaluation of mine-safety symbols, in *Proceedings of the Human Factors Society 27th Annual Meeting* (Human Factors Society, Santa Monica, CA, 1983); L. F. Laux, D. L. Mayer, and N. B. Thompson, Usefulness of symbols and pictorials to communicate hazard information, in *Proceedings of the Interface 89* (Human Factors Society, Santa Monica, CA, 1989).

13. S. S. Godfrey, L. Allender, K. R. Laughery, and V. L. Smith, Warning messages: Will the consumer bother to look? in *Proceedings of the Human Factors Society 27th Annual Meeting* (Human Factors Society, Santa Monica, CA, 1983); M. S. Wogalter, J. W. Brelsford, D. R. Desaulniers, and K. R. Laughery, Consumer product warnings: The role of hazard perception, *Journal of Safety Research, 22,* 71–82 (1991).

14. M. S. Wogalter, D. J. Brems, and E. G. Martin, Risk perception of common consumer products: Judgments of accident frequency and precautionary intent, *Journal of Safety Research, 24,* 97–106 (1993); S. L. Young, M. S. Wogalter, and J. W. Brelsford, Relative contribution of likelihood and severity of injury to risk perceptions, in *Proceedings of the Human Factors Society 36th Annual Meeting* (Human Factors Society, Santa Monica, CA, 1992).

15. M. S. Wogalter, S. T. Allison, and N. A. McKenna, Effects of cost and social influence on warning compliance, *Human Factors, 31,* 133–140 (1989).

16. T. J. Ayres, M. M. Gross, C. T. Wood, D. P. Horst, R. R. Beyer, and J. N. Robinson, What is a warning and when will it work, in *Proceedings of the Human Factors Society 33rd Annual Meeting* (Human Factors Society, Santa Monica, CA, 1989); R. L. McCarthy, J. P. Finnegan, S. Krumm-Scott, and G. E. McCarthy, Product information presentation, user behavior, and safety, in *Proceedings of the Human Factors Society 28th Annual Meeting* (Human Factors Society, Santa Monica, CA, 1984).

RECOMMENDED READING

Laughery, K. R., Wogalter, M. S., and Young S. L. Eds. (1994). *Human Factors Perspectives on Warnings: Selections From Human Factors and Ergonomics Society Annual Meetings 1980–1993* (Human Factors and Ergonomics Society, Santa Monica, CA).

Miller, J. M., Lehto, M. R., and Frantz, J. P. (1995). *Warnings and Safety Instructions: An Annotated Bibliography* (Fuller Publications, Ann Arbor, MI).

30

Dean Delis, John Fleer,
and Nancy H. Kerr

Memory for Music

Subjects created imaginal interpretations of classical music passages in accordance with themes which were either concrete and comprehensible or abstract and difficult to comprehend. Recognition memory for the musical passages was found to be superior in the former condition. The results support the hypothesis that meaningful interpretation of stimulus material is a major determinant of memory accuracy. The implications of the results for comparisons of music and language are also discussed.

The present experiment is concerned with the effect of people's meaningful interpretations of musical passages on their subsequent memory for them. Meyer (1967) has distinguished between two types of meaning in music, calling the melodic properties of a passage the "embodied meaning" and the images and ideas that a passage may evoke the "designative meaning." Meyer has noted that the structural characteristics of "embodied meaning" of a musical passage affect an individual's memory for the music, and recent research supports his observation (Dowling, 1973; Dowling & Fujitani, 1971; Dowling & Hollombe, 1977; White, 1960). Thus, just as one tends to remember familiar and well-organized visual (Goldstein & Chance, 1971) and linguistic (Miller & Selfridge, 1950) patterns, one also has better memory for musical passages which have coherent "embodied meaning." The current study was designed to determine whether the "designative meaning" of a musical passage also affects memory for the music itself.

The possibility that designative meaning may affect memory for music follows directly from recent research which indicates that the meaningful interpretation of a stimulus material is an important determinant of memory accuracy. For example, both Bransford and Johnson (1972) and Bransford and McCarrell (1974) tested recall for linguistic materials and found that memory for sentences was enhanced when the subject had been provided with a meaningful context for the sentences. Wiseman and Neisser (1974) used ambiguous pictures as stimuli in a recognition experiment and found that subjects had better memory for those pictures perceived as faces than for those perceived as meaningless patterns of black and white. Bower,

From Dean Delis, John Fleer, and Nancy H. Kerr, "Memory for Music," *Perception and Psychophysics,* vol. 23, no. 3 (1978), pp. 215–218. Copyright © 1978 by The Psychonomic Society, Inc. Reprinted by permission.

Karlin, and Dueck (1975) found that recall of potentially meaningless pictures (droodles) was improved when subjects were given a verbal interpretation which gave the pictures a meaning. All of these studies share the same general experimental procedure: (1) subjects are presented with stimulus materials which are difficult to "understand"; (2) a record is kept of which of the stimulus materials are meaningfully interpreted by the subjects; and (3) the subjects are given a memory test for the material. The studies all have shown that memory for a stimulus is superior when the subjects "understand its underlying meaning," supporting the hypothesis that memory performance is not a function of the surface characteristics of the stimulus alone (the medium), but that the subjects' understanding of the meaning of the stimulus (the message) is an important determinant of memory for the material.

Since music can be thought of as having both a surface string of notes and an underlying designative meaning, musical stimuli can be used in an experiment on memory analogous to the experiments described above. However, there is one important difference between the symbolic properties of music and those of language and pictures. Unlike words and pictures, musical notes do not act as socially agreed upon referents to objects and events in the physical world, and thus there is no guarantee that one person's designative interpretation of a musical passage will be similar to another's. Early research (Downey, 1897) demonstrated that, although emotional reactions to music may be similar across individuals, the images, thoughts, and ideas which listeners associate to a particular passage are generally very different. Thus, while in previous research employing linguistic and visual stimuli the material had an inherent deep meaning which could be "discovered" by the subjects, in an experiment employing musical stimuli the subjects' task would be to *create* their own designative interpretations. This suggests the hypothesis that subjects can improve their memory for musical passages by creating richer, more elaborate designative interpretations of the passages.

In order to test the hypothesis, the following experimental procedure was developed. Subjects were asked to make designative interpretations of musical passages by constructing visual images while listening to them. Imagery was chosen as the

vehicle for making designative interpretations because it has been found that music readily lends itself to the evocation of visual images (Seashore, 1967), and because visual imaging has been found to be a powerful strategy in general for enhancing memory for linguistic material (Paivio, 1969). The subjects' designative interpretations of the musical passages were manipulated by presenting the same musical passages with several different titles, half of the titles referring to objects, scenes, or events which had been rated as highly "concrete" and "comprehensible," the other half, as "abstract" and "difficult to comprehend." By instructing subjects to try to imagine, as they listened to the music, those things to which the title of a particular passage referred, it was possible to test whether the easy-to-comprehend titles would encourage richer designative interpretations of the music than the difficult-to-comprehend titles, and if so, whether subsequent memory for the music would be enhanced.

METHOD

Subjects

The subjects were 36 students (9 females, 27 males) from introductory psychology courses at the University of Wyoming, who volunteered for the experiment to receive extra class credit. They were run in individual sessions.

Procedure and Materials

The subjects were individually presented with six 1-min passages of classical music. The passages were taken from a selection of 20 19th and 20th century symphonic pieces, all of which were full orchestral works. In order to minimize the possibility that some subjects might be familiar with particular works of music, thus giving them an advantage on the memory test, the 20 symphonic pieces were played to an independent group of psychology undergraduates (n = 32) who were asked to rate each passage on a scale ranging from "1" (very familiar) to "7" (never heard before). The six passages which received the lowest "familiarity" ratings were chosen for the experiment (Bartok's *Divertimento for Orchestra,* second movement; Berlioz's *Symphonie Fantastique,* first movement;

Mahler's *Symphony No. 2,* first movement; Prok-ofiev's *Love for Three Oranges,* part five; Nielson's *The Inextinguishables,* first movement; and De-bussy's *Prelude to the Afternoon of a Faun,* first movement. The mean "familiarity" rating was 5.49).

At the start of the experiment, a sheet listing six titles was placed before the subject, who was told that the titles were the composers' thematic interpretations of the music. Three of the titles had been rated independently by a group of psychology undergraduates (n = 33) as highly concrete and easy to comprehend, and three had been rated as abstract and difficult to comprehend (concrete titles: *Ocean Voyage, Peasants in the Field,* and *Winter Forest;* abstract titles: *Refuge in Truth, Philosophical Questions,* and *Rebirth of Justice*). The six titles were ordered randomly on six different sheets with the constraint that each title be paired equally with all six passages of music; the sheets were assigned randomly to the 36 subjects with the constraint that each title sheet be presented to six subjects. In this way, the same passage of music was paired equally with all six titles, with six subjects imaging to each music-title combination.

Before listening to a passage, the subjects were instructed to: read the title of that passage; listen to the passage and mentally visualize those things to which the title referred that possibly could be related to the sounds of the music; after hearing each passage, describe their images into a tape recorder; and rate their images for each passage in terms of how vivid they were, on the average. (Sheehan's 1967 adaptation of Bett's vividness of imagery scale was used.) The subjects were asked to describe their images of the passages as a check to be sure that they had understood the instructions. The vividness of imagery scale was used as the measure of the richness of the subjects' designative interpretations of the passages.

After the images to all six passages were described and rated, subjects were given an incidental recognition test, which consisted of 24 5-sec passages. Twelve of the 5-sec passages were taken from the test passages used in the imaging phase of the experiment (two 5-sec passages from each 1-min passage), and 12 were taken from other classical music sources (from symphonic pieces which also received low familiarity ratings: Sibelius' *Symphony No. 1,* first movement; Beethoven's *Symphony No. 3,* second movement; Stravinsky's

Firebird, first movement; Lalo's *Symphonie Espagnole,* fourth movement; Thompson's *Louisiana Suite,* pastoral; Rachmaninoff's *Symphony No. 3,* first movement. The mean "familiarity" rating of these passages was 5.04). The subjects were told to write "yes" if they recognized the 5-sec passage as taken from the six passages they had just heard, and "no" if they did not recognize the test passage. In addition, they were asked to rate their confidence in all of their answers using a 5-point scale, with "1" indicating very little confidence and "5" indicating high confidence. The unexpected recognition test was used to avoid the possibility that subjects might use strategies of remembering other than imaginal elaboration.

Apparatus

The six 1-min and 24 5-sec passages were played from a Teac tape recorder, Model A-2340. Subjects listened to the passages through Telex headphones, Model ST-20.

RESULTS

Vividness Ratings

Vividness ratings ranged from "1" (very vivid) to "7" (no image). A 6 (passages) by 2 (concrete vs. abstract title) within-subjects factorial design was used. Table 1 shows the mean vividness ratings for the concrete and abstract title conditions. Differences assessed using a within-subjects analysis of variance showed that images were rated significantly more vivid when associated with the passages that had been given concrete titles than when associated with those given abstract titles [$F(1,35)$ = 13.198, $p < .005$]; there were no other significant effects. This finding supports the hypothesis that concrete titles lead to richer, more elaborate, designative interpretations of the music.

Recognition Scores

Only the recognition test responses associated with the 12 5-sec passages taken from the original passages were analyzed for effect of title on passage recognition, since the 12 "new" distractor items were paired with neither a concrete nor an abstract title. A "yes" response to one of the original passages was therefore a hit, and a "no" response was a miss. Each recognition response was combined with its accompanying confidence rating (1-5) and assigned a numerical value from 1 to 10, 1-5 corresponding to incorrect responses, 6-10 to correct responses, and the deviation from 5 or 6 to the degree of confidence. Thus, a "yes" response with a confidence rating of 5 was assigned a value of "10," the *most correct* possible score, since the confidence rating indicates that the subject claimed not to be guessing; a "no" response with a confidence rating of 5 was assigned a "1," the *most incorrect* possible score, since the confidence rating indicates that the subject was not unsure of the response. A "yes" response with a confidence rating of 4 was assigned a "9"; a "no" response with a confidence of 4 was assigned a "2"; etc. Thus, the closer the confidence rating of a response approached 1, the more the subject was objectively/subjectively wrong.

The dependent measure is patterned after the method used in previous studies (Bransford, Barclay, & Franks, 1972; Bransford & Franks, 1971) to assess recognition memory in a completely within-subjects design. We employed a scale from 1 to 10, instead of a scale from −5 to +5 as had been used previously, to avoid artificial inflation of the difference due to the gap at the zero value between positive and negative scores.

Since the recognition test contained two 5-sec passages from each of the six original passages, each subject gave two responses in each treatment condition. The design was thus a 6 (passages) by 2 (concrete vs. abstract title) by 2 (recognition responses) within-subjects factorial. Table 1 shows the mean recognition scores for the concrete and abstract title conditions. A within-subjects, repeated measures analysis of variance revealed significantly better recognition when passages were given concrete rather than abstract titles [$F(1,35) = 11.87$, $p < .005$]. There was also a significant passage effect [$F(5,35) = 6.02$, $p < .01$]; however, there were no significant interaction effects, indicating that recognition scores were not inflated due to specific title-passage combinations. These results support the hypothesis that interpreting a musical passage in

Table 1

Mean Vividness Ratings and Recognition Scores for Musical Passages When Assigned Easy- or Difficult-to-Comprehend Titles

Titles	Vividness Ratings*	Recognition Scores**
Easy to Comprehend	2.92	6.77
Difficult to Comprehend	4.68	5.79

*Lower numbers indicate more vivid imagery.
**Higher numbers indicate better recognition memory.

accordance with easy-to-comprehend themes improves memory for the passage.

Since the observed effects of passage title are based on entirely within-subjects comparisons, there is no reason to believe that subjects' overall guessing strategies affected the two kinds of material differentially. Nevertheless, the possibility that response biases existed was tested by analyzing the responses to the distractor items using a system similar to that used for the experimental items. A "no" response to a distractor item was a correct rejection, and a "yes" response was a false alarm. A "no" response with a confidence rating of 5 was assigned a recognition score of "10," the *most correct* possible rejection of a distractor item; a "yes" response with a confidence rating of 5 was assigned a "1," the *most incorrect* possible false alarm. The recognition scores for distractor items thus ranged from 1 to 10, 1-5 corresponding to false alarms, 6-10 to correct rejections, and the deviation from 5 or 6 to the degree of confidence. The mean recognition score for distractor items was "6.1." That this value is greater than "5" indicates that the subjects did not have a general response bias to report "yes."

DISCUSSION

As Bower et al. (1975) have noted, experiments which show the importance of "understanding" the meaning of linguistic and pictorial material for memory accuracy are "intuitively obvious," their significance being to demonstrate weaknesses in theoretical orientations which address only the surface characteristics of the stimuli to be remembered. The present experiment addresses a question, however, whose answer is less obvious. Since the relationship between the surface string of notes and designative meaning in music is arbitrary, it is not readily apparent that "real world" interpretations would affect memory for music. Intuitively, it would seem that only the structural properties—the "embodied" meaning—would need to be addressed. However, the present study indicates that interpreting patterns of notes into comprehensible themes serves to impart organization upon the notes in much the same way that discovering "faces" in patterns of black and white (Wiseman & Neisser, 1974) serves to organize the patterns for more fluent assimilation into existing cognitive schemata. Presumably, subjects who are able to provide a coherent perceptual interpretation of a musical passage on its initial presentation are reminded of that interpretation on subsequent exposure and are able to report recognition of the music.

The present study also has implications for researchers and theorists interested in drawing analogies between language and music. Previous research has suggested that encoding strategies for music and language may be similar, but the empirical basis has been limited to evidence that stimulus characteristics, such as rhythmic grouping and rate of presentation, are systematically related to subjects' responses to both musical and verbal stimuli (Dowling, 1973). The current study extends previous findings by demonstrating that the processing strategies and skills that subjects use in a given experimental task may affect encoding of and memory for music as well as for verbal materials. Thus, just as a subject's memory for a verbal passage may be affected by the referential interpretation assigned by the experimenter of supplied by the subject (Bransford & McCarrell, 1974), memory for a musical passage may be similarly affected. The finding also provides an empirical base for the distinction between "embodied" and "designative" meaning in music by showing a significant and independent effect of "designative meaning" as a determinant of memory.

REFERENCES

Bower, G. H., Karlin, M. B., & Dueck, A. Comprehension and memory for pictures. *Memory & Cognition,* 1975, **3**, 216–220.

Bransford, J. D., Barclay, J. R., & Franks, J. J. Sentence memory: A constructive versus interpretive approach. *Cognitive Psychology,* 1972, **3**, 193–209.

Bransford, J. D., & Franks, J. J. The abstraction of linguistic ideas. *Cognitive Psychology,* 1971, **2**, 331–350.

Bransford, J. D., & Johnson, M. K. Contextual prerequisites for understanding: Some investigations of comprehension and recall. *Journal of Verbal Learning and Verbal Behavior,* 1972, **11**, 717–726.

Bransford, J. D., & McCarrell, N. S. A sketch of a cognitive approach to comprehension: Some thoughts about understanding what it means to comprehend. In W. B. Weimer & D. S. Palermo (Eds.), *Cognition and the symbolic processes.* Hillsdale, N.J.: Erlbaum, 1974.

Dowling, W. J. Rhythmic groups and subjective chunks in memory for melody. *Perception & Psychophysics,* 1973, **14**, 37–40.

Dowling, W. J., & Fujitani, D. S. Contour, interval, and pitch recognition in memory for melodies. *Journal of the Acoustical Society of America,* 1971, **49**, 524–531.

Dowling, W. J., & Hollombe, A. W. The perception of melodies distorted by splitting into several octaves: Effects of increasing proximity and melodic contour. *Perception & Psychophysics,* 1977, **21**, 60–64.

Downey, J. E. A musical experiment. *American Journal of Psychology,* 1897, **9**, 63–69.

Goldstein, A. G., & Chance, J. E. Recognition of complex visual stimuli. *Perception & Psychophysics,* 1971, **9**, 237–241.

Meyer, L. B. *Music, the arts, and ideas.* Chicago: University of Chicago Press, 1967.

Miller, G. A., & Selfridge, J. A. Verbal context and the recall of meaningful material. *American Journal of Psychology,* 1950, **63**, 176–187.

Paivio, A. Mental imagery in associative learning and memory. *Psychological Review,* 1969, **76**, 241–263.

Seashore, C. E. *Psychology of music.* New York: Dover, 1967.

Sheehan, P. W. A shortened form of Betts' questionnaire upon mental imagery. *Journal of Clinical Psychology,* 1967, **23**, 386–389.

White, B. Recognition of distorted melodies. *American Journal of Psychology,* 1960, **73**, 100–107.

Wiseman, S., & Neisser, U. Perceptual organization as a determinant of visual recognition memory. *American Journal of Psychology,* 1974, **4**, 675–681.

We would like to thank Sandy Wiseman and David Foulkes for their helpful comments on an earlier draft, and Hugh McGinley for his assistance with statistical analysis.

31

Stephen J. Ceci and Elizabeth F. Loftus

"Memory Work": A Royal Road to False Memories?

SUMMARY

In this reaction to Lindsay and Read, we raise three unanswered questions, and rebut three unquestioned answers. Specifically, we ask: (1) how compelling is the evidence for repression as a mechanism, as opposed to simple forgetting, infantile amnesia, or motivated forgetting?; (2) are trauma memories subject to the same type of alteration as nontraumatic memories?; and (3) should memory work techniques be used even if they entail some reliability risk, because to forsake them will result in unrecovered memories? The three unquestioned answers we address are: (1) painful, but nonsexual, genital experiences (e.g., vaginal catheterizations), do not get recovered in therapy because they are societally sanctioned, and therefore do not rise to the level of trauma that is associated with sexual abuse by a trusted loved one; (2) it is acceptable for therapists to pursue repressed memories if their 'index of suspicion' is raised by the presence of multiple symptoms of childhood abuse; and (3) the problem with incest resolution therapists has been overblown by focusing on a few bad apples.

Laura Pasley worked for the Dallas Police Department. One day, at the urging of a friend, she sought therapy for a life-long problem, bulimia. She was to emerge from that therapy with another problem—one for which she had no prior memory—namely, incest (Pasley, 1993). Pasley was hypnotized by her therapist. She joined group therapy and tore up phone books (an anger-venting exercise that is common in incest resolution therapy), and had flashbacks that her therapist insisted were actual data from her repressed past. Each dream she reported was, according to her therapist, an actual rendition of her past, no matter how bizarre. And they were very bizarre! Like other members of her group therapy, Pasley was urged to read *Courage to Heal, The Child Within* (Bass and Davis, 1988) and other so-called 'bibliotherapies'. Aided by these books and her therapist's interpretations of her dreams, she started 'remembering' having been sexually abused by animals, group human sexual abuse, and a dead man hanging from a rope (Pasley, 1993: p. 355). Pasley accused family members of these crimes, and broke off contact with them.

Laura Pasley's case is typical of the type that Lindsay and Read are most concerned about. Like many others, this case began when a grown-up child walked into a therapist's office to seek help for some problem that was not specifically tied to early incest (e.g., eating disorder, depression, low self-esteem). Eventually, following numerous therapy sessions in which the therapist employed memory retrieval techniques that modern researchers recognize as being potentially suggestive (e.g., visually-guided imagery inductions, hypnotic regression), clients begin to 'remember' early abuse. Of special interest to Lindsay and Read are those cases in which clients begin therapy without any memory of abuse, and may even have denied it, but eventually came to believe they repressed memories of their abuse.

'Repressed memory' refers to the exclusion from consciousness of painful experiences. Some believe that amnesia 'barricades' trauma victims from the conscious awareness of these painful memories. Repressed memories may be retrieved spontaneously (e.g., nightmares are claimed by some to represent a form of memory that emerges outside the barriers of repression) but, more often than not, repressed memories are elicited through therapeutic interventions that involve repeated suggestions, imagery inductions, journal writing, hypnosis, sodium amytal, etc.[1]

In expressing their case so eloquently, Lindsay and Read have accomplished the psychological equivalent of a triple crown. Their triple feat was: (1) to lay out a syllogism that is inert in most discussions of repressed memories, namely, incest occurs, it is associated with later psychological problems, and some of its victims purport to have no memory of its occurrence, at least by the time they are adults; (2) to explain that memory distortions are far from rare, the result of myriad cognitive and social mechanisms; and (3) to argue that therapists' confirmatory biases may have resulted in overlooking less esoteric explanations of memory failure than 'fierce repression'. Although Lindsay and Read start slowly, listing caveats and taking

great (and finally greatly redundant) pains to acknowledge their belief in the theoretical possibility of forgotten abuses, they sharpen their daggers as they inch along their journey—a journey that becomes a *tour de force* by its end. In all, Lindsay and Read provide a trenchant and much needed point of view that is animated by the desire to build bridges, not burn them.

Because we agree with the main points made by Lindsay and Read, in our commentary we shall focus on what we anticipate will be some flash points for those who disagree with them. Lest it gets lost amidst the counter-points that follow, we want to reiterate at the outset our admiration for the job Lindsay and Read did in crafting their argument and documenting it with careful analysis of the research. Our points of departure are extensions of their reasoning, not refutations of it.

Like Lindsay and Read, we too believe that it is possible to lose contact with memories for long periods of time. Although repression is a possible explanation, it may not be the best way to conceptualize these memory lapses. Indeed, repression is almost surely overused as an explanation of memory failure, with normal forgetting, deliberate avoidance, attentional overfocusing, and infantile amnesia providing both more prosaic and parsimonious explanations of encoding and/or retrieval problems.

Unlike the construct of repression, each of the above memory mechanisms is underscored by decades of empirical research; each has been shown to exert powerful effects on performance (e.g., it is inconceivable that an adult can have a verbal recollection of an infant experience that required interpretative analysis beyond the cognitive capability of the infant, such as that involved in high-level inferences).

In addition, the concept of repression runs into conceptual difficulties when accounting for differences in the retrievability of events that, on the one hand, are potentially traumatic and painful, and are non-sanctioned (e.g. the interdigitation of an infant's genitals or anus by a paedophilic caregiver) versus events that are, from an adult standpoint, socially sanctioned (e.g. insertion of anal suppositories, circumcision, tonsillectomies, voiding cystourethrograms (VCUGs)), but which from a developmental–cognitive perspective, ought to be as painful and traumatic and, hence, as frequently repressed (and subsequently retrieved in therapy) as the former. That memories of the latter types of experiences are seldom retrieved in incest resolution therapy raises questions about the presumptive mechanisms involved in both repression and its liberation in therapy. Anyone who has witnessed children undergoing invasive genital catheterizations (e.g. VCUGs) knows how traumatic such procedures can be, with the physically restrained child sometimes screaming for an absent mother and protesting tearfully that their bladder hurts (VCUGs entail filling the child's bladder with fluid to the point where it seems like it will explode, while a strange medical team member urges the child to urinate on a table in public, often while the parent is not present). Although genital catheterizations are fairly common among preschool children, it is not clear why they are not recovered in therapy as often as experiences that are construed by adults as sexual in nature, such as penile or digital insertion. While one could argue that the trauma associated with the medical procedures is insufficient to lead to repression, the bottom line is that the determination and interpretation of trauma and pain sufficient to result in repression seems more easily applied in retrospect.

None of this is meant to imply that we are claiming that the construct of repressed memory is invalid, only that it is undoubtedly overused when more mundane, better understood mechanisms exist to account for findings like those of Williams (in press). In cases such as Williams (in press), one wonders how much of the failure of adult victims of sexual abuse to remember their abuse was due to ordinary forgetting as opposed to repression. What do we know of adult recollections of childhood medical procedures? We suspect that if Williams employed a control group of children hospitalized for non-sexual problems, only some of these medical procedures would be recallable in adulthood. A failure to recall non-sexual experiences might have nothing to do with repression.

Like Lindsay and Read, we believe that false beliefs can be inculcated using the techniques employed by some therapists in the absence of a serious effort to verify empirically any uncovered memories. This is not meant to claim that all accounts of incest that are uncovered in therapy are false, or that all suggestive techniques will inevitably lead to the creation of false memories: they will

not, as our own research amply documents (many of our experimental subjects never succumb to erroneous suggestions). But it is to say at the outset that we believe that the creation of false beliefs is not just a cottage industry of memory researchers: vivid, confidently held beliefs about painful experiences can be induced even when they happen to be false. We shall say more about this later.

THE SYLLOGISM

At the start of their article, Lindsay and Read lay out the groundwork which they believe animates therapists' concerns. Briefly, they note that childhood sexual abuse occurs at a high rate, it is frequently associated with later developmental problems, and the adult survivors often have no conscious memory of the abuse experience. We can add to Lindsay and Read's list that incest survivors are claimed by some to exhibit behaviours in addition to psychogenic amnesia: for example, they are claimed to exhibit depression, diminished interest in sex, emotional reactions to certain stimuli, etc.

To some clinicians, the presence of these 'symptoms' raises their index of suspicion that a client is a survivor of childhood sexual abuse and has repressed all memory of the event. There is a thriving market for readers who suspect they may have been abused as children, and are trying to uncover their presumed abuse memories. Self-help books contain literally hundreds of 'symptoms', including: 'having had an abortion, affairs during marriage, alcoholism, asthma, bad dreams, bipolar disease, teeth grinding, masturbation, crying, denial of sexual abuse, downcast looks, early puberty, emotionally unstable spouse, environmental disease, family secrets, fear of being alone, fear of rape, fear of trusting God, fits of rage, guilt, hatred, homosexuality, "I'm sorry syndrome", inability to call God "Father", inability to forgive, insecurity, insomnia, jealousy, low self-worth, memory gap, migraines, missionary/social work, multiple divorces/marriages, overweight, multiple layers of clothing, pornography at home, preoccupation with sex, repugnance to sex, interracial marriage, workaholic, unmet emotional needs, tension, undiagnosed pains, and use of drugs' (Appendix D, Littauer and Littauer, 1992). The proponents of such symptom lists appear to have listed every problem exhibited by every client who has ever alleged to have been abused, without regard to diagnosticity or incremental validity of such symptoms. While the diagnostic folly of presenting such symptom lists may be immediately apparent to a social scientist, it is not clear that clients seeking help for their problems appreciate that such symptoms also occur among non-abused individuals, or that there is often a lack of such symptoms among truly abused individuals. For example, Kendall-Tacket, Williams, and Finkelhor (1993) report that there is no conspicuous syndrome in children who have been sexually abused, no symptom that is manifested by a majority of victims (p. 167), and significant numbers of victims are asymptomatic (p. 168).

WHAT DO WE KNOW ABOUT MEMORY DISTORTION?

First of all, as Lindsay and Read note, we know a great deal about the basic mechanisms underlying memory. While much of what we know is only indirectly relevant to the recovery of memories in psychotherapy, some of what we know is directly relevant. Lindsay and Read do a good job of reviewing the relevant evidence, therefore we will not rehash it here, save those aspects that they shortshrift. Before listing this research, however, we briefly review several of the points made by Lindsay and Read.

First, memory for non-events is far from rare, and subjects' staunch beliefs in the reality of these pseudomemories are also far from rare. Much research accords with this claim (Ceci, Loftus, Crotteau, and Smith, in press a; Ceci, Loftus, Leichtman, and Bruck, in press b; Loftus, 1993), some of it conducted by Lindsay and Read and their colleagues.

Second, false memories can be highly vivid, internally coherent, and contain many low-frequency perceptual details. None of these characteristics are to be found exclusively in true memories even if they are, at times, statistically associated with true memories.

Third, some critics of the relevance of basic memory research to the debate over the pervasiveness of repressed memory have argued that memories uncovered during psychotherapy are qualitatively unlike those constructed in experimental laboratories, and therefore insights gained from the latter

are not relevant to this debate (Franklin and Wright, 1991; Herman and Harvey, 1993; Wylie, 1993). For example, Wylie (1993: p. 43), the senior editor of the *Family Therapy Networker*, recently remarked:

> Traumatic memory seems to bear little resemblance to the tepid, anemic, and rather desiccated experimental laboratory paradigms of the memory researchers, and might be expected to leave a much deeper imprint.

While it is undoubtedly true that many memory researchers do not come close to capturing the intensity of experience alluded to in clinical case studies and anecdotes, this is not always the case. For example, many studies show that even highly salient events, such as the mass chaos that led to the death of 91 soccer fans in Hillsborough, UK, can be systematically distorted over time (Wright, 1993). Neither the salience nor the participatory nature of an event is sufficient to inoculate the rememberer from subsequent distortion about painful bodily experiences such as genital insertion during an exam, being lost in a mall, or being mutilated by captors, (Bruck, Ceci, Francoer, and Barr, in press; Ceci and Bruck, 1993; Wagenaar and Groeneweg (1990); Loftus, 1993; Oates and Shrimpton, 1991; Ornstein, Gordon, and Larus, 1992).

Fourth, merely repeating erroneous suggestions over time can make them more potent (Ceci *et al.*, in press b; Zaragoza and Lane, in press). While subjects may correctly refuse to accept erroneous suggestions as actual memories the first or second time they are suggested, at times they progressively slide into accepting them as real the more often they are imagined (Ceci *et al.*, in press b). Not all erroneous suggestions are equally potent in this regard; plausible erroneous suggestions become more believable than silly suggestions (Orenstein *et al.*, 1992). Finally, any instruction or creation of a mindset that causes a lowering of memory monitoring criteria will result in elevated false reports. Lindsay and Read provide a helpful description of how this can play out in the context of psychotherapy. This means that if we are interested in the reality of a client's 'memory', then it is important to avoid inculcating lax decision criteria; it is important to provide incentives to challenge and check the veracity of what is retrieved.

Fifth, memories of actual experiences are easier to retrieve than are memories of imagined events;

that is, initially they are retrieved faster and they are more vivid. Yet, as will be seen later, many 'bibliotherapy' sources claim that repressed memories that are uncovered during 'memory work' will be vague and sketchy and that the client ought not to worry about this because it is a sign of a real memory (Bass and Davis, 1988; Fredrickson, 1992). The authors of these self-help books seem to be unaware that false memories can also be vague and sketchy. As there is no clinical or experimental 'Pinocchio test' that can lead to a determination of whether a client's memory is real or false (Leichtman and Ceci, in press), the only prudent course of action is to seek external verification—if the reality of the uncovered memory is important to the client and therapist. And we believe that the most powerful way of knowing is by attempting disconfirmation. Thus, it would seem wise for therapists, in the course of supporting their clients during the difficult disclosure process, also to attempt to disconfirm memories as they arise. This can be done without calling into question the client's veracity or stifling the disclosure process. Indeed, falsification ought to be built in to therapy aimed at recovering hidden memories.

We turn now to a few questions that cropped up when discussing these issues with colleagues, some of whom are experienced therapists. We have chosen to make these comments in the style of a press conference, posing questions, expanding on them and, where warranted, providing counterpoints.

Q: If therapists do not actively pursue (with memory work techniques) the possibility that the client was abused as a child, then many clients will not make this discovery on their own, and won't this therefore preclude effective treatment?

A: This question entails a conflation of assumptions that warrant consideration. First, it is undoubtedly true that many clients may not make contact with actual abuse memories from their childhood in the absence of so-called 'memory-work' techniques such as repeated suggestions, journal-writing, hypnotic regression, and visually guided imagery inductions. Not to employ these techniques carries the risk of failing to uncover lost memories in some portion of adult survivors of early abuse. This is a real risk and should not be gainsayed. The

problem is that these same techniques, while effective in bringing to consciousness memories of actual experiences, also are effective in the creation of false memories. To expand on Lindsay and Read's medical analogy, it is as though we have a powerful drug that can cure cancer in those truly afflicted, but the same drug will induce cancer in those not afflicted. Would you administer the drug to a group of clients whose cancer proneness is unknown? It depends on the base-rate parameters, we think. If the chances of administering the drug to someone without cancer are slim, then the technique might be indicated (e.g. the same risk as administering an inoculation to a child for smallpox who, it turns out, already harbours the virus in her body). Unfortunately, there are no diagnostically probative symptoms that should give a therapist *confidence* that they are dealing with a survivor of childhood sexual abuse, notwithstanding claims to the contrary. There is simply nothing in the literature that indicates a majority of survivors can be described similarly in terms of symptoms. Routinely, it is reported that childhood abuse accounts for less than half of the variance on symptom patterns, and sometimes less than 30 per cent (e.g. Kendall-Tacket, Williams, and Finkelhor, 1993). This being the case, then clinicians are unable to justify using memory work techniques on the presumption that they will safely elicit memories of abuse in truly abused clients and avoid creating false memories among those clients who were not abused.

Second, the question also presupposes that we have good empirical grounds for asserting that the uncovering of childhood sexual experiences is a vital factor in treating adult mental health problems. Naturally, the assumption of a developmental linkage between childhood sexual experiences/fantasies and adult mental health problems has an illustrious past going back to Freud (Masson, 1984).[2] Assumptions of linkage between childhood sexual ideation or actual sexual behavior and adult psychopathology have not gone unchallenged. Recently, Crews (1993) has argued that Freud's case studies do not support his assumptions, claiming that Freud had taken liberties in recounting them. In addition, Albert Moll (1913), a contemporary of Freud's, argued forcefully that uncovering sexual offences committed against children and litigating them caused as much psychic harm to his clients as did the abuse itself. Moll is noteworthy because he was not only medically trained and knowledgeable about psychoanalytic techniques, but he had far greater experience working with children suspected of having been sexually abused than any of his contemporaries. To Moll (1913: p. 190) Freud's presumptions about the aetiological significance of childhood sexual abuse, or the fantasy of such abuse, rested on weak evidence and was 'fully explicable' in terms of the heavy-handed manner in which Freud made suggestions to his clients:

> It is out of the question that in every case of the above-mentioned neuroses, sexual experiences should be the cause; and it is equally erroneous to suppose that every sexual experience in childhood has the effects which he (Freud) assumes. It is true that Freud and his followers report cases which they regard as proving their thesis. But I am by no means satisfied with these clinical histories. They rather produce the impression that much of the alleged histories has been introduced by the suggestive questioning of the examiner, or that sufficient care has not been taken to guard against illusions of memory.

Moll (1913: p. 279) expanded on his discontent with Freud's claims, drawing on his ample experience providing therapy for sexual abuse victims:

> I believe that the general sexual etiology which he assumes to exist can from no point of view be regarded as sound, even with the limitation which he later imposed upon his own doctrine, namely, that it is not the sexual experience itself, but the reaction against this experience, which is etiologically significant. Recently, I have several times tried to treat by the psycho-analytic method some of the cases for which that method is supposed to be suitable, and as a result of my experience I have been forced more and more to the conclusion that . . . *the importance of the factor of sexual experiences in the causation of disease has been greatly over-estimated by Freud.* Moreover, I believe that the cures effected by Freud are explicable another way. A large proportion of the good results are certainly fully explicable as the results of suggestion (italics in the original).

Is interminable digging into a client's past necessary to achieve a positive mental health outcome? In support of an affirmative answer, some have of-

fered analogies. For example, one writer suggested that treating a client without excavating their past is akin to planting a garden on a toxic waste site (Herman and Schatzow, 1987). Whether this analogy ultimately proves to be correct, we should acknowledge that at present we have no scientifically adequate evidence for asserting that dredging up the past is a required step toward achieving a desirable mental health outcome. Clients who have uncovered memories of early sexual abuse in therapy do not always make a convincing case for the therapeutic benefit of such awareness: case studies are replete with the unbelievable suffering of some victims upon discovering (or thinking they discovered) evidence of early abuse (see Goldstein and Farmer, 1993). This is not to argue that therapists ought to ignore their client's developmental history during treatment, only that we need to be forthright about our evidence that this step is therapeutically required.[3] If we are modest, then we should also try to obtain external verification.

Finally, a much overlooked aspect of this argument needs to be made explicit: If unconscious memories of the past can cause physical and psychological symptoms, then we need to acknowledge the possibility that current conscious fixation on early abuse also can cause physical and psychological symptoms. As already noted, Moll (1913) felt that the uncovering experience was as much a source of current psychic problems as the sexual assault itself.

Some clinical traditions focus on current phenomenology rather than attempting excursions into the past. Who is to say this is wrong or leads to a less desirable mental health outcome than trying to uncover early memories that may or may not be true? At this stage in our knowledge it seems that the developmental perspective has been relatively better at claiming converts than cures; that is, many have adopted a developmental perspective even though little evidence can be cited to show that it works. Those of us who call ourselves developmentalists ought to acknowledge the limited support for some of our ideology, and while not abandoning the search for the developmental grail, advise the client to engage in various forms of reality checking.

Q: Why should I care about the reality of my client's memories? I am a therapist not a forensic investigator.

A: Admittedly, this is a worthwhile distinction to draw between the two roles. Some therapists have told us that their goal is to bring to fruition intrapsychic material—regardless of the external reality of this material. In contrast, forensic investigators are necessarily interested in the reality of retrieved material. A therapist who has used suggestive memory work techniques with a client who has decided to sever a family relationship or bring a legal action against a party as a result of recovered memories, has a responsibility, we think, to warn the client about the reliability risks that inhere in such 'memories'. To do anything less would be ethically impermissible, as it unleashes the potential for great harm to all parties. For many therapists who have encouraged clients to retrieve childhood memories of abuse, their goal is avowedly therapeutic; they do so for the restricted purpose of bringing to fruition unconscious causes of current problems, and they do not affirm or deny the validity of a client's recovered memories no matter how imploring the client is. For others, however, the retrieval of abuse memories is tied to a form of self-empowerment that entails legal mechanisms; these therapists assert that an integral aspect of the healing process is to regain control over the presumed victimization by such means as law suits. If this is the case, then the therapist may have a responsibility not merely to warn the client of the reliability risks of memories retrieved under such circumstances, but also to seek corroboration for the memories. Ethically, the matter ought not to be relegated to the purview of a forensic interviewer. If these memories are false, then great damage can be done.

Q: Where is the other side of the story, namely, that just because memory work techniques may lead to false disclosures, this does not mean that they must inevitably do so? Are you saying that it is impossible to recover real abuse memories in therapy?

A: No scientist who studies memory has ever claimed, nor should they ever claim, that it is impossible to retrieve memories of abuse that occurred long ago. The clinical literature is replete with accounts of clients making contact with long-forgotten memories of abuse, and even if we discard those cases that are problematic from the standpoint of repeated suggestions, there are other cases that are seemingly free of these problems. While many of these accounts are not compellingly documented, some are (e.g. the Professor Ross Cheit case in Providence R.I.). Importantly, there is no theoretical reason why true memories cannot be recovered using memory work techniques. This does not mean that recovered memories were repressed, however, because there is a vigorous debate over whether recovered memories have been repressed or were unavailable due to normal forgetting, motivated forgetting, infantile amnesia, denial, etc. The point is not that suggestive memory work techniques unalterably lead to false memory, but merely that they *may* do so, and that it is incumbent on those who employ them to acquaint themselves with the cognitive literature and to engage in safety checks to insure that their clients do not assume that the memories are veridical merely because they come to be hazy, sketchy, fragmented, etc. None of these characteristics of retrieved memories are dispositive of real memories; any of them can occur with false memories, too. Finally, an error that some make in this regard is to assume that because true allegations of abuse outnumber false memories, then it is desirable to 'tilt' the odds in favour of erring on the side of eliciting many memories even if it means that an occasional false memory might arise. To do otherwise, it is argued, is to miss the preponderance of true memories. This argument is not without merit—but only if researchers have some idea of the base rates among the population in question. However, no one knows what proportion of perpetrators exist among all those who insist on their innocence, rejecting plea offers and incurring large debts. And no one can possibly know the 'ground truth' among those who enter therapy for non-sexual problems (e.g. stress related to job loss, eating disorders, marital difficulties) only to emerge later with memories of abuse as a result of suggestive memory work techniques. Until the true and false base rates among these groups are known, it is irresponsible to urge that we rig the odds one way or another.

Q: As a clinician, my index of suspicion is raised when my client presents with certain symptoms. While these may not be diagnostic in the sense that they are unique signs of abuse, they are certainly consistent with abuse. Why can't I use memory work techniques to encourage my client to recover memories of abusive episodes, understanding that this is only one part of a larger pic-

ture that will lead to a determination of the validity of such memories?

A: The question presumes an additive, linear model of the way that evidence accumulates to determine a diagnosis. But is this true of recovered memories? There is no research showing that a symptom that is 'consistent with' abuse can be added to anything else that is 'consistent with' abuse to raise the log odds of making a valid abuse determination. This is the problem on incremental validity (Dawes, Faust, and Meehl, 1989; Wolfner, Faust, and Dawes, 1993), that is, demonstrating that any single piece of information adds to the diagnostic validity over and above that which is provided by another piece (e.g. the client's conscious memory). What does it mean for one to have a suspicion that a client is an incest survivor? What exactly are the scientifically-derived symptoms that are 'consistent with' abuse that lead a therapist to harbour such a suspicion?

The phrase 'consistent with' is frequently used in courtroom testimony to mean quite different things. It can refer to affirmative probative evidence (e.g. this symptom is related to sexual abuse), or it can refer to the lack of inconsistency between a symptom and an experience (e.g. while a symptom may not be dispositive of abuse in itself, it does not rule out such a possibility). One worries that jurors interpret the phrase 'consistent with' to mean the former when all that can be claimed is the latter. An index of suspicion could be based on an illusory correlation, resulting in clinical overconfidence.

What we are trying to say is that a scientifically acceptable foundation for an index of suspicion should be based on a 2 × 2 table, with real versus imagined experiences along one axis, and the presence versus absence of various symptoms along the other axis. A series of such 2 × 2 tables is needed, showing that each new symptom adds incrementally to the explained variance of the other symptoms. Without such evidence of incremental validity, it is possible to lapse into illusory causal attributions, as would be the case, for instance, if all depressed clients were also lacking social supports. Observing one symptom (e.g. depression), then adding weight upon observing another (e.g. lack of social support), runs this very risk whenever the two symptoms are not independent. We may think that we have accumulated lots of evidence for our diagnosis when all that we have done is uncover a spurious correlation. Only upon a showing of incremental predictive validity can we know in a scientifically adequate manner if our rising suspicions are warranted.

So, to return to the question, what symptoms are being used to drive the 'index of suspicion', given that recent reviews indicate that many survivors of sexual abuse are asymptomatic, and no as yet identifiable symptom cluster can account for a majority of adult survivors (Kendall-Tacket *et al.*, 1993)? If suggestive techniques that can lead to false memories are to be used with a client, then it would seem prudent to possess a scientifically adequate justification or else warn clients about the significant reliability risks that inhere in using these methods.

Q: Every field has a few bad apples. There are bad plumbers and bad doctors. Isn't it unfair to single out a few bad therapists and in doing so give the impression that their use of suggestive techniques is characteristic of the entire profession?

A: Is it really the case that it is only a small fringe group of therapists who use techniques that might unwittingly lead to the creation of false memories? And is it true that these questionable activities are not found among properly trained clinicians from accredited programmes? We think not. The very same 'memory work techniques' described by Lindsay and Read can be found in use by graduates of accredited clinical programmes, including 'cream of the crop' clinicians who contribute scholarly writings and conduct national workshops. One needs only to peruse books written by or interviews given by highly renowned clinicians to see the evidence for this claim. For example, one psychiatrist told a *Harvard Magazine* interviewer that she interprets a client's lack of memory of abuse this way: 'What they mean is, they don't remember anything with a penis in it ... Bit by bit, if you work at it, you can fill in the missing pieces' (Hawkins, 1991: p. 45). Similar analogies to finding missing pieces of a jigsaw puzzle have been used by other highly credentialed therapists from accredited programmes. For example, one wrote that 'Disparate, fragmented, evidence must often be pieced together, much like completing a giant jigsaw puzzle' (Courtois, 1992: p. 26), and that it is occasionally necessary for the therapist to 'put the pieces together and speculate about the emerging picture' (Courtois, 1992: p. 26). Although this clinician happily also emphasized the inappropriateness of a therapist conclusively informing the client of specific abuse experiences unless irrefutable evidence supports such a finding, one cannot help but wonder about the double-edged sword of the jigsaw puzzle analogy to memory excavation. A more troubling example is the message contained in a popular book written by another clinician with a PhD from an accredited programme:

If an abuse memory does not materialize spontaneously, it rarely surfaces as a recall memory. Survivors will have a series of realizations about their abuse that they find clear and believable, but rarely do they have a sense of having lived what is being felt or pictured. They call it a memory because the pieces fit into their sense of reality, not because they actually now remember experiencing the abuse (Fredrickson, 1992: p. 96)

... Repressed memories never feel the same as recall memories. You will not have a sense of having experienced the abuse you are remembering. Expect your repressed memories to have a hazy, dissociated quality to them, even after working with them over an extended period of time. You will gradually come to know that they are real, but not in the same way you remember something that was never repressed (Fredrickson, 1992: p. 100).

... Whether what is remembered around an (imagistic) focal point is made up or real is of no concern at the beginning of the process; that can be decided at a later date (Fredrickson, 1992: p. 109).

Such allegations are not accompanied by caveats or warnings that repeated induction of focal images can result in an image becoming more and more familiar, to the point where a client may gain confidence that it is real even when it is not. Nor is there any warning that true memories are not the only memories that may seem hazy and dissociated; false memories may also seem hazy and dissociated. Finally, there seems to be a lack of awareness that imagined versus actual mnemonic sources can become virtually impossible to disentangle 'at a later date'.

Lest one think that we have chosen outliers among the therapeutic writings on this topic, consider this advertisement of a workshop in the APA Continuing Education Calendar that carries six education credits:

Healing from Trauma: Recovering Repressed Memory Through Dream, Image, and Metaphor/Andover, MA/$95/6 CE credits: Obtain an understanding of the psychobiological foundations of memory repression of traumatic events; recognize cues and signals of repressed memories in clients, and learn how to access memory through the use of dream, image, and metaphor. (APA Monitor, 1993: p. 63)

In view of the above, it would appear disingenuous to suggest that the problems of concern to Lindsay and Read are confined to a few poorly trained mental health professionals. The problems are not specific to any training model or type of degree (PhD, CSW, PsyD), and they can be found in our own house—among the graduates of the most prestigious APA accredited doctoral programmes as well as the finest departments of psychiatry. Unless we acknowledge the pervasiveness of the problem, we cannot hope to change it.

TO END AT THE BEGINNING

Laura Pasley spent four years being tormented by her horrible new-found 'memories' of abuse. Eventually, she terminated therapy, then realized that her memories were false, sued her former therapist, collecting a sizeable six-digit settlement, and entered therapy with a new therapist. Her advice to others: 'If you have recovered an entire childhood, several pregnancies, repeated sexual abuse, I'd say you run, don't walk, to a competent counselor who deals with reality' (Pasley, 1993: p. 363). ' ... This therapy has snatched something from me that I can never get back: years off my life; years where I was emotionally distant from my family and my daughter' (Pasley, 1993: p. 361).

While we must never relax our effort to serve the mental health needs of true abuse survivors, we need to be sensitive to the potential problems that inhere in suggestive techniques. Specifically, we need to acknowledge the possibility that clients can be led to co-construct vivid memories of events that never transpired; repeated suggestions, imagery instructions, journal writing, and trance inductions are potent psychological mechanisms that we are beginning to realize can lead to false memories. Lindsay and Read have taken a significant step toward preventing more cases like Laura Pasley's from occurring. Such cases harm not only the therapeutic profession, but they dilute public sympathy for true cases of childhood abuse, and increase the suffering of real victims.

NOTES

1. It is common for authors of incest resolution therapy books to recommend a combination of repeated suggestions, journal writing, and imagery inductions: 'Take an event in your family history that you can never actually find out about. It could be your father's childhood or the circumstances in your mother's life that kept her from protecting you. Using all the details you do know, create your own story. Ground the experience or event in as much knowledge as you have and then let yourself imagine what might have happened.' (Bass and Davis, 1988: p. 154)

2. Actually, many writers have made distinctions about differing types of repression. In Loftus *et al.* (1994) the distinction was between complete and partial repression, while others have distinguished between partial and 'fierce' repression (Ofshe and Waters, 1993). Some have distinguished between repression associated with early Oedipal conflicts versus that associated with later trauma, with the former unavailable to verbal retrieval but allegedly manifested in unconscious behaviours such as dreams and slips of the tongue. For empirical researchers in this area, such distinctions amount to trying to hit a moving target because common terms are being used to convey different meanings by different writers. To make matters worse, many who provide incest resolution therapy use the term repression differently from both Freudians and memory researchers. Progress depends on all groups using similar definitions; moreover, all groups ought to be held to meeting reasonably convincing canons of evidence, providing empirical validation for their claims of differing mechanisms underlying various forms of repression.

3. At the 1994 annual meeting of the American Psychiatric Association, Spiegel (1994) reported the results of a small treatment outcome validity study. Eighteen subjects who had reported histories of sexual abuse were assigned randomly to one of two types of therapy, memory work or present focused (the latter actively resisting description and discussion of abuse memories, instead focusing on current interpersonal difficulties, peer relations, etc.). From Spiegel's results, no clear-cut advantage was evi-

dent after 6 months of therapy for either type. More research of this nature is needed.

REFERENCES

APA Monitor (1993, September). CE Calendar, 64.

Bass, E. and Davis, L. (1988). *Courage to heal.* New York: Harper & Row.

Bruck, M., Ceci, S. J., Francoer, E., and Barr, R. (in press). 'I hardly cried': Children's recollections of a painful experience. *Child Development.*

Ceci, S. J. and Bruck, M. (1993). The suggestibility of the child witness: A historical review and synthesis. *Psychological Bulletin,* **113,** 403–439.

Ceci, S. J., Loftus, E. F., Crotteau, M. L., and Smith, E. (in press). Repeatedly thinking about non-events. *Consciousness and Cognition.*

Ceci, S. J., Loftus, E. F., Leichtman, M., and Bruck, M. (in press). The role of source misattributions in the creation of false beliefs among preschoolers. *International Journal of Clinical and Experimental Hypnosis.*

Courtois, C. A. (1992). The memory retrieval process in incest survivor therapy. *Journal of Child Sexual Abuse,* **1,** 15–31.

Crews, F. (1993, November 18). The unknown Freud. *The New York Review of Books,* 55–65.

Dawes, R. M., Faust, D, and Meehl, P. (1989). Clinical versus actuarial judgement. *Science,* **243,** 1668–1674.

Franklin, E. and Wright, W. (1991). *Sins of the father.* New York: Crown Publishers.

Fredrickson, R. (1992). *Repressed memories: A journey to recovery from sexual abuse.* New York: Parkside Books/Simon and Schuster.

Goldstein, E., and Farmer, K. (Eds). (1993). *True stories of false memories.* Boca Raton, FL: Sirs Publishing.

Hawkins, J. (1991, March-April). Rowers on the River Styx. *Harvard Magazine,* 43–52.

Herman, J. L. and Harvey, M. R. (1993, April). The false memory debate: Social science or social backlash? *The Harvard Mental Health Letter,* 4–6.

Herman, J. L. and Schatzow, E. (1987). Recovery and verification of memories of childhood sexual trauma. *Psychoanalytic Psychology,* **4,** 518–537.

Horner, T. M., Guyer, M. J., and Kalter, N. (1993). Clinical expertise and the assessment of child sexual abuse. *Journal of the American Academy of Child and Adolescent Psychiatry,* **32,** 925–931.

Kendall-Tacket, K. A., Williams, L. M., and Finkelhor, D. (1993). Impact of sexual abuse on children: A review and synthesis of recent empirical studies. *Psychological Bulletin,* **113,** 164–188.

Lawson, A. H. (1984). Perinatal imagery in UFO reports. *Journal of Psychohistory,* **12,** 211–239.

Leichtman, M. D. and Ceci, S. J. (in press). The effects of stereotypes and suggestions on preschoolers' reports. *Developmental Psychology.*

Lindsay, D. S. and Read, J. D. (1994). Psychotherapy and memories of childhood sexual abuse: A cognitive perspective (this volume).

Littauer, F. and Littauer, F. (1992). *Freeing your mind from memories that bind: How to heal the hurts of the past.* San Bernadino, CA: Here's Life Publishers.

Loftus, E. F. (1993). The reality of repressed memories. *American Psychologist,* **48,** 518–537.

Loftus, E. F., Polonsky, S. and Fullilove, M. T. (in press). Memories of childhood sexual abuse: Remembering and repressing. *Psychology of Women Quarterly.*

Masson, J. M. (1984, February). Freud and the seduction theory. *The Atlantic Monthly,* 33–60.

Moll, A. (1913). *The sexual life of the child.* New York: Macmillan.

Oates, K. and Shrimpton, S. (1991). Children's memories for stressful and non-stressful events. *Medicine, Science, and the Law,* **31,** 4–10.

Ofshe, R. and Waters, E. (1993, March). Making monsters. *Society,* 4–16.

Ornstein, P. A., Gordon, B., and Larus, D. (1992). Children's memory for a personally experienced event: Implications for testimony. *Applied Cognitive Psychology,* **6,** 49–60.

Pasley, L. (1993). Misplaced trust. In E. Goldstein and K. Farmer (Eds), *True stories of false memories.* (pp. 347–365). Boca Raton, FL: Sirs Publishing.

Spiegel, D. (1994). Presenter: New research on child abuse. Annual meeting of the American Psychiatric Association. Philadelphia, PA.

Wagenaar, W. A. and Groeneweg, T. (1990). The memory of concentration camp survivors. *Applied Cognitive Psychology,* **4,** 77–88.

Williams, L. M. (in press). *Journal of Consulting and Clinical Psychology.*

Wolfner, G., Faust, D., and Dawes, R. M. (1993). The use of anatomically detailed dolls in sexual abuse evaluations. *Applied and Preventive Psychology,* **2,** 1–11.

Wright, (1993). Recall of the Hillsborough disaster over time: Systematic biases in flashbulb memories. *Applied Cognitive Psychology,* **7,** 129–138.

Wylie, M. S. (1993, September/October). Trauma and memory. *The Family Therapy Networker,* 42–43.

Zaragoza, M. and Lane, S. (in press). Source misattributions and the suggestibility of eyewitness memory. *Journal of Experimental Psychology: Learning, Memory, and Cognition.*

32

Ronald P. Fisher and
R. Edward Geiselman

Enhancing Eyewitness Memory With the Cognitive Interview

Abstract: *Basic principles of cognition were incorporated into an interactive interview format to try to enhance the recall of eyewitnesses to crime. Subjects observed a filmed simulation of a crime and were interviewed by experienced law enforcement agents two days later. Across several studies, the Cognitive Interview was found to elicit between 25–35% more correct information than did a standard police interview, without generating any more incorrect information. The Cognitive Interview is easily learned by novice and experienced interviewers and should be useful in a variety of investigative interviews.*

A major determinant of whether or not a criminal case is solved is the completeness and accuracy of the eyewitness account. Nevertheless, eyewitness reports are known to be incomplete and unreliable (e.g., Loftus, 1979). To compound the problem, law enforcement agents receive little formal training in effective methods to interview co-operative eyewitnesses (Harris, 1973). As a result, police interviews are guided more by common sense than by scientific principles of memory retrieval. Fisher, Geiselman, and Raymond (1987) found that the typical police interview begins with an open-ended question, requesting the respondent to recall as much as possible about the event. Somewhere in the middle of the respondent's narration, there followed a sequence of direct, short-answer questions about specific, relevant details of the event. When the respondent indicated that he or she could not recall, little assistance was provided by the interviewer to facilitate the respondent's memory. While no formal study has been undertaken to characterize the "standard" police interview, it is likely that such a common sense approach typifies many investigative interviews. Unfortunately, common sense is not always the best navigator, especially when the course is as complex as the human mind. The purpose of the present study, therefore, was to develop scientifically based interview methods to enhance the accuracy of eyewitness reports and to test these methods empirically in a controlled, yet ecologically valid, laboratory setting.

During the past twenty years, there has been a growing interest among experimental psychologists in the area of eyewitness testimony. In general, the focus of this interest has been to demonstrate the fallibility of eyewitness memory. Unfortunately, we have contributed very little on the positive side, developing techniques to assist the beleaguered witness. At first glance, it might appear that psychologists would have contributed extensively to this endeavor, since we have developed a wide variety of memory-enhancing techniques. Virtually all of these mnemonics, however, are applicable only at the encoding phase, during the crime, when victims are least likely to strategically control learning operations. Our primary goal, then, was to develop a set of retrieval mnemonics, which could be used during the post-event interview, when memory is more likely to be under strategic control.

One dramatic technique for eyewitness memory enhancement is hypnosis. Hypnosis has been reported to be useful in criminal cases especially when trauma to the witness is involved. Enhanced memory under hypnosis also obtains in some controlled laboratory experiments. On the whole, though, the evidence about memory under hypnosis is mixed. Many studies find no memory enhancement with hypnosis (see Smith, 1983, for a review). Of greater practical consequence, hypnosis may distort the memory process (see Orne, Soskis, Dinges, & Orne, 1984). As a result of the inconsistency in the empirical literature, and as a general safeguard against the potential problems encountered with memory under hypnosis, several United States states have placed restrictions on the admissibility of hypnosis recall in a court of law—although, note the recent Supreme Court decision reversing this ruling.

In order to develop an alternative memory-enhancing technique, free from the legal constraints of hypnosis, we sought to apply generally accepted principles of memory, as found by cognitive psychologists in controlled, laboratory studies. The theoretical underpinnings of the Cognitive Interview are based on two such principles. First, the effectiveness of a retrieval cue is related to the number of features it shares with the encoded event (Flexser & Tulving, 1978). Second, there may be several retrieval paths to the encoded event, so that information not accessible with one retrieval cue may be accessible with a different cue (Tulving, 1974).

Based on these two principles, we developed a memory-retrieval procedure for eyewitnesses called the Cognitive Interview that consists of four general retrieval mnemonics. Of these, two attempt to increase the feature overlap between encoding and retrieval contexts (a) mentally reinstating the environmental and personal context that existed at the time of the crime, and (b) reporting everything, regardless of the perceived importance of the information. The other two mnemonics encourage the use of many retrieval paths: (c) recounting the events in a variety of temporal orders (e.g., both forward and backward) and (d) reporting the events from a variety of perspectives (e.g., from that of the witness and also from that of a prominent character). These four principles are explained to the respondent before the interviewer asks the initial open-ended question requesting a narration of the crime scene. In addition, several specific mnemonics, geared to elicit specific details, are described. These include mnemonics for recalling names, physical appearance, numbers, speech characteristics, and conversation. Generally, these mnemonics are based on eliciting partial information when the complete form is inaccessible. For example, if respondents cannot think of a particular name, they are encouraged to think of the length of the name, number of syllables, frequency, ethnicity, etc.

EXPERIMENTAL TESTS

Since a primary goal of our research plan was to test the Cognitive Interview under ecologically valid conditions, the events to be remembered were simulated violent crimes, as depicted on Los Angeles Police Department training films and the interviews were conducted face-to-face by experienced law enforcement investigators. In the first major study (Geiselman, Fisher, MacKinnon, & Holland, 1985), we compared the Cognitive Interview with two interview procedures that have been used by police, the hypnosis interview and the standard police interview. Eighty-nine U.C.L.A. volunteer students viewed a 4-minute film of a violent crime and were interviewed 48 hours later in one of three methods: Standard, Hypnosis, and Cognitive. In the Standard condition, the interviewers were told to conduct the interview in the same fashion as they would a typical real-world interview. In the Hypnosis condition, the interviewers were instructed first to conduct a hypnosis induction and then to proceed with their standard interview. In the Cognitive condition, the interviewers were told to present the Cognitive Interview instructions first to the witness and then proceed with the interview. In all, over 120 hours of recorded interviews were generated for analysis. The results show that significantly more correct statements were elicited by the Cognitive (41.15) and Hypnosis (38.00) interviews than by the Standard interview (29.40). $F (2, 77) = 5.27$, $p < .01$. The Cognitive and Hypnosis interviews were not reliably different from one another. Since the number of correctly recalled events could be raised spuriously by simply lowering the witness's threshold for saying anything, correct or incorrect, we also examined the number of incorrect statements. There were no reliable differences in error rates across the three conditions, $F (2, 77) = 1.99$, $p > .14$. The superiority of the Cognitive and Hypnosis interviews held even when the results were scored only for the 20 facts with the greatest investigative value (e.g., suspect description). In a follow-up study of nonstudent witnesses, perhaps a more representative sample of the real world, the results replicated the earlier findings (Geiselman, Fisher, MacKinnon, & Holland, 1986).

Although the Cognitive and Hypnosis procedures were equally effective, the Cognitive Interview can be learned and applied with considerably less training than hypnosis. In addition, it took significantly less time to instruct the respondent in the general cognitive techniques than to perform a hypnosis induction. Thus, the Cognitive Interview is more efficient than hypnosis. Since one criticism of hypnosis is that it may heighten the suggestibility of the respondent to information embedded within a leading question, we next examined the effects of leading questions with the Cognitive Interview (Geiselman, Fisher, Cohen, Holland, & Surtes, 1986). Following a staged event, in which a classroom was interrupted, student witnesses were questioned about the event. Embedded within one of the initial questions, however, was a leading statement. For example, in the original event, one of two classroom intruders was carrying a blue backpack. The leading question was: "Was the guy with the green backpack nervous?" At the end of the interview, the witnesses were asked, "What color was the backpack?" The students who were questioned using the Cognitive Interview were less likely to change the color of the backpack from blue to green than were students who were questioned using the standard interview. Thus, unlike the effects of hypnosis, which enhances respondent's suggestibility to leading questions, the Cognitive Interview appears to reduce the biasing effects of leading questions.

NEW DEVELOPMENTS

Following several hours of interviewing respondents, analyzing experimental interview protocols, and perusing actual tape recorded police interviews, two sources of improving the Cognitive Interview became apparent. First, there were characteristic differences between effective and ineffective interviewers. To improve the Cognitive Interview, then, we modeled good and poor interviewers, to build in those attributes of good interviewers and to delete those faults characteristic of poor interviewers. One typical difference, e.g., is that effective interviewers asked more open-ended questions, whereas ineffective interviewers asked more direct, short-answer questions. We also noticed that, in many of the field interviews, the sequence of questions seemed unplanned and generally unrelated to the mental activities of the respondent. Furthermore, it appeared that this haphazard question order frequently created a barrier, which obstructed memory. To overcome some of this interviewer-induced forgetting, we developed further guidelines about the sequential order of the interview. This last development of the Cognitive Interview is too detailed to describe here, but let us summarize the major point. In essence, the interviewer's goal is to infer the respondent's mental representation of the event, and then structure the interview so as to be compatible with that representation.

In a recently completed study (Fisher, Geiselman, Raymond, Jurkevich, & Warhaftig, 1987), we compared the revised version of the Cognitive Interview with the simpler version used in the earlier studies. Student volunteers were trained to conduct eyewitness interviews either according to the original Cognitive Interview or the revised version. We followed the same general experimental technique as mentioned before: Volunteer eyewitnesses viewed a film of a violent crime and then returned to be interviewed 48 hours later. When the original Cognitive Interview technique was used, approximately the same number of correct responses (39.56) were generated as in earlier studies, which simply testifies to the reliability of the experimental method. With the revised version, the number of correct responses increased dramatically, by 46% (57.50). F (1, 14) = 7.60, p < .02. This was not caused simply by eliciting more responses, as the number of incorrect responses was almost identical for the two techniques. Rather, it reflects a more efficient method to search through memory.

It is always hazardous to compare the results across different experiments, but one of the more impressive findings is that in the most recent study, the three interviewers were high school and undergraduate students with no prior training in eyewitness interviewing. In the earlier studies, the interviewers were law enforcement personnel with several years of practice using hypnosis and interviewing eyewitnesses. Nevertheless, under comparable experimental conditions, the novice students, using the revised version of the Cognitive Interview, elicited considerably more correct information than did the experienced law enforcement interviewers conducting either a typical police interview or a hypnosis interview.

The revised version requires considerably more time to learn—a few hours—than does the original Cognitive Interview and demands more practice to reach proficiency. In addition, the interviewer must be more mentally active during the interview, as he or she must be sensitive to the respondent's output, and make instantaneous decisions about the course of the interview. Nevertheless, the demonstrated superiority of the revised technique seems to more than warrant the extra expense of learning time and effort.

PRACTICAL CONSIDERATIONS

It is not at all clear how much information may be stored in a witness's memory of a crime. It is clear, however, that the amount actually recalled will de-

pend heavily on the interview method. Furthermore, it is apparent that the common-sense approach to interviewing, as used by experienced, but untrained, law enforcement agents is not nearly as efficient as scientifically developed methods based on controlled laboratory studies. Finally, it should be noted that the theoretical basis for the Cognitive Interview is grounded in principles of memory, in general, not specifically eyewitness memory for details of crime. We might expect, therefore, that the Cognitive Interview, or a modified version of it, could be used to improve any type of investigative interview that depended on accuracy and extent of the respondent's memory.

REFERENCES

Fisher, R. P., Geiselman, R. E., & Raymond, D. S. (1987) 'Critical analysis of police interview techniques.' *Journal of Police Science and Administration,* in press.

Fisher, R. P., Geiselman, R. E., Raymond, D. S., Jurkevich, L. M., & Warhaftig, M. L. (1987) 'Enhancing enhanced eyewitness memory: Refining the cognitive interview.' *Journal of Police Science and Administration,* in press.

Flexser, A. & Tulving, E. (1978) 'Retrieval independence in recognition and recall.' *Psychological Review,* 85, 153–171.

Geiselman, R. E., Fisher, R. P., MacKinnon, D. P., & Holland, H. L. (1985) 'Eyewitness memory enhancement in the police interview: Cognitive retrieval mnemonics versus hypnosis.' *Journal of Applied Psychology,* 70, 401–412.

Geiselman, R. E., Fisher, R. P., MacKinnon, D. P., & Holland, H. L. (1986) 'Enhancement of eyewitness memory with the cognitive interview.' *American Journal of Psychology,* 99, 385–401.

Harris, R. (1973) *The police academy.* New York, Wiley & Sons.

Loftus, E. F. (1979) *Eyewitness testimony.* Cambridge, MA: Harvard University Press.

Orne, M. T., Soskis, D. A., Dinges, D. F., & Orne, E. C. (1984) 'Hypnotically induced testimony.' In G. L. Wells & E. F. Loftus (Eds.) *Eyewitness testimony: Psychological perspectives.* New York: Cambridge University Press.

Smith, M. (1983) 'Hypnotic memory enhancement of witnesses: Does it work?' *Psychological Bulletin,* 94, 387–407.

Tulving, E. (1974) 'Cue-dependent forgetting.' *American Scientist,* 76, 559–573.

INDEX